# D.B. COOPER

AND

# FLIGHT 305

## Re-Examining the Hijacking and Disappearance

Robert H. Edwards, PhD

SCHIFFER PUBLISHING®

4880 Lower Valley Road • Atglen, PA 19310

Library of Congress Control Number: 2020952589



Designed by Molly Shields
Cover design by Ashley Millhouse
Type set in Orpheus Pro/Times New Roman

ISBN: 978-0-7643-6256-9
Printed in China

Published by Schiffer Publishing, Ltd.
4880 Lower Valley Road
Atglen, PA 19310
Phone: (610) 593-1777; Fax: (610) 593-2002
E-mail: Info@schifferbooks.com
Web: www.schifferbooks.com

# DEDICATION

For Wayne Walker, who laid the foundations of this book.
For my wife, Nadia, for putting up with the construction.
For Tom Brown, who taught me to fly.
For Noel, who taught me how to jump from airplanes.
For the memory of my good friend, Tony Ford.

# EPIGRAPHS

My dear Watson, whenever you have eliminated the impossible, then whatever remains, however improbable, must be the truth. —Sherlock Holmes

It is futile to do with more things, that which can be done with less. —William of Ockham

• • •

I recall sayin to myself
"were going for a ride"
this plane has been "hijacked"
and I'm stuck here inside!

We get over by the terminal
these "FBI" guys ask our names,
it seems this guy "Dan Cooper's"
the one playin the big game!

I reckon for this o'le cowpoke
that "hijackings" close as I'll get
to stage holdups and outlaws
well, maybe a movie set!

—Daniel L. Rice, passenger on Flight 305, 11.24.1971

• • •

You don't trust me? I am from the government and here to help. How could you not trust an FBI agent; after all, I am the one that protects your rights as provided by the constitution of the United States. By the way, that book you checked out is two days late and at the moment your cell phone is off; just here to help. —"Ckret," FBI, post on dropzone.com

# CONTENTS

# PROLOGUE

## *Remember 1971?*

It was not the year of the summer of love, or the year of the moon landing, much less a year of a Pearl Harbor, a JFK, or a 9/11. Nothing happened in 1971 to change the world. No great events subverted the way we see things. India and Pakistan fought a war, Bangladesh was born. At the movies, we had *Dirty Harry*, *The French Connection*, and *A Clockwork Orange*. In music, 1971 was the year that gave us "Imagine," "American Pie," and "Stairway to Heaven." Floppy disks came on the market. Jim Morrison left this mortal coil.

But one event of 1971 has passed into legend and popular culture.

On the morning of Wednesday, November 24, 1971, the eve of Thanksgiving, Northwest Airlines Flight 305 departed Washington, DC, on a cross-country flight to Seattle, Washington. The airplane was a Boeing 727-100, with registration number N467US. It was one of the second generation of American jetliners, a descendant of the pathbreaking Boeing 707. On its way across the continent, Flight 305 stopped to disembark some passengers, and to receive others, at Minneapolis, Minnesota; Great Falls, Montana; Missoula, Montana; Spokane, Washington; and Portland, Oregon.

What followed is well known to everyone who has ever heard of Flight 305. Millions of words have been written on this subject in books, the press, and the archives of the FBI; at least four television movies have attempted to unravel the story; many gigabytes of text, images, and video have been uploaded to the internet. Debate continues to this day. Therefore, a brief description may suffice.

At Portland, the second-to-last passenger to board Flight 305 was a polite and nondescript man who, according to the remarkably consistent testimony of eyewitnesses, was between thirty-five and fifty years old, 5 foot 10 to 6 foot 1 tall, 170 to 190 pounds, of Latin or Hispanic complexion, conservatively dressed, and carrying a briefcase. Shortly before takeoff, he informed the cabin crew that he had a bomb. He asked for US$200,000 and four parachutes to be brought to the airplane on landing at Seattle.

After landing, the man allowed the other passengers and two of the cabin crew to disembark. He received the money and the parachutes. He instructed the air crew to fly to Mexico but agreed to a refueling stop at Reno, Nevada. N467US departed Seattle-Tacoma International Airport at 7:36 p.m. Pacific Standard Time (PST). When the airplane landed at Reno at 11:03 p.m. PST, the hijacker was gone, along with the money, the briefcase, and two of the parachutes. He was never apprehended or identified.

A factual point that is essential to the story is that in 1980, an eight-year-old boy found three bundles of $20 bills totaling about $5,880, unequivocally identified as part of the ransom money, in a sandbar on the east side of the Columbia River, 10 miles northwest of Portland International Airport. This location was upwind of the airplane's presumed flight path.

There is one technical detail that is germane, though not necessarily crucial, to this story. In 1971, several models of airliner were equipped with a ventral airstair: a passenger stairway that hinged downward from below the tail. In the 1970s, on the Boeing 727[1] and the Douglas DC-9[2] at least, the airstair could be opened in flight and would thus permit an exit by parachute. Northwest Airlines was by no means the hijacker's only choice; several US airlines were operating 727s or DC-9s closer to the Mexican border, if that is really where he wanted to go. But many miles of text and many hours of film and television have been devoted to the idea that he knew this critical detail of the Boeing 727.

On the website of the FBI, there is an image that is said to be of the ticket that the hijacker bought at Portland, which bears the name Dan Cooper. In the legend of this event, he is universally known by the name D. B. Cooper. There are several versions of how this came about, none of them important to our story. The outcome, however, is that the hijacker has become a modern version of Robin Hood, who in similar fashion might have metamorphosed from a real and banal Robyn Hode or Robert Hood. Decades of effort have been expended on imagining a history and personality for this mythical figure.

For exactly this reason, we might prefer not to refer to the hijacker by his mythic name. The FBI, in its forty-five-year investigation of the hijacking (suspended since July 2016), always referred to him prosaically as the "unsub" ("unknown subject"). If pressed to give him a name, if only for artistic license, we could take the facts as reported and surmise that he might have been Mexican or Hispanic American, and simply by selecting the most common Hispanic first names and surnames, we would come up with something like Luis Hernández or José Garcia. Or we might call him Daniél El Tonelero, which is a literal translation of Dan Cooper into Spanish; the man who fixes the hoops on barrels.

In any case, in this retelling of the story of Flight 305, our objective is not to identify the hijacker, even less to endow him with a character, a personal history, or a motivation.

What is much more interesting is to assemble the known facts, stripped of all myth, speculation, hearsay, and wishful thinking; to apply the tools of mathematics, statistics, aeronautics, and meteorology; and to construct a hypothesis of what really happened on the night of November 24, 1971. Thereby, we could develop a plan of action for further research or investigation. That, in turn, might persuade the FBI, or other interested public agencies or private parties, to deploy further resources toward a resolution of the case.

In this investigation and analysis, we may be guided by the principle of Occam's razor. William of Ockham was an English theologian and philosopher who lived from about 1287 to 1347. The statement that has come to represent Occam's razor is "Frustra fit per plura quod potest fieri per pauciora" ("It is futile to do with more things that which can be done with fewer").[3] In other words, let us not make complex assumptions if we can test our hypothesis with simpler ones.

Another maxim that serves our purpose well was expressed in various ways by Sherlock Holmes: "When you have eliminated the impossible, then whatever remains, however improbable, must be the truth."[4]

On a cursory inspection, the enigma of Flight 305 looks as impregnable as Mount Everest once seemed to be. We may recall, however, the words of George Mallory at the conclusion of the 1921 British reconnaissance expedition. He saw a route via the North Col and he said simply: "It will go."

**Figure 0.1.** Portland International Airport in the 1960s. *Image credit: Port of Portland*

# CHAPTER 1

# THE WITNESSES

In our prologue we proposed that we should not attempt to imagine an identity, a personality, or a personal history for the man who became known as D. B. Cooper. Nevertheless, he was a real person who left impressions, ranging from superficial to life changing, on those with whom he interacted on the afternoon and evening of November 24, 1971. Those impressions are an important part of our story.

Fourteen witnesses have left written records of their interactions with the hijacker.[1] Let us introduce the cast of characters.

Dennis Eugene Lysne was the Northwest Orient Airlines salesperson who sold the air ticket to the hijacker at Portland International Airport.[2]

Six crew members were on board Flight 305 for the segment from Portland to Seattle: three on the flight deck and three in the cabin. The flight crew consisted of Captain William A. Scott, First Officer William John (Bill) Rataczak (in the copilot's seat) and Second Officer Harold E. Anderson (acting as flight engineer). The cabin crew were Senior Stewardess Alice Carley Hancock, "B" Stewardess Florence Schaffner, and "C" (junior) Stewardess Tina Mucklow.

In addition, at least seven passengers were able to provide a substantive recollection of the hijacker. In approximate order of their degree of interaction with the hijacker, they were George R. Labissoniere, Cord Harms Zum Spreckel, William W. Mitchell, Robert B. Gregory, Nancy House, Richard Simmons, and Jack Almstad.

During the late evening of November 24 and the early morning of November 25, eleven witnesses told their stories to special agents of the FBI. Richard Simmons spoke to the *New York Times* on November 25. Dennis Lysne testified to the FBI on November 26. Tina Mucklow gave a second interview to the FBI on December 3.

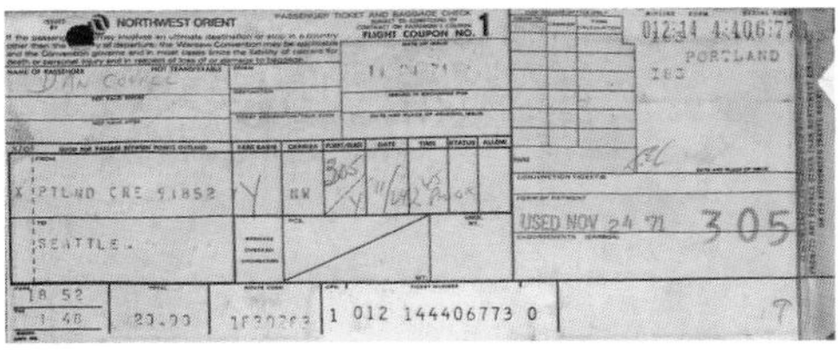


**Figure 1.1.** Portland International Airport, November 24, 1971: Northwest Orient Airlines ticket number 012 144406773 0. *Image credit: FBI*

Our script has stars, supporting actors, and walk-on parts. The star witness was undoubtedly Tina Mucklow, who, as we shall elaborate, was front and center in the interactions among the hijacker, the flight crew, the ground personnel, and the law enforcement authorities. Then came Florence Schaffner, who was the first recipient of the hijacker's demands. Third was Alice Hancock, who was a material witness to the proceedings. The six passengers contributed descriptions of the hijacker and recollections of the events between Portland and Seattle. Finally, the flight crew, who never saw the hijacker and had no direct interaction with him, recounted what they had understood through the intermediation of Tina Mucklow.

## *With this preamble, our story begins.*

At about 2:00 p.m.[3] on November 24, 1971, at Portland International Airport, the hijacker joins a long line of customers at the sales desk of Northwest Orient Airlines, where Dennis Lysne is serving. The hijacker waits patiently in the line. When he reaches the desk, he says something like "Can I get on your flight to Seattle?" Lysne is now about to spend more time face to face with the hijacker than any other witness with the exception of Tina Mucklow.[4]

The flight is due to depart at 2:45 p.m. Pacific Standard Time (PST) and to arrive at 3:21 p.m. at Seattle-Tacoma (Sea-Tac) International Airport, where it will terminate. It is a nonstop flight, with a daily frequency.

Lysne will recall that the man is not nervous. Lysne asks if he wants one-way coach (economy class), and the man says, "Yes." The fare from Portland to Seattle is $25 for first class and $20 for economy. The passenger hands over a $20 bill; Lysne will recall "probably with the right hand" but will not recall from which pocket the bill was drawn. Lysne asks the passenger's name.

He replies, "Cooper. Dan Cooper."

Lysne writes this name on the ticket, all in upper case.

Much later, after the internet is invented, a photograph of coupon 1 of this ticket will appear on the website of the FBI and, later still, will circulate on thousands of websites throughout the virtual world. The ticket bears the serial number 012 144406773 0. It is curious, however, that on the passenger manifest of Flight 305 for November 24, 1971 (at least the version that has circulated on the internet), the name Dan Cooper does not appear. Almstad, Gregory, House, Labissoniere, Mitchell, Simmons, and Zum Spreckel are all there. There is a Michael Cooper, but no one has claimed that he was the perpetrator.

The ticket that Lysne sold to "Dan Cooper" does not indicate a seat number; we presume that seating was not allocated, in that time and place.

Lysne will recall that this passenger has no checked baggage, but does not notice whether the passenger is carrying anything. The passenger receives directions to the departure area and leaves unremarked. The $20 bill is commingled with other bills and is lost to history.

Nothing in Lysne's testimony suggests that the hijacker inquired about the airplane. There is no reason why he should. Northwest Orient has published a system timetable, effective October 31, 1971. Probably there are many free copies on the sales desk, and for that matter at any Northwest office in the United States. The timetable indicates that Flight 305 is always operated by a Boeing 727. If the hijacker needs to know what kind of airplane he will be on, he does not need to ask. He knows already.

There are four flights from Portland to Seattle that depart later in the day. Flight 735 is another Boeing 727, departing 4:50 p.m. and arriving 5:26 p.m. Flight 537 is at 6:00 p.m. (a Boeing 707), Flight 723 at 9:15 p.m. (a Boeing 720B), and Flight 42 at 10:00 p.m. (a Boeing 707). It may or may not be significant, but Flight 305 is the last flight from Portland to Seattle that, on a November afternoon, will arrive before nightfall.

Sometime later (we guess, around 2:15 p.m.), the hijacker boards the airplane. Rataczak will remember the scene, if not the individual:

> **This was the time when the jetway, as we called them, was just being put in place. ... He boarded the airplane with all the other passengers through this jetway. I remember it was raining at the time.[5]**

At this stage we may collate the eventual descriptions of the hijacker.

He is white or Caucasian (six witnesses) or "white American" (Lysne), but Schaffner adds that he "appeared to be of Latin descent"; Robert Gregory will describe him with remarkable precision, or condescension, as "Caucasian, believed to be of Mexican-American descent with possibly some American Indian blood." His complexion is "medium, smooth" or "medium to dark" (Mucklow), "olive" (Schaffner and Hancock), "slightly darker, possibly olive" (Lysne), "dark" (Labissoniere), or "swarthy" (Gregory). But Mitchell, who will spend over two hours in the same row of seats as the hijacker, disagrees: "[swarthy?] I didn't notice that."

He is between 5 foot 10 and 6 foot 1 (here the testimony of Tina Mucklow, who herself is 5 foot 8, carries the most weight). Lysne, who has seen him standing for at least a minute or two, puts him at 5 foot 10 to 5 foot 11. Only two passengers, who could only have seen him seated, put him as short as 5 foot 9. He is consistently described as of medium build; Alice Hancock will remember him as slim, and Mitchell, who is 6 foot 2 and 220 pounds, will call him "slight ... I was way bigger than him." He is clean shaven. His hair is universally agreed to be very dark or black, short, combed close to the head, and parted on the left. Alice Hancock will remember his hair as "wavy"; Robert Gregory, with his eye for detail (or is it with distaste?), will recall it as "wavy, marcelled, greasy patent leather sheen . . . slightly receding in front."

Regarding the age of the hijacker, which is both the most critical component of any attempt at identification, and the most difficult attribute to guess: Tine Mucklow puts him in the midforties (later refining this to forty-four to forty-six), Florence Schaffner agrees, Alice Hancock proposes a range from thirty-three to forty-five, and Lysne guesses at midthirties but adds "possibly older." The flight crew (who never see the hijacker and most probably rely on Tina Mucklow) will send a radio transmission in which they say he is about fifty. Two passengers place him around thirty-five, and one at fifty. Simmons describes him as "middle aged."

Alone among all the witnesses, Bill Mitchell remembers a distinctive physical feature. Mitchell will tell the FBI that the hijacker has "a sagging chin," and, in an interview forty-two years later with the Washington State Historical Society, will elaborate a remarkable detail that, if the FBI had paid attention, would have enormously narrowed down the manhunt: "He had a . . . you know, a turkey gobble. It wasn't a double chin, but he had a loose skin under there."[6]

Last, but forty-one years after the events, FBI sketch artist Roy Rose will recall how he was sent at short notice from Washington, DC, to Northwest Airlines' headquarters in Minneapolis, to interview the cabin crew. He will contribute a detail that has never been documented in any public file of the FBI:

> **When I arrived at the airport in Minneapolis, I... talked to the two stewardesses. ... The two stewardesses differed a little bit on their description... They described the unknown subject as... ah, middle aged person, dressed in a suit, with a dark complexion, and, sort of a protruding lower lip. The rest of the face was rather nondescript, nothing unusual about it.[7]**

The hijacker's voice is low and has "no accent, possibly from the West or Midwest" (Mucklow), is normal and calm (Schaffner), is soft-spoken with no accent (Hancock), is soft (Lysne), or has no particular characteristics (Labissoniere). Mitchell, from whom we might have hoped for a brilliant playback, will only recall: "[sigh, breathing in] No. I couldn't [hear him speak]."[8]

To complete our image of the hijacker as he boards Flight 305: by general agreement, he is wearing one or more dark-colored outer garments (variously described as top coat, suit, business suit, trench coat, jacket, blazer, or raincoat); Lysne will remember what he believes to be a casual jacket, whereas Labissoniere uniquely will recall "a sporty vest underneath." He has a white or light-colored shirt and a dark necktie; no one will recall seeing a tie tack on him. He wears "brown ankle-length, pebble-grain shoes, not tie-type shoes" (Tina Mucklow); he has no hat, gloves, or rings. He is carrying a cheap-looking, dark-colored briefcase; whether it is in his right or left hand, no one has testified.

Lysne alone offers an intriguing guess at the passenger's background, which is at odds with his attire. The passenger, he will tell the FBI, gives the "overall impression of [a] laboring type man as opposed to [an] office worker." Does Lysne sense that the clothes are cheap or secondhand?

Florence Schaffner, who is checking the passengers boarding through the rear stairs, will later remember that the hijacker is the second to last to board Flight 305. She will testify that he "did not appear suspicious and did not attract her attention." The last passenger to board is, by his own testimony, Robert Gregory.

The passenger manifest for Flight 305 on November 24, 1971, lists thirty-six passengers, excluding "Dan Cooper." This particular Boeing 727 is configured with eighteen rows, of which probably rows 1–3 are first class with four seats abreast and rows 4–18 are coach (economy class), with six seats each (A–C on the port side and D–F on the starboard side). If so, the passenger capacity is ninety-six, and the airplane is operating at 39 percent of capacity.

The hijacker goes to the rearmost row of seats (row 18). The three seats on the starboard side (D–F) are empty, and he takes the middle seat (18-E). We presume that he wants a rearmost seat in order to be minimally conspicuous to the other passengers, and to have access to the cabin crew (some of whom will be seated in the rear galley) for conveying his demands. One wonders nevertheless why he has left it so late to board the airplane; could he have been sure that row 18 would be free?

Directly across from the hijacker, on the port side in row 18, is Bill Mitchell, who is twenty years old and is a sophomore at the University of Oregon in Eugene. He is probably in the window seat (18-A), with his homework spread out over seats 18-B and 18-C. He does not notice the hijacker at first.

One row forward, on the port side in row 17, is Cord Zum Spreckel. He will later recall, accurately, that "the man who he believes was the hijacker of the plane was sitting on the right-hand side of the plane in the last row of seats."

One or more rows forward, on the port side in an aisle seat, is Robert Gregory. Gregory will recall seeing the hijacker in a window seat; if so, at some point the hijacker must have shifted from 18-E to 18-F. Later, Gregory will have the idea that his own seat was in row 18, but he is wrong, because the hijacker is to his rear.

Labissoniere is sitting about six rows in front of row 18. At some point he notices the man in seat 18-E.

Nancy House is in row 15, on the starboard side, three rows in front of the hijacker. She will not notice the man until much later, but she will make a unique observation.

Jack Almstad, who is somewhere near the back, will never contribute a description of the hijacker. But he will recall a brief and extraordinary interaction with the man. In the holding pattern outside Seattle, in the aisle near row 17 while waiting for the restroom, Almstad cracks a joke about Thanksgiving. The man in 18-E turns toward him and smiles.[9]

## BOURBON AND 7-UP

Florence Schaffner takes up the story. After all the passengers have boarded the plane, but before the airplane starts to taxi, she begins serving refreshments. The first person she serves is the man in seat 18-E. He asks for a bourbon and 7-Up. This is an unusual drink: a variation of the Presbyterian, which is usually made with ginger ale and club soda. Is it a clue to his origins? Schaffner fixes the drink, which in dear departed 1971 costs $1.25; he proffers a $20 bill, she asks if he has anything smaller, and he says, "No, I'm sorry." She promises to bring his change after serving the rest of the economy section, which she does. He thanks her.

Shortly thereafter, the man in seat 18-E spills his drink. This is the first time that Mitchell notices him. Mitchell will say that "a dark-haired stewardess talked to the subject, and it appeared that they filled out a form." Neither Schaffner nor Hancock (who were then brunette) will mention this in their interviews. None of the cabin crew will ever refer to the spilled drink.

Moments later, Second Officer Anderson announces the takeoff.

While the airplane is taxiing to the takeoff position, Schaffner checks that the passengers' seat belts are fastened. She then takes the cabin crew seat in the rear galley. She is immediately behind and to the left of the man in seat 18-E. Within a minute, and while the airplane is still taxiing, he turns and hands her a plain white envelope with no writing on it. She thinks he is making a pass. She does not open the envelope. Several times he turns and looks at her, and she understands that he wants her to open the envelope, and she does so. Inside, there is a sheet of plain unlined paper, on which a message is written in black, apparently with a felt-tip pen. She will recall that the message read:

**MISS—I have a bomb here and I would like you to sit by me.**

The word "MISS" is written in capitals, and the rest is in neat cursive script.

Schaffner reads the note twice. She sees that the man is looking directly at her. She asks if he is kidding. He replies, "No, Miss; this is for real." She will later relate that his voice is "serious but calm."

Tina Mucklow at this moment[10] takes a beverage form to the aft jump seat. She notices the man in seat 18-E. Mucklow is facing what she calls "the barrier strip" (presumably a rope or a strip of material that separates the passenger section from the aft galley). She sees Schaffner drop a note, stand up, unfasten the barrier strip, and sit down next to the man in seat 18-E. Schaffner appears emotional. She is trying to speak to Mucklow; she is moving her lips. Mucklow will relate that "other than 'Tina,' no other words came out."

The note is lying on the floor at Mucklow's feet. She picks up the note and reads it. In her interview with the FBI, she will say that to the best of her recollection, the contents were as follows:

**Miss, I am hijacking this plane. I have a bomb. Sit next to me.**

Schaffner will have a slightly different recollection. She will recall that she stood up, handed the note to Mucklow, moved into the passenger section, and sat in the aisle seat (18-D) beside the hijacker; and that Mucklow read the note and went to the phone in the rear of the plane.

Flight 305 lifts off at 2:58 p.m.

The flight crew, as yet unaware of events in the cabin, transmit a message to the airline on the internal frequency,[11] reading (after translation into plain English):

> **Flight 305 out of Portland at 2253/2258, estimated time of arrival Seattle 2336.**[12]

**Figure 1.2**. Seattle-Portland, November 24, 1971: the ARINC teletype tape of Flight 305. *Image credit*: *Washington State Historical Society*

On the teletype, the times are expressed as Zulu or Universal time (eight hours ahead of PST). The first time is 2:53 p.m. and probably refers to engine start or push back; the second time is 2:58 p.m. and probably indicates liftoff. The landing in Seattle is scheduled for 3:36 p.m. The message is followed by a time stamp of 3:07 p.m. but has probably been sent immediately after takeoff.[13]

Meanwhile, Schaffner is sitting beside the hijacker. She asks him again if he is kidding. He replies, "No, Miss."

He has a briefcase on the window seat (18-F). He places it on his lap, opens it, and shows her the contents. For the purposes of our narrative, it is sufficient to relate that Schaffner believes she is looking at a bomb.

Schaffner asks the man what he wants her to do. He replies, "Take this down." She opens her purse and takes out a pen and notepad. The hijacker dictates a message, which she will tell the FBI was, in her recollection, as follows:

> **I want $200,000 by 5:00 p.m. in cash. Put it in a knapsack. I want two back parachutes and two front parachutes. When we land, I want a fuel truck ready to refuel. No funny stuff, or I'll do the job.**

Schaffner stops writing and looks at the man. He says, in a calm voice, "No fuss." Thinking that this is part of the message, she adds these words to the note. She says, "Okay." The man says, "After this, we'll take a little trip."

The narratives of Schaffner and Mucklow intersect at this point, and the order of events is not clear.

Mucklow is in the aisle near Schaffner and sees that Schaffner is writing on an envelope. Schaffner finishes writing and says to the hijacker that she will take the note to the cockpit, to relay the information to the flight crew. He says, "All right, go ahead." As she gets up, she asks, "Sir, is this all you want?" He replies, "Yes." She goes to the aft galley, where (in her recollection) Mucklow is talking on the intercom, and retrieves the original note. Mucklow offers to take the note to the cockpit, but Schaffner says no. Mucklow says to the hijacker, "Do you want me to stay here?," and he replies, "Yes," while Schaffner takes the two notes to the cockpit.

At this juncture, Tina Mucklow takes up the narrative.

Mucklow will recall that at this point, without leaving her seat, she reaches up to pick up the intercom in order to inform the flight crew of trouble. She does so with a prearranged signal of bells. The chronology may be out of sync. Most probably, she made this call earlier, from the aft galley seat (as Schaffner recalls), and not from seat 18-D (which would surely alarm the hijacker).

First Officer Rataczak now enters the narrative. He will testify that "he received an emergency signal from hostess Tina Mucklow on the intercom with a series of bells signaling that they had trouble on board." He makes a note of the time of this signal. Inexplicably, the FBI's notes will later record that he received the signal at 2759 Zulu time or 3:59 p.m. PST. Both times are wrong. Zulu time is based on a twenty-four-hour clock and goes up only to 2359, after which the next minute is 0000. Perhaps Rataczak will say 2:59 p.m. (2259 Zulu)—in other words, one minute after takeoff—and the FBI agent will record both times incorrectly.

Moments later, Mucklow communicates the fact of the hijacking to the cockpit. There are two different versions of this event.

According to Mucklow's second interview with the FBI, in her recollection she telephones the cockpit and says, "We're being hijacked; he's got a bomb and this is no joke."

According to First Officer Rataczak, almost immediately after the bell signal he receives a note from Mucklow advising that she thinks they are being hijacked and that she is not kidding. It is clear that he means that Mucklow came to the cockpit before Schaffner, because he goes on to say, "Subsequently, hostess Florence Schaffner brought a note . . . Hostess Mucklow then went back to the compartment and sat with the hijacker."

Neither Mucklow nor Schaffner will ever mention Mucklow's visit to the cockpit. The FBI never comments on the discrepancy between the three interviews.

Mucklow will not report ever seeing the contents of the note with the hijacker's demands. She learns only later that the note that Schaffner has carried to the pilot contains a list of demands. In her recollection, the hijacker himself later tells her that he wants $200,000 in "circulated US currency," two back and two front parachutes, and fuel trucks to meet the plane when it lands at Seattle.

Rataczak's recollections are almost identical: "Notations also containing the figure $200,000, two back parachutes, two chest packs, and under it a time of 5:00 p.m."

Up front, Schaffner gives the information to Captain Scott, who instructs her to stay in the cockpit. She will remain there until shortly before the airplane lands in Seattle.

Back in the passenger cabin, Mucklow has taken seat 18-D next to the hijacker, where Schaffner had previously been sitting. She lights a cigarette for the hijacker and tells him the crew will cooperate with him.

Mucklow will recall that the man said, "No kidding and no funny stuff"; it sounds like either she overheard his dictation to Schaffner, or he repeated this admonition for her benefit. She will recall that about this time, he partially opens the attaché case and she sees the contents. Like Schaffner, Mucklow is convinced that she is looking at a bomb.

The hijacker says that the ignition is an electronic device. He suggests that the crew use the aircraft radio as little as possible. He does not think radio transmissions "would bother it," but he wants to let the crew know. If this warning ever reaches the crew, it does not seem to overly concern them, since they continue to communicate with the airline on the company frequency; but whether by accident or design, their communications with air traffic control are sparse.

Mucklow calls the flight deck and describes the device. Evidently the hijacker does not object to this call. From this moment, it appears that the hijacker has decided on Mucklow as the intermediary between himself and all other parties.

At 3:13 p.m. the flight crew communicates with Northwest to the following effect:

**Passenger advises he is hijacking [us] en route to Seattle. Stewardess has been handed note requesting two hundred thousand and knapsack by 5 p.m. at Seattle this afternoon. Wants two backpack parachutes. Wants money in negotiable American currency.**

**Denomination of bills not important. Has bomb in briefcase and will use it if anything is done to block his request. En route to Seattle.**

The word "negotiable" has been seized by analysts of this event, as a word unlikely to be used by an American to refer to American currency, and therefore as evidence that the hijacker was a foreigner. But this word does not appear in the testimony of any of the witnesses to the FBI. Possibly the flight crew are using the word "negotiable" to paraphrase "circulated" as Mucklow reported, referring, in other words, to used bills rather than new ones.

Meanwhile, on the company frequency, the flight crew and Northwest Airlines exchange a flurry of messages. A plan begins to form. The flight crew will inform the passengers of "mechanical difficulties," which will require fuel to be burned off. The airplane will enter a holding pattern near Seattle until the money and parachutes are ready.

At 3:20 p.m. the flight crew transmit in abbreviated form: "Advise [that] the passenger that is hijacking the flight boarded at Portland." By now, they must know that his seat number is 18-E.

During this period, Mucklow is alone with the hijacker; she in seat 18-D, he still in 18-E, and the briefcase on 18-F. She makes what she imagines is light conversation with him. She asks him unwisely where he is from, which annoys him. She wonders aloud if they are going to Cuba, which makes him laugh. He is extraordinarily relaxed. He says they are not going to Cuba, but she will like where they are going. At one point he offers her a cigarette (probably one of his Raleigh filter tips), which she accepts although she has quit. He asks her where she is from; she says Pennsylvania, but living in Minneapolis, which he says is "very nice country." Could it be a foreigner's perspective, or a verbal mannerism, to describe an urban area of over two million people (in 1970) as "nice country"?

Throwing caution to the wind, Mucklow asks the hijacker why he selected Northwest Airlines. He laughs (again); he says, "It's not because I have a grudge against your airlines [*sic*]; it's just because I have a grudge."

Is that a typo in the transcript or does he say "airlines" instead of "airline"? If so, he is possibly a Spanish speaker who has inadvertently translated the word "aerolíneas."

Be that as it may, the hijacker is saying that Flight 305 suits his time, his place, and his plans. This is a weighty comment. He has a plan, and the rainy skies between Portland and Seattle, on the afternoon of November 24, 1971, are in conformity with the plan.

Apart from his original bourbon and 7-Up, which he spilled, the hijacker refuses all offers of food or refreshment. No witness will recall seeing him eat or drink anything.

At 3:54 p.m., the flight crew transmit this: "Name of man unknown; about 6'1" high, black hair, age about fifty, weight 175 pounds, boarded at Portland." This description must be from Mucklow via the intercom. They do not know his name because it is not on the manifest.

In row 18, the conversation is not uniformly airy. The hijacker reminds Mucklow repeatedly that the crew should attempt "nothing funny." Each time she reassures him that the crew will cooperate. Evidently, Mucklow thinks it wise to pass this on to the flight deck. At 4:12 p.m. the crew sends a further message: "The hijacker is advising that if anything [occurs] to hinder things [he] will definitely ignite the bomb."

## THE COWBOY

Somewhere between Portland and Seattle, a male passenger comes aft down the aisle. By this time the passengers have heard about the "mechanical difficulties." Mucklow leaves seat 18-D and intercepts the passenger around row 14. He says he is looking for a sports magazine. She takes him to the aft galley, evidently passing the hijacker on the way; the passenger accepts a *New Yorker* magazine and returns to his seat.

George Labissoniere has more on this story. Emerging from one of several visits to the aft restroom, Labissoniere finds himself blocked in the aisle by "a stewardess named Tina" (evidently he has seen her name tag) and a male passenger wearing a cowboy hat. The cowboy is "hassling" Tina for information about the "mechanical difficulties." The man in 18-E seems to enjoy the situation at first but becomes irritated and tells the cowboy to go to his seat. The cowboy takes no notice of the man in 18-E. Finally, it is Labissoniere who, by his own account, persuades the cowboy to return to his seat.

An intriguing reference to this dispute is buried in the files of the FBI:

> **One passenger scuffled briefly with hijacker. Second passenger pulled first passenger away from hijacker.**[14]

The FBI will quickly walk back this story. ASAC Paul R. Bibler will write on November 30:

> **This was a wrong choice of words . . . the word should have been "hassel" [*sic*] . . . there was actually no scuffle and the witness had not had to separate the two, but merely stepped in to end an argument.**[15]

The witness is undoubtedly Labissoniere, and the initiator of the "scuffle" or "hassle" is undoubtedly the cowboy. We recall that the passengers do not know of the hijack; yet, the hijacker takes the risk of speaking, for the first time, to anyone other than the ticket clerk and the two stewardesses. The cowboy is the only person who exchanges hot words with the hijacker; his testimony would be a gold mine. But Mucklow never reports the incident.

The cowboy is surely one of the passengers who boarded in Great Falls or Missoula, Montana, and an altercation of this kind is something the crew want to avoid. Rataczak, years later, will tell an interviewer:

> **I know we picked up some good old Montana mountain boys and they're pretty good sized, and they're sitting up in first class and they were on their second or third martinis. . . . we don't need them to look at each other and say, "Hey, let's go back and get a hijacker."**[16]

Quite possibly, Rataczak does not know about Labissoniere's testimony, which will not find its way into the public domain until 2016. If so, he may not know how close they came to finding out whether the bomb was real, or not.

A newsreel on KIRO-TV, dated November 25, 1971, records some of the passengers of Flight 305, apparently leaving Seattle Airport. Among them is the cowboy. He looks young, maybe under 30, average height, clean-cut and square-jawed; he is chewing gum. His hat is a dark color and so is his shirt. He does not look at all fazed by his experience.

The cowboy has never been identified.

## HOLDING PATTERN

When Mucklow is back in seat 18-D, the hijacker says, "If that is a sky marshal, I don't want any more of that." Mucklow assures him that there are no sky marshals on the flight. Does she know that for a fact?

Shortly afterward, the pilot calls Mucklow, who is now established as the intermediary. The pilot asks if he should inform the passengers of the situation. Mucklow asks the hijacker, and he says no.

At some point the hijacker instructs Mucklow to tell the pilot to return the note and envelope that he had given to Schaffner. In her first interview with the FBI, Mucklow will say that this occurred on the way to Seattle; later she will say it was after landing. In this context she will recall that at one time, she lit a cigarette for him with the last match in the paper match folder, and when she attempted to discard the empty folder, he "decisively took it from her and placed it into one of his pockets, stating he did not want her to throw it away." Finally, she will remember that he kept another book of matches, "Sky Chef" brand with a blue cover, which she had been using to light his cigarettes.

No doubt through Mucklow, First Officer Rataczak also hears this story. He will tell the FBI (one imagines a grudging respect for the hijacker's preparedness) that the hijacker "insisted on the return of the original note and the envelope and appeared especially careful to see that nothing of his was left behind. . . . [He] even insisted that a discarded match cover be returned to him."

At 5:15 p.m., two and a quarter hours into the flight, the airplane is in a holding pattern over Seattle. The hijacker becomes increasingly impatient. He reminds Mucklow that he had asked for his demands to be met by 5:00 p.m. At 5:22 p.m. the crew transmit: "[The hijacker] has inquired three times now about the chutes. He is not accepting the fact that they are not available locally."

By this time the crew have made arrangements for some of the parachutes to be delivered from McChord Field, which in 1971 is a US Air Force base. It is 33 miles by road from Seattle-Tacoma International Airport.

Somewhere around this time, in Mucklow's recollection, the hijacker makes two comments that seem to show that he knows the area. With reference to the parachutes, he mentions that it is about twenty minutes' drive from McChord to Sea-Tac. The crew seem to take his word for it: at 5:26 p.m. they transmit: "He is fully aware that McChord Field is 20 miles away." Even if they meant 20 nautical miles, they were greatly underestimating the distance; to make it in twenty minutes would require an average speed of 99 mph.

The second comment is also during the holding pattern. The hijacker looks out the window and says, "We're over Tacoma now." The crew has made no mention of Tacoma on the public address system.

At 5:37 p.m., Flight 305 transmits, "About 5 miles out on final [approach]," and the company replies, "Everything is ready for your arrival."

By 5:47 p.m., nearly two and a half hours after its scheduled arrival, Flight 305 is on the ground at Seattle. Following the hijacker's instructions, Mucklow leaves the aircraft, collects the money bag and the parachutes, and delivers them one by one to the hijacker. Again in accordance with the detailed directions of the hijacker, the aircraft is refueled. All the passengers disembark, except for the man in seat 18-E. Alice Hancock and Florence Schaffner, with the permission of the hijacker, leave the airplane; the three flight crew and Tina Mucklow remain on board. The first part of the hijacking is over.

To recapitulate: The hijacker is a middle-aged man, quite tall, of average build, and dressed conservatively to look like a businessman, but maybe this is a costume for the occasion. He is physically unremarkable in all respects except that he is dark complexioned and appears Hispanic. If he has an accent, it is undetectable to Americans. He is soft spoken, good humored, and courteous. He is preternaturally calm in a situation of extreme danger. He has planned the mission with great care and in great detail. He knows the Seattle area. He has chosen Flight 305 for a specific reason or reasons. For the moment, this is all we know of him.

Here we will advance a wild surmise. The hijacker has rehearsed this mission. He has taken Flight 305 before.

CHAPTER

# 2

# THE ESCAPE

In chapter 1, we saw how a middle-aged, soft-spoken, dark-complexioned man, holding a one-way ticket from Portland to Seattle, successfully extorted $200,000 from Northwest Orient Airlines. In this chapter we shall recount the events leading up to his escape with the money, never to be apprehended.

It is around 6:00 p.m. at Seattle-Tacoma International Airport on the evening of November 24, 1971. Aboard Flight 305, parked in a dark and remote corner of the airport, the passengers are awaiting the signal to disembark. Some of them have begun to entertain suspicions about the man in seat 18-E and his prolonged conference with the blonde-haired stewardess, but none is aware that there has been a hijacking.

At this point the ransom money arrives. Rataczak, in an interview 41 years later, will recall:

> **The money that was to be brought in by Tina [Mucklow] was brought in a hap sack, a bag. I'm not quite sure how to describe the bag other than it was a very coarse hap sack with a leather shoulder strap across it and a leather handle and the $200,000 was in that.**[1]

Cord Zum Spreckel, who has been sitting in row 17 on the port side, is probably one of the last passengers to disembark. He will tell the FBI:

> **After the plane landed, the blonde stewardess, who had been sitting next to the hijacker, got up and went forward and out of the forward exit of the plane. . . . She returned through the same door after several minutes, carrying a package which was made of**

> **off-white canvas. . . . The package was about two feet by one foot by one and one-half feet in dimensions. . . . The stewardess took the package back to the hijacker, and then the passengers were instructed to deboard.**

This package is undoubtedly the ransom money, collected from a waiting truck and delivered by Tina Mucklow in accordance with the hijacker's instructions. If Zum Spreckel's recollection is accurate, it looks like a bulky package. His dimensions give it a volume of about 3 cubic feet; however, the ransom consists of 10,000 $20 bills, which if stacked neatly would occupy only 0.4 cubic feet (roughly 1 foot by 1 foot by 4 inches). In this testimony, the sequence of events is that the front stairway is attached to the airplane, the front door is opened, Mucklow leaves through the front door and returns with the money, and the delivery to seat 18-E is made in full view of the passengers.

Robert Gregory will also recall the bag; his estimate of its dimensions agree with Zum Spreckel's, and furthermore he identifies it as a money bag. Although he is sitting only a few rows forward of seat 18-E, on the port side (and therefore well placed to see where the bag is going), he does not notice the delivery:

> **After the landing he noticed a blonde stewardess [Mucklow], one of the in-flight stewardesses, carrying a money bag about two feet tall. He did not see her give it to the man [in seat 18-E].**

Nancy House has been sitting in row 15. Up to now she has paid little attention to the man in 18-E. She now makes an observation that, later that evening, she will recount to the FBI, as follows:

> **Upon landing in Seattle, [the man in 18-E] got up from his seat and went into the restroom at the rear of the plane. He remained there for about one minute and then returned to the same seat which he had occupied throughout the flight. . . . When he exited the restroom and returned to his seat, he was carrying a dark-colored attaché case on its side in both arms. . . . On top of this case was a package which appeared to be a yellow paper bag . . . approximately four inches high and being about two inches shorter than the width of the attaché case.**

In a second interview with the FBI on December 2, Mrs House will remember the bag as cloth rather than paper:

> **Width and height approximately the same as the width and height of the attaché case. The bag was of cloth composition, possibly manila or burlap. The bag was of a light color, possibly very light yellow and possibly with a very light pink tinge . . . fairly smooth on the side, which was up.**

Mrs. House will testify that she never has a glimpse, and has no idea, of the contents of the bag. She evidently does not connect it with the money bag, which has been conspicuously carried onto the plane and delivered to seat 18-E.

Nevertheless, Mrs. House's paper or cloth bag must contain the money. The briefcase has been described (by Alice Hancock) as measuring about 12 by 18 inches. If the bag has the same depth and width and is 2 inches shorter, its capacity is 0.44 cubic feet, which is just about right for 10,000 $20 bills, neatly stacked.

From Zum Spreckel's and House's testimony, the purpose of the restroom trip is clear. The hijacker has received a burlap sack full of loose bundles of bills, and he takes them to the restroom in order to rearrange them neatly in the bag for minimum volume. He returns holding the briefcase in both arms, like a pizza box, and he has placed the bag on top because he has not yet found a way to secure the new arrangement of the bundles.

In two separate interviews, on November 24 and December 3, Mucklow will confirm the man's trip to the restroom.

In the first interview, the passengers have been requested to remain in their seats with their seat belts fastened. The hijacker closes the attaché case (which evidently has been open or partly open until now) and goes to the nearby lavatory, carrying the attaché case. He states that "he would return in a few minutes, at which time the stairway to the forward door should be ready." He comes out of the lavatory in three or four minutes and returns to seat 18-E.

In the second interview, Tina leaves through the front door to collect the money and other deliverables. At this point, the hijacker gets up with the attaché case and goes toward the aft lavatory. She returns with the money sack, which is made of white canvas. She sees that he is back in his seat. She drags (not carries) the money sack down the aisle and places it on seat 18-D next to the hijacker. He looks through the sack and says that it is all right for the passengers to leave the plane.

Between November 24 and December 3, Mucklow reverses the order of events. In the first interview, the hijacker expects the front stairway to be in place when he leaves the restroom; therefore it is not in place when he enters the restroom. In this case, Mucklow cannot have left the airplane to collect the money. In the second interview, the front stairway is in place when he enters the restroom. In neither case does Mucklow mention his carrying the money sack to the restroom. The special agents of the FBI never question this anomaly.

And what happened to the distinctive "hap" sack with a leather shoulder strap and a leather handle, that Rataczak described so precisely? It is never heard of again.

For the moment, we have to record this discrepancy for what it is worth, and move on.

The passengers are off the airplane. The money is in the hijacker's possession. We may now turn our attention to the four parachutes, which are the key to his escape.

Since the parachutes arrive after the passengers leave, Gregory must have overheard Mucklow, or another cabin crew member, talking about them. Incidentally, the parachutes are not a complete secret. Robert Gregory will say that he "heard some parachutes had been brought on board, but he did not see them."

Before going to collect the chutes, Mucklow asks the hijacker if he would prefer one of the flight crew to get them. He says that they are not that heavy, and she will not have any trouble.

The public records of the FBI will eventually provide two descriptions of the parachutes that Mucklow delivers to the hijacker. One is from a standard FD-36 form used by special agents, but it is undated, unsigned, and heavily redacted.[2] The other is from a statement by George Harrison, of Northwest Airlines Flight Operations at Seattle-Tacoma International Airport, who has been instrumental in securing the parachutes.[3] Harrison's statement relates only to the two backpacks and is also undated. Merging these two documents as best we can, we learn the following about the parachutes:[4]

- Two front chest chutes, twenty[-]four feet in diameter, all white nylon, model T-seven A, white shrouds, about fourteen feet long
- Number one[5] container has [redacted] written on it and is about ten by thirteen inches, olive drab.

- Number two container has [redacted; probably SSS #5 and COSS] written on a white patch[,] which is sewn to container.
- Two back packs ... two to three feet long, fifteen to eighteen inches wide [two handwritten lines redacted in the FD-36]
- Number one back pack chute described as civilian luxury type, tan soft cotton material outside, twenty[-]six[-] foot white canopy inside, and has a military chute inside of it [this is identical with Harrison's description], also one or two burp sacks,[6] and [the] usual lead seal. [Harrison adds: "The parachute has a foam pad; cushion, and a fray mark down the rib on the back from rubbing on metal."]
- Number two back pack chute was a military nylon type, olive drab green outside, twenty[-]eight[-]foot white canopy inside, with two burp sacks in back, lead seal. Seals had not been pulled." [Harrison confirms: "standard military olive drab green on outside ... also has a foam pad cushion."]

Harrison adds that both parachutes bear lead seals, which have not been broken.

Forty-nine years later, the FBI will finally publish a more explicit description of the two parachutes that the hijacker has taken:

1. Backpack #1: 28 foot, white nylon canopy, ripstop material, material 1.1 ounce weight, flat circular military, non-steerable, white shrouds; harness was civilian luxury type, soft tan. Backpack was Navy type 6, sage green nylon.
2. Chest pack #1: 24 foot, white nylon canopy, white nylon shrouds—14′ length model T-7A. Container was olive drab green, 10″ × 14″ × 6″, "Norm D" inscribed on container."[7]

A backpack chute, as all jumpers know, is the main chute that the jumper will deploy in the first instance. A chest pack or chest chute is the reserve, to be used only if the main chute fails.

The delivery to the hijacker, in short, consists of two backpacks and two chest packs, exactly as he has specified. The backpacks are of similar size, but one looks civilian and the other looks military; it is not apparent that he knows, or can discover, that both contain military chutes. We do not know whether the chest packs are similar to each other; we do know that one is olive drab in color, but the color of the other is not stated.

We shall now leap forward in time and space, to 11:25 p.m. the same evening at Reno Municipal Airport, where four special agents of the FBI are inspecting the airplane, now abandoned by crew and hijacker. They report the following findings:

**On the floor directly in front of seat number 18D, the exterior canvas cover for a chest[-]type parachute was observed along with the handle utilized for releasing this parachute.... The flap on this canvas exterior contained a sewn[-]on white label with the notation SSS #5 and COSS.[8]... An opened parachute which apparently had been removed from the canvas parachute cover described above was found spread out over seats 17C and 17B. This parachute was of a pink-orange color.**

**On seat 18B, an unopened back[-]type parachute was observed. A card in the pocket of this parachute reflected it to be a Conacol[-]type parachute number 60-9707 and made by the Pioneer Parachute Company." ["Conacol" undoubtedly should read "conical."]**

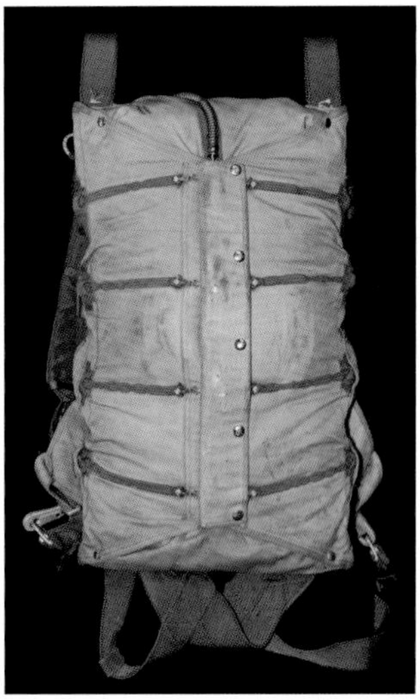

**Figure 2.1.** The number 1 backpack (left on airplane). *Courtesy of Washington State Historical Society. Image credit: FBI*

The four agents have evidently found the number 2 container for a chest chute, along with the chute that used to be inside it (except that the chute is pink orange in color, not "white nylon" as per the earlier FBI report). The agents have also found the number 1 backpack with its chute inside (since the pack is identifiable as a "civilian luxury" model).

We now know that the hijacker will depart the airplane with the number 1 chest pack and the number 2 backpack (to use the FBI's terminology). The chest pack is described as "olive drab," and the backpack as "military type" and also as "olive drab." He would almost look like a paratrooper, except that, as far as anyone knows, he is still wearing his dark suit and pebble-grain slip-on shoes. He has a 28-foot canopy for the main chute and a 24-foot canopy for the reserve (although this may not be known to him; we do not know whether the chute diameter is marked on the pack). At the risk of drifting into speculation, we might say that he chooses the equipment with which an ex-military man would be familiar.

Much has been made, on internet forums and elsewhere, of the claim that the hijacker has discarded the "civilian luxury" parachute. By this choice, it is argued, he adopts a nonsteerable military chute over a steerable civilian one and thereby loses flexibility in his descent path; therefore he cannot be an experienced jumper.

There are three possible rejoinders. First, there is no civilian parachute. Both main chutes are military, but one of them has a civilian-style cotton pack, or container. Possibly the hijacker checks the cotton pack and sees that this is the case. Second, it is possible that the hijacker does not check but nevertheless prefers the military-style pack. Third, even military parachutes are steerable; it's a matter of pulling on the shroud lines. They are simply less steerable than civilian chutes, because military chutes are usually intended to deposit large numbers of troops in roughly the same place.

An analogous argument has been made with regard to the chest pack. It has been claimed that the number 1 chest pack was unusable, because it was a dummy for classroom demonstrations, and the pack had been sewn shut. In this argument, the hijacker does not notice the state of the pack; he subsequently departs at the mercy of a single parachute, and therefore

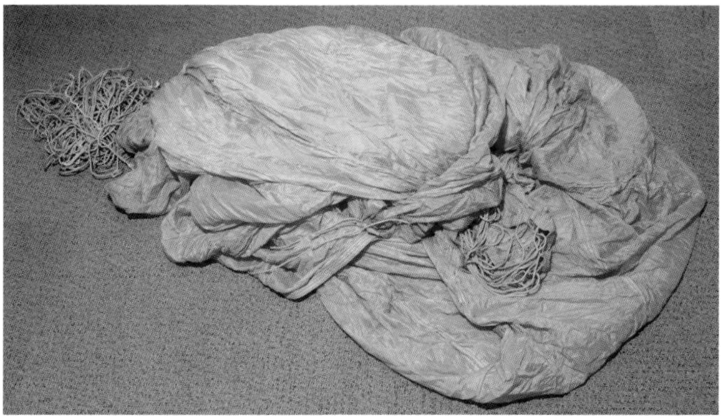

**Figure 2.2.** The number 2 reserve canopy (left on airplane). *Courtesy of Washington State Historical Society. Image credit: FBI*

**Figure 2.3**. The number 2 chest pack (left on airplane). *Courtesy of Washington State Historical Society. Image credit: FBI*

he cannot be an experienced jumper. Nothing in the FBI files supports the claim that the number 1 chest pack, as delivered, was inoperable. But if it is true, one can hypothesize that the hijacker does notice the state of the number 1 pack and that, preferring it for some reason to the other pack with the white label, he cuts the stitching and renders the pack usable.

Now that we know the nature of the parachutes that have been delivered to the hijacker, and the choices that he will make, we may return to the testimony of Tina Mucklow, who will shortly become the sole direct witness to the hijacker's actions.

Only seven persons—the three flight crew, the three cabin crew, and the hijacker—are aboard the airplane now.

Mucklow will recall that she brings one large backpack first. The hijacker instructs her to lower all the window shades in the rear section of the airplane. She leaves the airplane again to collect the two chest packs, which are smaller. Her last trip is to collect the second backpack. She leaves the four chutes with the hijacker, stacked on the seats in row 18. Upon delivering the fourth chute, she offers him a paper with instructions on how to jump. This is probably a plant by the FBI, to test whether he is an experienced jumper or not. He says that he does not need the instructions. He starts inspecting the parachutes; he appears to be completely familiar with them.

The hijacker now permits cabin crew members Hancock and Schaffner to depart the airplane. He instructs Mucklow and the three flight crew to remain on board. He gives detailed instructions for the next leg of the flight (which we shall elaborate in another chapter).

Earlier, sometime during the refueling, the hijacker has complained to Mucklow that since the money has been delivered in a cloth bag and not in a knapsack as he has requested, he is obliged to use one of the parachutes to rewrap it. He now tries to do so. He opens one of the packs (Mucklow will later recall that the canopy is colored bright orange, which agrees with the description by the four FBI agents in Reno). The hijacker makes an attempt to arrange the money in the pack. Mucklow assumes that he wants to attach the pack to his body, with the money inside in place of the canopy. She will recall that he produces a "small jack knife" from a pocket and cuts some part of the gear, either the pack or the canopy.

The hijacker mentions that he will cut the shroud lines so that when he lowers the aft airstair, Mucklow can use the lines to secure herself to the aircraft. During the actual event, she will not need to do so.

Later, in Reno, special agents of the FBI will find the reserve chute with several shroud lines severed.

In Mucklow's recollection, the hijacker does not make any modification to either of the two large backpacks.

In summary:

- The hijacker disables one reserve chute, possibly thinking to use either the pack or the canopy as a money bag (which in the end he does not, since he leaves both the pack and the canopy on the airplane), or possibly with some function in mind for the shroud lines.
- He dons the other reserve chute (which is later claimed to be unusable, but maybe he has noticed this and fixed it).
- He rejects the backpack that the FBI will describe as a "civilian luxury" model (but he may know or discover that the chute inside is military).
- He dons the other backpack, which is unmistakably a military model.
- He secures the money to himself in some unknown fashion (but clearly it is not with a chest pack or canopy).

So far, this is the essence of our direct knowledge of the parachutes and how the hijacker intends to use them.

Here we call an expert witness. His or her name is unknown, because it has been redacted from the documents on the FBI's website. He or she is evidently a highly experienced parachutist. The FBI's interview with this person, dated December 3, 1971, is a masterpiece of clarity, which makes it extraordinary that this interview has never been widely disseminated. It could have extinguished decades of uninformed speculation. The following is a series of extracts from the interview[9] (and more will follow in later chapters, in which we shall discuss the flight path and the jump zone).

**Q. Based on the information we have discussed, here, does this jump present any problem to an experienced jumper?**

A. None whatsoever.

**Q. Do you think this man made this type of jump before?**

A. I would say he has made some high[-]altitude jumps before. . . . The jumper was an experienced high[-]altitude parachutist. . . . It is my opinion that this jumper was experienced[,] and I would say having at least 150 jumps.

**Q. What would the possibility be of the jumper suffering ankle or leg injuries in wearing Oxford street shoes?**

A. No more than if he had jump boots on. It shouldn't create any problem. [redacted] . . . Footwear for an experienced jumper is inconsequential.

**Q. What would your guess be as to the number of jumpers in the country that could pull this type of jump off?**

A. At least [10,000] people.[10] In the "Parachutist" put out by the U.S. Parachute Association, there are listed the names, and [the] state from which they are from, for every individual which has obtained a license, whether it is Class A, B, C, D, or I. A Class C jumper could have made the above jump.[11] There are currently 7192 licensed Class C jumpers—to say nothing of Class D or I. As of this month, there are 3094 Class D jumpers. Class I is not given. The above figures do not include military personnel that have done high[-]altitude free-fall jumps. There is no way to determine how many jumpers would be in that category.

**Q. Would accepting an unfamiliar chute present any problem to this person?**

A. It wouldn't bother me. I would certainly check it over[,] as would any experienced jumper.

**Q. This would take less than ten minutes?**

A. Yes.

**Q. [redacted] would you discuss the age factor of a man 45 to 50 in parachute jumping? How many are active?**

A. Very few. However, high[-]altitude jumpers in that age group would be extremely limited. These would be officials of jump clubs or parachute governing bodies and/or instructors.

**Q. Bringing the age factor into this, would that change your estimate of the excess [*sic*] with which this jump could be performed?**

A. No, because of the fact it requires no special physical condition to pull off a jump if you know what you're doing.

This testimony has the ring of experience and adds powerful support to the statements of the flight crew and cabin crew, to the effect that the hijacker was generally very familiar with airplanes and with parachuting.

The Boeing Airplane Company confirms the benign nature of the jump. The day after the hijacking, Boeing spokesman John Wheeler will tell the press:

**It would be a very safe drop. He'd be away from flaps and other engines and go straight down.**[12]

Contrary, therefore, to much ill-founded commentary on internet forums and even by agents of the FBI, at this point we can surely conclude that the man who hijacked Flight 305 had made many parachute jumps, including high-altitude jumps, and that the execution of his escape from the airplane is the least of his concerns. His age, his street attire, his comfortable shoes, and the unfamiliar parachutes are in no way obstacles to his escape.

Perhaps one speculation is permissible. The hijacker is an experienced jumper, and there is some indication that he is ex-military. If he has been a paratrooper, many or most of his jumps in military service will have been with a static line. This is a line that is attached at one end to the structure of the airplane, and at the other end to the ripcord. With a static line, the jumper does not need to pull the ripcord. The chute will be deployed as soon as the jumper has fallen the length of the line, which will be within a second of leaving the airplane. Has the hijacker cut the shroud cords in order to make a static line?

We shall now metaphorically leave the parachutes aside and turn to the final element in the hijacker's escape: the ventral airstair.

To recapitulate: The ventral airstair is the stairway that hinges downward below the tail and allows passengers and crew to enter and exit the airplane without the need for an external bridge or staircase. As we observed in chapter 1, at the end of 1971, over a thousand jet airliners in the United States had this feature. More than half of them were Boeing 727s, but there were over three hundred DC-9s, as well as a few British-made BAC-111s.[13] Every one of the eleven trunk carriers, and nine of the ten local-service carriers, had some of these airplanes. The largest operator of such airplanes was Eastern, with 183; Northwest had only fifty-six. The possible reasons for the hijacker's choice of Flight 305 will be the subject of another chapter. However, on the subject of the ventral airstair, we recall our expert witness to the stand.

**Figure 2.4**. Schiphol Airport, 1970: a Douglas DC-9-30 with ventral airstair, operated by KLM. *Courtesy of Key Aero. Image credit: Jur van der Wees*

> **Q. [Redacted] given the following set of circumstances, the Boeing 727 which you are generally familiar with, the rear stairway . . . Would this be an ideal type aircraft from which to make a daylight or night jump?**
>
> A. Yes.

We return to the testimony of Tina Mucklow and the flight crew.

Earlier, at 6:21 p.m., while still on the ground at Seattle, the flight crew have transmitted a message that must have been relayed through Mucklow:

**Aft passenger loading door will be open and will remain in that position and aft stairs [the ventral airstair] are to be lowered after take off.**[14]

Minneapolis Flight Operations know already that Flight 305 is proposing to fly with landing gear and flaps down. They reply immediately:

**The drag will be such that you cannot make the Mexican border even with the aft stairs up.**

But in a moment, they add:

**The plane is operable with the aft stairs extended.**

The crew have a brief negotiation with the hijacker. They report back:

**The third girl [Mucklow] is to stay with the aircraft. He wants her to manipulate the stairs for him after the plane is airborne. We have tried to tell him we are unable to operate with the stairs lowered after take-off. We are trying to get him to let us lower the stairs partially for take-off.**

Minneapolis does not like this idea at all. They reply:

**We don't know of any way to lock the stairs in the intermediate position.**

The ARINC time stamp registers 6:28 p.m.

Flight 305 comes back with another idea. It is not clear whether this has originated with the hijacker, or whether they are reading from an operations manual.

**Reading the proposed order [?] [he?] says the stairs will open about 20 degrees at 120 knots. Is that enough for an individual to escape the aircraft?**

Minneapolis thinks that this will work:

**With him on the stairs, they will open possibly [enough] for him to get out . . . slow to ERTL speed[15] before you try to extend the stairs.**

And an unidentified party transmits:

**Slow to threshold speed [landing speed]. Try with either gear up, or if unable, with gear down.**

It is now 6:40 p.m. The flight crew are not at all comfortable about flying with the airstairs down. Many years later, Rataczak will remember:

**We needed to know how that airplane was going to fly if the aft stairs were lowered in flight --is the airplane going to tip over, is it going to roll and what's going on?[16]**

Someone in Minneapolis (probably Paul Soderlind, whom we will introduce later) has an action plan:

**You will have no control problem when [the ventral stairs are] extended. There may be some slight pitch-up[,] but it will be very controllable. The plane has been flown this way. They have [dropped] large boxes of 200 to 300 lbs through the door.**

The term "pitch-up" is strange. When the stairs are lowered, they will generate drag below the centerline of the airplane. That will push the tail up and the nose down; in other words it will create a "pitch down" force. However, Rataczak does not question the advice from Minneapolis, and he seems reassured. Recounting this exchange many years later, he will recall that he learned (either then or later) that the information came from Boeing:

**Interestingly, Boeing had tested that plane before it was certified in flight with the stairs down. So, I knew exactly what it was going to do and I can confirm that it did exactly what they told us it would do. It was a very stable introduction to our clean airplane when the stairs were lowered."[17]**

When Rataczak says "clean," he is using an aeronautical term meaning that there are no devices or surfaces protruding into the airstream. Strictly speaking, the airplane would not be "clean" when the stairs were lowered. It would have the landing gear and flaps down, in other words, it would be in what pilots call a "dirty" configuration.

Nevertheless, the crew of Flight 305 have a doubt. Should they take off with the stairs down, as the hijacker demands?

**He seems to be insistent with the stairs in [1 degree?]**

But Minneapolis is adamant:

**It's impossible to take off with the stairs extended[,] but full up [is OK].**

Evidently the hijacker concedes this point. Flight 305 transmits:

**He wants the girl [Mucklow] to initiate the stairs after take off. Should we tie her down to the structure?**

Minneapolis agrees that this is a good idea. They issue a final admonition:

**Advise him that you cannot take off with [the aft] door down.**

Flight 305:

**Roger.**

It is now 7:05 p.m. Tina Mucklow takes up the story.

## THE AFT CABIN DOOR

As a last action before takeoff, Mucklow opens the aft cabin door and locks it in the open position.

Or does she? In Reno, when the hijacking is over, she will tell the FBI:

**The hijacker also indicated that he wanted take-off made with the rear door open and the stairs extended for take-off.**

**The crew ... informed the hijacker that take-off in that aircraft with the door open and stairs extended would be an impossibility ...**

**... it was finally agreed that take-off would be made with the door closed, stairs retracted and Miss Mucklow would remain on board to lower the door and stairs after the aircraft was airborne.**

**... as soon as this lowering of the door and stairs were accomplished in flight, she would be permitted to go to the pilot's compartment.**

**... After the plane was airborne, there was conversation between Miss Mucklow and the hijacker regarding her opening the rear door and extending the stairway.**

**... Shortly thereafter he asked her to demonstrate to him the procedure for opening the rear door and extending the stairway. She did this and was under the impression that he understood how to do it."**

In this testimony, there are at least six references to opening a door and extending the stairs, as if these are separate operations. But the only door that is separate from the stairs is the aft cabin door. We are practically forced to assume that the takeoff will be made with this door closed.

Nine days later, in her second testimony to the FBI, Mucklow will apparently set the record straight:

> **She opened the aft door and locked it open and the pilot started the engines and taxied towards the runway.**

In spite of all the previous references, we are now obliged to believe that on takeoff from Seattle, the aft cabin door is open, and is locked in that position.

This action essentially disables the pressurization of the airplane. In normal circumstances, flight engineer Harold Anderson would manage the cabin pressure via the controls on his upper panel (as shown in figure 2.5). He has an automatic pressurization control, which he can set at any cabin altitude up to 10,000 feet; or a manual control knob which he can turn to increase or decrease the cabin pressure relative to the outside air. But with the aft door open, it does not matter what he does. There might as well be a hole in the fuselage (which, in a sense, there is). No matter what setting Anderson applies to the pressurization system, the cabin air pressure will now remain the same as the outside air pressure. An aerospace engineer explains:

> **The aft entry door is part of the rear pressure bulkhead and is completely independent from the airstair, whose entire assembly exists outside the bulkhead. According to Mucklow, this door was secured open during the entire flight from takeoff, so there could not have been a pressure differential.**[18]

Another 727 expert confirms:

> **With the door open, [it] wouldn't make any difference what the F/E did. [The airplane] would be totally depressurized. The outflow valve(s) are tiny, the door area is huge. The Press system would be unable to pressurize the airplane—tho there might be a lot of airflow and some pressure variations.**[19]

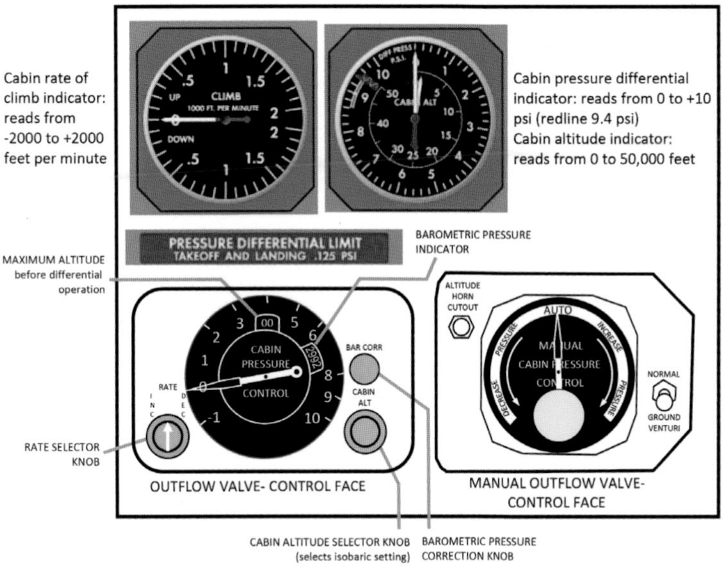


**Figure 2.5**. Boeing 727-51: diagram of pressurisation indicators and controls on flight engineer's upper panel. *Graphic by author based on Northwest Orient Airlines, Boeing 727-51/251 Maintenance Training Manual, ca. 1963, pp. 21–39 RevE and 21–42, by courtesy of avialogs.com; and Alfredo Ramirez, B727 Pressurization – General Description, August 3, 2016, at https://www.youtube.com/watch?v=J3qDknQaQp4*

## TAKEOFF

At 7:36 p.m. (according to the FBI), Flight 305 lifts off again from Seattle International Airport.

In the public domain, there is no transcript which might confirm this time. Flight 305 should be on the Seattle Tower frequency for takeoff, followed by Seattle Departure, followed by Seattle Center, but there is no record of communications with either Tower or Departure. By 7:37:11 p.m. Flight 305 is communicating with Seattle Center, so the plane is certainly airborne at this point.

After takeoff, Mucklow talks to the hijacker about her extending the stairway. (As we know, the aft cabin door is open, and if Mucklow and the hijacker look rearward into the stairwell, they can see the hinged portion of the stairs, in its raised position.) She tells him that she is afraid of being sucked out of the airplane, and he proposes to secure her with the cords that he is cutting, or has cut, from the canopy.

The hijacker asks her to demonstrate the procedure for extending the ventral stairway. She does so (but without actually operating the stairway). In her subsequent testimony to the FBI, there is no record that she elaborates this procedure; but we can reconstruct it. She must open the panel on the right-hand side of the stairwell, and show him the control lever. Probably she reminds the hijacker to squeeze the trigger on the control lever (this is a different system from other 727-100s, which have a push button on the end of the lever). This action will force the lever out of the "raise" detent. Then she should tell him to push the control lever to the "lower" detent and hold it there. That will apply hydraulic power to the stair and lower it to the fully extended position. If he keeps the control lever in the "lower" detent, the stairs will lock down under hydraulic power. Later she will recall that he seems to understand the procedure.

Less than five minutes after takeoff, as she will recall, the hijacker evidently decides that he does not need her to lower the airstair. It is at this point that she receives his instruction to go to the flight deck and not to return. Here her testimony ends.

## THE FINAL ACT

To reconstruct the final act of the hijacker's escape, we now have only what we can reconstruct of the exchanges between him and the flight crew. These exchanges take place via the intercom and the public address system, and the flight crew describe them to Minneapolis, Seattle, and other stations on the ARINC network. Occasionally, the crew make additional terse messages to air traffic control in Seattle; these messages are retained as audio recordings and will later be transcribed.

The communications relating to the ventral stair are as follows and represent the entirety of our knowledge about the hijacker's physical escape.

Four minutes after takeoff, at 7:40:06 p.m., Flight 305 advises Seattle Center:[20]

**Three oh five [climbing] through sixty[-]five hundred [feet] ah trying to get the steps down back there ah . . .**

At 7:40:37, Flight 305 speaks again to air traffic control:

**One oh five ah three oh five we're gonna level off here for a while at seven thousand [feet] he wants the steps down and ah we're gonna have er about down to a hundred and sixty knots.**

Clearly, air traffic control knows that there is a hijacker on board and that he wants the aft steps to be lowered. They must be expecting a resolution of this situation, one way or the other, and surely they have a need to know. Extraordinarily, from this moment onward the flight crew never breathe a word to air traffic control about the hijack. Henceforward, the transcriptions of the air traffic messages from Flight 305 are nothing more than position and altitude reports, radio and transponder frequencies, and the technical exchanges that would accompany an everyday flight. On the other hand, there is a veritable Babel of chatter between Flight 305 and Northwest operations via the ARINC frequency. Why air traffic control was not in the loop remains unknown.

Between the time stamps for 7:40 and 7:42 p.m. (which evidently have a delay of around two to four minutes), the ARINC operator transcribes a transmission from Flight 305 to Northwest, which reads, verbatim:

**305 OUT SEA . . . 14 MILES ON V23 OUT SEA HE IS TRYING TO GET THE DOOR W DOWN . . . STEW IS WITH US HE CANNOT GET THE STAIRS DOWN.**

And in our interpretation:

**We are outbound from Seattle at 14 miles DME[21] on airway Victor 23 out of Seattle. The hijacker is trying to get the aft door down. The stewardess [Mucklow] is with us. He cannot get the aft stairs down.**

If the hijacker is struggling with the airstairs, he must have told the flight crew so on the interphone.

Moments later (the transcriber does not break the line), it is apparent that the hijacker has found the way to work the controls:

**We now have an aft stair light on.**

Here we need to insert a technical note. The aft stair is powered by the B hydraulic system and is operated by interconnected control levers: the upper lever in the aft stairwell (to be operated by the cabin crew), and the lower lever in a panel on the outside of the airplane (to be operated by the ground crew). Each lever has a RAISE and a LOWER detent.

The operation may be described broadly as follows:

**The 727-100 aft airstairs operated a little differently than the 727-200. When you released the control handle, both -100 and -200 [airstairs] will unlock and drop to the ground, and there will be an amber light. The -100 will stop when the stairs are down, but will not lock over center unless [hydraulic] B-system is pressurized and a thumb switch (on the control handle) is held in to lock the stairs down.[22]**

However, this particular airplane does not have a thumb switch on the control lever:

**Some 727-100s (including N467US) had a trigger on the shaft of the control handle for the airstair, while some had a pushbutton on the end. Depressing the trigger would**

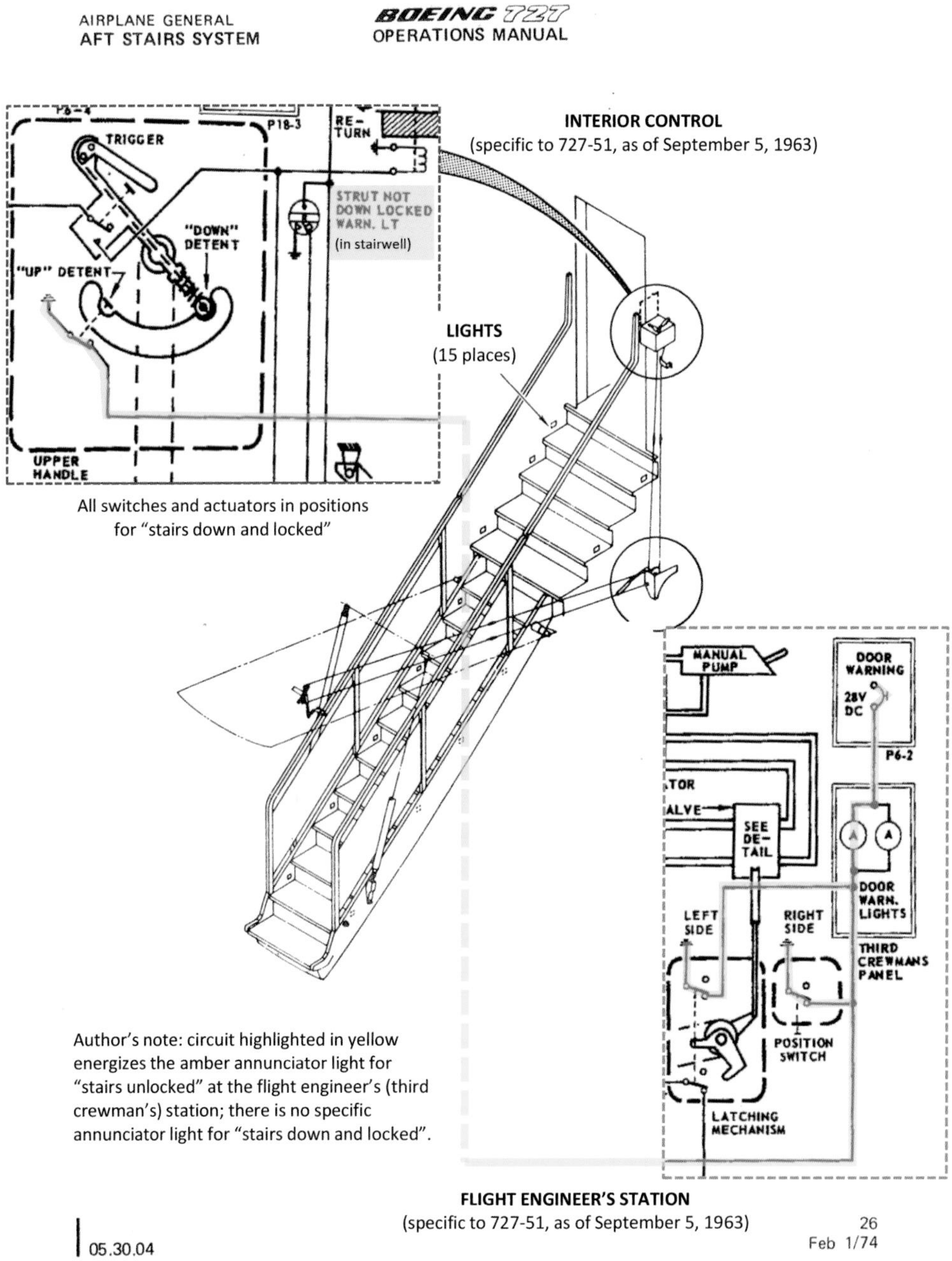


**Figure 2.6**. Boeing 727: diagram of the aft (ventral) airstairs, showing locking struts and interior controls. *Main image by courtesy of Washington State Historical Society, image credit: Boeing Airplane Company. Lower and upper inset images adapted by author from Northwest Orient Airlines, Boeing 727-51/251,* Maintenance Training Manual, *chapter 52, pp. 52–72, by courtesy of avialogs.com; image credit: Northwest Orient Airlines*

**force the handle to leave the "up" detent, but it was ultimately the position of the handle, not the switch, that operated the airstair.[23]**

From the flight deck, the crew cannot operate the airstair, but they can monitor its position. The flight engineer's station includes a panel with a bank of annunciator (indicator) lights. On the 727-100 series, one of these lights (an amber light) indicates the condition of the aft airstair. An aircraft engineer explains:

**The aft-airstair light on the flight engineer's panel illuminates whenever the airstair is not downlocked or uplocked. ... While it is true that the [727]-100 has no specific indication of downlock, the annunciator light will go out under that condition, as it will for uplock. So there is an indirect indication. ... So the annunciator's still being lit would indicate that the airstair is partially deployed.[24]**

We know that N467US is one of the 727-100 series, specifically the 727-51 model. This airplane has only one light on the flight deck for the aft airstair. When illuminated, it signals "stairs unlocked." If it subsequently goes out, it signals "down and locked" or "up and locked."

Tina Mucklow will later recall, in her testimony to the FBI, that "she observed the red indicator light go on the second officer's [flight engineer's] panel indicating that the stairs had been lowered ..." This must mean that the stairs are unlocked.

The B hydraulic system, which powers the airstair among other systems, is functioning. The crew could have disabled the hydraulic power to the airstair by pulling a circuit breaker in the cockpit, but Anderson will later confirm that they did not:

**We didn't want to disable the airstairs by defusing electrical power to [the] hydraulic actuators. We wanted the bastard to get off our ship ASAP.[25]**

Therefore the hijacker, if he understands the controls, has the means to lock the stairs down.

At 7:40 p.m., someone in Flight Operations makes a note:

**Cockpit door closed. Stew [Mucklow] in cockpit.**

At 7:40 p.m. another person in Flight Operations, probably listening in to the radio in real time, makes a note as follows:

**No contact [with hijacker]. Aft stair light on.**

We know therefore that not later than 7:40 p.m., the stairs are out of the up and locked position. We do not know whether they are down and locked.

At 7:42 p.m. someone records, probably reading the teletype and referring to a transmission from some minutes earlier:

**He is trying to get stairs down.**

Between the 7:42 and 7:44 time stamps, the ARINC operator transcribes another message from Flight 305, seemingly confirming the observers' notes:

**305 STILL AT 7THSD FT 19 DME S V23 DUNNO NO COMMS WITH HIM BUT HAVE AN AFT STAIR LITE.**

In plain English this means::

**We are still at 7000 feet at 19 miles DME south of Seattle on airway V-23. Don't know, we have no communications with him but we have an aft stair light on in the cockpit.**

This must be another reference to the amber light.

At 7:44 p.m. another handwritten note is made in Seattle:

**Air stair light.**

At 7:44:22 p.m., Flight 305 reports to air traffic control:

**Okay we'll hold at seven [thousand feet] here we got the back steps down now**

Something has changed between 7:40 and 7:44:22 p.m.; but what?

The only way that the crew can make this statement is by reference to the single annunciator light on the flight engineer's lower panel. If the light has been illuminated since 7:40 p.m., then the stairs are still unlocked, but there is no point in making a new transmission. The B hydraulic system is functioning and operates at 2800 to 3100 psi; therefore the stairs are probably fully extended.

There is something else, that possibly the hijacker knows. Here's another 727 engineer:

**There is a trick that not many people know of. You do not need hydraulics to lock the stairs down. You can simply lean on the support struts and they will go overcenter and lock.[26]**

If the hijacker has either understood the controls or knows the trick, he can lock the stairs down. But he has not yet done so, because as we shall see in a moment, the amber light has not gone out. As of 7:44:22 p.m., that is all that we know.

Sometime between the 7:48 and 7:54 time stamps, the ARINC operator keys the teletype (but this must be a long delayed report of an earlier conversation on the flight deck, because Tina Mucklow has been in the cockpit since 7:40 p.m.):

**Miss Mucklow said that he apparently has the knapsack around him[,] and she thinks that he will attempt a jump.**

At 7:52 p.m., someone in Minneapolis or Seattle repeats this message, with some elaboration that does not appear on either the teletype or in the communications with air traffic control:

**Stew [Mucklow] says he has knapsack on (?) planning to jump. Think he[']s going to leave any time. We want to give him as much time as possible.**

However, Mucklow has now been on the flight deck for between six and fourteen minutes and has not seen the hijacker's final configuration for the jump. Her reference to the "knapsack" seems to refer to the backpack for the main parachute. As to whether he attaches the chest pack, and how he stores the money on his person, that remains unknown to this day.

Between 7:54 and 8:05 p.m., the transcript reads as follows:

**We have attempted on two occasions to make contact with the individual. He did not reply. Then [he came on] the Public Address system and he said that everything is OK.**

At 8:05 p.m., two persons in flight operations write down notes to this effect:

**Attempted 2 times to contact, just responded [underlined] he said everything was OK. No answer on Interphone. Response on PA. [underlined]**

## THE OSCILLATION

Between 8:10 and 8:12 p.m., the ARINC transcriber keys a new message:

**We are getting some oscillations in the cabin. [The hijacker] must be doing something with the [aft] air stairs.**

This message can probably be narrowed down to a moment not later than 8:11 p.m., at which time two persons in Flight Operations make notes as follows:

**Unknown author: Cabin fluctuating xA**

**Bob Lowenthal: . . . 305 At the present cabin is fluctuating [underlined] playing with air stair . . . fwd [forward?] cabin lites on.**

The unknown first author's use of the term "xA" (or possibly "zA" or "≈A") might mean what an engineer would call "delta A" and if so, possibly means "change in altitude." In that case, it is probably a reference to the cabin rate-of-climb indicator on Harold Anderson's upper panel.

Over 18 months later, an FBI summary report dated May 30, 1973, written by an unknown author in the Seattle office, will add to our understanding of this event. The author has listened to audio recordings which he or she describes as "conversations between Flight 305 and Ground Control." This is a misunderstanding: the crew of Flight 305 are not talking to Ground Control at that moment; they are talking to Northwest operations in Minneapolis on the ARINC frequency. The FBI report reproduces the crew's crucial message as follows:

**O.K, fine uh, at the present time [redacted; perhaps the flight engineer's name] uh, uh!**

**[here the FBI report inserts: "co-pilot, who is speaking, turned to look at the cabin rate of climb meter because of an increase in cabin pressure and in doing so his ear plug was pulled from his ear"] . . at the present time we're getting some uh, the uh, cabin uh rate uh . . . uh, scuse me, my ear plug came out and I uh, at the present time we're getting some oscillations in the cabin rate of climb indicator and uh, apparently he (unsub) must be uh attempting to do something with the uh, the airstairs back there.[27]**

The reference to the "co-pilot" (a title not used by Northwest Airlines) must mean First Officer William Rataczak.

Rate of climb is measured by reference to air pressure. Flight engineers speak of "cabin altitude" to mean the altitude that the cabin feels like, in terms of its air pressure. We airline passengers can breathe comfortably in the cabin because it is pressurised to feel like an altitude of (say) 10,000 feet, rather than the (say) 33,000 feet where the airplane is, and at which altitude, we could not breathe.

When a flight engineer says that the cabin is climbing, he or she means simply that the air pressure is decreasing; and if descending, that the air pressure is increasing.

As we recall, Flight 305 has left Seattle in an unpressurised condition; and since Tina Mucklow has locked the rear cabin door in the open position, and has been ordered to retreat to the flight deck, there is no way to change that. No one on the flight deck can operate the rear cabin door; so the entire cabin and cockpit are exposed to the outside air. At any given altitude, the cabin pressure is the same as the outside pressure; therefore the cabin's rate of climb is the same as the airplane's rate of climb. The airplane is on autopilot; the crew have most probably set the autopilot to keep a fixed altitude of 10,000 feet, as the hijacker has demanded.

If the cabin is showing fluctuations in altitude, then either the airplane has climbed or descended momentarily from 10,000 feet (in which case the autopilot will have tried to adjust); or the cabin pressure has changed momentarily relative to the outside pressure.

If the airplane is changing altitude, the cabin rate-of-climb indicator should register a change, but the cabin pressure differential should not. If the airplane is not changing altitude but the cabin pressure is changing relative to the outside pressure, then both gauges should register a change.

From the ARINC transcripts, and from the handwritten notes, we do not know whether one or both gauges have registered an oscillation. However, as we shall see, the crew, and later Northwest and the FBI, apparently will come to believe or to recall that only one gauge has reacted, namely the cabin rate-of-climb indicator. In that case, since the cabin is open to the outside air, the airplane has climbed or descended.

Bob Lowenthal, in reference to the oscillations, quotes the flight crew's curious use of the term "playing with [the] air stair." The phrasing seems to imply that the hijacker is not necessarily on the stair, and that he is testing the stair in some way. It could be interpreted that he is raising and lowering the stair, or that he is putting weight on the stair at different points, or even that he has descended partway and returned.

We should add that these two authors may not be receiving their information in real time. They may be watching a teletype with a delay of two to four minutes. In that case, the oscillations that they are noting down could have occurred between 8:07 and 8:09 p.m., or earlier.

There is no official document in the public domain that elaborates the nature of the oscillation. Over forty-two years later, in January 2014, Harold Anderson will tell private researchers that there was a series of minor fluctuations in the cabin rate-of-climb indicator, but not in the cabin pressure differential gauge. This seems to imply that the airplane itself is alternately climbing and descending. This is as one might expect if the lowered airstair is creating drag, the autopilot is trying to correct the pitch of the airplane, and the airstair (if not locked down) is in turn reacting to the changed pitch. Elsewhere in the same interview, he will say "gauges," implying that the pressure differential is also changing.

In his 2014 interview, Anderson will give three descriptions of the events, which we reproduce below in approximately the order in which they occur:

... it wasn't a one time event but a series of fluctuations which attracted our attention. ... These were minor oscillations. We detected [them] on the gauges only.

... The oscillations continued, as I remember, but were smoother and we hadn't heard anything from [the hijacker]. Bill [Rataczak]called back to him and he finally answered. He said everything was "OK." [This exchange is recorded in the ARINC transcript between the time stamps for 8:03 and 8:05 p.m.]

... it wasn't totally smooth even before the oscillations started. What we noticed was the pattern of the oscillations was continuing and there was a very minor disruption of the slipstream. ... I saw it first then alerted [Captain] Scott and [co-pilot] Bill [Rataczak] ... ...Scott said at first he wasn't feeling anything for sure, then a little later he thought there was more drag and the nose was deviating a little.

More time passed. And then suddenly came that "bump" ... a single pressure event we felt in our ears, and nothing following, not even more fluctuations.... After the final "bump" which we felt with our ears, we all discussed it for awhile, waiting for another bump. It never repeated, ... I just don't recall how much time lapsed between feeling the final "bump" and reporting it to NWA via radio.[28]

The ARINC transcript records the oscillations but not the "pressure bump" (and does not seem to be redacted at this point). Of the six note-takers who are in the ARINC loop, two make notes of the oscillations (both writing down the time as 8:05 p.m.), but neither records the "pressure bump." Most probably, that final radio call is never made.

Rataczak, also many years after the events, will confirm his recollection of the physiological sensation:

... We felt a tremendous amount of pressure bump in our ears ...[29]

Today, in the era of intelligent airplanes which do not spill our drinks, the phrase "pressure bump" is not a widespread technical term. But we airline passengers still sometimes notice that, particularly as an airplane descends from the cruising altitude, we may feel a discomfort in our ears. The cabin pressure is rising and our inner ears are not adjusting quickly enough. In the 1960s, with jet airliners starting to fly well above 30,000 feet, the Boeing Airplane Company was well aware of the phenomenon. An article in the long-defunct Boeing Airliner magazine reads as follows:

Pressure changes or pressure "bumps" of sufficient magnitude and duration can cause passenger discomfort. Proper operation of the various controls of the air conditioning and pressurization system can significantly reduce the magnitude and duration of these bumps ... Maximum sustained rates of change of pressure generally accepted for commercial aircraft are 0.263 psi per minute decreasing and 0.158 psi per .minute increasing pressure.[30]

The Boeing 727 was not such a smooth-riding airplane as those to which we are accustomed today. We may quote from a 727 engineer with reference to the pressurisation system on the 727-100 series:

Pneumatic Control System ... is still around and in use on a great number of aircraft, mostly [727-]100's. ... There are two control panels, again at the flight engineers panel. One for automatic control and one for manual mode. You set these by markings on the instrument and it is then entirely controlled by sensed pressures

**and venturi's. It's basic, but robust, though pressure bumps are quite a common feature of this system.**[31]

And finally … Rataczak after decades will remember something that he has never mentioned to the FBI, and which seems to occur after, or simultaneously with, the "pressure bump":

**We also got confirmation on the Flight Engineer's panel indicating that the stairs had momentarily closed.**[32]

This can only mean that the amber annunciator light has gone out, and then has illuminated again. Therefore the airstairs are, at least for a moment, locked in the up position or in the down position. From the flight deck, the crew cannot know which. This airplane, N467US, is a 727-51 which does not have the green light to confirm the locked position. It is practically impossible for the airstairs to lock and then unlock, except by operation of the control lever.

There are now four possible scenarios.

- The stairs lock, even momentarily, in the "up" position, after the pressure bump. In this case, the hijacker has returned the control lever to the "raise" detent and held it there till the stairs uplock. When the pressure bump occurs, he must be on board. Later when the annunciator goes out, he is at the top of the stairwell.
- The stairs lock in the "down" position after the pressure bump. In this case, the hijacker has either held the control lever in the "lower" detent (which he can only do at the top of the stairs), or he has manually forced the stairs into the downlocked position (in which case, when the annunciator goes out, he is on the stairs). When the pressure bump occurs, he has not taken either of these actions and must still be on board.
- The stairs lock in the "up" position" before the pressure bump. Again, the hijacker has to be at the top of the stairwell to achieve the uplock. If he then unlocks the stair, he has to wait until the hydraulics or gravity extend it. Depending on how long that takes, he may descend the airstair and the pressure bump may be linked with his movements on the stair or with his departure. More than that, we cannot say.
- The stairs lock in the "down" position before the pressure bump. Either the hijacker successfully operates the control lever, or forces the downlock; his subsequent movements create the pressure bump. This scenario yields the highest probability of a link between the pressure bump and the hijacker's departure. However, this requires the stairs subsequently to escape from the downlocked position and return to the unlocked state; the scenario itself is improbable. An aerospace engineer explains:

**Perhaps enough turbulence could have shaken them out of the downlocked position or broken the mechanism altogether, but I would consider that exceedingly unlikely, especially if the control handle remained in the DOWN position.** [33]

In summary, the probabilities tend to favor an interpretation that the momentary extinction of the annunciator is a temporary uplock, not a downlock; and that this uplock is due to the hijacker's moving the control lever to the "raise" position, which he subsequently reverses. As we shall see later, the "pressure bump" will subsequently became synonymous, in the minds of Northwest Airlines and the FBI, with the time and place of the hijacker's departure. But a senior test pilot from Boeing would tell the FBI:

**If the rear stairs on a 727 is [*sic*] lowered in flight at an altitude of less than 10,000 feet a change in pressurization occurs and this could be felt by the crew if the door leading into the cockpit is open. If the cockpit door were closed, it is doubtful that the crew would experience the change in pressurization.**[34]

As we know, when Tina Mucklow retreats to the cockpit on the hijacker's instructions, she closes and locks the cockpit door behind her. Then where does the "pressure bump" come from?

Although some of our scenarios allow for the pressure bump to be synchronous with the hijacker's departure, prudence would have called for a clear-eyed look at the probabilities, before committing resources to the consequences of this assumption.

## LAST CONTACT

The flight crew, Mucklow, and Flight Operations do not know it now, but there will be no further communication between the hijacker and Flight 305. This has possibly dawned on someone listening in Flight Operations, who writes against the time 8:05 p.m.:

**Last contact with hijacker.**

This note is squeezed in between two previous notes and is evidently a later insertion, added at some unknown time when the hijacker's departure has become evident.

It is clear that at 8:05 p.m., the hijacker is on board the airplane. From 8:11 p.m. onward, and throughout the rest of the flight to Reno, Nevada, the crew of Flight 305 and the observers in Flight Operations will believe that he is still on board. The following selection of notes, jotted down by unknown authors in Flight Operations, tell the story of their bewilderment:

**8:30 p.m. PST: have stew communicate with man.**

**9:00 p.m.: 305 No comms with man. Last contact 55" ago [8:05 p.m.]. Have decided not to contact him till near Reno.**

**9:20 p.m.: FBI suggest communicating as much as [possible]. [Flight] crew decided no. Communications have not been good. His objective is Mexico City. We'll ask him to raise stairs to land(?) at Reno**

**9:32 p.m.: negotiate clean [aircraft] [gear and flaps up] out RNO to Mexico City.**

**9:40 p.m.: Cool [the] cabin appreciably [it] will slow his reflexes.**

**9:59 p.m.: Is aft door lite on—Affirm (?) entry & airstair**

On the descent toward Reno, at 10:36 p.m. Flight 305 finally gives air traffic control a heads-up on their situation:

**Okay ah we're trying to make contact with the back now and ah we're going to get these steps up before we can make our landing**

In fact if, as they believe, the hijacker is still on board, the crew have no way to raise the stairs. There is no control lever on the flight deck. Evidently their idea is to ask the hijacker if he will cooperate. Tina Mucklow calls the hijacker repeatedly on the interphone. Later she will tell the FBI that her final message was:

**Sir, we are going to land now, please put up the stairs. We are going to land anyway but the aircraft may be structurally damaged and we may not be able to take off after we've landed.**

From the passenger cabin, there is no reply.

Reno Tower asks:

**Northwest three zero five what's the status of the stairs now sir.**

But there is no communication from row 18. At 10:43 p.m., Flight 305 informs Reno Tower:

**Ah we haven't been able to get ahold of anybody yet uh trying to contact him and ah they're still down so I, we haven't decided yet an we might come in and land with them down, there'd be some sparks, so . . .**

Back in Flight Operations, notes are made:

**10:38 p.m.: attempted call man [with] call button and P.A. no contact.**
**10:46 p.m.: tried call again no contact.**

At 10:48 p.m. the flight crew made the decision to land with the airstairs down, taking the chance that the airplane will be damaged and they will not be able to take off again:

**[Reno] Approach, ah three zero five we can't seem to raise him back there, if he is there, we kind of hate to, we'd just as soon land with the thing hanging down, it isn't all the way down, and then probably [it] won't have any pressure on it, so we hope it'll [unintelligible] free . . .**

This is possibly the most inexplicable transmission that the crew will make in the course of the flight. For the first time, we have a suggestion that the stairs are not fully deployed. This can only be by reference to the light on the flight engineer's panel. We know that none of the crew has gone aft to check. They could not have disabled the hydraulic "B" system, which powers several essential flight controls. How do they know that the stairs are not "all the way down"? Neither Northwest nor the FBI will ever report these crucial details.

Here we may mention that landing with the stairs down is no big deal. A 727-100 engineer recalls:

**I saw quite a few [727s] land with the steps down . . . No damage. There was a skid plate . . . Most of the occasions when they dropped was due to extreme low temp cold soak. . . The control cables would droop allowing the control valve to move on the impact of landing.**[35]

At 11:02 p.m., Flight 305 is on the ground at Reno. The tower reports seeing a few sparks from the airstair:

**I do see some ah sparks now, just a few, ah trailing you as you're taxiing in.**

To which Flight 305 replies, possibly in jest:

**Our ah passenger tried to disembark.**

Until this point at least, the flight crew are completely convinced that the hijacker is still onboard. They park the airplane. Ignoring the entreaties of Reno Tower not to touch anything on the airplane, they go back into the passenger cabin.

Somehow Flight Operations (and probably the FBI) are first with the scoop. If their timepieces are correct, they know the outcome before Flight 305 has rolled to a stop:

**11:03 p.m.: terminated at Reno no psgr [passenger] no damage**
**11:10 p.m.: no psgr [passenger] no briefcase.**

At 11:13 p.m., Flight 305 reports to Reno Tower:

**Okay sir, be advised that ah, we apparently ah, our passenger took leave of us somewhere between here and Seattle, we have ah, made a rather cursory examination of the aircraft for the ah, brief case, and ah, we are unable to do this . . . we're going to take leave of the aircraft . . .**

Reno Tower wants the crew to wait in the airplane until the front stairs arrive, but the flight crew is having none of that:

**Okay ah, be advised ah, we got no front steps and ah, we just soon not have anyone come out here ah, we'll go down the back steps and ah, ah, we'll be taking leave of the aircraft . . .**

Reno Tower asks (but why do they want to know?) whether the crew can remember when they last saw the hijacker. The crew have undoubtedly already communicated, through Flight Operations, with the FBI, and they are not talking:

**I'm sorry I ah, ah, we have ah, been given orders if you'll, if you'll pardon us for ah, not cutting you short but we've been given orders not to, not to ah, answer any questions at this time.**

With that, they tread in the footsteps of the hijacker, out of the airplane, and down the ventral airstair, and for now, their testimony ends.

In short, sometime between 8:05 p.m. and 11:02 p.m. on November 24, 1971, the hijacker and the ransom money have departed from Flight 305. In a later chapter, we will examine the flight path and will attempt to narrow down the point at which he made his escape.

## POSTSCRIPT: THE SQUAWK

Before we turn to the flight path, due diligence compels that we address one of the many mysteries surrounding Flight 305: namely, the missing squawk.

In this day and age, and indeed at any time in the last fifty years, a commercial pilot faced with a hijacking will reach out a hand, as soon as he or she is able, for the dials of the transponder. The name is short for transmitter responder. This device does what it says on the tin; when it receives a radio signal on the frequency of 1030 MHz, it transmits a reply in the form of a radio signal on the frequency of 1090 MHz. The combination of receipt and reply enables the interrogator (who typically is an air traffic controller) to identify the aircraft and match it with a voice transmission.

A transponder, when in use, has to be set to a four-digit code, which is usually specified by air traffic control. Pilots and controllers universally refer to this code as the "squawk."

If an aircraft is in any kind of distress, without waiting for air traffic control the crew can set one of three specific codes that will tell controllers the nature of the distress. These three codes were originally set by the International Civil Aviation Organization and, since the mid 1970s, have been adopted by the US Federal Aviation Administration:

7500 Hijack in accordance with FAA Order JO 7610.4

7600 Radio failure in accordance with FAA Order JO 7110.65, paragraph 5-2-8

7700 Emergency in accordance with FAA Order JO 7110.65, paragraph 5-2-7[36]

Today, therefore, a pilot confronted with a hijack would normally squawk 7500 and could expect law enforcement officers to monitor his or her flight and to be present, if needed, at the point of arrival.

Until September 1976, the US aviation industry was not using ICAO codes for distress situations.[37] At the time of Flight 305, the squawk code for a hijacking was 3100. It was therefore logical for the crew, the moment they knew that they had a hijacker on board, to discreetly set the transponder to this code. The hijacker could not know that the code had been set.

This opportunity arose at the moment that Tina Mucklow, "with a prearranged signal of bells" as she later testified, informed the flight crew that there was a hijack in progress. By her account, this must have been minutes after takeoff from Portland. There might even have been an earlier opportunity, since Florence Schaffner apparently received the "bomb" note while the airplane was still taxiing to the takeoff position.

We can imagine, therefore, the bewilderment of the official at Seattle Air Route Traffic Control Center (whose name was redacted but who was probably Chief Gerald Osterkamp), whose testimony to the FBI, on December 30, 1971, reads as follows:

> **The Seattle Center worked Flight #305 on the way in to Seattle from Portland, but had no indication that a hijack had occurred[,] and the aircraft did not squawk any signal as to a hijack situation. They were not aware of the hijack until they handed off the plane to the Seattle-Tacoma Tower.[38]**

The transcripts of the conversations between Flight 305 and Seattle Center, which Osterkamp shared with the FBI, reveal that the crew were discreet in the extreme when alluding to their situation. They wanted to hold about 20 miles from the airport but did not want to say why. Over the period from 3:15 p.m. to 4:11 p.m., their transmissions to Seattle Approach Control were along the following lines:

> **Okay, we've got a bit of a problem up here. We'd like to, ah, have you give us some holding instructions or something where we can go out in a holding pattern where we're not going to be involved in your traffic, ah.**
>
> **... We'd like to hold, ah. if we could hold at about, ah 20 [DME] 15-20, something like that if that is not going to be in your approach pattern, we'd appreciate that.**

**... Ah, we could just find ourselves a place to hold out here somewhere in the 20 [DME] range would be okay. Looks like it'll keep us in the clear and smooth.**[39]

If Approach Control knew what was going on, they did not say so. Only after close to an hour of these circumvolutions did Flight 305 tiptoe into the heart of the matter:

**Pilot: I don't know, I think it's free ... free to call us, ah, nobody's giving us any trouble up here. He's in the back.**

**Control: We won't bother you unless we absolutely need to.**[40]

It is understandable that Captain Scott and his colleagues did not want a massive delegation of law enforcement to greet them on landing. After Flight 305, Captain Scott never talked to historians and only with the utmost brevity to the press; he passed away in 2001, so we shall never know his reasoning. With hindsight, we know that no one was harmed, and hardly any passengers knew they had been hijacked until they were interviewed by the FBI. Still, it is a mystery that Flight 305 did not squawk 3100 between Portland and Seattle; the more so since, as we shall see in a later chapter, they were asked to squawk, and did so, on the next leg of the journey from Seattle to Reno.

## POSTSCRIPT: THE AIRSTAIR

As we have seen in the course of this chapter, at 7:44:22 p.m., the crew believed that the airstair was down. The hydraulic system was operational and should have driven the stair to the fully extended position. The hijacker had at least two means of locking it. Yet at 10:48 p.m., on the approach to Reno, they told air traffic control that the airstair was "hanging" or only partly extended.

Later, for the FBI's attempt to replicate the flight conditions, it should have become vital to know whether the stair had been down and locked. An immediate inspection at Reno would have resolved this issue. But whether such an inspection was done, nothing in the public domain permits us to know.

CHAPTER

# 3

# TAKHLI

The hijacker of Flight 305 was not the first person to parachute from a Boeing 727. In this exploit, he was preceded by at least five fearless Americans.

To elaborate this story, we must first introduce an airline that to the vast majority of the American public is known only though an eponymous and predominantly fictional film released in 1990, starring Mel Gibson and Robert Downey Jr., and currently scoring 13 percent on Rotten Tomatoes: *Air America*.

The true and extraordinary story of Air America has been told elsewhere, most comprehensively in Dr. Joe F Leeker's *History of Air America*.[1] For our purposes, it suffices to introduce Air America as an airline once registered in the pre-Communist Republic of China under the name Civil Air Transport (CAT). Dr Leeker records that "the name of CAT Inc was changed to Air America Inc with effective date of change 31 March 1959."[2]

Without further preamble, we quote a formerly secret and now-declassified memo of the Central Intelligence Agency, dated November 7, 1962:

> **Review of Air Support Activities:—A. The Pacific Corporation | B. Air America, Inc. | C. Air Asia Company Limited | D. Civil Air Transport Company Limited | E. Southern Air Transport, Inc. [author's note: this last name was handwritten]**
>
> **. . . In 1950 the Agency purchased all of the assets of Civil Air Transport, a partnership that had been operating on the Chinese Mainland. This purchase . . . was principally for the purpose of denying the Chinese Communists the aircraft and other assets of Civil Air Transport. . . . These assets were used as investment in kind in what has become the above-listed family of Companies—Tab I.**

**At the outset[,] operational use of aircraft and personnel was of secondary importance, but the continued political instability of the Far East has provided sufficient target for the Agency to have determined during periodic reviews that the continued operation of the project was desirable.[3]**

In short, Air America was an asset of the Central Intelligence Agency.

The operational objectives of Air America were as follows:

**Air America (formerly called CAT Incorporated), a Delaware corporation also organized on July 10, 1950, in turn was organized to overtly conduct and to carry on, directly and through domestic and foreign subsidiary and affiliated companies, a scheduled Chinese flag airline, contract U.S. and foreign flag airlift, and contract maintenance engineering activities in the Far East and in other parts of the world.[4]**

We shall now pursue the trail from Air America to the Boeing 727. A colorful description of this trail may be found in the testimony of Lawrence R. Houston, former general counsel of the CIA, to the Senate Intelligence Committee:

**As the operations of Air America developed, problems arose involving large cargo carriers. . . . Air America did not maintain any jet equipment at that point. . . . In the early 1950s, Air America became deeply involved in a military Air Transport System. This system was originally known as MATS, and later as MAC. . . . In 1956 MATS changed its policy and required that bidders on their contracts be certificated. Because Air America could not become certificated, the Agency decided to purchase Southern Air Transport.[5]**

Dr. Leeker has more on this story:

**Like Air America, Southern Air Transport was controlled by the CIA. . . . Airlines that wanted to operate under the MATS contract . . . had to operate under Part 42 of the CAB [Civil Aeronautics Board] and had to participate in the Civil Reserve Air Fleet Program (CRAF). . . . The CIA decided to acquire control of a company that already had all those qualifications and was for sale. . . . The airline chosen was Southern Air Transport.[6]**

Back to Lawrence R. Houston of the CIA:

**While this corporation was technically a separate entity, not involved with Air America, it was actually an integral part of the complex from a management perspective. All management decisions for Southern Air Transport were made by the same CIA consultant and advisory team that established Air America policy. Eventually, MAC decided to require that bidders not only be certificated, but, that they also have equipment qualified for the Civil Reserve Air Fleet, i.e., jet aircraft. As a result, the Agency acquired Boeing 727s.[7]**

Thanks to Dr. Leeker, we know when these acquisitions took place:

**Although three Boeing 727s had been ordered by Air Asia, none of them was ever operated by Air America, but all of them were used by Southern Air Transport on an MAC contract.[8]**

| Type | Registration | Serial no. | Date acquired | Origin | Disposition |
|---|---|---|---|---|---|
| Boeing 727-92C | N5055 | 19173 | 3 Oct. 1966 | bought new; acquired via Air Asia | leased to Southern Air Transport, Miami, on 3 October 1966 |
| | N5092 | 19174 | 5 Nov. 1966 | bought new; acquired via Air Asia | leased to Southern Air transport, Miami, on 5 November 1966 |
| | N5093 | 19175 | 10 Dec. 1966 | bought new; acquired via Air Asia | immediately sold to Southern Air Transport . . . bought [back] by Air America on 16 January 1968 |

The final step on the trail, however, is in the wrong place, or the wrong time. In 1976, Lawrence R. Houston would testify to the Senate Intelligence Committee:

> **The [Central Intelligence] Agency . . . convinced Boeing to modify the 727 by enlarging the ventral exit, enhancing its air drop capability.[9]**

This statement is an anomaly. As we have seen, the agency (or Air America, acting on the agency's behalf) acquired the three Boeing 727s in 1966. But Boeing had already enhanced and tested the air drop capability of the Boeing 727 in 1963 and 1964. Here's how we know (by courtesy of the FBI):

> **In 1963–1964, the Boeing Company had a team of 20 to 30 engineers and test pilots experimenting with the airstairs of the Boeing 727 to determine the plane's adaptability for dropping cargo or personnel.[10]**

## THE BOEING AIR DROP TESTS

So, two or three years before the CIA acquired their 727s, who asked the Boeing Company to do the air drop tests? The FBI's files are silent on this point. Today, there is no reference to these tests anywhere on the website of the Boeing Airplane Company, and inquiries to Boeing's media office yield no reply. One can imagine that Boeing sales managers might have initiated these tests themselves, with a view to pitching the 727 to military customers (and Boeing did indeed eventually sell at least three 727-100s to the Air National Guard, under the military designation C-22). But in that case, Boeing would not have required the CIA to convince them.

A retired Boeing engineering manager gives us a clue to part of the story:

> **... the 727 ... could take off, fly, and land with the airstairs deployed. That was demonstrated by Boeing to the government at our test field at Moses Lake (Washington). The plane did not rotate on take off but just gained enough airspeed for the lift generated to clear the plane from the ground. The same level landing kept the airstairs from touching the ground.**
>
> **... in the "Manuals and Handbooks Group" ... all the details were available about the airstairs. We even had a full scale 727 airstair mechanical systems test attached to the 727 full scale flight controls test rig.[11]**

The reference to Moses Lake presumably means Larson Air Force Base, five miles northwest of the city of Moses Lake, Washington. It was at Larson that Boeing, from the mid-1940s onward, had been testing military aircraft such as the B-47 Stratojet, the B-50 Superfortress and the B-52 Stratofortress. Larson eventually closed in 1966 and became Grant County International Airport.

It was evidently for prospective customers in the US government that Boeing tested the 727 with the airstair down. For which agency of the US government, we do not know. However, FBI Agent Larry Carr would much later write cryptically on a skydiving forum:

> **The lead test pilot for the 727 project [stated that] they had done several tests deploying them for a certain company that was interested in doing "food" drops. (I'll leave that one alone.)[12]**

May we be forgiven for floating here the names "Air America" and "Southern Air Transport."

The tests of the Boeing 727 at Larson AFB were not the only experiments with the airstair. It may have been for a different customer, or for an internal requirement, that Boeing removed the airstair completely, and made air drops from the second 727 prototype (registration N72700). At least one of these tests was conducted over the Pacific off Ocean Shores, Washington, as shown in figure 3.1.

In any event, after Flight 305 the FBI took a profound interest in the Boeing air drop program. On June 8, 1972, barely six months into the investigation of Flight 305, the FBI recorded:

> **The Boeing Company is in the process of pulling the personnel files of those individuals involved in the research work done on the Boeing seven two seven with particular reference to the air stairs, and each file being reviewed to consider employee as a suspect.[13]**

These efforts eventually generated a list of thirty-one persons: thirty Boeing employees and one employee of the FAA. One, Charles M. Clark, was by then deceased; five others were identified by name: William Lee Gray, Edward Ferdinand Hartz, Richard Llewellyn (Dix) Leosch Jr. (who had been Chief of Flight Test for the 727), Erik Stanley Lund, and Charles Edward McOmber (all eliminated for reasons of age, facial features, or both). Twenty-two others, whose names have been redacted, were eliminated because they were not thought physically to resemble

**Figure 3.1.** An air drop test from the second prototype Boeing 727-22 (N72700), off Ocean Shores, Washington, 1963 or 1964. The altitude appears to be about 2,000 feet and the flap setting appears to be 40 degrees down. The airstair has been removed. *By courtesy of Scott Carson via Bob Bogash. Image credit: Harold C. (Kit) Carson. Used by permission*

the hijacker. The FBI's notes reveal that a "swarthy" complexion was a key element of resemblance; anyone who did not have such a complexion was eliminated forthwith.

As of July 27, 1972, three persons from the test team had not yet been eliminated.[14] There, as far as we know from the FBI files, the matter rested.

The FBI did, however, glean—from among the hundreds of pages of Boeing test reports—the two following, and apparently contradictory, statements:

> **In the tests conducted *the air stairs were removed* [our emphasis] and packages were dropped from the plane using an especially designed chute" [three following lines redacted].[15]**
>
> **The following information was obtained from the Boeing report: . . . *the air stair was quite stable when it was down* [our emphasis] and no airplane control problems were experienced. No excessive cabin pressure transients were noted with the aft entry door open and the stair extended. The environment near the aft entry door allowed it to be safely opened[,] and the stair retracted at speeds up to 300 knots.[16]**

We are compelled to conclude that Boeing conducted not one but two series of tests: one with the airstairs removed, and one with the airstairs retained but lowered and raised in flight. This vital distinction seems to have escaped the FBI completely; if they had noticed it, they would surely have focused their investigations on the engineers and pilots involved in the raising and lowering of the airstairs.

Be that as it may, the second question that the FBI wanted to resolve was whether the flight parameters of the Boeing tests in any way resembled those of Flight 305. The response that seems to have made the greatest impact on the FBI reads as follows:

> **On 7/31/72, [redacted; probably a Boeing employee] made available a copy of the Boeing tests summary report dealing with the flight configuration of the 727 during testing. The following is a summary of the configuration used during the Boeing air stairs test:**
>
> **Speed—125 knots**
> **Flaps—25 degrees down**
> **Altitude—10,000 feet[17]**

Here we may legitimately ask: Only that speed? Only that flap setting? Only that altitude? And no other? No aeronautical test program is conducted that way. As an example, we have only to look at the highly successful test program of the North American X-15 research airplane, which lasted from March 10, 1959, to December 12, 1968, and encompassed 336 powered and unpowered flights, including eleven flights piloted by future astronaut Neil Armstrong. The X-15 was flown at every speed from 200 knots (the landing speed) to a record-breaking 3,927 knots, and at every altitude from ground level to the edge of space at 354,000 feet.[18] Put another way: any Boeing customer who asked for tests of air drops would surely want to anticipate the range of flight conditions that would occur in real-life operations. And if there had been only one set of flight parameters, the testing would have lasted one day and would not have spanned part of 1963 and part of 1964.

In any case, the Boeing statement quoted above confirms beyond doubt that the tests encompassed a range of airspeeds up to 300 knots, and that at this speed, the airstairs were certainly in place.

A range of airspeeds implies a range of flap settings. The lower the setting, the faster the airplane can fly, and vice versa. Above about 250 knots, and certainly at 300 knots, the flaps would have to be retracted (set to 0 degrees); if not, they would probably break off. So the tests must have encompassed flap settings from 0 to 25 degrees. The full test reports might confirm this, but as far as is known, the FBI never saw these reports and Boeing has never released them.

Seven or eight years later, the hijacker of Flight 305 would specify an altitude of 10,000 feet (identical to the sole test altitude that Boeing disclosed to the FBI); he would not ask for a specific airspeed, but he would demand a flap setting of 15 degrees, which is probably within the range of the Boeing tests. In the segment in which he was presumed to have departed, Flight 305 for the most part maintained indicated airspeeds between 155 and 180 knots: again, within the Boeing test range of 125 to 300 knots.

We have the impression that the respondents at Boeing gave the FBI incomplete information, which would dilute the FBI's interest in their tests. They were counting on the FBI's presumed ignorance of aeronautics. If so, it worked. The FBI seemed to accept that the Boeing tests were not a precursor to Flight 305:

> **It is apparent therefore, that the configuration requested by UNSUB [the unknown subject] is not the same as used in Boeing air stair testing.**[19]

As we have argued, this conclusion is not sound. The configuration that the hijacker demanded was well within the Boeing test range and, in the case of the altitude, identical with the one figure that Boeing chose to disclose.

In short, the responses given by the Boeing people seem to have been intended to disassociate the company from the hijacking. The FBI recorded on July 26, 1972:

> **[Author's note: redacted, but surely a Boeing employee] advised that if the hijacker was a member of, or had consulted with a member of the Boeing test team, he would have known that the seven two seven could not have taken off with the air stairs down, nor would it have been necessary since the air stairs can easily be lowered in flight.**[20]

This is a fair comment, although it requires us to make assumptions about the knowledge of a typical Boeing engineer or pilot. Most probably, the operations manual for the Boeing 727 prohibits takeoffs with the airstairs down, and probably the manual says nothing about lowering the stairs in flight (since no normal flight would call for such an action). An average engineer or pilot would know about flying according to the manual. Only a test pilot would know about flying outside the envelope. We recall, from Tom Wolfe's *The Right Stuff*, the remark of the hotshot pilot who takes to the air after a night on the tiles and lives to brag about it:

> **I don't advise it, you understand, but it can be done.**[21]

Even if we accept that the hijacker was not a party to the Boeing tests, the FBI's respondent cannot exclude the possibility that the hijacker saw the test reports or saw the tests underway, either from the air or from the ground.

Absent information to the contrary, we are also obliged to assume that the Boeing tests were solely concerned with air drops of physical objects. There is no indication that Boeing ever asked a parachutist to jump from a 727.

The Boeing people had the last word:

> **[Redacted] further stated that the Boeing test results occupy many volumes[,] and because of the many copies made and length of time since test conducted (8 years), it is not possible to determine the names of all persons who might have had access to the test results.[22]**

Equally, no one could determine how many persons might have seen parachutes descending from a commercial airliner, over a densely populated area of the United States.

## SOUTHERN AIR TRANSPORT

We know at this point that as of 1964, thirty Boeing employees and one FAA employee had participated directly in tests of air drops from a Boeing 727, probably somewhere in the Pacific Northwest; unknown numbers of others, probably working for Boeing or their customers or the FAA, knew of these tests from the engineering reports, and unknowable numbers of others, including members of the public, saw the tests from the ground, and perhaps among them was one who formed an idea in his mind.

However, before Flight 305 came to pass, there was at least one other series of tests that would demonstrate that it was possible not only to drop cargo, but to jump, from a Boeing 727. We return to Air America, and specifically to its sister company Southern Air Transport.

There are at least four public documents that establish that Southern Air Transport tested the capability of the Boeing 727 for air drops via the ventral exit.

One is an internal memo of the CIA, date-stamped November 29, 1971 (five days after the hijacking of Flight 305, which we have to believe was a coincidence), but approved for release only on September 24, 2009: nearly thirty-eight years after it was written. In this memo, the special assistant to the deputy director for support writes to his or her boss (both names redacted) to summarize the operations of Southern Air Transport, which we know was a CIA asset. The memo states that:[23]

> **Southern operates . . . two leased Boeing 727 convertible (passenger and cargo) jet aircraft[24] which are used primarily on Military Airlift Command (MAC) operations in the Far East. . . . The Boeing 727 aircraft also has drop capabilities out the ventral exit which can be opened in flight and Southern has crews trained in this procedure.**

**Figure 3.2.** Saigon Airport, May 1967: Boeing 727-92C, registration number N5092, operated by Southern Air Transport. "92" is the customer number and "C" means convertible. *Courtesy of Wayne Mutza. Image credit: Rodger D. Fetters*

The two Boeing 727s must be those with tail numbers N5055 and N5092, since Southern Air Transport had sold N5093 back to Air America in 1968. We know therefore that by November 1971, Southern Air Transport had tested one or both of these airplanes for their air drop capabilities.

The second document is the film *Flying Men, Flying Machines*,[25] directed and produced by John Wilheim and apparently produced around 1970. In a memo dated 2003 from the CIA to the National Archives, it is described as an "Air America publicity film."[26] This film focuses on Air America's humanitarian operations in Southeast Asia. It includes a sequence of about two minutes, starting at the 1 hr., 7 min., 47 sec. mark, on air drops and parachute jumps from Boeing 727s in an unidentified location. Some of the airplanes are identifiable as Boeing 727Cs (passenger/cargo convertible); it is not clear whether there is more than one individual airplane, or whether the whole segment was filmed in the same place. There are no markings on the airplanes, apart from possibly the legend "Boeing 727C" on the engine nacelles. If these airplanes were operating on behalf of Air America, they were most probably one or both of the two 727s leased to Southern Air Transport.

The narration of this segment includes the following commentary:

> **The Boeing 727 can be adapted for aerial deliveries. On arrival at the drop zone, the cabin can be depressurized, the ventral exit opened, and after the drops are accomplished, the cabin can again be pressurized for return to base at jet altitude.**

The video accompanying this narration has two distinct segments. One segment shows a Boeing 727 flying at low altitude (probably under 2,000 feet) under a cloudy sky, in an unpressurized condition (since the ventral exit is open). The shot is taken from a chase plane that seems to have a swept wing (maybe another 727). The ventral airstair is not visible and has evidently been removed. A jumper emerges from the exit, clearly on a static line since his or her parachute deploys immediately. The landscape in the background is relatively flat, with low, green hills and no sign of urban development (so the segment was probably not filmed around Seattle and was probably not from the Boeing tests to which we earlier referred).

The other segment is a ground-to-air shot of a 727 against a clear blue sky, showing a series of pallets with blossoming parachutes, emerging from the ventral exit. Following the 727 is a chase plane that looks like a twin-engined Beech Model 18.

In the third document, we begin to comprehend that these segments of the Air America film were probably filmed in Southeast Asia, and most probably at Takhli Royal Thai

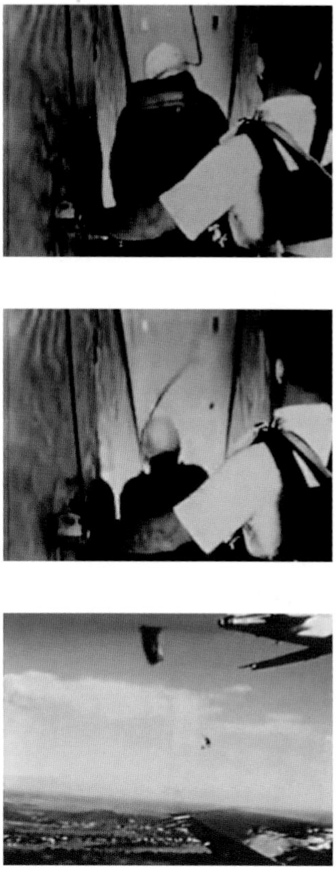

**Figure 3.3**. Southeast Asia, 1970: a sequence of screenshots from *Flying Men, Flying Machines* showing a jump from the ventral exit of a Boeing 727. The ventral airstair has been removed. The jumper is using a static line, which deploys the parachute on exit. The landscape resembles that around Takhli Air Base, Thailand; the wing of the chase plane is consistent with that of the Volpar 18 that was used at Takhli. *Image credits: John Wilheim Productions*

Air Force Base, 240 kilometers northwest of Bangkok. We refer to Professor William Leary's interview with Air America pilot Thomas C. Sailer:

> **Sailer later tested 727s at Takhli for airdrops [with] conveyer belt and rollers. Airplane could be pressurized until drop. System worked well but never used in operation.[27]**

This story is confirmed by our fourth document: *Smokejumpers Magazine*, the journal of the airborne firefighters who keep wildfires under control in the North American wilderness. The January 2014 issue summarizes the mission:

> **[John P.] Kirkley was later selected as one of seven air-freight specialists sent to Takhli, Thailand, on a secret mission to train to jump and drop freight from a commercial Boeing 727 jet. "There was unrest in Tibet on the Chinese border[,] and the CIA wanted to do some tests to see if it was feasible to make high-altitude drops of paratroopers and cargo from a 727," he said. After making a few jumps and dropping several loads of cargo, Kirkley said the mission was eventually scrubbed.[28]**

By way of context: since 1951, it had been standard practice for the CIA to recruit smoke jumpers for their operations in Southeast Asia and elsewhere. No doubt, one day the story of smoke jumpers and the CIA will be told in the fashion that it deserves. Jim Veitch (MSO-67),[29] who ran the CIA's unit in Saravane, Laos, explains the concept:

**Figure 3.4.** Over Takhli, Thailand, 1966: a training jump from a C-123. *Image credit*: *John P Kirkley*

> **There have been a lot of smokejumpers involved in [Central Intelligence] Agency work over the years[,] and basically no one knows about it. . . . I think it was because we could go anywhere, anytime, and do a tough, confusing job and then keep our mouths shut. I think smoke-jumpers have what it takes. They are not just fit and strong but have the ability to think independently and work towards a solution, no matter what the odds . . . the war in Laos was so much like fighting a forest fire.[30]**

Here we are grateful to John P. Kirkley (CJ '64) himself for his personal recollections, and for his generous sharing of stories from the few surviving smoke jumpers from Vientiane, Laos, who tested the Boeing 727 in Thailand.

Kirkley confirms that he was one of the seven air freight specialists (or "kickers") working at the time for Air America in Vientiane, who were recruited for a series of tests of the 727 at Takhli in June 1968. The team was headed by Lou Rucker, a CIA officer and veteran of the Office of Strategic Services, who had handled parachute training for Nationalist Chinese troops in Xiamen in the 1950s.[31] His deputy was T. J. Thompson, a smoke jumper (MSO '55) who had been with the CIA since 1960.[32] Jack Manska was the third representative of the CIA. The pilot of the 727 was Bill Welk, probably on the payroll of Southern Air Transport; most likely Thomas C Sailer and one other were among the flight crew. The chase plane was a Volpar 18, an elegant modification of the Beech 18S with two turboprop engines and a tricycle undercarriage; the legendary Air America pilot Jim Rhyne was at the controls, accompanied by T. J. Thompson and a professional photographer.

Completing the team of jumpers and kickers were Fred Barnowsky (MSO '42), Billy Bowles (RDD '57), Robert Herald (MSO '55), Kirkley, possibly Lyman Knopp, and one other whose name has escaped memory.

From Kirkley's description, it is clear that the airplane was one of the two 727-92Cs then operated by Southern Air Transport, either N5055 or N5092, since N5093 had by then been sold back to Air America:

> **This project was the first of its kind. We were to drop cargo and jump out of a Southern Air Transport "sanitized" Boeing 727 jet. The tail number was the only markings on this stark aluminum plane. In the briefing room we were told that the training was for testing the capabilities and feasibility of making aerial deliveries in Tibet. . . . The tests were only conducted with AFS [air freight specialists] from Vientiane and a couple of CIA case officers (customers). No Tibetans were involved in this test operation.[33]**

Unlike the Boeing Airplane Company's tests four or five years earlier, the ventral airstair was removed completely. There was no plan to raise or lower it in flight.

> **The passenger compartment of the 727 was fitted with roller conveyers to hold and transport the cargo out the rear for drops. The rear stairwell was removed and retrofitted with stainless sheet metal to make a sliding board.[34]**

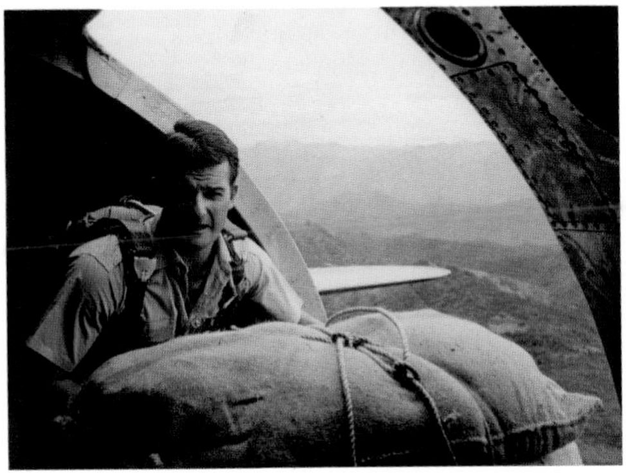

**Figure 3.5**. Over Laos, 1960s: John P. Kirkley preparing an air drop of rice from an Air America C-46. *Image credit*: *John P. Kirkley*

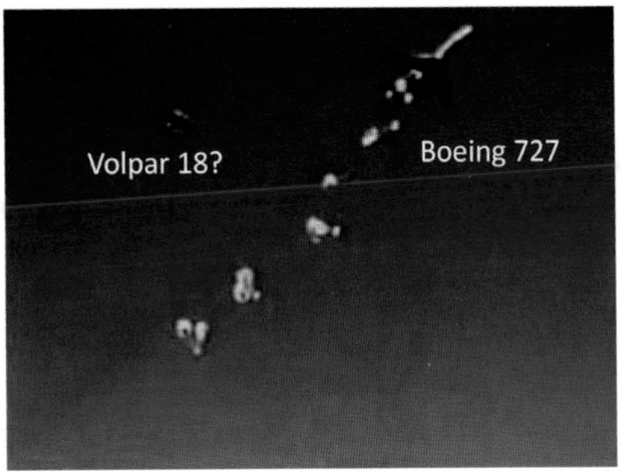


**Figure 3.6**. Southeast Asia, 1970: a screenshot from *Flying Men, Flying Machines*, apparently depicting drop tests at Takhli, Thailand. Image shows a Boeing 727 and a Volpar 18 chase plane. *Image credit*: *John Wilheim Productions; text by author*

The configuration of the airplane and the airspeed were very similar to those that, three years later, would prevail on Flight 305:

> **The test were done in the morning . . . and the outside air temperature at Takhli was warm (70–80°). The cargo drops went without a hitch[,] then we suited up for our parachute jump. We leveled off at 1200 feet. The flaps were set at about 15° and the landing gear was lowered to create drag to maintain 150 knots.[35]**

As we recall from chapter 2, Flight 305 set the flaps to 15 degrees and kept the landing gear down at the hijacker's bidding, exactly as in the Takhli tests. In the segment wherein the hijacker was thought to have departed, the pilot held the airspeed in a range between 155 and 180 knots. Unlike in the Takhli tests, the hijacker ordered Flight 305 to maintain 10,000 feet, and he departed under a dark sky in a temperature around –5 degrees C.

Nevertheless (and as expert jumpers would later confirm to the FBI), the jump from the ventral exit of the Boeing 727 was perfectly benign. At least five members of the team did the jump: Barnowsky, Bowles, Kirkley, Manska, and Rucker:

> **When we got over the jump spot[,] the pilot gave the signal and we slid out the rear of the plane. Compared to jumping out of a prop plane[,] it was quiet. There was no noise or prop blast like from a reciprocating engine[,] and hardly a jerk when the static cord released. We floated down with the greatest of ease.[36]**

With that, the Takhli tests came to an end, never to be translated into military or intelligence operations:

> **Knowing what to expect[,] we were all excited to make a second jump. The tests went well, [and] the project was approved and ready to go; however, as it turned out the funding was cut and the 727 Tibet project was cancelled to our chagrin. . . . As far as I know[,] drops were never made from [a] 727 in Tibet.[37]**

As with the Boeing tests in 1963 and 1964, we have no way of assessing how many people knew of the Takhli operation. What we know is that the team included seven smoke jumpers (one of them on the CIA payroll), two other CIA officers, probably four flight crew members, and a photographer; at least one person filmed the drops from the ground, and the director and editors of *Flying Men, Flying Machines* had access to the film footage. As of April 30, 1971, Southern Air Transport had fifty-five office staff and fifty-six mechanics and technical service staff;[38] some of them had to know of the tests at Takhli. In 1968, Takhli Air Force Base was host to the 355th Tactical Fighter Wing of the US Air Force. Probably hundreds of USAF personnel could have observed the distinctive unmarked 727 conducting its takeoffs and landings, and some of them possibly could have also seen the air drops and jumps and the recovery of the pallets and jumpers. What we cannot know is whether, among the witnesses to the Takhli tests, there was a soft-spoken, middle-aged, dark-complexioned man who, three and a half years later, would board Flight 305.

## POSTSCRIPT

John Kirkley well recalls the morning of November 29, 1971, when two FBI agents called on him at the Polar Bar that he owned in Anchorage, Alaska, and advised him that they knew he had jumped from a 727 for Air America. Later he heard that the FBI had also interviewed Louis A Banta (CJ '51), another smoke jumper who had worked with Air America. Neither of these interviews is among the public files of the FBI. In over 24,000 pages of documents, the one interview that is clearly with a smoke jumper is dated July 18, 1975, and reads in part as follows:

> **[Name redacted] Oklahoma, [was] formerly employed by Air America. . . . He stated [that] most [redacted; probably air freight specialists] for Air America had parachute backgrounds in that 30% of the freight handled by Air America was parachuted for delivery. . . . He did not recall a film on parachuting from a 727 airplane; however, he had heard that several employees of Air America had parachuted from such a plane with no problems[,] and he believed it could be done with relative ease depending on the minimum speed of the aircraft (this speed unknown to [him]).[39]**

We could thereby assume that by 1971, and probably long before then, the Takhli tests were common knowledge among the employees of Air America.

## ANOTHER POSTSCRIPT

For over fifty years, the sleepy city of Vientiane, on the Mekong River, was the capital of the territory of Laos, one of the five components of French Indochina (along with Annam, Cambodia, Cochinchina, and Tonkin). On October 22, 1953, Laos became an independent kingdom, but the French community lived on. In the late 1960s, about the time that the seven American smoke jumpers were working in Vientiane for Air America, the city had a colorful nightlife, enriched by a sprinkling of old French establishments.

Let us imagine an evening scene in such an establishment—let's say the French officers' mess, the former Cercle des Officiers—in the spring of 1968. A soft-spoken, dark-complexioned man, approaching middle age, is sitting at a corner table. Most of the customers are drinking cheap red wine, but he prefers a bourbon and 7-Up. Moments ago, he was chatting to a pilot who works for Air America, which, as everyone knows, has a hub in Vientiane and is engaged in an unofficial war against the North Vietnamese. This pilot was talking about a project that is coming up, across the border in Thailand. Some smoke jumpers have been recruited to jump out of a commercial jetliner, a Boeing 727. The bourbon drinker reflects on that. He has done a few jumps himself, with the US Air Force back in Korea.

He looks around for something to read. The French officers' mess has bookshelves stuffed with magazines. He picks up a graphic novel, which of course is in French. It seems to be about a test pilot in the Canadian air force. He looks at the cover, which depicts an airplane exploding in midair: he translates the title as "The Secret of Dan Cooper."[40] He stares at it for a long time.

This scene is of course fictional.

CHAPTER

# 4

# THE PLAN

At around 6:25 p.m. on November 24, 1971, while Flight 305 was refueling at Seattle, someone at Flight Operations in Minneapolis sent the following message to the crew:

**Ability to jump out of a 707 with a parachute on is nil.**[1]

This statement was perfectly correct. However, the sender was unaware, or had forgotten, that Flight 305 was not operated by a Boeing 707. It was a Boeing 727: a completely different design. As such, it was perfect for the hijacker's mission.

With that preamble, we may pose the question: What plans or preparations had the hijacker made that led to his choice of Flight 305?

We submit the following hypotheses as probable criteria for the mission plan:

- The airplane had to have a ventral airstair.
- The flight had to be within the continental United States.
- The airline had to be a trunk passenger carrier.
- The flight had to terminate at its next destination.
- The flight had to be of very short duration.

We shall now explain why each of these criteria could have led to the choice of Flight 305.

## THE VENTRAL AIRSTAIR

As we alluded in our prologue, the hinged airstair below the tail of the airplane was key to a safe exit by parachute. Within the jet airline fleet in the USA, this type of airstair was found only on airplanes with rear-mounted engines. Airliners with wing-mounted engines, such as the Boeing 707 and the Douglas DC-8, had only side doors. Even if these doors could be opened in flight, a jumper would be in grave danger of striking an engine or the tailplane. With a ventral airstair, tucked under the tail and protected by the fuselage from much of the air blast, it would be possible to make a clean jump without the risk of collision with the airframe.

In the United States in 1971, only three models of jet airliner possessed a ventral airstair: the Boeing 727, the Douglas DC-9, and the British Aircraft Corporation 1-11. At the end of 1971, US air carriers were operating at least 1,030 aircraft with this feature: 638 Boeing 727s, 334 Douglas DC-9s, and fifty-eight BAC 1-11s.[2]

On November 24, 1972, exactly one year after Flight 305, the Federal Aviation Administration issued Regulation 25.809, governing emergency exit arrangements for transport aircraft.[3] This regulation stated, inter alia, that

> When required by the operating rules for any large passenger-carrying turbojet powered airplane, each ventral exit and tailcone exit must be
>
> (1) designed and constructed so that it cannot be opened during flight; and
>
> (2) marked with a placard readable from a distance of 30 inches and installed at a conspicuous location near the means of opening the exit, stating that the exit has been designed and constructed so that it cannot be opened during flight.

This regulation led to the development of a simple mechanical device that came to be known colloquially as the "Cooper vane." It does what the FAA mandated: it blocks the ventral airstair when the aircraft is airborne.

However, on November 24, 1971, as we know with hindsight, at least on the Boeing 727 and probably also on the Douglas DC-9 and the BAC 1-11, it was possible for the ventral airstair to be lowered in flight.

We may now pose this question: In 1971, was this public knowledge?

Certainly, Northwest Flight Operations knew. Around 6:59 p.m. on November 24, 1971, with refueling underway at Seattle, Flight Operations and Flight 305 were in conversation on the company frequency about the hijacker's demand to take off with the airstair down. Flight Operations had this to say:[4]

> You'll have no control problem when [the airstair] is extended. There may be some slight pitch up, but it will be very controllable. The plane has been flown this way. We have had large boxes of 200 to 300 pounds through the door in this configuration. The landing flaps must be down. The speed is not too critical. Any flap position between 5 and 40 degrees, and speed up to 120 knots.

If this was common knowledge in Flight Operations, we could hazard the presumption that it was also common knowledge among people with flight experience, as the hijacker of Flight 305 appeared to be.

As we learned in chapter 3, in 1963 and 1964 the Boeing Airplane Company had done tests to establish that the 727 was capable of air drops via the ventral exit, and that the airstair could easily be lowered and raised in flight. In June 1968, probably at the request of the CIA, Southern Air Transport had repeated these tests at Takhli Air Force Base in Thailand and had further established that jumpers could safely depart from the ventral exit. By around 1970, the film *Flying Men, Flying Machines* had documented some of these experiments, and this film was known to the FBI, who referred to it in their investigations of Flight 305.

Extraordinarily, we have found no record in the public domain that after the hijacking of Flight 305, the FBI interviewed anyone who had flown for Air America, Southern Air Transport, or any other proprietary airline of the CIA. It would seem an obvious avenue of investigation, for example, to ask Air America or Southern Air Transport how widely it was known that a Boeing 727 could be used for air drops or jumps. There were at least three candidates for interview: C. W. "Connie" Siegrist, the celebrated chief pilot of Air America; Thomas C. Sailer, another Air America pilot who, as we noted in chapter 3, might have flown Boeing 727s at Takhli; and Merrill D. "Doc" Johnson, who recorded in his pilot's logbook that he flew 727s for Southern Air Transport on various dates between May 29, 1970, and June 24, 1971.[5] Only the unnamed Air America smoke jumper from Oklahoma City, whom we cited in the postscript to chapter 3, is on record as saying that he had heard about jumps from a 727.

In the absence of any public record of such interviews, we cannot draw any inferences about the hijacker's knowledge of Air America or Southern Air Transport operations, or about his previous experience or employment.

What is still a mystery is how Northwest Flight Operations knew about the air drop capability of the 727. When on the evening of November 24, 1971, they told Flight 305 on their private frequency that "we have had large boxes of 200 to 300 pounds through the door in this configuration," they surely did not mean that Northwest themselves had done such tests. Perhaps a Boeing employee, or an FBI agent with access to CIA files, was sitting in on the conversation and inserted this advice. We do not know.

Nevertheless, we can defend the hypothesis that the hijacker knew about the airstair and expected that if he boarded a Boeing 727, a DC-9, or a BAC-111, it would serve his purpose.

If this had been his sole criterion, he had a choice of over 1,000 airplanes within the United States, as table 4.1 illustrates.

**Table 4.1. Turbojet airliners with ventral airstair, in US-certificated air carrier operations, December 31, 1971**

| Carrier group and carrier | Boeing 727 | Douglas DC-9 | BAC-111 | Total |
|---|---|---|---|---|
| Total | 638 | 334 | 58 | 1,030 |
| Trunk carriers: Big Four | 423 | 101 | 27 | 551 |
| American | 100 | 0 | 27 | 127 |
| Eastern | 101 | 82 | 0 | 183 |
| Trans World (TWA) | 72 | 19 | 0 | 91 |
| United | 150 | 0 | 0 | 150 |
| Trunk carriers: other | 181 | 110 | 8 | 299 |
| Braniff | 40 | 0 | 8 | 48 |
| Continental | 20 | 19 | 0 | 39 |
| Delta | 0 | 77 | 0 | 77 |
| National | 38 | 0 | 0 | 38 |
| Northeast | 21 | 14 | 0 | 35 |

**Table 4.1. Turbojet airliners with ventral airstair, in US-certificated air carrier operations, December 31, 1971**

| | | | | |
|---|---|---|---|---|
| Northwest | 56 | 0 | 0 | 56 |
| Western | 6 | 0 | 0 | 6 |
| Local service carriers | 3 | 112 | 23 | 138 |
| Air West | 0 | 19 | 0 | 19 |
| Allegheny | 0 | 31 | 0 | 31 |
| Frontier | 3 | 0 | 0 | 3 |
| Mohawk | 0 | 0 | 23 | 23 |
| North Central | 0 | 15 | 0 | 15 |
| Ozark | 0 | 17 | 0 | 17 |
| Southern | 0 | 15 | 0 | 15 |
| Texas International | 0 | 15 | 0 | 15 |
| Intra-Hawaii carriers | 0 | 8 | 0 | 8 |
| Hawaiian | 0 | 8 | 0 | 8 |
| International and territorial | 28 | 3 | 0 | 31 |
| Alaska | 4 | 0 | 0 | 4 |
| Caribbean Atlantic | 0 | 3 | 0 | 3 |
| Pan American | 24 | 0 | 0 | 24 |
| All-cargo carriers | 3 | 0 | 0 | 3 |
| Airlift International | 3 | 0 | 0 | 3 |
| | | | | |

Source: FAA, *Statistical Handbook of Aviation 1972*, table 5-13, pp. 120–121.

## THE LOWER 48

In the USA in the innocent 1970s, an air passenger could generally board an airplane with no documents, no baggage control, and no questions asked.

However, in his mission planning, the hijacker would surely have excluded flights to or from Alaska, Hawaii, or international destinations. A jump over Alaska would probably land him in rugged terrain, with nighttime temperatures well below freezing, and no easy escape overland. An exit over Hawaii could end up in the sea, and again, Hawaii would be an impossible place in which to hide. A flight involving an international destination would require some form of identification at the time of departure.

This criterion would narrow down the target airline to the Big Four trunk carriers (American, Eastern, Trans World, and United), the seven other trunk carriers, and the nine local service carriers that operated the right kind of airplane within the lower forty-eight states.

## TRUNK CARRIERS

Our hypothesis is that the hijacker would quickly have excluded local service carriers. First, their routes would have a limited number of destinations, and many of these destinations would be small airports where a stranger would be conspicuous. Possibly, also, these airports would not be in the right part of the USA for his mission. Second, they would have small fleets, and the hijacker could not be sure of finding a flight with the right type of airplane. In 1971, the largest of these carriers, Mohawk, had only twenty-three BAC-111s. Third, and probably most important, a local service carrier might not be able to raise $200,000 in cash on short notice.

This criterion would have further focused the planning on the Big Four and the seven other trunk carriers. Each of these carriers had an extensive domestic-route network, in many cases from coast to coast and from the Canadian border to the frontier with Mexico.

The question would now arise: Would it be possible to identify the flights that were operated by a Boeing 727, a Douglas DC-9, or a BAC-111?

It would not be smart to ask this question at the ticket counter. It would be an unusual question, and it would attract attention: the more so if the airplane were the wrong type, and the prospective passenger walked away. One could not do that many times before law enforcement would take an interest.

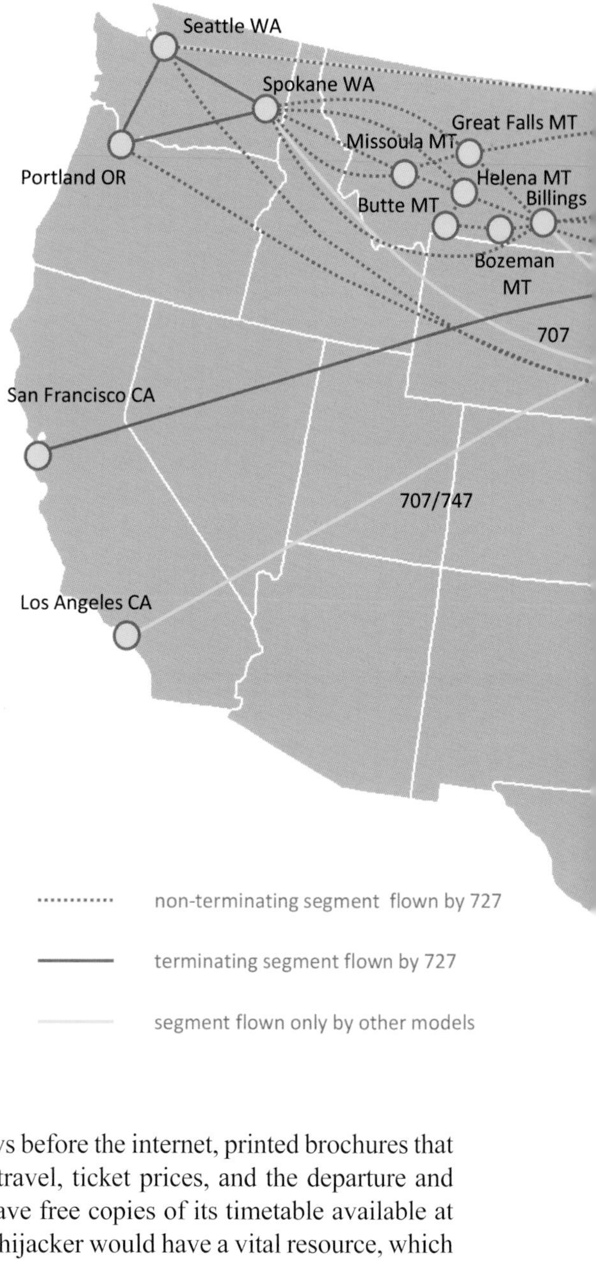


However, in the 1970s, all US airlines published system timetables. These were, in the days before the internet, printed brochures that included network maps, terms and conditions of travel, ticket prices, and the departure and arrival time of every flight. Every airline would have free copies of its timetable available at each of its offices throughout the country. Here the hijacker would have a vital resource, which he could browse in privacy and at his leisure.

It would be necessary for him to select airlines that identified the type of airplane on each route.Braniff, Trans World, and Western did not, and that would exclude them. Continental and Eastern identified the airplane type only if the flight was operated by a Boeing 747; United identified flights operated only by a Boeing 747 or a Douglas DC-10. That would not be sufficiently specific; an unspecified type of airplane could prove to be a Boeing 707 or 720, which would not work.

However, five airlines publicly specified their flights with sufficient precision that a passenger could be sure of flying on a Boeing 727 or a DC-9:[6]

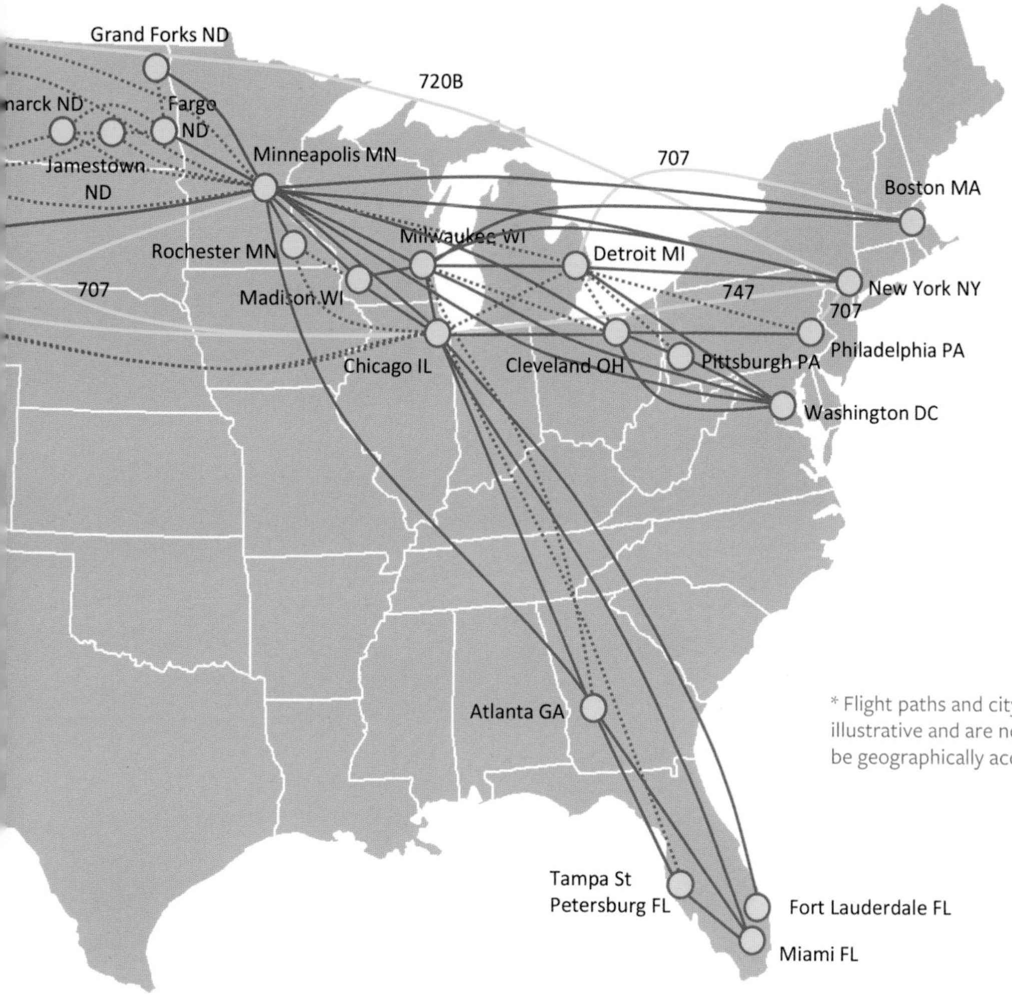


**Figure 4.1**. US lower forty-eight states, October 31, 1971: Northwest Orient Airlines route network. *Base map from Wikipedia; graphics by author*

| | |
|---|---|
| American | BAC 111-400, Boeing 707, Boeing 727, Boeing 747 |
| Delta | Boeing 747, Convair 880, Douglas DC-8, Douglas DC-9 |
| National | Boeing 727, Boeing 747, Douglas DC-8, Douglas DC-10 |
| Northeast | "jet" flights specified = Boeing 727 or Douglas DC-9 |
| Northwest | Boeing 707, Boeing 720, Boeing 727, Boeing 747. |

There may have been other airlines that operated the right kind of airplane; but these five airlines would have qualified for the hijacker's short list.

At this point, for a mission intended to terminate in Mexico, Northwest Orient Airlines would not have seemed an obvious choice. In 1971, Northwest had only four destinations that were anywhere near Mexico. Three were in Florida: Fort Lauderdale, Miami, and Tampa / St. Petersburg. Diverting an airplane to Mexico from any of these airports would entail a long flight over water, with no place for an early jump, and ample time for law enforcement to prepare a welcome party on arrival. The fourth possibility was Los Angeles, which would be just minutes from the Mexican border, but other criteria, as we shall see in a moment, would rule it out.

## A TERMINATING FLIGHT

As we have seen in earlier chapters, the hijacker of Flight 305 succeeded in presenting and securing his demands in the course of a flight between Portland and Seattle, without any of the other passengers realizing that a hijack was in progress. At Seattle, the other thirty-six passengers disembarked in the belief that the long and tiresome delay was nothing more than a consequence of "mechanical difficulties." The hijacker had known they would do so, because Seattle was the final destination of the flight. Everyone (except the hijacker) was bound to disembark.

We can imagine the situation if Flight 305 had been scheduled to continue to another destination. This would have been the case if the hijack had been initiated at the origin point at Washington, DC, or at any of the intermediate airports: Minneapolis–St. Paul, Minnesota; Great Falls, Montana; Missoula, Montana; or Spokane, Washington.

The passengers disembarking at those airports would not cause a problem, any more than did those who left at Seattle. But those who remained on board would be witnesses to the unfolding drama and, sooner or later, would realize what was happening, with unpredictable consequences. Even worse, those who attempted to board at the intermediate airports would certainly be turned away and would not know why. A prolonged and segmented flight of this nature would trigger a chain reaction among law enforcers, who would reach the hijacker's destination long before he did.

The hijacker was clearly a careful planner. He must have anticipated the obstacles that would arise to a successful mission if there were other passengers still on board and aware of the situation. In his presumed search through the airline timetables, he must have eliminated all the flights with subsequent segments and focused on those that would terminate at the next airport.

This would have still presented the hijacker with a wealth of choice. Up to now, we are assuming that the starting point in the USA was not important to him (as his ultimate choice of Portland, taken at face value, seems to suggest). In the Northeast Airlines timetable, for example, there were 243 city-to-city segments operated by either 727s or DC-9s, of which 170 were terminating flights.[7] Northwest Airlines had 538 segments, of which 352 were operated by Boeing 727s and 200 were terminating flights.[8] With five or more airlines on the shortlist, there were probably over a thousand flights to choose from.

The final decision, it seems to us, must have involved the duration of the flight, and plausibly the time of the arrival.

## A SHORT FLIGHT IN THE AFTERNOON

The hijacker of Flight 305 greatly simplified his mission by choosing a flight that was scheduled to last only thirty-six minutes. He initiated the hijack by 2:58 p.m., within moments of taking his seat and before the airplane had taken off, and he allowed the airline until 5:00 p.m. for his demands to be met. This gave him the maximum time to ensure the fulfillment of his demands, and the minimum time for law enforcement authorities to respond. By 5:30 p.m. the money and the parachutes were on hand at Seattle, and law enforcement officers, although present at the flight's arrival, were unable to intervene.

We hypothesize that the duration of the flight was one of the criteria that the hijacker used to arrive at the final selection of Flight 305.

If so, he had a wide choice of flights of a similar duration to Flight 305. Northwest Airlines had forty-nine flights of one hour or less. The Northeast Airlines timetable offered ninety-nine flights of an hour or less. The shortlist of specific flights was probably taking shape but still numbered in the hundreds.

An ultimate or penultimate criterion, we can imagine, might have been the time of arrival. The hijacker knew that Flight 305 was scheduled to arrive at Seattle at 3:21 p.m.; with hindsight we know that it eventually departed Seattle, with the hijacker and the ransom money, at 7:36 p.m. By then it would have been dark, and we can readily believe that a nighttime exit from the airplane was central to the hijacker's plans.

If so, we may postulate that the final shortlist was as follows:

- a flight operated by American, Delta, National, Northeast, or Northwest
- a Boeing 727 or a Douglas DC-9
- a flight with both the origin and the destination in the continental United States
- a flight terminating at the next airport
- a flight of less than one hour (maybe less than forty-five minutes), arriving between about 3 p.m. and 5 p.m.

Table 4.2, below, presents a selection of such flights. This table illustrates that if we have approximated the hijacker's iterative process of selecting airplanes, airlines, and specific flight segments, at the end of the day there would be a number of flights with similar characteristics to those of Flight 305.

Northwest itself had another Boeing 727 (Flight 735) departing from Portland to Seattle-Tacoma and arriving at 5:26 p.m.; perhaps this was the backup flight, in case the hijacker was unable to board Flight 305. Northwest also had afternoon flights terminating at Detroit, Michigan; Chicago, Illinois; and Madison, Wisconsin. Northeast Airlines had short-duration flights terminating in the afternoon at Keene, New Hampshire; Tampa / St. Petersburg, Florida; Portland, Maine; and Boston, Massachusetts. American, Delta and National undoubtedly offered similar opportunities. Any of these flights should have presented an opportunity for diversion to Mexico, with no greater difficulty than that which the hijacker experienced on Flight 305.

**Table 4.2. November 24, 1971: Selected terminating flights in US lower forty-eight states, under forty-five minutes in duration, and arriving between 2:45 and 5:20 p.m.**

| Aircraft | Routing from | Routing to | Days of week | Flight no. | Dep. | Arr. | Duration |
|---|---|---|---|---|---|---|---|
| Northwest Orient | | | | | | | |
| 727 | Portland, OR | Seattle-Tacoma, WA | daily | 305 | 14:45 | 15:21 | 0:36 |
| 727 | Portland, OR | Seattle-Tacoma, WA | daily | 735 | 16:50 | 17:26 | 0:36 |
| 727 | Cleveland, OH | Detroit, MI | daily | 353 | 15:40 | 16:19 | 0:39 |

**Table 4.2. November 24, 1971: Selected terminating flights in US lower forty-eight states, under forty-five minutes in duration, and arriving between 2:45 and 5:20 p.m.**

| | | | | | | | |
|---|---|---|---|---|---|---|---|
| 727S | Madison, WI | Chicago ORD, IL | ex Sa | 444 | 16:35 | 17:15 | 0:40 |
| 727S | Chicago ORD, IL | Madison, WI | ex Sa | 439 | 15:00 | 15:40 | 0:40 |
| Northeast Airlines | | | | | | | |
| 727/DC9 | New York LGA, NY | Keene, NH | ex Sa | 960 | 14:30 | 15:15 | 0:45 |
| 727/DC9 | Jacksonville, FL | Tampa/St. Petersburg, FL | daily | 151 | 14:40 | 15:23 | 0:43 |
| 727/DC9 | Boston, MA | Portland, ME | daily | 530 | 16:40 | 17:13 | 0:33 |
| 727/DC9 | Newark, NJ | Boston, MA | Sa Su Mo | 76 | 16:35 | 17:20 | 0:45 |
| | | | | | | | |

Sources: Northwest Orient and Northeast Airlines system timetables, October 31, 1971.

Finally, we may be permitted to speculate that, after all, there was something specific to Portland, Oregon, that underlay the choice of Flight 305. We know that the hijacker was familiar with the Seattle area, and specifically that he recognized Tacoma from the air and knew the distance from Seattle to McChord Air Field. He demanded an outbound flight at or below 10,000 feet but did not specify the flight path; it is logical to infer that he knew of the existence of the Victor 23 airway, which passes nearly overhead Portland International Airport.

At one point prior to the departure from Seattle, the ground controller, who knew that the hijacker had boarded at Portland, offered a suggestion that was perhaps facetious:

> **(GC): Or maybe you can get him into down towards Portland[;] he might get homesick and want to land there again.**

## THE TRACK RECORD

We may reasonably suppose that the hijacker was aware of the multitude of hijackings that had taken place in the previous ten years. It had been the golden age of hijacking, in the USA and throughout the world. In the period from May 1, 1961 to October 25, 1971, there had been 126 attempts to hijack US-registered aircraft. These attempts had involved 196 persons including the principal hijackers and their families or companions. Of these persons, 151 had succeeded in reaching their destination (although not always with a happy conclusion at that end).

The hijacker probably would not have had access to FAA databases (which did not appear until around 1975), nor to personal spreadsheet software (which would come onto the market in 1983). But no doubt he read the newspapers. With sufficient patience and diligence, and a big pad of legal-size paper, he could have developed a database along the lines that we summarize in table 4.3 below.

He could not have avoided noticing that the majority of would-be hijackers wanted to go to Cuba. That destination would not have interested him; but he might have observed that hijackings to Cuba had a remarkably high rate of success. It must have seemed that the airlines saw a diversion to Cuba as little more than an inconvenience, adding a bit to the fuel bill. No one wanted to put security barriers in the way of the booming airline business. Most of the

Cuban trips passed off without injuries. It was not unheard of for additional passengers, ostensibly unrelated to the hijackers but surely forewarned, to jump ship at Havana.

If he was doing his homework, he would have noticed that the choice of airline seemed to make a difference. Among the trunk carriers that were frequently targeted for hijacking, Eastern, United and National seemed to work very well from the hijacker's point of view. On Delta and Trans World, the hijackers did not fare so well. As far as the choice of airplane was concerned: his focus would be on the two widely used airliners with the ventral airstair: the Boeing 727 and the Douglas DC-9. The Boeing 727 was the hijackers' favorite, unsurprisingly since it was the most common airplane in the whole US civil fleet. It was followed by the Douglas DC-8, which had only side doors and would not work for the purpose at hand. The DC-9, for no obvious reason, was not among the previous hijackers' favorites.

In terms of airports of embarkation, five stood out as origins of almost half the hijackings: Chicago O'Hare, Los Angeles, Miami, New York JFK, and Newark. For that reason, we can imagine that the hijacker might have evolved a strategy to avoid large airports such as these, and to focus on smaller airports which were not used to, and maybe unprepared for, passengers wielding threats and weapons. For what it is worth: as of November 24, 1971, Portland had never experienced a hijacking.

The hijacker might have noted that two kinds of flight offered him a good chance of success: very short ones (up to 100 nautical miles), or very long ones (over 800 nautical miles). Some of the successful short hijacks involved small private planes, charter flights, even a sightseeing flight from Key West to the Dry Tortugas. He could not hope to pick up a ransom from a small-scale operator; but the short flights demonstrated that a hijacker could secure his or her demands before law enforcement could react. For what he had in mind, statistics such as these might have consolidated the strategy in favor of a very short flight, wherein events would happen quickly.

**Table 4.3. Hijackings of US-registered aircraft, May 1, 1961–October 25, 1971**

| | | | | |
|---|---|---|---|---|
| **Characteristics of hijacking** | | **number of persons involved** | | |
| | | **total** | **successful** | **success rate** |
| | | | | |
| ***Hijacker's destination/objective*** | | | | |
| Cuba | | 156 | 139 | 89% |
| other | | 40 | 12 | 30% |
| total | | 196 | 151 | 77% |
| | | | | |
| ***Big Four airlines*** | | | | |
| American | | 2 | 2 | 100% |
| Eastern | | 48 | 40 | 83% |
| Trans World | | 18 | 12 | 67% |
| United | | 13 | 12 | 92% |

**Table 4.3. Hijackings of US-registered aircraft, May 1, 1961–October 25, 1971**

| | | | | |
|---|---|---|---|---|
| ***Other trunk carriers*** | | | | |
| Braniff | | 2 | 0 | 0% |
| Continental | | 4 | 1 | 25% |
| Delta | | 13 | 7 | 54% |
| National | | 41 | 34 | 83% |
| Northeast | | 5 | 5 | 100% |
| Northwest | | 2 | 2 | 100% |
| Western | | 1 | 1 | 100% |
| ***Other airlines or carriers*** | | 47 | 35 | 74% |
| | | | | |
| ***Type of aircraft hijacked*** | ***no. in operation*** | | | |
| Boeing 707 | 365 | 16 | 11 | 69% |
| Boeing 727 | 665 | 67 | 56 | 84% |
| Boeing 737 | 155 | 4 | 1 | 25% |
| Boeing 747 | 104 | 5 | 5 | 100% |
| Convair CV-880 | 41 | 5 | 2 | 40% |
| Douglas DC-8 | 265 | 52 | 48 | 92% |
| Douglas DC-9 | 341 | 14 | 5 | 36% |
| Lockheed L-188 | 60 | 2 | 1 | 50% |
| others | – | 31 | 22 | 71% |
| | | | | |
| ***Airport of origin*** | | | | |
| Chicago | | 17 | 15 | 88% |
| Los Angeles | | 17 | 16 | 94% |
| Miami | | 22 | 20 | 91% |
| New York | | 20 | 16 | 80% |
| Newark | | 16 | 14 | 88% |
| others | | 104 | 70 | 67% |
| | | | | |
| ***Distance as per flight plan*** | | | | |
| under 100 nm | | 20 | 16 | 80% |
| 101 to 200 nm | | 23 | 15 | 65% |
| 201 to 400 nm | | 14 | 6 | 43% |
| 401 to 800 nm | | 30 | 20 | 67% |

| Table 4.3. Hijackings of US-registered aircraft, May 1, 1961–October 25, 1971 | | | | |
|---|---|---|---|---|
| 801 to 1600 nm | | 75 | 62 | 83% |
| over 1600 nm | | 34 | 32 | 94% |
| | | | | |
| *Source*: author's analysis based on Robert T. Turi, Charles M. Friel, Robert B. Sheldon and John P. Matthews, *Descriptive Study of Aircraft Hijacking*, Criminal Justice Monograph Vol. III, No. 5 (Huntsville, Texas, 1972); and Federal Aviation Administration, Office of Civil Aviation Security, *Aircraft Hijackings and Other Criminal Acts Against Civil Aviation, Statistical and Narrative Reports, Updated to January 1, 1983* (Washington, DC, May 1983) | | | | |

Finally, although he could not change who he was and where he had come from, he might have observed that, as we have illustrated in table 4.4 below, the most successful hijackers were between twenty and forty years old, and foreign-born (which in most cases meant Cuban or other Hispanic). He might have wondered if he was too old for this game, although we know that in the event, he went ahead. We of course do not know where he had been born; but if he was Hispanic, he had a track record in his favor.

| Table 4.4. Hijackers of US-registered aircraft, May 1, 1961–October 25, 1971 | | | |
|---|---|---|---|
| | | | |
| **Characteristics of hijacker(s)** | **number of persons involved** | | |
| | **total** | **successful** | **success rate** |
| | | | |
| ***Age of principal hijacker(s)*** | | | |
| less than 20 | 20 | 13 | 65% |
| 20 to under 30 | 66 | 51 | 77% |
| 30 to under 40 | 36 | 27 | 75% |
| over 40 | 17 | 10 | 59% |
| total of known age | 139 | 101 | 73% |
| | | | |
| ***Place of birth of principal hijacker(s)*** | | | |
| USA | 66 | 41 | 62% |
| foreign | 78 | 70 | 90% |
| unknown | 52 | 40 | 77% |
| | | | |
| *Source*: author's analysis based on Robert T. Turi, Charles M. Friel, Robert B. Sheldon and John P. Matthews, *Descriptive Study of Aircraft Hijacking*, Criminal Justice Monograph Vol. III, No. 5 (Huntsville, Texas, 1972); and Federal Aviation Administration, Office of Civil Aviation Security, *Aircraft Hijackings and Other Criminal Acts Against Civil Aviation, Statistical and Narrative Reports, Updated to January 1, 1983* (Washington, DC, May 1983) | | | |

## THE HIJACKER'S ORIGINS

A theory that is widely accepted in the social sciences is the concept of "distance-decay." In broad terms, the theory states that for any two locations, the scale of human interaction between them decreases as the distance increases. This applies to any kind of physical human activity: trade, tourism, investment, marriage, friendship. The farther apart are the locations, the less likely are these interactions. The theory applies in particular to crime.

For the most common types of crime, like violence against persons and theft of property, it is well established from empirical evidence that the crime is less likely to happen, the farther it is from the criminal's place of abode.

The "distance-decay" phenomenon allows us to reflect on the place of residence of the hijacker of Flight 305.

Firstly, we need to acknowledge that hijacking is not a common type of crime. The rewards and risks are relatively large, and could overwhelm the obstacles of distance. Nevertheless, we have a database of hijackings, of the kind which we have imagined in the hands of the hijacker of Flight 305, and we can try using it for a purpose that he would not have intended: to work out where he came from.

Among the 394 persons who were involved in hijackings of American airplanes between May 1961 and December 1982, there were 165 who had a known birthplace in the United States. For each of these persons, we can calculate what law enforcement officers call the "journey-to-crime" (JTC) distance; although we are obliged to use the place of birth rather

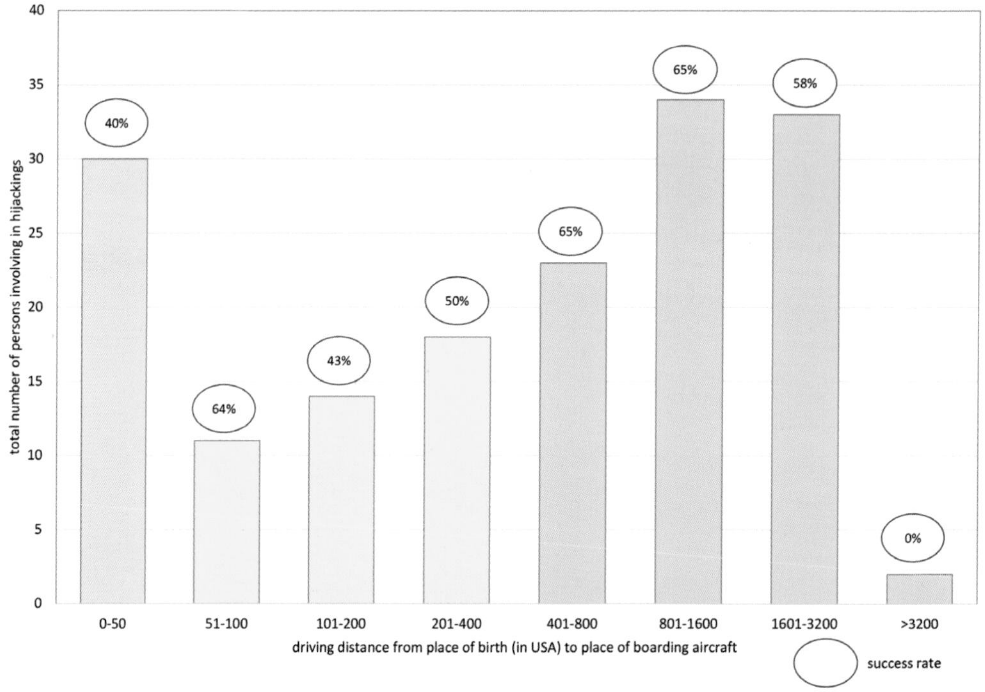


**Figure 4.2**. Hijackings of US-registered airplanes by US-born persons, 05.01.1961 to 01.01.1983, by journey-to-crime distance. *Source: analysis by author based on FAA databases*

than the place of residence at the time of the crime, for which data are not readily available. We summarize the results in figure 4.2 above.

Here we can see that in the history of hijacking from the 1960s through the early 1980s, there were three broad types of American hijacker. There was what we might call the "backyard hijacker," who initiated the crime within 50 miles of his or her home town, accounting for 18 percent of the events. There was a much-larger group (56 percent), which we could call the "hijacker at large," whose crime was over 400 miles from his or her birthplace, although we do not have enough data to know how many had traveled to reach the crime scene, and how many were already nearby. The rest (26 percent) were persons who started the hijacking at intermediate distances, between 50 and 400 miles from their place of birth.

The "backyard hijackers" had a success rate of only 40 percent; we might surmise that they were generally opportunists without a clear plan of action. In one such incident, in Evansville, Indiana, a nineteen-year-old man commandeered a Cessna 150 and ordered the pilot to dive into the ground. The pilot fought back and pushed the hijacker out of the airplane. The hijacker's objective was recorded as "suicide."

The "hijackers at large" averaged a success rate of 61 percent. Their rate of success increased with distance from the home town, peaking at 65 percent for hijackings at a distance between 800 and 1,600 miles from home. There was no obvious reason for this, unless their roaming had taught them street smarts and mission planning.

The hijacker of Flight 305 could not have known it at the time, but in the 1970s there would be a "sweet spot" for people operating between 50 and 100 miles from their home town, who scored a success rate of 64 percent.

For what it is worth, this author has tested the statistical relationships between the journey-to-crime distance and several other measurable aspects of the crime. In terms of predicting where the hijacker came from, none of the relationships was very strong. The age and ethnicity of the hijacker were not predictors of the journey-to-crime distance. Eastern Airlines was more likely to attract "backyard hijackers"; National tended to attract "hijackers at large." The longer the scheduled flight distance, the more likely it was that the hijacker was far from home.

If the hijacker of Flight 305 was US born, other things being equal, the statistics would place his most probable birthplace in the eastern third of the country, anywhere between the Midwest and the East Coast. If not, he might have been a man from northern Oregon or southern Washington. More than that, we cannot say.

CHAPTER

# 5

# THE FLIGHT PATH

Leaving aside all speculation, conspiracy theory, and wishful thinking, and working exclusively from source documents in the public domain, we may summarize a few facts that we know with some confidence about the path of Flight 305 from Seattle to Reno on the night of November 24, 1971.

First, the hijacker transmitted explicit instructions to the crew of Flight 305 about the configuration of the airplane and the altitude at which they were to fly.

Second, Seattle air traffic control gave Flight 305 an advisory route, which the controllers felt would take the airplane safely at least as far as Northern California, and which the flight crew could follow at their discretion.

Third, while airborne the flight crew talked (but very sparingly) to air traffic control at Seattle Center, followed by Oakland Center and finally by several controllers at Reno. On a more continuous basis, and on a private frequency, they talked to Northwest Flight Operations, where at least six employees of Northwest were taking notes, and agents of the FBI were sitting in.[1] To air traffic control, the crew reported their altitude but never their location. Presumably they knew that the controllers could see them on radar; perhaps they suspected that the hijacker had a radio tuned to the traffic control frequency. Meanwhile, the crew monitored their position by reference to various navigational beacons and, from time to time (but infrequently, as we shall see), reported their location to Northwest on the private frequency.

Fourth, we know that the flight data recorder was recovered and studied, although nothing of its contents has ever been disclosed.

Fifth, a report exists that one witness on the ground saw the airplane pass overhead.

Sixth, some thirty-six years later, the FBI published a map that purported to show a series of radar plots, furnished by the US Air Force, of Flight 305 on its path southward.

Seventh, Portland Airport picked up Flight 305 on radar.

Finally, we have the testimony of one of the four air traffic controllers who handled Flight 305 from Seattle Center.

We shall examine each of these sources of information in turn.

## THE INSTRUCTIONS

On the ground at Seattle International Airport, while refueling was underway, Tina Mucklow for the first time received the hijacker's instructions on the nature and destination of the outbound flight. In her interview with the FBI, at Reno Municipal Airport on the night of November 24, two special agents recorded the following:

**Miss Mucklow said that she obtained one of her pay sheets and by this time did have a pencil and took down the following instructions from the hijacker: "Going to Mexico City—or, anyplace in Mexico—nonstop—[landing] gear down—flaps down—don't go over 10,000 feet altitude—all cabin lights out—do not again land in the States for fuel or any other reason—no one behind the first[-]class section."**

In a second interview, conducted at Trevose, Pennsylvania, on December 3, Mucklow added her further recollections:

**He said, "We're going to Mexico City, [landing] gear down, flaps down, you can trim the flaps to 15, you can stop anywhere in Mexico to refuel, but nowhere in the United States. The aft door must be open and the [ventral] stairs to be down. The altitude under 10,000 feet; they know they can't go over that. Cabin lights out and everyone is to be forward of the first-class curtain."**

Sometime between 5:47 p.m. and 6:21 p.m., the flight crew confirmed these instructions by ARINC radio to Northwest Flight Operations and the listening FBI:[2]

**We have instructions from the individual; he wants to go to Mexico City, to fly with [landing] gear down and flaps at 15 degrees after we are underway. All lights to be turned out in the aircraft. We cannot land in the US for fuel or any other reason. No crew member is to go aft of the first[-]class curtain.**

By accident or design, the flight crew omitted to mention the proposed altitude of up to 10,000 feet.

We can see that the hijacker's instructions had a clear intent. With landing gear and flaps down, the aircraft would have to fly slowly, probably not above 160 knots. The flap setting refers to the control surfaces on the rear of the wings, which provide extra lift when needed. A flap setting of 15 degrees is good for slow, level flight; higher settings such as 30 or 40 degrees are used only for takeoff and landing. The hijacker clearly knew this; he was not only a jumper but, we infer, had also spent time on flight decks, maybe as a pilot or as a second or third crewman.

The altitude of 10,000 feet (or below) is also safe, and in some ways desirable, for a parachute jump. It is high enough to give flexibility in the descent path (which can be several minutes, depending on how soon the jumper pulls the ripcord). It is also high enough to clear most of the terrain on the way to Mexico (but not all of the terrain, as we shall see). This altitude is also low enough that an oxygen mask is not required. Let us recall our expert witness:[3]

**Q. This would have no material effect on the jumper physiologically at this altitude?**

A. No, not at 10,000 feet.

**Q. This would be a very practical altitude in which to jump?**

A. Certainly.

The one parameter that the hijacker might have been expected to specify, but did not, was the flight path. Did he not care? Was he ready to jump from the airplane wherever it might be above the American continent? Or did he know, or believe, that an altitude of 10,000 feet would impose a certain route on the airplane? We do not know, but as we have said, we suspect that he knew about Victor 23.

## THE FLIGHT PLAN

Having received these instructions, the crew turned to air traffic control for a solution. Their discussion was primarily with Ground Control at Seattle (here abbreviated as GC).[4] There may have been other parties on the same frequency; the transcript does not make this clear.

**(305): . . . He seems to know a little bit about an airplane. He says we'll have to go unpressurized, though: he seems to—I don't know where he picked that up. He said we'll have to go below 10,000 [feet].**

**(GC)(?): Al [this is addressed to Al Lee, Northwest's operations manager in Seattle], we checked on altitude here in Reno and the minimum obstruction altitude is 15,000 [feet]. . . . First league [leg?] is 15,000 [feet] going J-5.[5]**

Here the first obstacle appeared. Someone on the Ground Control frequency was proposing a "J" (Jet) airway, but these airways start at a minimum altitude of 18,000 feet. This would not conform to the hijacker's instructions. Since the hijacker had not specified a route, Flight 305 had to find one that would stay below 10,000 feet. Capt. Scott offered an alternative suggestion:

**(P): Well[,] we may have to go down the coast and come in from another route possibly . . . we'll have to pick a flight plan in the air. You get us headed the general direction: put us southerly out over the, somewhat along the coast.**

**(GC): Okay, we'll start you out here heading toward Portland and then we'll get your clearance cornered.**

At that point the plan was simply to fly south, though not really following the coast, but rather the Willamette Valley, which is about 50 miles inland and runs through Oregon over a distance of about 150 miles, from Portland in the north to Eugene in the south. The valley is bounded by the Cascade Range on the east, rising to over 14,000 feet, and on the west by the much-lower Oregon Coast Range, which does not exceed 4,101 feet. A flight along the Willamette Valley, at 10,000 feet, would offer plenty of opportunity to cut across to the coast if need be.

We recall from chapter 3 the cryptic, or facetious, message from Ground Control:

**(GC): Or maybe you can get him into down towards Portland[;] he might get homesick and want to land there again.**

Moments later, air traffic control suddenly came up with a possible solution:

> **(CG):[6] Northwest 305 . . . refer to Portland Vector [*sic*] 23, maintain 10,000 [feet] and remain in this [frequency] until advised and [set transponder to] 3100[7] until the other codes advises. . . . And 305 checking on the maps Vector 23 all the way south the highest mountain is 10,000 [feet] that looks about like the best to get you down and that goes all the way into Sacramento at 10 [thousand feet] or less.**

## VICTOR 23

In the context of our story, this is the first known reference to Victor (not Vector) 23, the airway that later became part of the Flight 305 mythology. To this day, there is a small-batch brewery and pub in Vancouver, Washington, named "Victor 23," with a parachute logo and a collection of Northwest Airlines paraphernalia.

In real life, Victor 23, or V-23,[8] is a low-level federal airway, defined by the Federal Aviation Administration as a route served by VOR (very high-frequency omnirange) navigational beacons. Victor airways are located throughout the United States and Canada, are intended mainly for general aviation, and serve to keep low-flying airplanes out of the way of the high-level airline traffic. Victor 23 runs from the Canadian border at its northern end to Mission Bay, California, in the south. On the segment southbound from Seattle, Victor 23 follows the 197° radial (17 degrees west of due south).

In this instance, Seattle Ground Control evidently felt that Victor 23 would route Flight 305 safely at least as far as Sacramento, California, if the airplane maintained an altitude of 10,000 feet.

When the Victor airways were first conceived and implemented, back in the 1950s, they had a width of 10 statute miles (8.68 nautical miles). The FAA chronicles the official introduction of these airways as follows:

> **June 1, 1952: Forty-five thousand miles of very-high-frequency (omnirange) airways, referred to as "Victor" airways, were put in operation. Like the then existing 70,000 miles of Federally maintained low-frequency airways, the "Victor" routes were 10 statute miles in width.[9]**

In 1964, the FAA reduced the width of the Victor airways from 10 statute miles to 8 nautical miles.

> **The final rule was published on July 7, 1964. Section 71.5 established the width of 4 miles either side of centerline. Section 71.19 adopts nautical miles as the measurement. Both sections are on page 8472 of the rule.[10]**

This system, which is still in use today, gives Victor airways a standard width of 8 nautical miles, provided that the navigational beacons that serve the airway have intervening distances of less than 102 miles.[11] In the segment of Victor 23 between Seattle and Sacramento, there are eight such beacons; the spacing of each consecutive pair of beacons is well under 102 miles. Therefore, the protected space of the Victor 23 airway was in 1971, and is today, up to 4 miles on either side of the centerline.

The 8-mile width of Victor 23 is significant because to this day there is a school of thought, among researchers of Flight 305, that favors a narrative known as the "western flight path."

According to this narrative, Victor 23 in 1971 was 10 nautical miles wide, and an airplane within, or just outside, the Victor 23 corridor could have passed over a sandbank on the Columbia River, known as Tena Bar. To this narrative, which we believe is erroneous, we shall return.

The flight crew was not at first entirely convinced of the plan to fly Victor 23, and there was a brief debate with Ground Control:

**(P): Okay, fine . . . but of course somewhere along the coast would be best. . . . It wouldn't add appreciably to our Reno way by going doglegging it.**

**(GC): Yeah, Vector 23, you're over the valley most of the way. It's populated most of the way so it might be Vector 23 all the way down. It looks to us like the best.**

**(P): Okay, fine that's all right; as long as we got the [unintelligible] that's all that matters.**

**(GC): And 305, ground, if en route there's any problem on communications, why don't we just clear you to Sacramento; that looks a little bit longer than Reno not much. Let's clear you to Sacramento to maintain 10,000 [feet].**

**(P): Okay, clear to Sacramento and maintain 10,000. How about rerouting Vector 23; we haven't got the maps out here and haven't really had a chance to look at it.**

**(GC): That'll be Vector 23 all the way to Sacramento.**

There was clearly something about Victor 23 that bothered the flight crew. Perhaps it was a concern about flying over a populated valley, with a presumed bomb on board. Perhaps they wanted to be over the sea, so that if the bomb went off, they might have a chance to ditch the airplane in the water. Perhaps they had been paying attention when Ground Control mentioned terrain rising to 10,000 feet. FAA rules would mandate a terrain clearance of at least 2,000 feet, and the flight would have to climb to 12,000 feet or more. The crew would have to assume that the hijacker had an altimeter and would know if they exceeded 10,000 feet.

Whatever it was, they did not say. Capt. Scott finally asked for some flexibility on the altitude:

**(P): Okay . . . be advised that I will be trying to make her up to altitude anyway we can here now before . . . any other restrictions that may be imposed upon us.**

**(GC): No restrictions at all. You fly in the best way you can do her. . . . Altimeter can be missed at least 4,000 feet if it will help you . . . if you do get on top of 10,000 [feet] let Center know.**

In the end, it looks as though air traffic control sent Flight 305 on its way with no more than an advisory to follow Victor 23, and with the freedom to go to 14,000 feet or above if they needed to. We know, and Flight 305 knew, that military aircraft would be dispatched to follow them, and maybe that was the motive behind the insistence on Victor 23. But that is another story.

## THE POSITION REPORTS

At this juncture, we may attempt to determine what path Flight 305 actually took on its journey southward. Our third resource is their position reporting. We have noted already that this information is sparse. Most of what we know comes from handwritten notes made by up to six persons in Northwest Flight Operations (among whom, only Bob Lowenthal can be identified), and by transcriptions of internal radio messages, with uncertain timing. The data in the public domain may be summarized as follows.

- At 7:36 p.m.,[12] by the estimate of the FBI, the aircraft took off from Seattle-Tacoma International Airport. For the takeoff, Flight 305 had to be under control of Seattle Tower, followed shortly thereafter by Seattle Departure and then by Seattle ARTCC (Seattle Center). A full transcript of the exchange with Seattle Center has been published, but no records of the communications with Seattle Tower or Seattle Departure have ever been released.
- At 7:37:11 p.m. (as we know from the transcripts), Flight 305 made its first communication with Seattle Center. The aircraft was clearly airborne at that moment, but the crew did not say where they were. Center did not ask, but they did not need to, because they had Flight 305 on their radar screens. The controller at position R2 simply asked them to squawk "ident" and to verify that they were assigned an altitude of 10,000 feet: "Northwest three zero five ident verify assigned one zero thousand."
- By pressing the "ident" button on their transponder, the crew would ensure that their radar return would be identified as Flight 305.
- At 7:40 p.m., someone in Flight Operations made a note that Flight 305 was at an altitude of 7,000 feet AMSL, within Victor 23 at a position 14 miles from the Sea-Tac beacon.[13] This did not pin down their location but it put them on an arc somewhere between Lakewood and Puyallup, Washington. We can call this reporting point 1.
- At 7:44 p.m., two independent observers in Flight Operations made notes to the effect that 305 was still at 7,000 feet within Victor 23, but now 19 miles south of the Sea-Tac beacon.[14] This would place them on an arc to the east of Lakewood, Washington, and close to Gray Army Air Field. We'll call this reporting point 2.
- At 7:47 p.m., a note was made that Flight 305 was beginning the climb from 7,000 feet; at 7:51:51 p.m. the flight crew came on the radio to Seattle Center, to report passing 9,000 feet; and at 7:53:34 p.m. they reported leveling off at 10,000 feet.[15]
- It is at this point, entering level flight, that another position report would have been most sorely needed. The airplane would now speed up; the crew's subsequent reports of indicated airspeed would be generally in the range 165 to 175 knots, which corresponds to 195 to 208 knots true airspeed. But the absence of a position report at 7:53:34 p.m. means that we do not know where this higher speed took effect, and therefore we do not know accurately where the airplane was during the following half hour.
- There would now be no further position or altitude reports for twenty-five to twenty-nine minutes, either through ARINC or on the Seattle Center frequency. This was the crucial period during which the crew reported the "oscillation," which, as we shall see, came to dominate the thinking of the FBI.
- At 8:18 p.m.,[16] an unknown author in Northwest Flight Operations made a note of a new position report. The crew were now reporting with reference to another beacon: what was then known, perhaps misleadingly, as PDX (Portland) and is now labeled, more accurately, as BTG (Battle Ground). They advised that they were 23 miles south of PDX. Their altitude was still 10, 000 feet. Let's call this position reporting point 3. At this point, Flight 305 had overflown Portland and was well south of the city, approximately overhead Tualatin, Oregon.

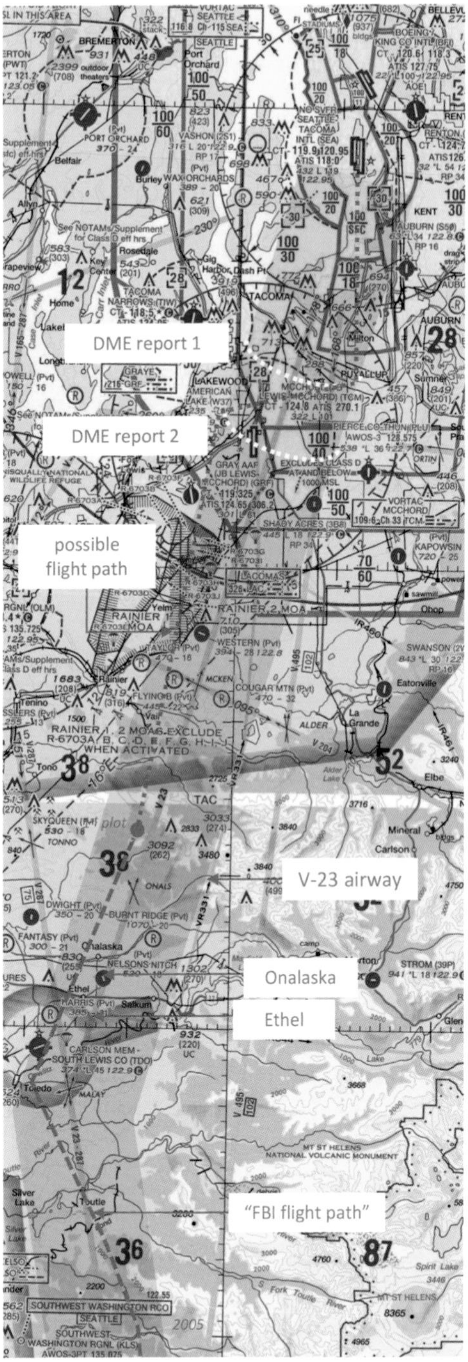


**Figure 5.1**. Seattle flight region: Flight 305 reporting points 1 and 2, Victor 23 airway, and FBI map of flight path. *Base map from FAA Sectional Chart no. 97, Seattle; graphics by author*

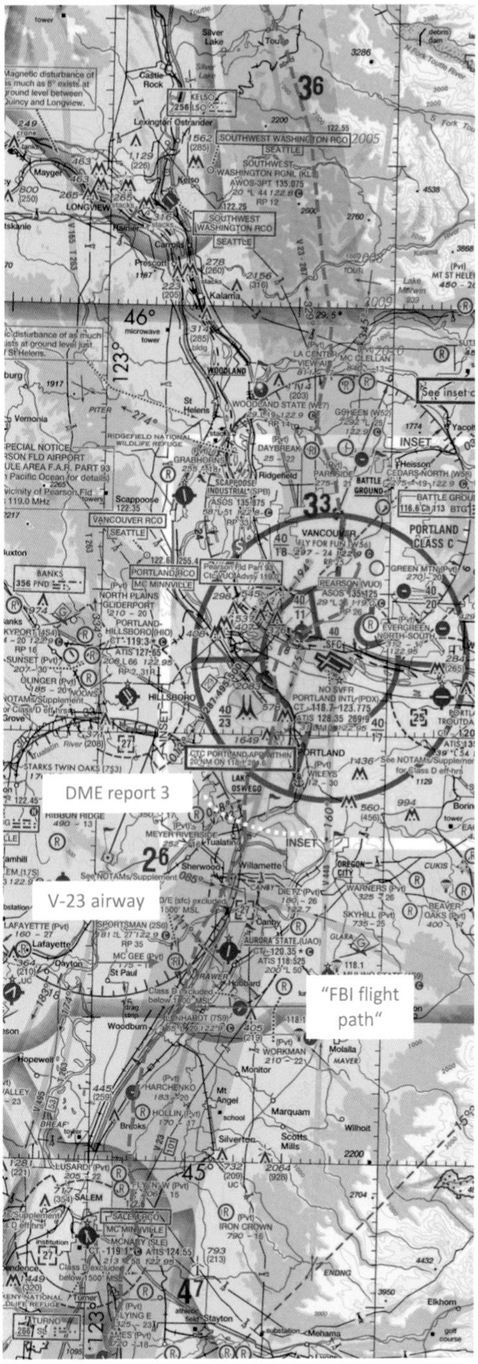


**Figure 5.2**. Seattle flight region: Flight 305 reporting point 3, Victor 23 airway, and FBI map of flight path. *Base map from FAA Sectional Chart no. 97, Seattle; graphics by author*

**Figure 5.3.** Battle Ground, Washington: BTG VORTAC navigational beacon. *Image credit: Michael Grigsby*

## BATTLE GROUND

The navigational beacon known as PDX in 1971 (but now renamed BTG) is quite central to our story because it anchors our knowledge of the position of Flight 305 in the few minutes before and after the moment when the hijacker is said to have jumped.

BTG is located near Battle Ground, Washington. It is housed in a futuristic circular white building at the end of a dirt track. At one juncture, it caused perplexity among the residents of Battle Ground because it was listed on Google Maps as a nightclub (later corrected to "radio station").[17]

BTG is 106.6 flying miles from Sea-Tac along the Victor 23 airway. Portland International Airport is 9.5 miles farther south on the 160° radial. A point 23 miles south of BTG would be approximately 130 flying miles from Sea-Tac.

## POSITION REPORTS

We shall attempt at this point to determine whether the positions reported by Flight 305 were consistent with the hijacker's instructions and with the advice of air traffic control. We need to consider how much we know, and what the accuracy of our knowledge is:

- The crew reported their position by reference to an instrument on the airplane known as the DME (distance-measuring equipment). This device transmits a pair of radio pulses to a transponder in a ground station; the transponder retransmits a pair of pulses on a slightly different frequency. The interval between the transmission and the reply permits a calculation of the distance. This calculation gives the slant distance between the airplane and the ground station; the horizontal distance will be slightly less. For example if the airplane is at 10,000 feet (about 2 miles up) and the DME reads 14 miles, the horizontal distance will be about 13.9 miles.[18] According to the US government, the overall system error of a DME is not greater than ±0.5 nautical miles or 3 percent of the distance, whichever is greater.[19]

- It is almost certain that N467US had only one DME (later versions of the 727 would have two). On N467US, this instrument would have had two displays (with the same information), one on the captain's side and one on the copilot's side. This means that the crew could not triangulate their flight against two beacons; they would have to fly with reference to one beacon, and then would switch to another.

- Over Washington and Oregon, the crew transmitted their DME on three occasions. Let us recapitulate: 14 miles south of Sea-Tac; 19 miles south of Sea-Tac; and 23 miles south of BTG (about 130 miles south of Sea-Tac). On each of these three occasions, they reported a number in whole miles. We believe that on the Boeing 727-100 series, the DME shows tenths of a mile.[20] It is probable that the crew of Flight 305 reported the nearest whole miles that they saw on the instrument.[21]

- We have therefore two sources of error: plus or minus half a mile in the DME itself, and plus or minus half a mile in the crew's reporting of the DME reading. This introduces an uncertainty of up to a mile into our estimate of the aircraft's position at any given moment.

- Our working assumption therefore is that each of the position reports, as recorded in Flight Operations, had uncertainties of plus or minus half a minute in timing and plus or minus a mile in position. Only the times of the radio transmissions to air traffic control were accurate to the second.

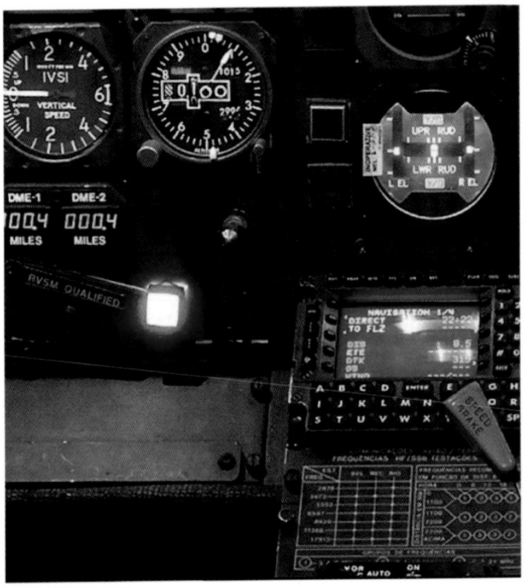


**Figure 5.4.** Boeing 727-243: part of the instrument panel, showing two DME gauges. *Image credit*: *Haroldo Fiuza Jr.*

- We can now summarize what we know about the three reporting points, as follows:

- Reporting point 1 was between 13 and 15 miles south of Sea-Tac and was timed not later than 7:40 p.m.

- Reporting point 2 was between 18 and 20 miles south of Sea-Tac and was timed not later than 7:44 p.m.

- Reporting point 3 was between 22 and 24 miles south of BTG, or if the airplane had followed the centerline of the airway, between 128.6 and 130.6 miles flying distance from Sea-Tac, and was first timed by Northwest at 8:18 p.m.[22]

- During this segment of the flight, on only two occasions did the crew of Flight 305 confirm that they were within the

Victor 23 airway: first at the 14-mile point, and again at the 19-mile point. Their navigation equipment would have told them their radial: that is, their compass bearing from Sea-Tac; thereby they would have known how far they were from the centerline of Victor 23. But they did not report their radial at any point, either to Northwest or to air traffic control. At the third reporting point, they gave their distance but did not say whether they were within the airway or not.

- Whether by design or otherwise, the flight crew were more communicative about their flight level. Periodically during the segment from Sea-Tac to point 3, they reported their altitude. At 7:40:06 p.m., they told air traffic control that they were climbing and passing 6,500 feet; at 7:40:37 p.m., they reported leveling off at 7,000 feet; at 7:47 p.m., a teletype message arrived to say that they were starting a slow climb from 7,000 feet; at 7:51:31 p.m., they were passing 9,000 feet; and at 7:53:34 p.m., they leveled off at 10,000 feet, where they would remain.

At this juncture, all that we can say is that the position reports are consistent with the hijacker's instructions and with the original advisory from Seattle Ground Control. Where Flight 305 was on the map of Washington and Oregon, we do not know with confidence. We do know that prior to takeoff, they had wanted to do a "dogleg" to the coast and back inland, but nothing in their reports tells us whether they did or did not do so.

## THE BLACK BOXES

Our fourth resource is one that we do not have, and to this day, has never been released: the contents of the flight recorders, or "black boxes" as they are colloquially known. Since 1966, all US-registered jet airliners have been required to carry two such boxes: the flight data recorder (FDR) and the cockpit voice recorder (CVR).

Although N467US had a cockpit voice recorder, under prevailing US law it was only required to record the last 30 minutes of flight. In the case of Flight 305, that would have covered part of the segment between Red Bluff, California, and Reno, Nevada. The recording would at least have helped investigators confirm the flight path, which by that time was beyond the range of the radar at McChord.

Regarding the flight data recorder, here is the testimony of USAF master sergeant Wally Johnson, who during the following January would be involved in an attempt to simulate the conditions of Flight 305:[23]

> **I was the NTOIC [probably should read NCOIC], chief of the airdrop section at McCord [McChord]. . . . The 727 that he skyjacked only had one black box [this was incorrect; it had two]. Now days they all have two, they have a voice[,] and they have a mechanical. . . . [On that 727] it is all connected into the mechanical system. Everything is built in sections[,] you know, one for environmental, the altimeters, stuff like that. The other one is how the engines operate[,] and then they also have . . . sections of the dash, one which covers the safety of the aircraft and that. . . . I mean [you] never got a 1,000 foot you automatically get a change. The main part of the black box is made of stainless[-]steel wire. Instead of tape, that is what it's got. Sent to Washington[,] DC, taken care of. They read it out there.**

The flight data recorder, would have recorded all the important flight parameters, including the ones most critical to an understanding of the flight path: indicated airspeed, altitude (above sea level), and heading (the angle of the airplane's axis relative to magnetic north).

The flight data recorder would not record the ground speed or the track (the path of the airplane over the ground), and therefore would not directly yield the position of the airplane; for that, it would be necessary to know the speed and direction of the wind along the flight path. But the flight data would be the first step toward plotting that path.

Inexplicably, there is no evidence that Northwest ever shared the raw flight data with the FBI, or that the FBI ever asked for these data. All that is known in the public domain is that on November 26, 1971, SA Reese H Chipman reported to the SAC in Seattle that Northwest were sending (apparently to the FBI office in Minneapolis) the following:

1. **A log of ever[y]thing that happened during the flight from Seattle to Reno, all conversations etc. This should reflect the exact time the pilot mentioned the change [in] pressure, oscillation in the plane etc.**
2. **A vector chart (radio range chart), which also may be helpful in locating the spot where subject bailed out.**[24]

The phrases "vector chart" and "radio range chart" are not standard aeronautical terms, and do not sound like radar plots. They might be a reference to a time series of radio transmissions, each one with a distance (and maybe a bearing) from some ground station. In any case, this author's FOIA request to the FBI for the "vector chart" returned the response "no records found." Whether these data were preserved, and whether the data still exist, no one outside Northwest knows.

## THE "FBI MAP"

Our next resource is a document that has come to be known, at least on internet forums, as the "FBI map." In the archives of the FBI, dating from the year 2007 but still on the FBI website at the time of writing,[25] there is a low-resolution photograph of an annotated map. The underlying documents appear to be aeronautical charts covering Washington and Oregon States, of unknown vintage. There seem to be at least two versions of this map: the one which appears to this day on the FBI website, and another version of which two sections, much more clearly scanned, were shared with the Washington State Historical Society in 2013. From a comparison of the two, it appears that the website version was pasted together from several charts.

Superimposed on the map is a crude hand-drawn line, apparently marked twice with a felt-tip pen, starting south of Sea-Tac (but in different places on the two versions) and ending just south of the Oregon-California state line.[26] At the northern end of this line (but only on the WSHS version), there is a manual annotation that reads "1st plot." On both versions, the line is marked at intervals in a southerly direction by crosses and the numbers "2005," "2010," and a very faint "2011." It is clear that these numbers stand, respectively, for 20:05, 20:10, and 20:11 PST and refer to estimates of the positions of Flight 305 at those times, as assumed or calculated by the unknown author.

The FBI offers no explanation or attribution but, on its website, captions the map cryptically: "This map was made to help investigators figure out where Cooper landed." The FBI has never claimed to be the author of this map.

The map contains an anomaly that is puzzling but not critical. It seems to have been pasted together from several sheets of a series of topographic maps. In the southernmost portion of the map, the sheets have not been properly aligned. The path of Flight 305, as drawn, passes directly in a southeasterly direction from the *Roseburg Quadrangle* to the *Crater Lake Quadrangle* (to use the USGS definitions). This is not possible because the

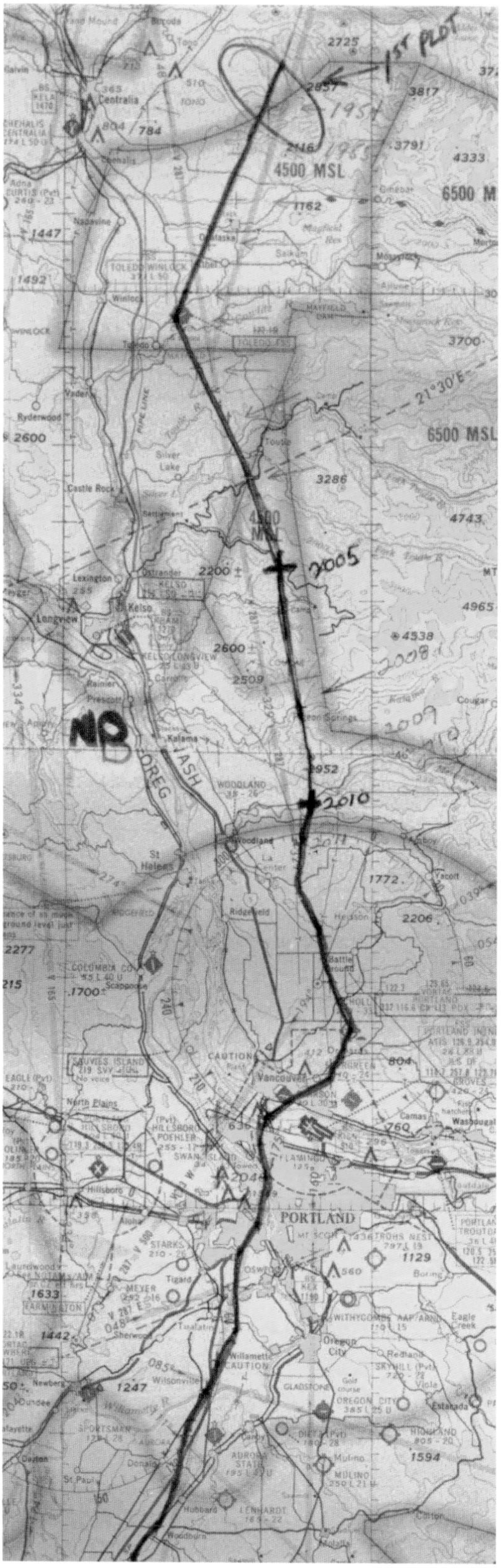


*Diamond Lake Quadrangle*, not the *Crater Lake Quadrangle*, is the next sheet east of the *Roseburg* sheet. Consequently, about 10 miles of the flight path is either missing or has been drawn on the wrong sheet (as shown in appendix 5).

Thanks to documents released by the FBI between March 2017 and May 2018 (over forty-five years after the event), we may begin to have an idea of the genesis of this map.

On November 25, 1971, the day after the hijacking, Special Agent (SA) Held of the FBI's Minneapolis office wrote to Special Agent in Charge (SAC) James E. Milnes in Seattle. Held told Milnes that he had spoken to Northwest Airlines, probably at the airline's headquarters in Minneapolis. Northwest had studied the "log" of Flight 305 (probably referring to the flight data recorder) and had concluded that the last point when the hijacker was known to be in the airplane was over Merwin, Washington, at the center of a triangle formed by Amboy, Cougar, and Pigeon Springs. There is no inhabited place by the name of Merwin; Northwest was presumably referring to Lake Merwin, which fits the geographical description. From the radio transmissions, we can put a time to this point: 8:05 p.m. This seems to be the first attempt at a time-coordinated map of the flight path.

On the same day, ASAC Paul R Bibler wrote a note to SAC Milnes, reporting on a conversation between the Minneapolis office and Northwest (probably the same conversation that Agent Held had reported to Milnes). Bibler had something new: an estimate of the jump point:

**Figure 5.5**. Seattle flight region: extracts from two versions of the "FBI map" of the path of Flight 305, from first radar plot to approximately overhead Tualatin, Oregon. *Left-hand image from www.fbi.gov. Right-hand image by courtesy of Washington State Historical Society. Image credits: FBI*

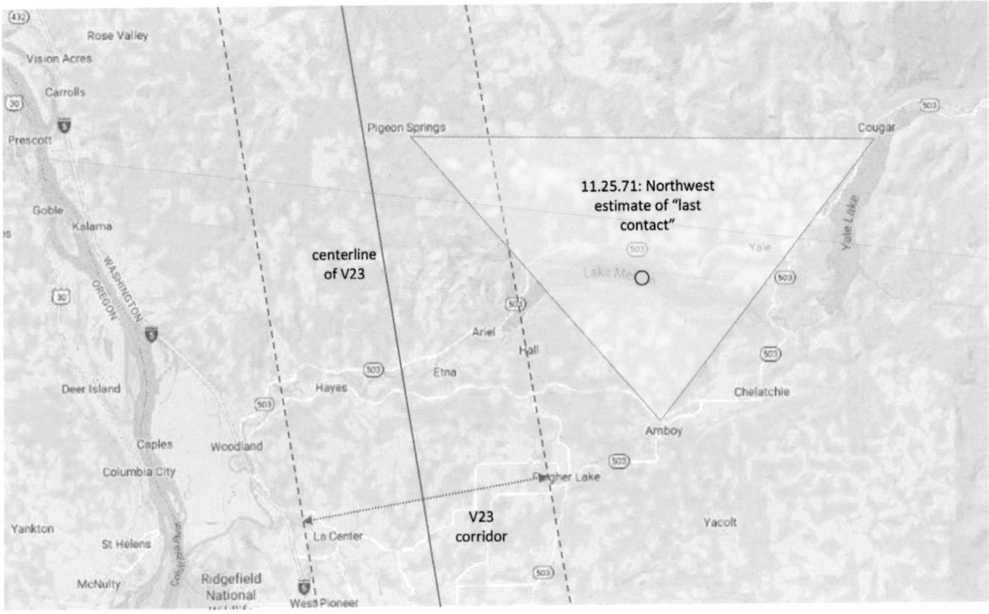


**Figure 5.6**. Amboy–Cougar–Pigeon Springs triangle: first Northwest Airlines estimate of the path of Flight 305. *Base map © 2020 Google Maps; graphics by author*

**... Northwest Airlines had figured out by pressure changes [relating to?] the rate of descent, [that] one reference point should be north[-]northwest of Crawford, Washington, about four miles just west of Highway I-S [*sic*]. The second reference point is two miles south southwest of Ariel [handwritten], Washington. A line drawn between these two points should cover the place of descent of the Unsub.**[27]

This message was strange. Crawford is not a town; it is a suburb of Venersborg, Washington. There is no Highway I-S. There is a highway I-5, but a line drawn north-northwest from Crawford will never cross the I-5. At least we know that Northwest had already downloaded the contents of the flight data recorder: data that they would never share with anyone.

The same day, the Seattle office prepared a press release stating that the FBI "was concentrating its search for the missing hijacker of Northwest Airlines Flight 305 in the vicinity of southwestern Washington in an area generally near Aeriel [*sic*], Merwin, Amboy and Crawford, Washington" and "urged anyone in the public having knowledge of a parachutist landing on the route between Aeriel [*sic*], Washington, and Reno, Nevada, to notify the FBI immediately."[28]

The press release was never made. Crawford was never mentioned again. Even more intriguing, at around this time and place, a witness saw a low-flying airplane. On November 26, Milnes wrote to the SAC in Minneapolis with the following report (the insertion was handwritten):

**During search today[,] witness "near Amboy Washington" recalls that at approximately eight p.m., twenty-fourth instant, he recalls a low[-]flying jet plane flying south at an unusually low altitude[,] and that all lights, including navigation and cabin lights[,] were going on and off.**[29]

However, if Flight 305 was where Northwest thought it was, it was way off course. The Victor 23 corridor was 8 miles wide. Both Northwest's "triangle" and the witness sighting placed Flight 305 around 4 miles outside the corridor, toward the east.

Northwest Airlines were quick to refute the idea that anyone near Amboy could have seen their airplane. On November 27, one of the flight crew told the FBI's Minneapolis office:

> **[Redacted] advised that their flight path would have been approximately seven nautical miles from Amboy, Washington[,] and the plane was at ten thousand feet indicated, eight thousand above ground, flying in clouds.**[30]

With that, the official view of the flight path shifted toward the west. For whatever reason, the Amboy, Cougar, and Pigeon Springs triangle was never mentioned again.

Meanwhile, on November 26, the US Air Force had entered the picture. On that date, the SAC at Portland wrote to Milnes in Seattle. His report, in its entirety, was as follows:[31]

> **There is attached a map which has been prepared by the Air Force showing the route taken by the airplane from Seattle to the California-Oregon line.**

Forty-nine years later, there is nothing in the public domain that explains who approached the Air Force, or whether the Air Force intervened, or whether the "Air Force map" is the one that now appears on the website of the FBI (although it probably is).

Briefly, another section of the flight path, much farther south, came into focus. On December 2, the Sacramento office of the FBI reported:[32]

> **Map describing route of flight captioned aircraft obtained from FAA, Oakland, Calif. . . . determine from FAA or Reno airport officials precise route of captioned flight over Calif, after released [*sic*] by Oakland, and forward map to Sacramento with route from Portola to Nevada.**

As the transcripts from Reno air traffic control confirm, at 10:34 p.m., Flight 305 was sighted on radar, 42 nautical miles west-northwest of Reno; that would place it overhead or close to Portola, California.

Evidently the FAA received these radar plots from Oakland Center and passed them on to the FBI. However, the FBI would quickly lose interest in this segment of the flight. In any case, the map of this segment has never been released.

## BLACKBIRD

By this time, the Sacramento office of the FBI was seeking the help of the 9th Strategic Reconnaissance Wing at Beale AFB, California, which at that time hosted the Lockheed SR-71 Blackbird spy plane. The plan was to have an SR-71 duplicate the entire path of Flight 305 and photograph the ground at resolutions down to 2 feet, with a view to locating the hijacker's parachutes and any other sign of his landing. For this plan to work, Sacramento would have to supply Beale with a map of the flight path. The Seattle office evidently had such a map to hand over. FBI internal communications dated December 3, 1971, make it clear that the outfit that had tracked Flight 305 was the Air Force's SAGE network (Semi-automatic Ground Environment) and, specifically, the SAGE Direction Center at McChord Air Force Base, just south of Tacoma, Washington:

- **ASAC Paul R. Bibler to Milnes: "I had one of the maps which we obtained from SAGE sent to him [an unnamed agent in Sacramento] by courier on the night of 12/2/71."[33]**
- **Sacramento to Seattle: "map of Northwest flight over Washington and Oregon territory forwarded to Sacramento by United Airlines night Dec. two, last, hand-carried to Beale AFB this am."[34]**
- **Milnes to J. Edgar Hoover: "Map of flight path has been furnished to Sacramento as prepared by Mc Chord AFB, Seattle."[35]**

The US Air Force evidently made several attempts to do this photographic flight, without success:

> **The Air Force has flown its SR Dash Seven One over the drop area in southwestern Washington on five separate occasions, but no photographs have been taken. . . . they were unable to find conditions without some cloud cover."[36]**

With that, the Blackbird mission came to an end. Either the FBI gave up or the Air Force withdrew its offer:

> **Plans for photographing with SR-seventy-one, discontinued, as aircraft committed for military missions.[37]**

## BACK TO THE DRAWING BOARD

Meanwhile, Northwest Airlines had returned to the mapping process. On December 6, SA Charles E. Farrell wrote to Milnes:

> **A facsimile copy of a memo prepared by [redacted], which was accompanied by a map, which is also a facsimile, were received at 6:05 P.M., 12/4/71, from Minneapolis. The map shows the course of the aircraft from slightly north of the Kelso-Longview area to just south of Battle Ground.[38]**

If the author of this memo and map was in Minneapolis, it was almost certainly someone at the head office of Northwest Airlines. But if so, between November 25 and December 4, Northwest had radically changed their view of the flight path. Lake Merwin is 8 miles east of the V23 centerline, while the Kelso-Longview area is about 12 miles west of the centerline. Either Northwest abandoned the Lake Merwin hypothesis, or Flight 305 did a 20-mile dogleg to the east to reach Lake Merwin and then cut back west to join the airway. In the absence of the map to which the FBI referred (which has never made it into the public domain), we do not know.

As Christmas 1971 approached, the mapping process slowed down. On December 23, Milnes wrote to the SAC in Minneapolis as follows:

> **The original and one copy of an Air Force map of the flight path was delivered to Northwest Airlines, Seattle, today to be dispatched on flight twenty[-]four, leaving at five fifty p.m., addressed to NW Airlines, Minneapolis.[39]**

It is not clear what the purpose of this delivery was. Perhaps the Air Force and Northwest Airlines had different views of the flight path, and the FBI wanted to put them on the same page.

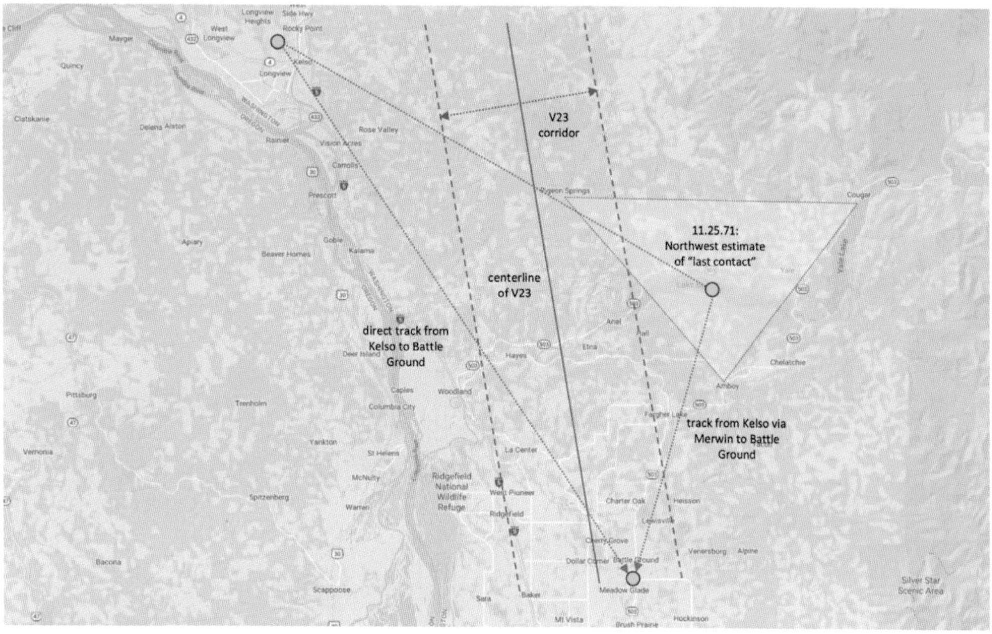


**Figure 5.7**. Kelso-Longview area to Battle Ground, Washington: possible tracks of Flight 305. *Base map © 2020 Google Maps; graphics by author*

In any event, Northwest reacted. On December 27, an executive of Northwest called Milnes twice: first to say that he would be arriving in Seattle to prepare for a replication of Flight 305, and second, to quote Milnes:

> **He . . . asked if it is possible to determine the identity of the person who drew up the flight chart map from McChord AFB so that he can discuss with them the time schedule and minute variations and locations of the flight at given times during the night.**[40]

Milnes gave instructions for this to be done, but it remains unknown whether anyone from Northwest ever met the unnamed radar operator from McChord.

As of January 6, 1972, the FBI still seemed to be acting as the intermediary between the Air Force and Northwest. From Seattle, Charles E. Farrell wrote to Hoover to report the following:

> **Refinements of the map of the hijacked aircraft originally made by the Air Force are underway and will be plotted by Air Force personnel[,] then furnished to Northwest Airlines for further coordination of precise times as logged by Northwest flight equipment.**[41]

Finally, Northwest came up with what appeared to be a definitive map. The FBI website today contains a three-page document dated January 9, 1972, and signed by someone at Northwest whose name has been redacted (but who we know now was Paul Soderlind). It has two pages of text and a black-and-white copy of a map titled "La Center Quadrangle, Washington," without a scale but resembling the 1:62500 charts issued by the United States Geological Survey. On the map is superimposed a short segment of the flight path, about 11 miles long. This path starts about 3 miles northwest of Ariel in Cowlitz County and ends about 2 miles east of La Center in Clark County. The path appears to be a segment of the "Air Force map." The text states inter alia:

**Aircraft position from USAF radar data from McChord AFB furnished by [redacted].**[42]

Another version of this text, which possibly originates from a now-abandoned website named n467us.com (after the tail number of the hijacked airplane), reads "furnished by Captain Thomas Spangler."[43]

We shall meet Captain Spangler again, in chapter 8, in connection with the "sled test" flight of January 9, 1972, where he will be identified as a C-141 pilot.

In any event, Northwest seem to have relinquished their first two versions of the flight path, and to have accepted the "Air Force map." Since this map became the basis for Northwest's assumptions on the hijacker's exit point, and consequently on the area that the FBI would search on the ground, the coalition around the Air Force version would have profound consequences for the manhunt. That is another story, to which we shall return in a later chapter.

Neither Northwest Airlines nor the FBI nor the US Air Force has ever disclosed the radar data on which the map was based. To this day, McChord Air Force Base denies that it has the data, on the grounds that under the Air Force Records Information Management System (AFRIMS), radar data once "superseded" are destroyed at the latest after ten years.[44]

There is, however, a coda to the story of the radar data. Over a year passed after the consensus on the Air Force map, during which exhaustive searches on the ground produced nothing. On January 23, 1973, the SAC in Seattle wrote to the SAC in Alexandria, voicing his concern that the computations of the search area could have been in error. He added:

**On 1/12/73 [redacted; possibly Brig.Gen. Van N. Backman, commander of the 62nd Military Airlift Wing] McChord Air Force Base, advised [that] [redacted, probably Capt. Spangler] has been transferred to the Far East. [Redacted] further advised that he is in possession of the Radar Data and calculations used by [redacted] to estimate UNSUB's drop area. [Redacted] advised he could not make this information available to the FBI personnel without the prior approval of the National Military Command Center.**[45]

As a working pilot, Captain Spangler could not have been the radar operator who tracked Flight 305. He must have acquired the data from a colleague in the radar room, and shared it with Northwest Airlines. Dare we surmise that this generosity was unauthorised? And that for his pains, Spangler was shipped to the Far East?

The FBI in Alexandria evidently took their quest for the radar data to the Pentagon. On February 1, 1973, Alexandria reported back to Seattle as follows:

**Representatives of the National Military Command Center, Pentagon, contacted 1-29-73, by SA [redacted] regarding release to Bureau [FBI] of radar data and calculations in possession of [redacted, base commander?] McChord Air Force Base, Washington. Matter referred to Joint Chiefs Of Staff (JCS) personnel. . . . [Redacted] US Army, JCS, advised telephonically conference held 1-31-73, between himself, [redacted] Air Force staff, Judge Advocate Generals office, Washington, DC, and other pertinent air force officers throughout the country regarding instant matter. Results are [that] Bureau [FBI] will be furnished the desired information.**[46]

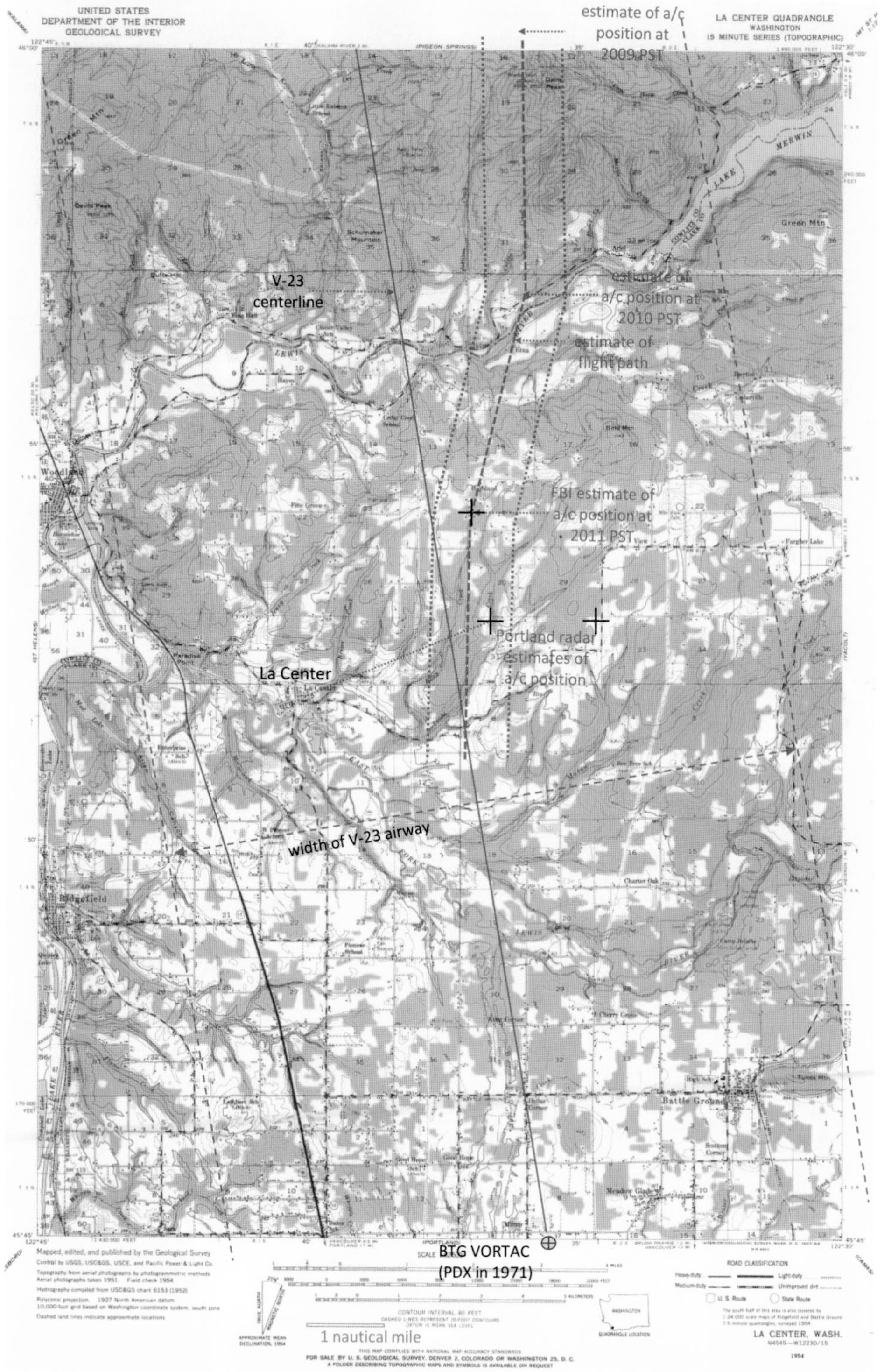


**Figure 5.8**. *La Center Quadrangle*, Washington: the "FBI map" of the flight path, as proposed by Northwest Airlines. *Base map from USGS, La Center Quadrangle, scale 1:62500; graphics by author*

In the end, it appears that after a fight with the Air Force and half the US military establishment, the FBI laid their hands on the radar data. But here the trail goes cold. Forty-seven years on, the data have never been published, and officially at least, the Air Force map has never been questioned.

Be that as it may, at least between Seattle and the Oregon-California state line, the flight path shown on the Air Force map is not greatly divergent from the centerline of the Victor 23 airway. This matters, because many commentators on the case have argued that Flight 305 at some point took a wide detour from Victor 23. To this argument, we shall return.

According to the Air Force plot, Flight 305 made the following maneuvers during the first 200 miles or so after leaving Seattle:

- SAGE radar at McChord picked up the aircraft about 50 miles out of Seattle, after which it followed a straight track on approximately the 198° radial (i.e., 18 degrees west of due south), drifting up to 2 miles to the west of the centerline of Victor 23, but still well within the corridor.
- It reached Toledo, Washington, where it made a turn of about 45 degrees to port.
- It crossed the centerline of Victor 23 from west to east overhead Toutle, Washington.
- It remained slightly east of the centerline until overhead Vancouver, Washington, where it made two successive turns of about 45 degrees to starboard, taking it back to the centerline of Victor 23 and avoiding an overflight of Portland International Airport.
- Thereafter it tracked Victor 23, not diverging from the centerline by more than a few miles east or west, as far as the California state line.

In short, the Air Force map of the flight path looks like a normal commercial flight within an airway prescribed by air traffic control. The path is entirely within the 8-nautical-mile width of the airway. While the Air Force has not been transparent with its source data, no evidence has ever been produced to invalidate this mapping. Therefore, if we believe the Air Force map, we are obliged to assume that Flight 305 followed Victor 23, or nearly so.

It is worth restating: we cannot exclude the Air Force version of the flight path unless new data require us to do so. For example, we might at some point discover that the underlying radar data were erroneous, or that the Air Force made errors in transposing those data to a map. To date, no such errors have been identified.

## PORTLAND RADAR

Flight 305 was also tracked at various times by at least four civilian radar stations: Seattle Center, Portland, Oakland Center, and Reno.

Not one data point from the civilian radar has ever been published, and as we shall see later, the FAA claims to this day that the data from Seattle Center were deleted within forty-five days. However, one fragment of the radar tracking emerged from Portland and was passed via Northwest Airlines to the FBI. On November 28, 1971, Paul Bibler wrote to his SAC:

> **[Redacted] Northwest Flight Dispatch Center, called twice. . . . The first time he advised that . . . a more accurate pin-pointing of the possible place of descent of the hijacker would be three statute miles east northeast of La Center, Washington, on a bearing of 080 degrees, true.**[47]

As shown in figure 5-8 above, this would place Flight 305 about half a nautical mile east of the Victor 23 centerline, and about 2 nautical miles south of Highland. Nothing in Bibler's memo indicated the source of Northwest's estimate, or the time to which the dispatcher was referring. Bibler, however, continued:

> **He [Northwest] called back subsequently and said that he had talked to the man who was working the radar at Portland[,] which was very accurate since it was very close to the plane at the time[,] and determined that the plane was actually one to two miles east of the center of this particular fly-way.**

This second estimate implied that when Flight 305 passed La Center, it was 1–2 miles (nautical or statute, we do not know) east of the centerline of Victor 23.

Bibler's memo did not make it clear whether Northwest were referring to Portland Tower (KPDX) or Portland Terminal Radar Approach Control (TRACON). Most probably it was the latter, since Tower had no reason to expect a landing at Portland, whereas TRACON would want to track an overflight.

In any event, this snibbet of data broadly supported the FBI version of the flight path. Both of Northwest's position estimates were east of the Victor 23 centerline, and within a few miles of where the FBI, by this time, believed the hijacker had jumped.

## CLIFFORD AMMERMAN

Our final witness is one of the four air traffic controllers at Seattle Center who handled Flight 305 on the evening of November 24, 1971. For sharing his recollections, we are grateful to Mr. Clifford A. Ammerman.

On the night of the hijacking, Ammerman was on duty at Seattle Air Route Traffic Control Center in Auburn, Washington. The chief of the center at that time was Gerald H. Osterkamp (who eventually signed off on the transcripts of all communications between the center and Flight 305). Four controllers spoke to Flight 305, one after another; on the transcripts, they are listed as positions R2, R5, R6, and R10. Ammerman was at position R5; the names of the other three controllers are unknown.

We asked Ammerman whether the transcripts were complete:

> **Q: Do the breaks in the transcript denoted by series of dots indicate redactions, or are they periods of silence.**
>
> A: It appears to me that the dashes (dots) are just used to bookend each conversation with NW305. There would be no reason to redact anything; however, many more transmissions would have been made to other aircraft that are not included in the transcript.[48]

Ammerman makes it clear that Flight 305 must have been airborne when it first opened communications with Seattle Center:

> **The take-off would have been handled by Seattle Tower[,] who would have sent the aircraft to Seattle Departure Control[,] who would have subsequently sent the aircraft to Seattle ARTCC at sector 2 (R2). The time of take-off would have been before 0337:11 Zulu. [7:37:11 p.m.]**

Ammerman recalls the duty roster as follows:

**Yes, I was one of the controllers and I occupied the position of R5. To avoid any confusion about sectors—I was working sectors 4 (R4) and 5 (R5) combined. Sector 4 covered from Mayfield intersection (now Malay) to the Portland, Oregon[,] airport from the surface up to 23,000 feet. Sector 5 covered from the Portland, Oregon[,] airport to Eugene, Oregon[,] from 10,000 to 23,000 feet. The two sectors were combined because of light traffic due to the stormy conditions.**

Seattle Center's low-altitude sectors, as they exist today, are shown in the map in figure 5.9 below.

From documents in the public domain, we have not been able to determine whether Seattle Center's low-altitude sectors had the same boundaries in 1971 as they have today. If they did, the sequence of communications is logical: first R2, followed by R5 (who was also handling R4), then R6, and finally R10. These four controllers were working approximately a north–south axis, which is consistent with the southbound track of Flight 305.

If so, it follows that in order for a controller to talk to Flight 305, it was not necessary for the airplane to be physically within the boundaries of his or her sector; only to be relatively close to the sector. We can see from the map that Victor 23 passed through the modern sectors 36 and 30 (which we assume also existed in 1971), but there is no reference in the transcripts to any communication with the controllers of those sectors. It is possible that, like Ammerman, those controllers were working multiple sectors; for example, R6 might have also handled R30, and R10 might have handled R36.

In any event, the times of handover from one controller to another (which we know) do not give us precise information about the position of Flight 305.

Ammerman's voice channel to Flight 305 was opened at 7:59:10 p.m., when the controller at R2 asked Flight 305 to switch to the frequency of 133.9 MHz. Flight 305 immediately acknowledged. This would have been the frequency to talk to Ammerman at R5. However, fourteen minutes would pass before Flight 305 made that call. During that time, Ammerman would have heard nothing from them. At 8:13:14 p.m., Flight 305 called him:

**Center four oh five (unintelligible) twenty point nine ten thousand.**

The unintelligible part of this message was probably a correction of the call sign to "three oh five." The meaning of "twenty point nine" is not clear; it is not a speed or a heading and does not seem to be shorthand for an altimeter setting, since Flight 305 should have been on the Toledo setting of 29.98 inches, as earlier instructed by position R2. "Ten thousand" was the altitude. A controller would not know whether the captain or another member of the flight crew was speaking.

Ammerman's first message to Flight 305 was brief and asked them to press the "ident" button on their transponder:

**Northwest three zero five ident.**

By this time, Flight 305 must have been over or close to Portland. At 8:15:52 p.m., Ammerman transmitted a new altimeter setting of 30.03 inches:

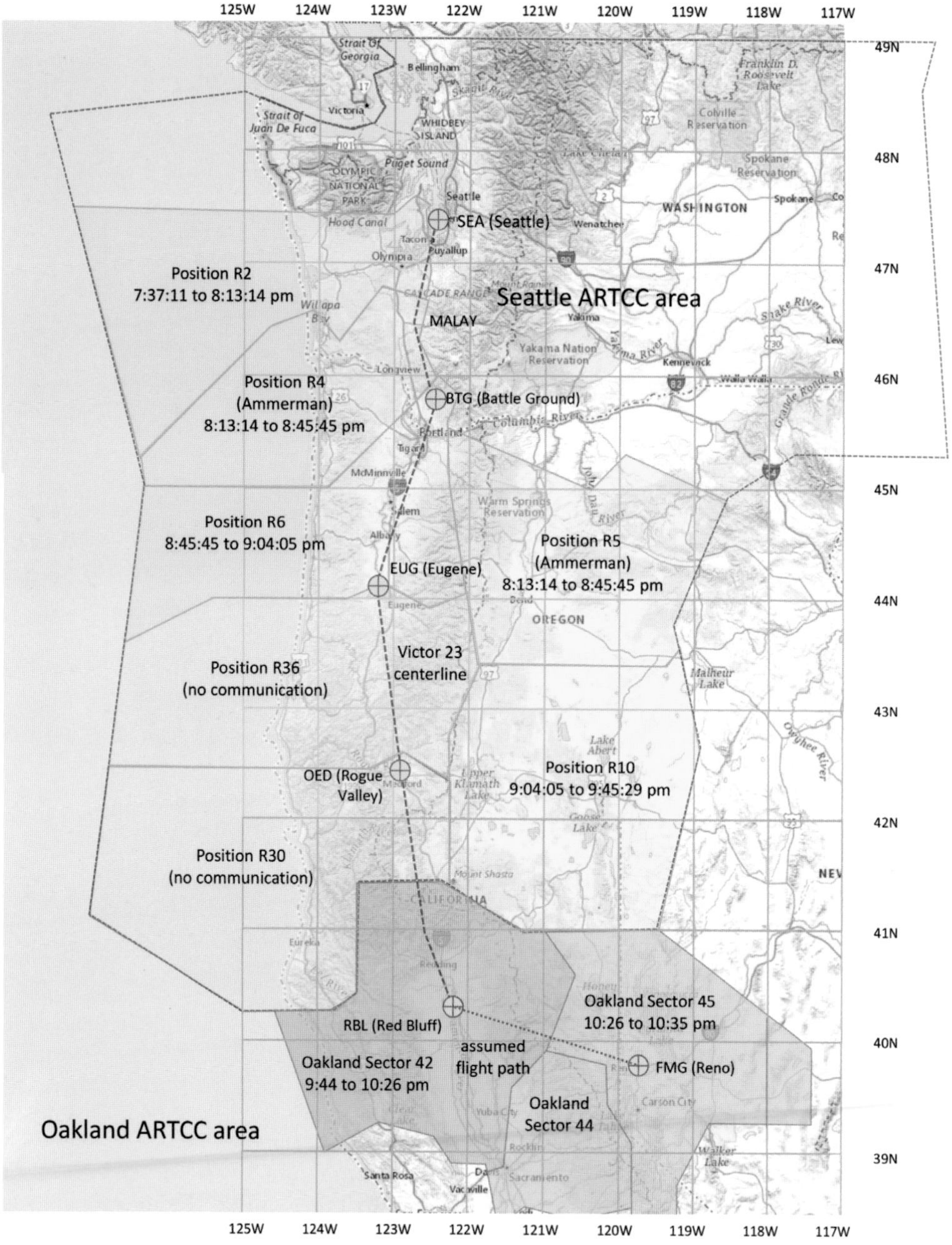


**Figure 5.9**. Seattle ARTCC and Oakland ARTCC low-altitude sectors, Victor 23 airway, and timeline of communications with NWA305 on November 24, 1971. *Base map from USGS; Seattle ARTCC sector boundaries (effective July 14, 1999) from Willamette Aviation; Oakland ARTCC sector boundaries (effective March 10, 1988) from FAA; timeline from WSHS; graphics by author*

**Northwest three zero five the Portland ah altimeter three zero zero three.**

This new setting would ensure that Flight 305 maintained the correct altitude of 10,000 feet, with allowance for the slight difference in air pressure between Toledo and Portland.

Eighteen minutes then passed with no communications between Ammerman and Flight 305. In this period the airplane would have covered about 55 nautical miles. At 8:33:36 p.m., Ammerman asked Flight 305 to switch to the frequency of 125.8 MHz in order to talk to position R6:

**Northwest three zero five contact Seattle Center one two five point eight.**

The controller at R6 asked Flight 305 to set its altimeter for Eugene, Oregon.

The geographical parameters of Ammerman's voice channel to Flight 305 are, in his recollection, as follows:

**I had voice communication with NW305 from about Toledo, Washington[,] until some distance north of Eugene, Oregon.**

If so, we might reasonably conclude the following:

- At 7:59:15 p.m., when Flight 305 switched (or acknowledged the request to switch) to Ammerman's frequency of 133.9 MHz, the airplane was near Toledo, Washington.
- At 8:33:46 p.m., when Flight 305 acknowledged the switch to R6 on 125.8 MHz, the airplane was north of Eugene, Oregon.
- In the intervening thirty-four and a half minutes, at a ground speed of about 3 nautical miles a minute, the airplane would have covered about 103 nautical miles; if we take Toledo, Washington, as the starting point, this would place the handover to R6 near Albany, Oregon.

We asked Ammerman whether there had been any loss of radar tracking:

**Q: Am I correct in thinking that Seattle ARTCC had radar tracking of NW305 from Seattle-Tacoma to south of Medford, and that Oakland had radar tracking from there at least as far as Red Bluff, and therefore that there was no gap in radar tracking.**

A: I personally did not maintain radar monitoring south of Eugene, Oregon[,] because of my radar coverage area and because it would have been the responsibility of sector 6 (R6) and sector 10 (R10). . . . I cannot speak to radar coverage south of Medford because that was a different area in which I never controlled. However, in the transcript R10 never advised NW305 that radar contact is lost[,] so a handoff to Oakland must have been made while NW305 was still in radar contact.

One might reasonably have assumed that all of this could be checked by reference to the archives of Seattle ARTCC. Ammerman expressed the view that the radar data should have been preserved:

**Seattle was required to keep all of the information relating to NW305[,] including not only radar data but also radio transmissions. Whether these files still exist[,] I do not know.**

However, this author's requests to the FAA under the FOIA received the following responses:

**You requested a copy of radar data for NWA305, a Boeing 727-051, on November 24, 1971, between 1936 Pacific Standard Time (PST) and 2022 PST. A search for records was conducted at the Portland Airport Traffic Control Tower (PDX) and Seattle Airport Traffic Control Tower (SEA). This search revealed no records pertaining to your specific request.[49]**

**You requested a copy of radar data for NWA305 from Seattle Air Route Traffic Control Center (ZSE) on November 24, 1971. A search for records was conducted at ZSE. There were no records responsive to your request because the request was received outside the 45[-]day record retention period. The incident was classified as a 45-day file, and no formal accident package was prepared.[50]**

Incredibly, the FAA was admitting that it had deleted evidence pertaining to a federal crime under the jurisdiction of the FBI: a crime that certainly had not been resolved within a period of forty-five days (or, for that matter, within forty-five years).

Finally we asked for Ammerman's view on whether Flight 305 had at any point departed from the Victor 23 corridor. He first confirmed that, as reported by the FBI, Flight 305 had passed over or close to the towns of Onalaska, Ethel, Toledo, Pigeon Springs, Ariel, Highland, Battle Ground, and Vancouver (all in Washington State). All of these towns are well under 3 nautical miles from the centerline of Victor 23 except Toledo, which is about 5 nautical miles from the centerline. Ammerman went on to say:

**Yes I have made the statement that NW305 never left the "confines" of Victor 23. NW305 did in fact stray a bit off of the centerline of Victor 23 but was still within the confines of the airway.**

Ammerman's recall of the flight path leaves no doubt that, under his control, Flight 305 was never more than 4 nautical miles from the centerline, and that between Pigeon Springs and Vancouver, it could not have been more than 3 nautical miles from that line.

As a coda (which is not central to our analysis), we must acknowledge Ammerman's main responsibility, which was to position the military chase planes:

**Most of my work load during this time was not in monitoring NW305 on radar but in positioning the F106s above and behind NW305 and trying to keep them 5 miles in trail by s-turning them because they could not fly as slow as the B727 was flying. Just north of Portland a T-33 was made available[,] so I was moving the F106s out and putting the T-33 in trail. I was able to slow the T-33 down to 150 knots at 11,000 feet[,] which then matched the speed of the B727.**

## RED BLUFF TO RENO

At about 9:35 p.m., south of Medford, Oregon, and about 7 nautical miles inside California, Flight 305 flew out of the range of the radar operator at McChord AFB. At that point, the plots on the "FBI map" come to an end.

Between 9:46 and 9:47 p.m., Flight 305 spoke to Oakland Center to report their plans for the final leg:

**(NWA305): "We want to go direct Red Bluff to Reno and uh we can either do it on our own navigation or accept a radar vector if you want to give it to us."**

**(Oakland ARTCC at Red Bluff): "Uh roger Red Bluff direct Reno is approved. I'd like you a little bit farther south and clear a few more of the hills at one one thousand prior to going direct.**

All parties seemed to be in agreement on flying overhead Red Bluff and possibly staying on Victor 23 a little longer to clear the mountains.

At this point, a military C-130, code name Rescue 983, was trailing Flight 305, probably without their knowledge. Oakland Center was talking to the C-130, but on the military UHF frequency:

**Oakland ARTCC at Red Bluff: "Northwest three zero five Oakland Center radio check. Rescue nine eight three I'm transmitting only on UHF now. I don't believe the Northwest can uh copy—uh you can monitor on one two zero point four but transmit on three zero six point nine."[51]**

At 9:52 p.m. or shortly before, the crew of Flight 305 transmitted a final position report to Northwest Flight Operations: today, no transcript is known to exist that might confirm this report, but two observers in Operations made handwritten notes of it, as follows:

**Author F (unknown): 0552 [Zulu time] 58 DME "NORTH OF" [inserted] from RBL[52]**

**Bob Lowenthal: 0554 [Zulu time] 58DME 325°R RBL 11000[53]**

These two notes establish that at 9:52 PST, Flight 305 was 58 nautical miles north of the Red Bluff VORTAC at an altitude of 11,000 feet. Bob Lowenthal was no doubt reading the teletype with a lag of two minutes. Lowenthal's report placed Flight 305 on the 325° magnetic radial from Red Bluff. In 1971, the magnetic declination at Red Bluff was about 18 degrees east of north. If we correct for the declination, we can calculate that Flight 305 was on the 343° true radial from Red Bluff: in other words, within one mile of the centerline of Victor 23.

Between 9:53 and 9:55 p.m., controllers at Oakland Center were also exchanging views on the position of Flight 305:

**Oakland ARTCC (Position E04): Yeah he's fifty northwest of Red Bluff Victor twenty three.**

Within a few minutes they were overflying the Red Bluff beacon, and turning onto a heading of 090° (due east) for Portola, California:

**10:05 p.m., Oakland ARTCC (position E04): "Northwest ten [miles] northwest Red Bluff"**

**(Watch supervisor): "Okay and vector what"**

**(E04): "Be zero niner zero out of Red Bluff."**

**10:07 p.m., NW305: "This Northwest three zero five er we start our turn ninety that okay"**

**10:11 p.m. (E04): "Okay he's over Red Bluff turning."**

With that, Flight 305 started the last leg of their journey to Reno. As far as anyone knows, they still believed that the hijacker was on board. Only at Reno would they discover that he was gone, and probably long gone.

## DID FLIGHT 305 LEAVE VICTOR 23?

To this day, we have no definitive knowledge of how far Flight 305 diverged from the Victor 23 centerline. Here then, let us summarize what we know.

- Seattle Ground Control gave Flight 305 a clearance to fly Victor 23 at least as far as Sacramento, but at the same time a free hand to fly the route and the altitude that they thought best.
- In the entirety of the published transcripts of the communications between Flight 305 and en route air traffic control, including Seattle Center, Oakland Center, and Reno, there is only one reference to Victor 23, and this was when Flight 305 was 50 miles northwest of Red Bluff.
- Capt. Scott at least twice expressed an interest in flying down the coast or making a dogleg to reach Reno (which, if he had carried out his idea, would have taken him at least 50 miles from Victor 23).
- The crew made two position reports referring to Victor 23, recorded in the ARINC transcripts, at 14 miles and 19 miles from Seattle. These reports were heard and logged by at least two observers in Northwest operations and subsequently were filed by the FBI. After that, the crew made no further reference to Victor 23.
- However, the "FBI map" or "Air Force map" (of which neither the FBI nor the Air Force has ever claimed authorship) placed Flight 305 firmly within 4 nautical miles of the Victor 23 centerline all the way from Seattle-Tacoma to the Oregon-California state line. (We have replotted this course on USGS quadrangle maps in appendixes 6 through 14, and the segment from Medford to Reno on an FAA sectional chart in appendix 15.).
- Clifford Ammerman has stated that Flight 305 was within the Victor 23 corridor in the segments for which he had the flight under his control, which he recalls as being from near Toledo, Washington, to north of Eugene, Oregon.
- Flight 305's final DME report, at 58 miles from Red Bluff, placed it squarely in the corridor of Victor 23.
- When the Oakland controller picked up Flight 305 at a point 50 miles northwest of Red Bluff, he specifically mentioned Victor 23.

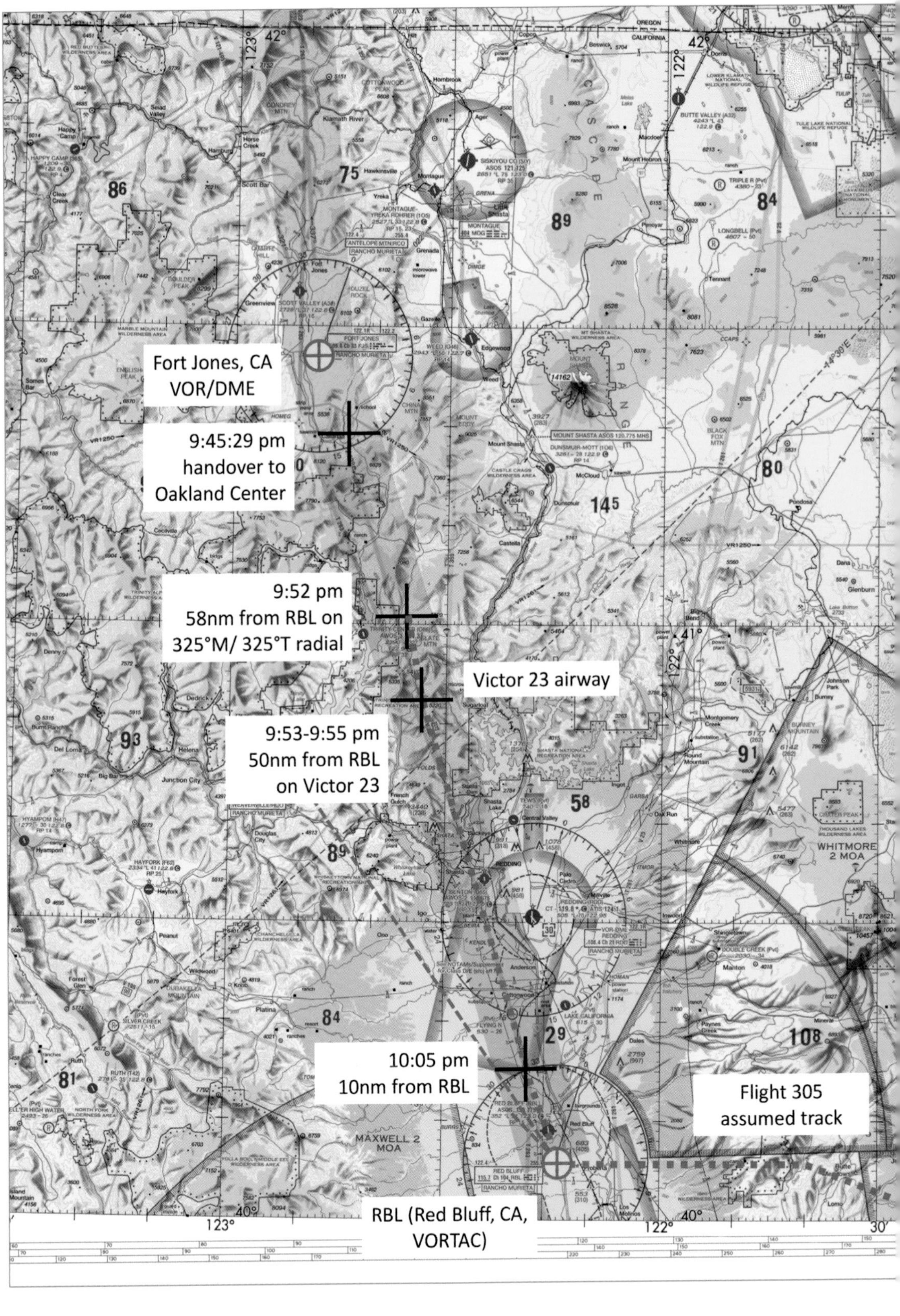
Fort Jones, CA
VOR/DME
9:45:29 pm
handover to
Oakland Center
9:52 pm
58nm from RBL on
325°M/ 325°T radial
Victor 23 airway
9:53-9:55 pm
50nm from RBL
on Victor 23
10:05 pm
10nm from RBL
Flight 305
assumed track
RBL (Red Bluff, CA,
VORTAC)

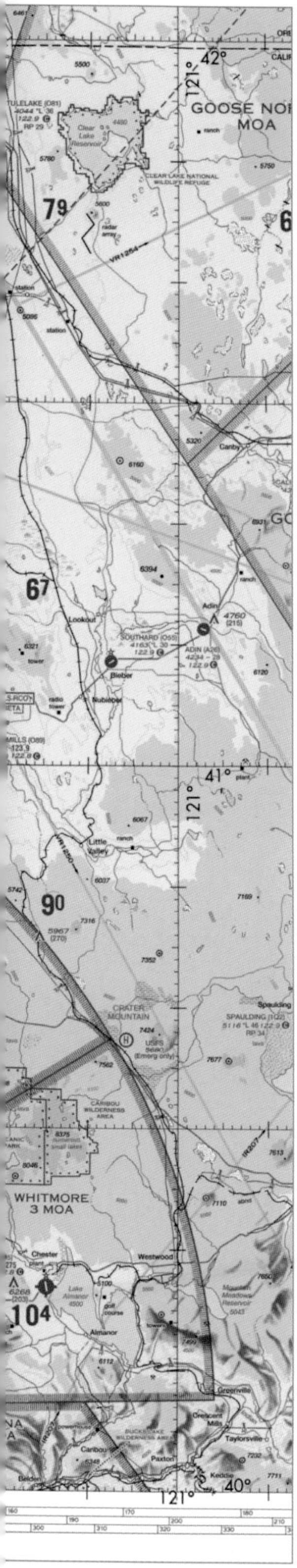


In short, the preponderance of evidence supports a flight path that remained within 4 miles of the Victor 23 centerline, in particular during the crucial period within which, according to all official narratives, the hijacker made his escape.

## POSTSCRIPT: AUTHOR F

On November 24, 1971, George Harrison was working for Northwest Airlines in an executive capacity at Seattle airport. In 2013, a representative of his estate provided the Washington State Historical Society with 23 pages of handwritten notes relating to Flight 305, which Mr. Harrison and his heirs had preserved for almost 42 years. These notes had never previously appeared in the public domain.

The notes appear in the main to be derived from communications between Flight 305 and Northwest on the ARINC frequency. From variations in the handwriting and the time periods covered, it seems that there were six different authors. The one who wrote pages 19 to 23 made a unique observation; we have called him (we suppose it was a man) "Author F." His notes, as furnished to the WSHS, cover the period from 3:30 p.m. to 10:19 p.m. PST.

At 8:18 p.m., Author F made the note "23 DME PDX."

He was recording that Flight 305 was 23 nautical miles from the PDX (Battle Ground) beacon. This information could only have come from a transmission on the ARINC frequency. Two other colleagues made essentially the same note, but they recorded this event at 8:22 p.m. The FBI later repeated the time of 8:22 p.m. Neither the transcripts from air traffic control, nor the ARINC transcript, nor the WSHS curators' report on the physical rolls of ARINC teletype, make any reference to this event.

Flight 305 was traveling at a ground speed of about 3 nautical miles per minute. If the airplane was 23 nautical miles from PDX at 8:18 p.m. (and if we assume that this was in a southerly direction, as the FBI map shows), then it could not have been overhead Highland, Washington, at 8:11 p.m., and the whole FBI narrative would unravel.

It is therefore a critical part of our investigation to determine whether Author F was keeping correct time.

Author F recorded the takeoff from Seattle as 7:36 p.m. So did Author C, and so did the FBI. No public transcript mentions the takeoff. Author F made his note out of chronological order, between his observations for 8:18 p.m. and 8:30 p.m., so he may have obtained the information from someone else. We have to leave this observation aside.

**Figure 5.10.** Victor 23 airway from Fort Jones to Red Bluff, and assumed track of Flight 305. *Base map from FAA sectional charts for Klamath Falls and San Francisco; graphics by author*

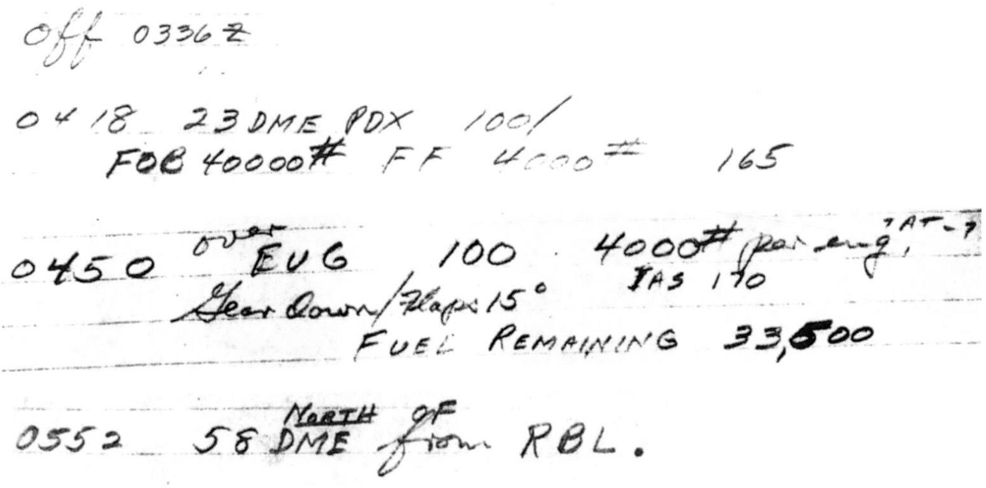
off 0336 Z

0418 23 DME PDX 100/
FOB 40000# FF 4000# 165

0450 over EUG 100 4000# per eng TAT-7
Gear Down/Flaps 15° IAS 170
FUEL REMAINING 33,500

0552 58 NORTH OF DME from RBL.

**Figure 5.11.** The four reports of the position of Flight 305, as noted by the unknown Author F. *Source; Washington State Historical Society, document 2013.5.23.1, pages 19–23. Image credit: the estate of George Harrison*

At 8:50 p.m. Author F wrote down another position report:

> **0450 [Zulu time] over EUG 100 4000# per eng TAT-7 Gear Down/Flaps 15° IAS 170 FUEL REMAINING 33,500.**

And on another line he wrote "(Bob Lowenthal)." The essence of this note, for our purposes, was that Flight 305 was overhead the navigational beacon at Eugene, Oregon. He was apparently quoting his colleague Bob Lowenthal, who later made an almost identical note:

> **0452 [Zulu time] Over Eugene VOR 10,000' 4000FF FOB 33500 TAT-7 170 IAS gear down 15 Flaps.**

But Lowenthal's reference to 0452 (Zulu time) meant 8:52 p.m. The ARINC transcript for this period has not been preserved.

Here we might hope for air traffic control to pin down the time. But the transcript from Seattle Center makes no mention of a passage overhead the Eugene beacon. All that we know about the approach to Eugene is that at 8:45:45 p.m. the controller at Position R6 called Flight 305 with the words "Northwest three zero five Eugene altimeter three zero zero six." This was a routine transmission to alert the crew to adjust their altimeter setting for the air pressure at Eugene. If Author F timed the overflight correctly, Seattle Center had given Flight 305 just over four minutes' notice of their arrival at the Eugene beacon.

At 9:52 p.m. Author F made one final note regarding the position of Flight 305: "0552 [Zulu time] 58 DME from RBL" with the words "NORTH OF" inserted; in other words, he had heard a transmission on the ARINC frequency that Flight 305 was 58 nautical miles from the Red Bluff beacon in an approximately northerly direction. Bob Lowenthal and another colleague made substantially identical notes at 9:54 p.m.

Oakland air traffic control were not on the ARINC frequency and therefore their transcript gives no corresponding position report; but between 9:53 p.m. and 9:55 p.m. (most probably near 9:54:40 p.m., at the normal speed of human speech) the controller at position E04 in Oakland told a colleague: "Yeah, he's fifty northwest of Red Bluff Victor twenty three." The intervening eight nautical miles would have taken about 2 minutes 40 seconds.

We conclude that Author F was keeping accurate timing. Probably, he was hearing the radio transmissions on ARINC in real time, while his colleagues were watching a teletype printout with a delay of between two and four minutes. We believe that his report at 8:18 p.m. was correct, and that the FBI, to their misfortune, made the wrong call.

CHAPTER

# 6

# HIGHLAND

In the previous chapters, we presented the following facts relating to the movements of Northwest Flight 305[1] and its unwanted passenger on the evening of November 24, 1971:

- After departing Seattle-Tacoma International Airport, the aircraft flew south, with clearance from air traffic control to follow the Victor 23 low-level airway at 10,000 feet, at least as far as Sacramento, California, but also with permission to diverge in routing and altitude at the crew's discretion.
- Northwest Airlines subsequently obtained radar data from McChord Air Force Base, which either they or the Air Force used to construct a hand-drawn plot of the aircraft's flight path, covering the whole of the flight between Seattle and the Oregon-California border, plus a few miles within California. Northwest transmitted a map depicting this plot to the FBI, which apparently accepted and took ownership of the map (since a low-resolution copy of the map appears on the FBI's website to this day).
- The hand-drawn plot was not greatly divergent from the centerline of the Victor 23 airway. According to the plot, between Seattle and northern California the aircraft was never more than 4 miles[2] west or 4 miles east of the centerline.
- No data have ever been presented to invalidate the hand-drawn plot of the flight path; indeed, it has come to be known as "the FBI map," although the FBI probably played no part in its construction.

- By the unanimous testimony of the flight crew and of airline personnel who followed the radio communications, the hijacker was on board the airplane at 8:05 p.m. PST[3] and was not on board when the airplane landed at Reno, Nevada, at 11:03 p.m. PST.

We now seek to establish what consequences followed for the identification of the hijacker's point of departure from the airplane, and of his point of landing.

## SPEEDS AND DISTANCES

In this and the following chapter, we shall be interested in the speed and direction of the wind that prevailed along the path of Flight 305. The reason is simple. Once the hijacker departed from the airplane, using a military canopy with limited steering, only the wind would determine where he would go.

The flight crew of an airplane in flight have no direct way of knowing the wind. They will have received a report of the surface wind at their airport of departure, and probably a forecast of the winds aloft on their flight path. But the actual wind that they encounter cannot be directly measured by any of their instruments. Their engines propel them relative to the air, and this is what their instruments show. How the air itself is moving, their instruments cannot tell.

However, if a flight is observed relative to the ground (either by the flight crew or by observers on the ground), then it is simple to calculate the ground speed and the direction of travel over the ground. A comparison with the airspeed and heading, as measured by the instruments, then enables us to infer the nature of the wind. This we shall elaborate later.

First, some aeronautical terminology.

- The speed that any aircrew read from their instruments on the flight deck is the indicated airspeed (IAS). This is not the same as true airspeed (TAS). A conversion from IAS to TAS requires a correction for the altitude, the air pressure, and the outside air temperature. At 10,000 feet and −5 degrees centigrade, the TAS will be significantly higher than the IAS. For example, in these conditions 160 knots indicated will translate to 186 knots true.[4]

- Between Seattle and Reporting Point 3, we can identify seven distinct reports of the indicated airspeed, as recorded by Northwest through the ARINC network. There were two separate periods in which the airplane entered a climb: a 4-minute period from ground level to 7,000 feet, and a second 4-minute climb from 7,000 feet to the cruise altitude of 10,000 feet. The slowest indicated airspeed that the crew reported was 150 knots; the highest, briefly, was 170–180 knots.[5] If we assemble these reports and weight them according to their timing, it looks as though the average indicated airspeed in this segment was about 164 knots. Allowing for the altitude and temperature, this translates to an average true airspeed of about 193 knots.[6]

- We believe that after departure from Sea-Tac, Flight 305 followed the runway heading, in other words almost due south, for several minutes; and reached the eastern edge of the V-23 airway at the 14-mile mark. The crew then had to make, or chose to make, an abrupt turn to the west to stay within the airway. They probably reached the western edge of the airway at the 19-mile mark and made another turn to the south before stabilizing within a couple of miles of the centerline, near the MALAY waypoint. If this reconstruction is accurate, these divergences put some extra miles on the flight, compared with a strict adherence to the centerline. On this track, by our estimates, the flying distance from Sea-Tac to Point 3 was about 133.6 miles (plus or minus a mile).

- The FBI recorded the departure of Flight 305 from Sea-Tac as 7:36 p.m. This time seems late if, twice in the next minute and a quarter, the crew were able to change frequencies with air traffic control, and by 7:37:11 p.m. were talking to the en-route controllers at Seattle Center. The subsequent arrival at Point 3 was timed by one observer, whom we believe reliable, at 8:18 p.m. If we allow for a departure from Sea-Tac between 7:35 and 7:36 p.m., and an arrival at Point 3 between 8:18 and 8:19 p.m., the airplane covered this distance in between 42 and 44 minutes. If so, the average ground speed from Sea-Tac to Point 3 was in the range 181 to 192 knots.
- We can see that the ground speed was up to 12 knots lower than the true airspeed, depending on our data and assumptions. The best that we can say is that most of the time between Seattle and Point 3, Flight 3 was probably flying into a mild headwind.
- Subject to the accuracy and the timing of the airspeed and position reports, the average headwind might have been up to 12 knots in the direction of the airplane's track.

The headwind did not necessarily prevail at every point along this flight path. In particular, we do not know whether there was a headwind at the moment the hijacker departed the airplane. As a working hypothesis, let us assume that it did. If so, with our estimate of the wind speed, we have a starting point for estimating the horizontal distance that he would have covered from his departure to his landing point. It is to his exit from Flight 305 that we now turn.

## THE HIJACKER'S DEPARTURE

To an even-greater extent than the flight path, our knowledge of the point of departure of the hijacker is constructed from fragments of information and subject to great uncertainty. The following is what we know with some degree of confidence.

From the departure from Seattle until the landing in Reno, the crew of Flight 305 was in continuous communication, though the ARINC system, with Northwest Airlines operations in Minneapolis and Seattle-Tacoma. A number of Northwest employees, and evidently some FBI agents, were party to these communications and made handwritten notes. Some of these notes are now in the archives of the Washington State Historical Society in the form of a twenty-three-page document,[7] gifted by the estate of George Harrison, who in 1971 was operations manager for Northwest Airlines at Seattle International Airport.

From the diversity of the handwriting, it is clear that there were at least six authors of the notes, of whom at least four were either listening to radio transmissions or were watching a teletype printout.[8] All those who took sequential notes recorded the times in GMT; we have converted these to PST.

In addition, the Washington State Historical Society has a certified transcript of radio communications between N467US and Seattle Air Route Traffic Control Center, covering the period from 7:37:11 p.m. to 9:45:29 p.m.[9] These communications are populated with aeronautical terms, and we have therefore paraphrased the raw transcript into a plain English version.[10]

Finally, the Washington State Historical Society has the original teleprinter tape of the communications via ARINC between N467US and Northwest Airlines operations, along with an incomplete transcript furnished by the FBI,[11] to which the historical society added some notes on the FBI's omissions. The transcript was written in an improvised shorthand, evidently in real time, and where the inevitable errors occurred, they were followed by series of Xs and then by the corrected text. Many aeronautical terms would be unfamiliar to the lay reader. As with the radio traffic, we have developed a paraphrase of the transcript in plain English.[12]

It should be noted that the time of each transmission can be specified only as a range defined by the preceding and succeeding time stamps.

From these communications, as we recounted in chapter 4, it is clear that the hijacker was on board the airplane at 8:05 p.m., and upon landing at Reno at 11:03 p.m., he was gone. Where he left the airplane, and where he landed, is the question to which we now turn.

## THE EXIT POINT

As far as we have been able to determine, the physical search for the hijacker was initiated on the basis of the document to which we referred in chapter 4.[13] It was dated January 9, 1972, and although the signature was redacted, we know now that it was signed by Paul Soderlind of Northwest Airlines.

Here we need to introduce Paul A. Soderlind. He was no ordinary Boeing driver. He was born in Billings, Montana, in 1923, and received his pilot's license on his eighteenth birthday, the earliest age permitted at that time. At age nineteen he was already an instrument flight instructor with Northwest Airlines. After Navy service in the Second World War, he returned to Northwest where he became, at age twenty-three, the youngest airline captain in America. At Northwest he had a brilliant career as a pilot, instructor, and eventually Director of Flight Operations (Technical). In 1996, he was inducted into the Minnesota Aviation Hall of Fame.[14]

As we shall demonstrate, Paul Soderlind was the architect of the flight path map which the FBI came to accept. He designated the time and place of the hijacker's departure, and he defined the parameters of the descent path and the boundaries of the presumed landing point. He thereby became the strategist of the FBI's immense manhunt on the ground in Washington state, which as we know, was ultimately fruitless.

And yet … although Soderlind passed away in 2001, in over 24,000 pages of public files of the FBI on the case of Flight 305, nowhere does his name appear. In places where we may deduce that his name should be, it is redacted. In the archives of Northwest Airlines, and at the Minnesota Aviation Hall of Fame, there is no mention of the work that Soderlind did for the FBI. Whether his and his colleagues' analysis was right or wrong, we could reasonably assume that they gave it their best shot. Their contribution however has been expunged from history.

With regard to the hijacker's exit from Flight 305, the key phrases in Soderlind's letter to the FBI are as follows, reproduced verbatim with our annotations in square brackets:

- Aircraft position from USAF radar data from McChord AFB[15] furnished by Captain [redacted; author's note: Thomas Spangler]
- Probable jump time (0411 GMT) [8:11 p.m.] from an analysis of the recorded communication from the flight relative to the cabin pressure fluctuation. Flight tests conducted on January 6 [1972] confirmed that the pressure fluctuation almost certainly occurred at the time the HJ [hijacker] left the airplane.
- Time correlation from the above USAF radar information and from the NWA communications network tape recording
- The north–south span of possible jump positions is a product of the radar position tolerance of ±.5 mile, and the possible communication time determination tolerance of ±1 minute.

There are at least three key assumptions embedded in these statements.

First, Northwest Airlines believed that a critical event occurred at the moment when the crew reported "oscillations in the cabin."

We recall that at 7:44:22 p.m., Seattle air traffic control had recorded the crew's radio transmission of "We got the back steps down now."[16] In the teletype tape, between the time stamps 8:10 and 8:12 p.m., there are two lines that read (in our paraphrase) "305 getting some [oscillations] in the cabin," followed by "[must] be doing something with air stairs."[17]

We recall also that at 8:11 p.m., Bob Lowenthal and a colleague in Northwest Airlines operations jotted down their notes about "cabin fluctuations."

The ARINC tape and the Northwest notes say nothing about pressure. Later on (as we recall from chapter 2), it became clear that the oscillations referred to cabin pressure. We know that the airstair had been down earlier, and according to Bob Lowenthal's note it was still down, but we do not know whether the crew thought the hijacker was raising it, putting weight on it, or doing something else.

We recall that from that point until the landing in Reno, according to all the transcripts, the crew and the FBI continued to believe that the hijacker was still on board the airplane.

The second assumption was that the "oscillation" was a reproducible event. To this end, on January 6, 1972, three days prior to the date of this document, Northwest Airlines, the FBI, and the US Air Force had conducted a test with the same airplane over the Pacific, in which they dropped one or more weighted sleds from the ventral airstair. The "sled test" has never been described in detail by the FBI, Northwest Airlines, or the US Air Force; we shall piece together the story in chapter 8. It was reported that at the moment when the sled fell from the airstair, a fluctuation was recorded in the instruments on the flight deck. Northwest Airlines and the FBI concluded that they had simulated the hijacker's departure.

The third assumption was that the possible errors in the estimation of the point of departure were limited to the following:

- an uncertainty in the radar data of plus or minus 0.5 miles in the north–south direction, and apparently also in the east–west direction
- an uncertainty of plus or minus 1 minute in the reporting of the "oscillation"

In any event, the FBI concluded that the hijacker had departed at the moment of the "oscillation"; that is, 8:11 p.m. This became the central premise of their investigation.

According to Northwest's interpretation of the radar data, the airplane's location at 8:11 p.m. was a point 10,000 feet above sea level, almost overhead Highland, Clark County, Washington, 98629.

Highland, Clark County, is not to be confused with another Highland, in Benton County, Washington, 99337. Google Maps shows Highland today as little more than a crossroads, at the intersection of NE 399th Street and NE Christensen Road, about 7 miles east of Woodland. It is 810 feet above sea level and 10 miles north of the Battle Ground navigational beacon.

Here is an issue to which we shall return.

According to the notes of the Northwest Airlines team listening to the radio transmissions, the crew's subsequent position report was 23 miles south of the Battle Ground beacon, roughly overhead Tualatin, Oregon. At this position, the crew said that their indicated airspeed was 165 knots (corresponding to a true airspeed of 195 knots). But the time of this report is subject to a four-minute variation: Bob Lowenthal (author D) and the unknown author C both noted 8:22 p.m., while the unknown author F wrote down 8:18 p.m. All three authors agreed on all other aspects of the Tualatin report (altitude, fuel on board, fuel flow, and indicated airspeed),

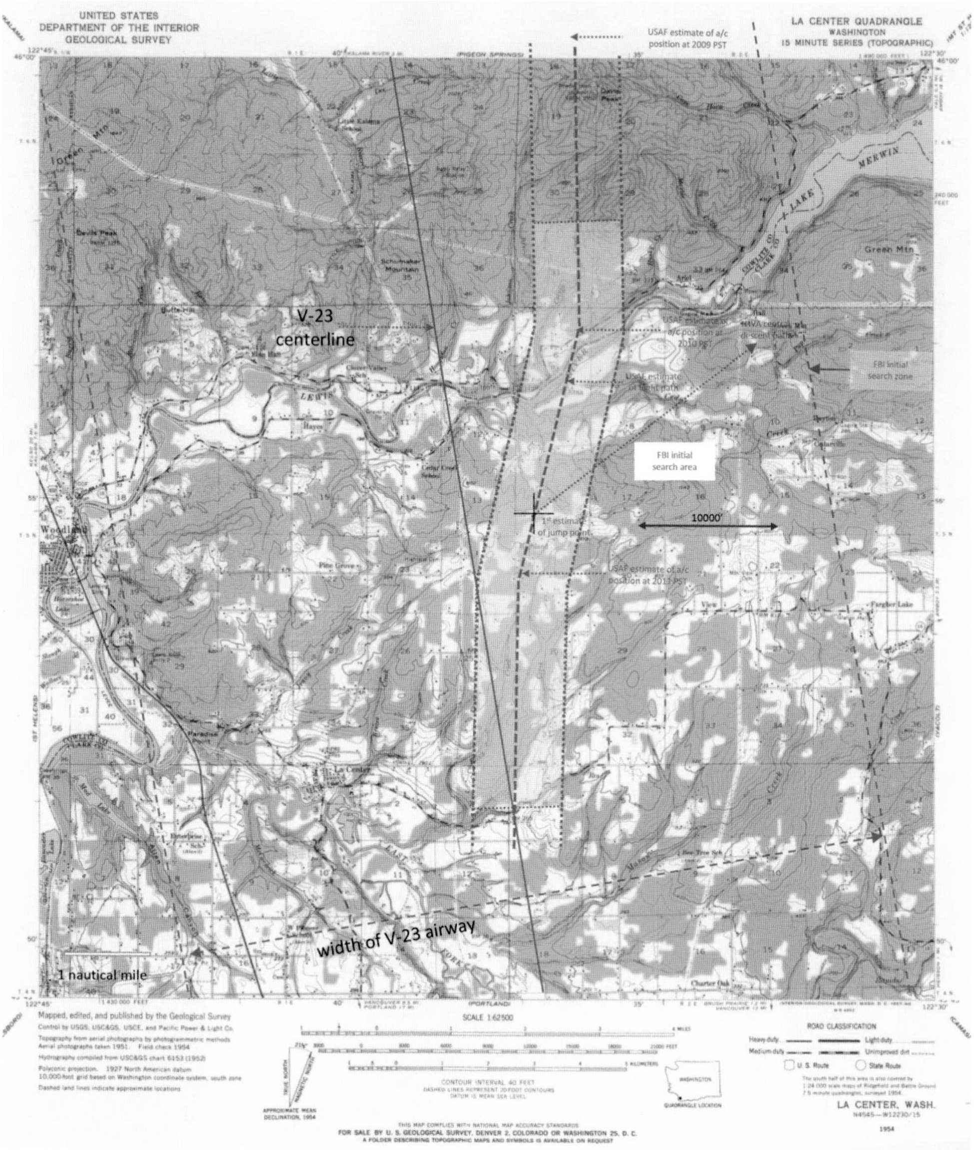


**Figure 6.1**. *La Center Quadrangle*, Washington, January 9, 1972: Northwest Airlines and FBI estimate of hijacker's jump zone. *Base map from USGS, La Center Quadrangle, scale 1:62500; graphics by author*

as well as on the times of previous transmissions. This particular position report (and only this one) is absent from the transcripts of the transmissions through ARINC.

In 1971, digital clocks were not yet on the market. When we visualize the Northwest team crowded around the radio, we must imagine them checking wristwatches and wall clocks (all analog devices), and noting the closest number to the minute hand. If so, Bob Lowenthal could have written down a time of 8:22 as early as 8:21:30 or as late as 8:22:30, and author F could have noted down 8:18 as early as 8:17:30 or as late as 8:18:30.

Let us suppose for the moment, as Northwest and the FBI came to believe, that Flight 305 was overhead Highland, Washington, at 8:11 p.m.

The next position report for Flight 305 was what we have called DME reporting point 3, approximately overhead Tualatin, Oregon. For this point, there is no timing on the ARINC transcript; the relevant section has been either redacted or lost. We are therefore dependent on the note takers at Northwest operations.

It is probable that author F was correct in recording the arrival of Flight 305 overhead Tualatin at 8:18 p.m., four minutes earlier than his or her colleagues. This would require only that author F was listening to the voice transmissions in real time, whereas Bob Lowenthal and author C were watching the teletype. Again, we can allow author F, whom we imagine consulting an old-fashioned timepiece, to be off by plus or minus half a minute. Here, however, the numbers go haywire. If we still believe that flight 305 was overhead Highland at 8:11 p.m., Flight 305 would have to cover the 33 miles to Tualatin in only 6.5–7.5 minutes. That would place the average ground speed in the range 264 to 304 knots. Since we have estimated the average true airspeed at 195 knots, we are implying an improbably strong *tailwind of 69 to 109 knots*. In this case, the hijacker's descent path would have commenced in a spectacularly southerly direction—the opposite of what Northwest Airlines believed.

At the end of the day, the congruence of the place of Highland and the time of 8:11 p.m. is entirely implausible.

If the hijacker jumped overhead Highland, it could not have been at 8:11 p.m. His departure would have had to be several minutes earlier, which would mean just after his last communication with the crew (for which their best estimate was 8:05 p.m.) and before the crew experienced the fluctuation in cabin pressure (for which the best estimate was 8:11 p.m.).

Conversely, if the hijacker jumped at 8:11 p.m., it could not have been overhead Highland. It would have had to be up to 12 miles farther south, in which case the FBI, and the military and law enforcement agencies who helped them, searched in the wrong place.

The uncertainties that pervade the source documents demonstrate a kind of "butterfly effect." Errors measured in minutes can radically alter our view of where the hijacker departed the airplane and, to an even-greater extent, of where he landed. We have seen that a variation of a few minutes can turn a headwind into a tailwind, which reverses the direction of the hijacker's descent path.

## THE OSCILLATIONS AND THE PRESSURE BUMP

Possibly the greatest ambiguity in Northwest's assumptions, and by extension those of the FBI, related to the distinction between the "oscillations" and the "pressure bump."

We have seen that on the ARINC frequency, the crew reported "oscillations in the cabin." On the ARINC transcript, this report was transcribed between the time stamps for 8:10 p.m. and 8:12 p.m. We know that two observers at Northwest made notes of "fluctuations," which must be a verbatim reference to the words of the crew, and which they timed at 8:11 p.m. The FBI would later state, without apologies in the light of their unproductive manhunt:

> **Log reconstructed from tape recordings of the conversations between Flight 305 and Ground Control: ... There is a time correlation check on this tape and through careful play back and sequencing the time of oscillations caused by the airstairs closing after unsub departed was calculated at 8:11 p.m.[18]**

The FBI were actually referring to an audio recording from the ARINC transmissions, not from air traffic control; but the time of 8:11 p.m. is consistent both with the surviving ARINC transcript and with the notes that emerged forty-two years later from the archives of George Harrison.

However, Harold Anderson, the man who first saw the oscillations on his instruments, had an entirely different interpretation of the events.

As we recounted in chapter 2: decades later, Anderson would recall a series of oscillations, that he could not feel, but that he could see on one of the gauges on the flight engineer's panel. He remembered that he discussed these oscillations with Captain Scott and with copilot Rataczak, and that they waited some time, while the oscillations continued, before deciding to report them to Northwest. Rataczak made this report on the ARINC frequency, and it is most probably to this transmission that the transcript and the observers' notes referred.

Anderson's recollections give the impression that the oscillations continued on the instruments, but for how long, he could not remember. He remembered that at some point, Captain Scott sensed some physical perturbation of the airplane. But the climax was the "pressure bump," which Anderson recalled as a physical sensation felt by all of the crew. There was only one "pressure bump," and there were no more oscillations. Only when the flight was over did the "pressure bump" become, in the minds of the crew, the moment of the hijacker's departure. By that time, the "oscillations" and the "pressure bump," which were originally distinct phenomena, had merged into one, never to be disentangled.

## NO SECOND THOUGHTS

We have seen that the FBI ignored these uncertainties and ambiguities. They quickly became locked in to a time for the hijacker's departure; equally quickly, they bolted this time to a place, and from that moment, they were committed to a search strategy that permitted no second thoughts.

At this point in our story, we are not convinced either by the time or the place in the official narrative of the hijacker's leap from Flight 305. We need to examine the spectrum of times and places that are consistent with the evidence: not only the flight path, but also the other physical evidence that existed in 1971 or that later became available.

We have seen in this chapter that the wind on Victor 23 is a factor of great uncertainty. We propose, therefore, to search for a robust estimate of the wind speed and direction, not only at the presumed exit point but also at other points that fit the evidence, and not only at the probable departure altitude of 10,000 feet but also at intermediate altitudes down to ground level. We shall address this issue in the next chapter.

CHAPTER

# 7

# THE WIND

Within days of the hijacking, Northwest Airlines had come to the conclusion that the hijacker had jumped at 8:11 p.m. and that his jump point had been at an altitude of 10,000 feet overhead Highland, Washington, 94.7 miles south of Seattle-Tacoma International Airport. Somewhat reluctantly and with reservations, as we have seen, the FBI came to accept this view and took it as the basis for their expensive and ultimately fruitless search on the ground in Cowlitz and Clark Counties.

Having committed to a view of where the hijacker had left the airplane, the FBI had to start thinking about his path of descent. There was at least one imponderable: Had he deployed the chute at the moment of his exit from the airplane, or had he fallen to a lower altitude before he pulled the ripcord? If the latter, he would have covered a relatively short distance over the ground. If the former, he could have drifted several miles.

This question in turn engendered another doomed speculation. Was the hijacker an experienced skydiver, or had he the barest minimum of jumping experience?

The hypotheses went back and forth. Tina Mucklow had vouched that the hijacker had seemed very comfortable with the parachutes. An experienced jumper, one could speculate, would have deployed the chute right away, to have the maximum time to steer to a supposed landing point, or even to a rendezvous. On the other hand, an ex-paratrooper or smoke jumper with relatively little experience might have done the same, out of familiarity with jumps on a static line. On the other hand, a sports skydiver might have fallen until the last moment before pulling the cord, to minimize his time in the air and the chances of being spotted. On the other hand . . .

The FBI acknowledged this dilemma from the outset. On November 30, Milnes wrote to the SAC in Cincinnati:

**There is no specific knowledge as to what previous experience unsub [the unknown subject] had as a parachute jumper.[1]**

With that, the FBI put aside all speculation as to whether the hijacker had made a slow or fast descent and, correspondingly, had covered a short or a long distance to his landing. All that they could be sure of was that he had jumped into the prevailing wind, and that the wind had carried him to his landing point. To identify the landing point, it became essential to estimate the wind speed and direction at the presumed location of the jump.

The FBI had already started talking to meteorologists. On November 27, Charles Farrell had spoken to the National Weather Service at Seattle-Tacoma International Airport and had collected reports on the weather at Seattle on the afternoon and evening of November 24. They were not much help; the reports gave only the surface winds at Sea-Tac, which between 7:00 p.m. and 8:00 p.m. had been 10 knots coming from the south or south-southeast.[2] That would not give much clue to the wind at the presumed jump point, 10,000 feet up and 95 miles to the south.

By November 30, SA Thomas Manning had picked up some more pertinent information from the weather service at Portland International Airport:

**Winds at 7,000 feet along the flight path of the aircraft were blowing from the west and were from 25 to 30 knots.[3]**

And from the FBI's search teams that were already deployed:

**Investigation on the ground in the search area reflects that weather conditions were a wind blowing from the west and a light misty rain falling with wind velocity 10 to 15 knots.**

By December 3, Manning had spoken to the US Weather Bureau in Portland and was able to report as follows:

**Contact [redacted] ... to determine exact weather from 7,000 feet to ground level on 11/24/71, reflects generally conditions previously furnished to case agent, except that some of these winds both at 7,000 feet and on the surface could have been coming from 225 to 235 degrees, a general southeast [author's note: he meant southwest] wind.[4]**

This was the first reference to the "southwest wind," which would come to dominate the thinking of the FBI and lead them on a wild-goose chase.

With regard to the upper-level winds, Manning was evidently referring to the following report from an unidentified special agent:

**[redacted] Portland International Airport, Portland, Oregon, furnished sheets containing read[-]out information and key to aviation weather reports for weather conditions between 7:00 and 9:00 p.m. on November 24, 1971. ... [redacted] also stated that to secure average of below[-]listed information for Woodland, Washington, an average of the two sets of information would give a close estimate of conditions at Woodland. The information below is for the times between 8:00 p.m. and 9:00 p.m., on November 24, 1971.[5]**

| Location | Altitude Feet [AMSL] | Wind direction deg [from N] | Wind speed knots | Temperature [deg C] |
|---|---|---|---|---|
| | | | | |
| Salem | surface | 235 | 15 | 10 |
| Salem | 2,000 | 235 | 20 | 6 |
| Salem | 5,000 | 230 | 25 | -1 |
| Salem | 7,000 | 230 | 30 | -4 |
| Portland | surface | 235 | 15 | 8 |
| Portland | 2,000 | 235 | 20 | 2 |
| Portland | 5,000 | 230 | 25 | -5 |
| Portland | 7,000 | 225 | 20 | -8 |

Woodland (where the FBI had made the headquarters of its ground search) does not have an airport or a weather station, so the FBI could not hope for weather reports that would closely reflect the area that they planned to cover. But it is not at all evident why the unnamed respondent would tell the FBI that the weather at Woodland could be approximated by an average of Portland and Salem. Portland is 23 miles southeast of Woodland as the crow flies, and Salem is 51 miles farther south. It would have been more logical to average the weather data at Portland (south of Woodland) and Seattle (north of Woodland), or, better still, an average of the data for Portland and Gray Army Air Field.

Be that as it may, if the FBI took this advice and did the mathematics, they would have come up with the following estimates for the weather at Woodland, which presumably would then have become a proxy for point A, the hijacker's jump point:

**Table 7.1. Woodland, Washington, November 24, 1971, 8:00 p.m. to 9:00 p.m.: Reconstruction of FBI estimate of wind speeds and directions**

| Location | Altitude feet AMSL | Wind direction degrees from N | Wind speed knots | Temperature degrees C |
|---|---|---|---|---|
| | | | | |
| Woodland | surface | 235 | 15 | 9 |
| Woodland | 2,000 | 235 | 20 | 4 |
| Woodland | 5,000 | 230 | 25 | -3 |
| Woodland | 7,000 | 227.5 | 25 | -6 |
| | | | | |

*Source*: estimates by author derived from FBI, "D. B. Cooper," Part 20 of 48.pdf, pp. 240–241

We can see how a southwest wind (more precisely, a wind from 227.5 degrees), with a speed of 25 knots, was shaping up as the FBI's central assumption. Although the hijacker was known to have jumped from 10,000 feet, it looks as though the FBI would use their estimate of the wind at 7,000 feet as a measure of the average wind throughout the descent path, from 10,000 feet down to the ground.

By December 4, the consensus on the southwest wind was formalized, and maps were sketched out for the ground search. Minneapolis wrote to Seattle with a two-page memo and a map, prepared by Northwest Airlines and signed by Paul Soderlind. The memo and map designated the hijacker's exit point as "point A" and added:

> **If it is assumed that the HJ [hijacker] was a highly expert parachutist, and would thus free-fall as far as practicable to insure [*sic*] the best accuracy of his touchdown point, he would land slightly to the NE of point A due to his drifting with the wind from the point of chute opening. . . . If the HJ opened his 'chute as soon as he left the airplane, he would drift along the line A–B and would touch down at B. All lines parallel to A–B are lines along which the HJ would drift if he opened his 'chute relatively early. . . . The most likely landing point for the HJ is at, or slightly NE of Point A.[6]**

The assumption that an expert parachutist would free-fall is not self-evident. In a free fall, the jumper has little control of his or her track over the ground. A free fall is not the way to land accurately (unless there is no wind).

In any case, the southwest wind was now locked in to the FBI's assumptions for all scenarios regarding the point of exit and the speed and direction of the descent.

## THE CONTINENTAL PILOT

For the sake of due diligence, this is perhaps a good a moment as any to relate an intriguing story that would come to light more than five years later. The narrator was the pilot or copilot of a Continental Airlines jet, which, he claimed, had been on the same route and the same airway as Flight 305 on the night of November 24, 1971.

On February 22, 1977, this unidentified pilot was interviewed by an unnamed FBI agent at Portland International Airport. He told this story:

> **[Redacted] advised that he departed Seattle-Tacoma Airport en route for Portland shortly after Northwest Flight 305, which was being hijacked, and that he followed the same course flown by Northwest Flight 305 but was approximately four minutes behind the Northwest flight when it arrived at Portland. . . . He recalls that night of 11/24/71, as being the most rapid and severe weather change in his experience. He said that when he was approaching Portland, along Victor 23 airways flying a course of approximately 166 degrees, he was experiencing a wind directly from 166 degrees at 80 knots of speed at his altitude[,] which was 14,000 feet. He said that the wind at 10,000 feet was approximately 65 knots and from a direction of from 160 to 170 degrees.[7]**

There are already some anomalies in this story. We may ask how this pilot could have known the wind (since there is no instrument on the flight deck that measures the wind); what he was doing on Victor 23, knowing that he was behind a hijacked airliner and several shadowing Air Force interceptors; and why it took him five years to come forward. The FBI agents seem also to have been perplexed, since they interviewed him again a month later. On March 29, 1977, he elaborated his recollections as follows:

**He was flying on Continental Flight 306 . . . estimated time of departure was 6:10 p.m., but he actually left Seattle at about 7:09 p.m. to fly back to Portland, Oregon. . . . When he landed at Portland the wind was from 160 degrees at 35 knots[,] and this was approximately 7:49 p.m. During the flight down to Portland, [redacted] noticed that [at] his cruising altitude of about 13,000 feet that he was flying into a headwind of about 60 knots. [Redacted] explained that on the way to Seattle from Portland ground speed was 480 knots, but on the way back down to Portland his ground speed was only 420 knots. According to [redacted] the wind apparently was shifting from approximately 160 to approximately 200 degrees.[8]**

Perhaps the FBI agent misheard or misunderstood, but most of these numbers do not stack up at all. If the Continental airplane left Seattle at 7:09 p.m., it was 25 minutes ahead of Flight 305, which departed at 7:36 p.m. When the Continental landed at Portland at 7:49 p.m., Flight 305 was still somewhere around Olympia, Washington. The Continental was never behind Flight 305. Second, the distance from Seattle to Portland is 112 miles; if the Continental airplane took forty minutes to cover this distance, its average ground speed was 168 knots, not 420 knots. Third, a ground speed of 480 knots on the previous leg would have brought Flight 306 from Portland to Seattle in fourteen minutes, which should have made the newspapers.

For what it's worth, the Continental Airlines timetable for October 31, 1971,[9] does show a Flight 306 departing Portland at 5:00 p.m. and arriving at Seattle at 5:35 p.m., and a Flight 307 (probably the same airplane and crew) departing Seattle at 6:10 p.m. and arriving at Portland at 6:45 p.m.

Whatever this pilot meant to say, nothing more was ever heard from him, at least not in the files of the FBI, though to this day, internet forums continue to juggle his story.

## THE FLIGHT DATA

There is one readily available source of data whereby we can assess whether the FBI was, to mix metaphors, on solid ground in its estimates of the wind.

As we related in an earlier chapter, we estimated that between Seattle-Tacoma and Tualatin, the airplane had an average ground speed up to 12 knots slower than the average true airspeed. This indicates a headwind, or more precisely, a headwind component. Relative to the axis of the airplane, the wind could have been from the port or the starboard, but the component along the airplane's axis, and slowing the airplane down, was an average of up to 12 knots.

So far, therefore, we have two estimates for the segment from Sea-Tac to Tualatin:

- the FBI's assumption of a wind of about 25 knots from the southwest at Woodland, which relative to the airplane's average track of 188 degrees (8 degrees west of south), would imply a headwind component of about 20 knots;
- and our own inference that there was an average headwind component of up to 12 knots, which would be consistent with any wind from the southwest, or the southeast.

## THE WIND TRIANGLE

If, for the moment, we accept the FBI's estimates of the wind, we are in a position to perform the trigonometric calculations, which are familiar to every pilot in the world, from ground school onward.

Pilots reach their destination by setting an airspeed and a heading. The airspeed is the speed of the airplane relative to the air mass; the heading is the direction in which the plane is pointing. These two parameters, combined with the wind speed and direction, yield the track (where the pilot wants to go) and the ground speed (the speed of the airplane relative to the ground). In short, there are six parameters of flight:

- true airspeed (measured normally in knots)
- heading or bearing (measured in degrees from true north)
- wind speed (measured in knots)
- wind direction (measured in degrees from true north)
- ground speed (measured in knots)
- track or course (measured in degrees from true north)

If we know any four of these, the other two can be calculated. In the old days, a pilot would have done this with a manual flight computer (a form of circular slide rule); now we can do it online.

We therefore tested the FBI estimates, at least for consistency, in respect to the flight segment from Seattle-Tacoma to Tualatin, the longest segment for which we had a good database of position and time reports.

For this segment, we had calculated an average ground speed of 183 knots. The true track from Seattle-Tacoma to Tualatin is 188 degrees, and to simplify, we treated this segment as a straight line. We took the wind as 25 knots from 227.5 degrees, as per the FBI estimate, throughout this segment. Our calculations of the flight settings then came out as follows:[10]

**Table 7.2. Seattle-Tacoma to Tualatin, November 24, 1971: Calculated airspeed and flight heading based on FBI estimates of wind speed and direction**

| | | | | | |
|---|---|---|---|---|---|
| movement over ground | wind (as per FBI) | => | crew's flight settings | | |
| ground speed: 183 kt | speed 25 kt | => | true airspeed: 203 kt | => | indicated airspeed: 175 kt |
| track 186.7 degrees | from 227.5 degrees | => | heading: 192 degrees | | |

Source: estimates by author

In other words, given the airplane's movement over the ground (which, more or less, we know), and if the wind was as the FBI believed (which, for the moment, we assume), in order to fly the desired track in a straight line with no en route adjustments, the crew would have had to set the average heading to 192 degrees (5.3 degrees to starboard of the track) and to maintain an average indicated airspeed of 175 knots.

This airspeed is about 10 knots higher than most of the crew's reports. If they had averaged 175 knots, we would have expected from time to time to see several reports in the range 170 to 180 knots, but there was only one such report. This suggests that the wind was either weaker than the FBI thought, or in a different direction.

This prompts us to construct another wind triangle: one in which we know the airspeed and we also know the wind speed (which we will take as 25 knots), but not its direction. The calculation then looks like this:[11]

**Table 7.3. Seattle-Tacoma to Tualatin: calculated wind direction and flight heading based on FBI estimates of wind speed and crew reports of airspeed**

| | | | | | |
|---|---|---|---|---|---|
| movement over ground | wind (as per FBI) | <= | crew's flight settings | | |
| ground speed: 183 kt | speed 25 kt | <= | true airspeed: 189 kt | <= | indicated airspeed: 163 kt |
| track 186.7 degrees | from 267 degrees | <= | heading: 194 degrees | | |
| | | | | | |
| *Source*: estimates by author | | | | | |

In other words, if the wind was really 25 knots, and the crew were holding an average of 163 knots indicated (as their reports seemed to imply), then they could have flown the track only if the wind was coming from 267 degrees (almost due west).

Finally, we can build a wind triangle in which again we know the airspeed, and we assume that the FBI estimate of the wind direction (227.5 degrees) is correct, but we do not know the wind speed. The calculation is as follows:[12]

**Table 7.4. Seattle-Tacoma to Tualatin: calculated wind speed and flight heading based on FBI estimate of wind direction and crew reports of airspeed**

| | | | | | |
|---|---|---|---|---|---|
| movement over ground | wind | <= | crew's flight settings | | |
| ground speed: 183 kt | speed 8 kt | <= | true airspeed: 189 kt | <= | indicated airspeed: 163 kt |
| track 186.7 degrees | from 227.5 degrees | <= | heading: 188 degrees | | |
| | | | | | |
| *Source*: estimates by author | | | | | |

In this case, if the wind was from the southwest as the FBI believed, Flight 305 could have flown the track only if the wind was averaging 8 knots.

In all three cases, we have reason to doubt that the FBI's estimate of the wind could be consistent both with the track as flown (in terms of distance and time) and with the crew's reports of their indicated airspeed.

## RADIOSONDES

At this point, we had some basis to challenge Northwest's and the FBI's view that the wind along Victor 23, and specifically at the jump point, at an altitude of 10,000 feet, was in the region of 25 knots from the southwest.

We needed then to explore whether we could verify independently the official estimate of the wind vector, and whether we could throw light on the wind vectors at lower altitudes, between 10,000 feet to the ground, that the hijacker encountered on his presumed descent.

As it transpires, we can.

For over 115 years, the US Department of Commerce has been recording, assembling, and distributing data on weather conditions from the surface to the upper atmosphere, throughout the United States and from many weather stations throughout the world. These data are now held by the National Oceanic and Atmospheric Administration (NOAA), which characterizes the data as follows:

> **These data are obtained from radiosondes, which are instrument packages tethered to balloons that are launched from the ground, ascend through the troposphere into the stratosphere, and transmit back to a receiving station on the ground. These observations include vertical profiles of temperature, humidity, wind speed and direction, atmospheric pressure, and geopotential height.**[13]

The radiosonde data are currently disseminated through NOAA's Integrated Global Radiosonde Archive, data set 2 (IGRA2). As of August 2019, the IGRA2 database contained data from 558 weather stations in the USA, plus 2,230 stations in other countries, with a total of over forty-eight million observations going back to the year 1905.[14]

Remarkably, neither Northwest Airlines nor the FBI, throughout the forty-five-year investigation of the Flight 305, made any public reference to the NOAA database.

Our first step was to identify the NOAA weather stations in closest proximity to the Victor 23 airway, and specifically to the segment of Victor 23 between Seattle (where N467US commenced its flight) and Salem (the southernmost reference for Northwest's weather estimates).

The four stations that met these criteria, and for which data were available for the 1970s, were as follows:

- Seattle-Tacoma International Airport, Washington, latitude 47.5 N, longitude 122.3 W, elevation 137 feet: data available for 1944–1981
- Gray Army Airfield, Washington, latitude 47.1 N, longitude 122.6 W, elevation 71 feet: data available for 1920–1986
- Portland International Airport, Oregon, latitude 45.5 N, longitude 122.7 W, elevation 8 feet: data available for 1928–1972
- Salem/McNary Field, Oregon, latitude 44.9 N, longitude 123.0 W, elevation 62 feet: data available for 1956–2019.

Our second step was to assemble, into a single Excel file, all the available weather data for these four stations for the months of November and December 1971. Our intention was to bracket the flight of N467US with up to thirty days of weather data before and after the event.

Here we encountered a surprising setback: for Portland International Airport, there were no data between June 1, 1956, and November 1, 1972. We contacted the NOAA, which informed us that

> **the upper-air period of record for Portland, Oregon was from 1928-1972. . . . It is possible months were missing near the end of the available period of record. Salem, located about 60 miles south[,] is the replacement site.**[15]

We therefore do not know on what basis the FBI's informant obtained the estimates of the wind overhead Portland, which he or she advised the FBI to average with Salem to arrive at estimates for Woodland, Washington. Evidently these estimates were not from the NOAA. However, the NOAA's data did include Salem/McNary Field, and we could at least compare the FBI's estimates for Salem (as of 8:00–9:00 p.m.) with the closest comparable data from the NOAA (which were for 4:00 p.m.). This comparison is illustrated in figure 7.1 and table 7.5 below.

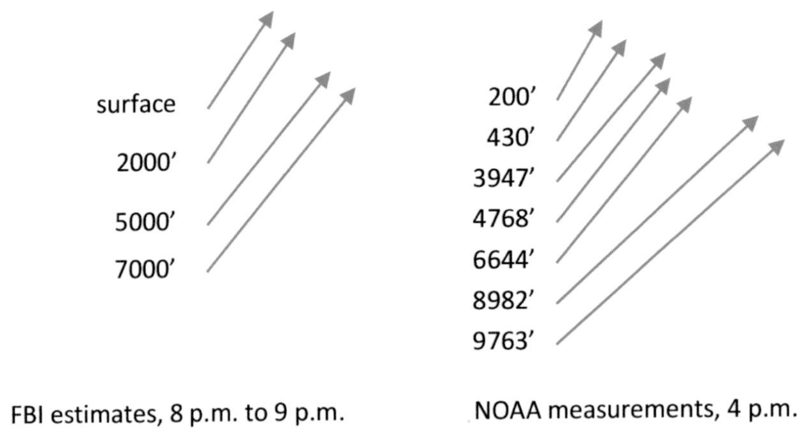


**Figure 7.1.** Salem, Oregon, November 24, 1971: graphical representation of wind speed and direction, as estimated by FBI and as measured by NOAA. *Graphics by author. Source data: FBI, D.B. Cooper Part 20 of 48.pdf, pp. 240–241; and NOAA, www1.ncdc.noaa.gov/pub/data/igra/data/data-por/USM00072694-data.txt.zip*

**Table 7.5. Salem, Oregon, November 24, 1971: Wind direction, wind speed, and temperature at surface and overhead, as estimated by FBI and as measured by NOAA**

| Altitude | Wind direction (degrees from N) | | Wind speed (knots) | | Temperature (degrees C) | |
|---|---|---|---|---|---|---|
| feet AMSL | FBI | NOAA | FBI | NOAA | FBI | NOAA |
| | 8 p.m.–9 p.m. | 4 p.m. | 8 p.m.–9 p.m. | 4 p.m. | 8 p.m.–9 p.m. | 4 p.m. |
| | | | | | | |
| 0 | 235 | | 15.0 | | 10.0 | |
| 200 | | 240 | | 11.7 | | 9.8 |
| 430 | | 235 | | 15.6 | | 8.7 |
| 2,000 | 235 | | 20.0 | | 6.0 | |
| 3,947 | | 229 | | 21.4 | | 0.4 |
| 4,768 | | 231 | | 23.3 | | −1.2 |
| 5,000 | 230 | | 25.0 | | −1.0 | |
| 6,644 | | 230 | | 27.2 | | −4.4 |
| 7,000 | 230 | | 30.0 | | −4.0 | |
| 8,982 | | 222 | | 35.0 | | −10.1 |
| 9,763 | | 221 | | 38.9 | | −11.4 |
| 10,492 | | 222 | | 38.9 | | −12.5 |
| | | | | | | |

*Source*: FBI, D.B. Cooper Part 20 of 48 .pdf, pp. 240–241, and US Department of Commerce, NOAA, www1.ncdc.noaa.gov/pub/data/igra/data/data-por/USM00072694-data.txt.zip

In summary, from a visual inspection the FBI estimates for Salem appeared quite consistent with those of the NOAA.

There remained the following unexplained issues with the FBI's estimates:

- where the FBI's sources had obtained their weather estimates for Portland, in the absence of radiosonde data
- why they had not used hard data for Salem when radiosonde data were available from the NOAA
- why they considered Portland and Salem (respectively, 23 miles and 80 miles south of Woodland) as the best proxies for Woodland, and if these were the closest weather stations, why they had not also used data for Gray AAF and Seattle-Tacoma (respectively, 80 and 95 miles north).

Since we could not answer these questions, we returned to our data set with a view to assembling the most-relevant data (in time and space) to the weather conditions on and below Victor 23 on the evening of November 24, 1971. The four weather stations that we had selected (Seattle-Tacoma, Gray AAF, Portland, and Salem) bracketed the airway in a spatial sense. The months of November and December 1971 bracketed the events of November 24. To compensate for the absence of event-specific data for Portland International Airport, we incorporated data for Portland for the months of November and December 1972.

When we started this phase of the analysis, we had 2,600 observations from the four weather stations, each observation including the date of sounding, the hour of the sounding (which we converted to PST), the latitude and longitude of the IGRA station, the geopotential height at which the observation was made, the reported wind direction, and the reported wind speed.

## MODELING THE WEATHER ON VICTOR 23

The weather is universally known to be variable in the extreme. It was not surprising, therefore, that our data, examined graphically, resembled clouds in the sky. Within these clouds, we looked for patterns. Our objective was to be able to make statements of this nature: "If the weather is like this at point A and time X, then within some range of probability, it is like that at point B and time Y."

More specifically, we wanted to reach a point where, if we knew the weather at Seattle, Gray, Portland, and Salem throughout November and December 1971, we could make a statement about the weather overhead Highland at 8:11 p.m. on November 24, 1971. If we could construct a model that would yield such statements, the same model would enable us to make corresponding statements in which 8:11 p.m. was replaced by another time, and Highland by another location.

The next step was to look for what mathematicians call correlations: that is, relationships between variables such that if one variable increases, the other variable increases (or decreases) in a predictable way.

Correlations are all around us in daily life. A child grows taller with time. In the Northern Hemisphere, the temperature rises as we travel south. Richer people are happier (or so it's claimed).

Specifically, we were searching for correlations that would explain, even if broadly, the speed and direction of the wind. Mathematically, we posed the following questions:

- Is the wind linked with latitude? Does it become stronger or weaker, or does it change direction, in some predictable way, as we move from north to south?
- Is the wind linked with longitude? Does it change predictably as we move from east to west?
- Is the wind linked to our altitude above sea level? Does it change speed or direction as we descend (under our parachute, for example, in the night sky) from 10,000 feet to the landing spot below?
- Is the wind linked with the time of year? If we had jumped a week later, or a week earlier, could we have expected a different trajectory?
- Is the wind linked to the time of day? Would an hour earlier, or an hour later, make a difference to the speed or the direction of the descent?

To set the record straight: we are not claiming for a moment that the hijacker made these calculations or was even aware that they could be made. As we said in chapter 1, we are interested in what really happened on the night of November 24, 1971. The key to this understanding is the path of descent, and one of the keys to this path is the wind.

Within the boundaries of its time and space, and within the limits of statistical significance, our data set yielded the following insights:[16]

- The time of year made no difference to the speed or direction of the wind.
- The time of day made no difference to the speed of the wind.
- The time of day had an effect on the direction of the wind. For every hour that passed, on average the wind could be expected to back (to use the nautical expression); that is, to change in a counterclockwise direction. It was not a big effect, but it was such that if the wind were from the southwest in the morning, it would be closer to southerly in the evening.
- Both the latitude and longitude had significant effects on the wind speed. The southwesterly path of Flight 305 would tend to increase the speed of the wind. For example, between Battle Ground and Eugene (40 minutes' flight time), our central estimate of the speed of the wind at 10,000 feet would increase from 27 knots to 33 knots.
- Both the latitude and longitude had significant effects on the direction of the wind. For a flight in a southwesterly direction, the effect was to turn the wind counterclockwise. We estimated that between Battle Ground and Eugene, the direction of the wind at 10,000 feet would shift from 244 degrees to 254 degrees.

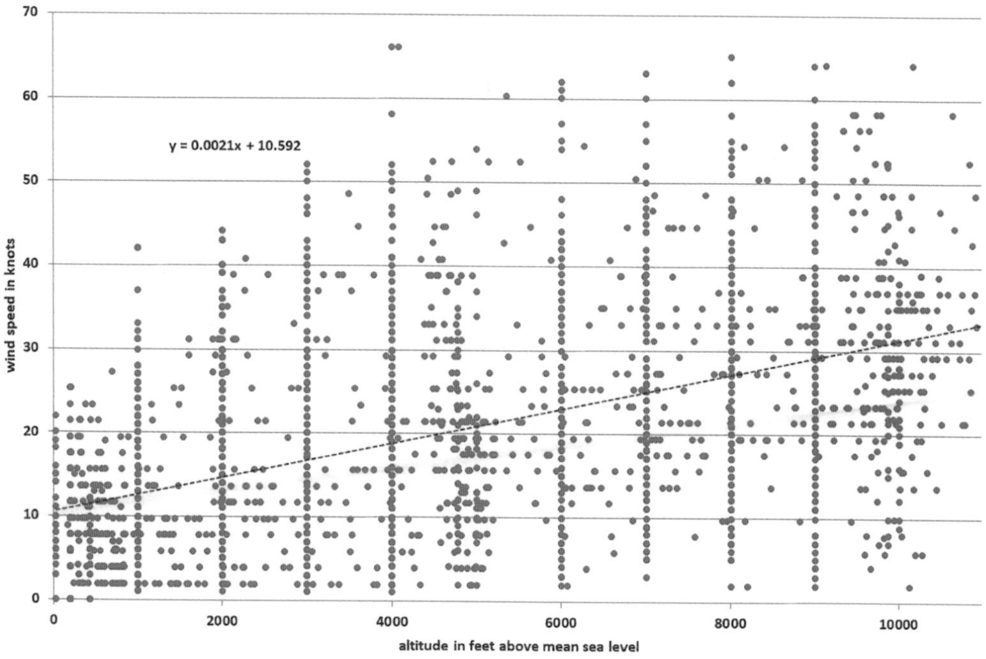


**Figure 7.2.** Four NOAA stations adjacent to Victor 23 airway, November and December 1971: graphical representation of data on wind speed versus altitude. *Graphics by author. Source: analysis by author based on NOAA, IGRA2 data set for Gray AAF, Portland (November–December 1972), Salem and Seattle-Tacoma*

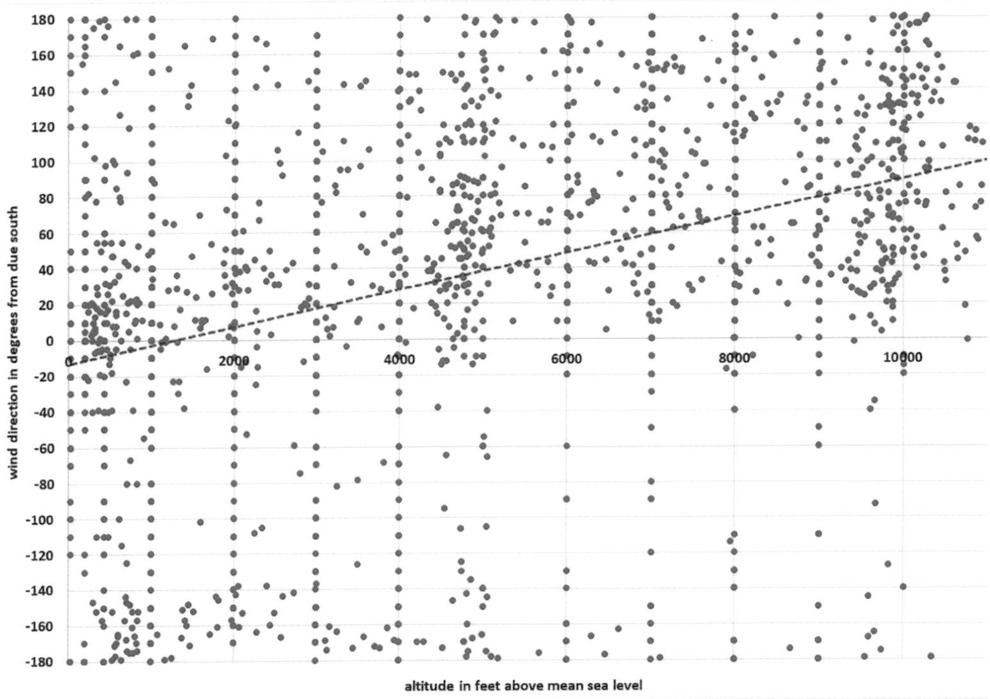


**Figure 7.3.** Four NOAA stations adjacent to Victor 23 airway, November and December 1971: graphical representation of data on wind direction versus altitude. Directions from 0 to 180 are west of south; from 0 to −180 are east of south. *Graphics by author. Source data: analysis by author based on NOAA, IGRA2 data set for Gray AAF, Portland (November–December 1972), Salem and Seattle-Tacoma.*

- However, the most-significant effects (in statistical terms, the strongest correlations) were those of altitude on both the speed and the direction of the wind. These relationships are already illustrated in the graphs above for Salem, even though those graphs are based on only a handful of points. With the full data set of 2,600 points of data, we found that the correlations were clearly demonstrated. On and below the Victor 23 airway, between Seattle-Tacoma and Salem, every 1,000 feet reduction in altitude would—other things being equal—reduce the wind speed by 2 knots and back the wind by 10 degrees.

If, as an example, we adopt the central scenario of Northwest Airlines and the FBI and assume that the hijacker deploys his parachute at 10,000 feet at Northwest's point A, overhead Highland:

- At the moment of exit, he encounters a wind of 25 knots from 247 degrees (in this respect, our model supports the FBI's estimate).
- At 217 seconds later, he is at an altitude of 5,000 feet, in a wind of 18 knots from 198 degrees (the wind is close to south-southwesterly and he is traveling slightly north-northeast).

- At 412 seconds after deployment, he reaches the ground, 810 feet above sea level, carried by a light wind of just 11 knots from 159 degrees (the wind is south-southeasterly and he is traveling north-northwest).
- He lands at a point not on a straight line northeast of his exit point, as in the Northwest/FBI scenario, but slightly west of north, having covered a curved trajectory over a horizontal distance of 13,124 feet.

We can now draw alternative landing zones for a range of scenarios, with alternative assumptions on both the time and the location of the exit point. This we shall do in a later chapter.

CHAPTER

8

# THE SLED TEST

In January 1972, the FBI embarked on an experiment that would create a dominant narrative of the case of Flight 305 and thereby would lock them into a futile search strategy from which they would not be able to extricate themselves. The experiment became known as "the sled test."

We begin the story eight years after the experiment, with the recollections of retired FBI agent Tom Manning, who had supervised the fruitless search for traces of the hijacker along the Lewis River and around Lake Merwin in Washington State. That search has been well documented elsewhere, and it is not part of our story. What is intriguing is how the FBI came to be searching there in the first place.

On February 13, 1980, perhaps by coincidence at exactly the time that other FBI agents were searching the beach at Tena Bar, Manning talked to his local newspaper, the *Daily News* of Longview, Washington, about the "oscillation theory."

As we recall from chapter 5, the ARINC transcript of Flight 305, at some moment between the time stamps for 8:10 and 8:12 p.m., recorded the crew as saying that they were experiencing an "oscillation" in the cabin. An FBI report dated May 30, 1973, would state that there was a "time correlation check" on this audio recording, and that by this means, the time of the oscillation was calculated to have been 8:11 p.m.

Back in November 1971, the details of this transmission apparently were not known to the FBI investigators.

We know that in the moment, neither the crew of Flight 305 nor Northwest Airlines nor the listening FBI associated this "oscillation" with the departure of the hijacker. All parties remained convinced that the hijacker was still on board, and they made repeated attempts to communicate with him. Agent John Detlor remembered it well, even after forty-one years:

**At the time of the hijacking[,] nobody expected, really nobody expected him to jump. When he did jump, the plane arrived in Reno, [we] discovered he wasn't there.**[1]

As early as November 26, 1971, the FBI was receiving contradictory messages, attributed to the crew of Flight 305, erroneously making it appear that the crew had promptly linked the oscillation with the departure of the hijacker:

**The last contact with him was at approximately 8:05 PM. Within the next 10 minutes, the crew experienced oscillation in the plane and speculated that it was caused by the subject departing the plane by way of the rear door. The crew of the above airline has now spotted a possible area for this suspected departure of the hijacker to be over Merwin Lake, near Woodland, Washington.**[2]

Paul R. Bibler, assistant SAC in Seattle, wrote to Director J. Edgar Hoover the same day to confirm that the ground search was already underway:

**Air search conducted in area where hijacker believed to have left plane . . . a limited ground search also conducted . . . [flight log] entries reflect oscillation at eight ten pm, at which time plane in area approximately two to three miles southwest by west from Lake Merwin dam, Washington.**[3]

However, J. Earl Milnes, special agent in charge at Seattle, seemed to be unconvinced. On November 29, he spoke to an unidentified person (probably Paul Soderlind) at Northwest Airlines in Minneapolis and the following day recorded this conversation as follows:

**I had examined the log of this flight very carefully. . . . However, I was curious to know if the pilot would be able to detect a difference in the trim of the plane, caused by the added weight brought about through the hijacker's descent on the stairway. [Redacted] said this would very likely be detected by the pilot were it not for the fact that the plane was on "automatic pilot" during the flight, which he described as being a normal procedure. He continued, however, and said he had examined minutely the flight recorder record and was unable to detect any similar occurrence in the airplane at the site we are presently searching.**[4]

The response from Northwest, as transcribed, does not make sense. Did the person from Northwest say "at the site" or "other than at the site"? We do not know.

It appears very probable that this conversation was the genesis of the official narrative that the "oscillation" had been the moment of the hijacker's leap from Flight 305. However, to this day there is no document in the public domain that makes explicit who first conceived the "oscillation theory."

## BOYLE'S LAW

We recall from chapter 5 that Flight Engineer Anderson was quite clear (although over forty-two years after the events) that there had been two distinct aerodynamic phenomena:

- a series of oscillations manifested only on the needle of the cabin rate-of-climb indicator, but not felt physically, and occurring over an unspecified period of time;

**Figure 8.1.** January 6, 1972: Boeing 727, registration N467US, ventral airstair. *Courtesy of Washington State Historical Society. Image credit: John Detlor, FBI*

- and later a "pressure bump" which he felt in his ears (and which his instruments might also have registered, but he did not say so)

First Officer Rataczak's transmissions on the ARINC frequency confirmed the oscillations, but did not mention the "pressure bump." Rataczak, again decades after the events, would eventually confirm Anderson's recollection of the "pressure bump." As far as the public record shows, neither airman ever clarified to the FBI, or was ever asked to clarify, these distinct phenomena. As we shall see, the FBI seized on the oscillations, and ignored or never understood the "pressure bump," which for all we know, could have occurred minutes later (and the airplane was traveling at 3 nautical miles a minute).

Of the oscillations, absent data from the flight recorder, we can say very little. The lowered airstair would certainly have created some additional drag below the centerline, and therefore would have generated a pitch-down force on the airplane; and the autopilot would have corrected with a pitch-up command. That would raise the nose, lower the tail, and add to the drag on the airstair. One could see in principle how this could make the airplane alternately climb slightly and descend slightly. If so, that should register both on the cabin rate-of-climb indicator and on the airplane rate-of-climb indicator. But these data were never reported; we do not know whether the data were recorded; and even if we did, we would need to fly another 727 or do a wind-tunnel test to understand the data.

Regarding the "pressure bump," there is at least a way to test its connection with the airstair. It is an admittedly crude application of Boyle's law: which states that the pressure of a given mass of gas is inversely proportional to its volume. As an example in layman's terms: if we squeeze a fixed amount of a gas into half the space, its pressure will double.

We estimate that the interior space of the airplane was about 4,050 cubic feet, consisting of the cabin plus the aft stairwell which, with the cabin door open, was effectively part of the cabin. The hinged portion of the airstair was 3 feet wide and 10 feet long, and therefore, if fully extended, would enclose an air volume of at most 125 cubic feet external to the airframe. If an abrupt movement of the airstair were to force this additional mass of air into the cabin space, it would be like compressing 4,175 cubic feet into 4,050 cubic feet. This would reduce the volume of the air by about 3 percent. So the pressure would increase by 3 percent.

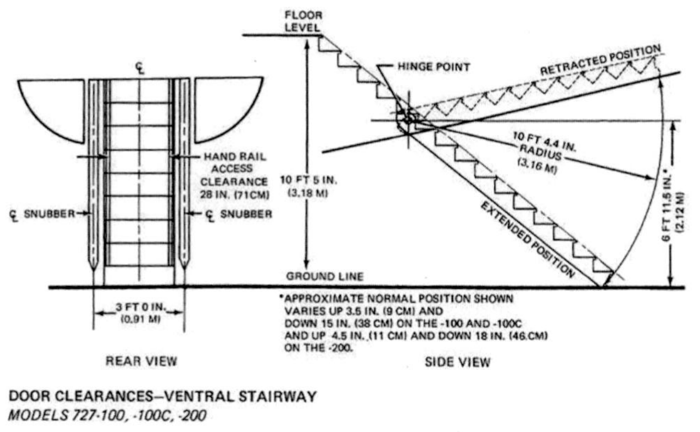


**Figure 8.2.** Boeing 727-100 series, dimensions of ventral airstair. *Source: Boeing Commercial Airplane Company, 727 Airplane Characteristics for Airport Planning, document D6-58324, page dated February 1969, p. 27*

This is of course the maximum effect; in practice some or most of the air enclosed by the airstair would escape and the pressure bump would be less, perhaps much less.

At 10,000 feet with no pressurization, the cabin pressure would have been about 10.1 psi (pounds per square inch). The most violent movement of the airstair would add at most 0.3 psi. From *Boeing Airliner* magazine, we recall that an increase of 0.158 psi, if gradually experienced over a minute, was thought to be about the limit for passenger comfort. So a sudden bump of 0.3 psi, if it were transmitted through the cabin and through the cockpit door, should certainly be detectable, even uncomfortable, in the human ear.

Be that as it may, there is no evidence that the FBI did these calculations. What they did, which was entirely logical, was to think about replicating the flight.

## REPEATING THE FLIGHT

It seems to have been someone in FBI Division 6 (General Investigative Division, as it was then known) who first came up with the idea of testing the oscillation theory with a repeat of the flight. On November 30, Bibler reported to Milnes on a conversation with that unnamed person:

> **He also wanted to know if we had given consideration to hiring a professional parachutist or make a simulated drop with a dummy and following it to the ground. . . . I pointed out to him that anything we did by way of simulating the conditions would be a very broad approximation since we didn't know exactly where the plane was, assuming that the hijacker did go out at 8:12 PM, when they felt the "oscillation." Since this would vary with such factors as wind direction, which side of the flyway the plane happened to be on at the time, etc.[5]**

By mid-December, once it had become clear that the initial ground and air search had been fruitless, the FBI's attention returned to Northwest Airlines, which must by that time have felt responsible for directing the FBI to the Lake Merwin area. Milnes clearly expected a more proactive involvement from Northwest. Writing to Director Hoover, he could not be troubled to conceal his exasperation with what, so far, had been a wild goose chase:

> **Seattle [office] has conducted an extensive search of what was considered the prime area into which the subject might have parachuted, all with negative results. This area was considered prime due to calculations by Northwest Airlines of their flight recorder**

**and other instruments aboard the plane[,] plus the experiencing of an quote oscillation unquote by pilot. Northwest Airlines has offered to simulate the same conditions of the aircraft as prevailed during the hijack and will fly over the same course from Seattle to Reno.**[6]

By the end of December, the FBI had probably found that a parachute drop over populated areas would be impractical and possibly illegal; a repeat of the flight from Seattle to Reno had evidently been ruled out. Attention therefore shifted to involving the military, which would have both people trained in air drops, and places where the drop could be done. Milnes wrote again to Hoover on December 29:

**Arrangements are being made to have voluntary Air Force personnel parachute from the identical plane involved in this case. Arrangements involve Air Force and Northwest Airlines[,] and jumps will be made at an Air Force training area near Moses Lake, Washington. Purpose of this experiment is to determine if it is possible to pinpoint the time when unsub [unidentified subject] actually left the aircraft and whether this was cause of oscillation and cabin pressure change experienced by crew.**[7]

With that, we return to Tom Manning's conversation eight years later with the *Daily News*:

**Using the same aircraft, we made some tests three days after the hijacking, and the results gave credence to the theory that he jumped in the area the crew told us about.**[8]

Manning's recollection of the date was adrift; actually the tests took place forty-three days after the hijacking, on January 6, 1972.

Manning recalled that he personally had been aboard the airplane, that the pilot in command had been the chief pilot of Northwest Airlines, and that the team had included the "flight engineer" of Flight 305. Manning did not give the names of the two persons from Northwest. In the crew's initial depositions to the FBI on the evening of November 24, 1971, none had identified himself as a flight engineer (their job titles were pilot, first officer, and second

**Figure 8.3**. January 6, 1972: on board Boeing 727, registration N467US, preparation for sled test. *Courtesy of Washington State Historical Society. Image credit: John Detlor, FBI*

officer), but in a photograph of the "sled test" crew, the first person from the right in the back row is Harold Anderson, who had been second officer and flight engineer on Flight 305. The two other crew members of Flight 305, Captain William Scott and First Officer William J. Rataczak, are not in the photograph. The person to whom Manning referred as the "chief pilot" was Paul Soderlind, director of flight operations (technical) at Northwest Airlines.

Manning related that the plane had been flown over the Pacific Ocean off the Hoquiam bombing range for the tests.

> **We took along some wooden sleds with sandbags to approximate the weight of Cooper, the parachutes given him[,] and the ransom money and dropped them from the plane when the flying conditions were the same as they were at the time he bailed out. . . . The engineer said the plane reacted the same as it had before when the weight was released.**

What Manning was describing seemed to be an "oscillation" similar, or identical, to what the crew of Flight 305 had experienced between 8:06 and 8:11 p.m. on November 24, 1971.

It is remarkable that at this juncture the FBI seemed to be unaware of the two previous series of air drop tests with a Boeing 727, the first done by the Boeing Airplane Company in 1963 and 1964, and the second by Southern Air Transport for the CIA in 1968 (as we recounted in chapter 3). We know from the transcripts from Seattle air traffic control, on the evening of the hijacking, that tests of this nature were discussed with the crew of Flight 305. Specifically, someone on the Seattle Ground Control frequency had reassured the crew that they would have no flight problems with the rear airstair down, and that "we" (but who?) had dropped loads of 200 to 300 pounds from the rear exit. They could only have been referring to the tests done by Boeing or the CIA.

Forty-one years later, the Washington State Historical Society interviewed retired FBI agent John S. Detlor, who had been aboard the sled test flight. He confirmed that:

**Figure 8.4**. Seattle, January 6, 1972: some of the FBI agents, USAF personnel, and Northwest crew who formed the team for the "sled test" flight of N467US. First from right, standing: is believed to be Harold Anderson. *Image courtesy of Washington State Historical Society, document number 18031. Image credit: FBI*

**of course the speculation comes whether somebody can jump out of a 727 and survive[,] and nobody was right sure; I think we discovered later the military, CIA[,] or somebody had done some tests and had people jump.**[9]

Evidently, as of January 1972 the FBI needed to see an air drop from a Boeing 727 with their own eyes.

For the FBI's first terse account of the "sled test," we quote from their record for January 6, 1972:

**Experimental flight was made today using the same Northwest Airlines aircraft as hijacked, during which two sleds, made to somewhat approximate the size of a man and weighing approximately two hundred thirty five lb[.,] were dropped over Pacific Ocean. The effect of these dummies definitely recorded a cabin pressure change and, according to [redacted; undoubtedly Harold Anderson] of the hijacked aircraft, the reaction today was identical to that which occurred during the hijacking.**[10]

For more on this story, we turn to the recollections of Wally Johnson, retired senior master sergeant, US Air Force, as recorded in 2013 by the Washington State Historical Society. Johnson and MSgt David A. Saiz were the two loadmasters on the "sled test" flight.

**I am the one that designed and deployed the test drop for that. . . . I am the one from Clovis Air Force base. . . . I was a senior load master. . . . Saiz and I were both flight examiners for all different types of loads and everything[,] especially airdrops; we were very proficient at that. . . . The unit that we airdropped? . . . We built it and we weighted it with sandbags to almost the exact weight compared to what the [chute] weighed, what he weighed, this that and the other, money, the whole works. I would say that we were probably within fifty pounds. . . . He weighed approximately 200 pounds and each [chute] and the money [he] had with him. All together probably between 275 and 300 pounds, with all the extra stuff.**[11]

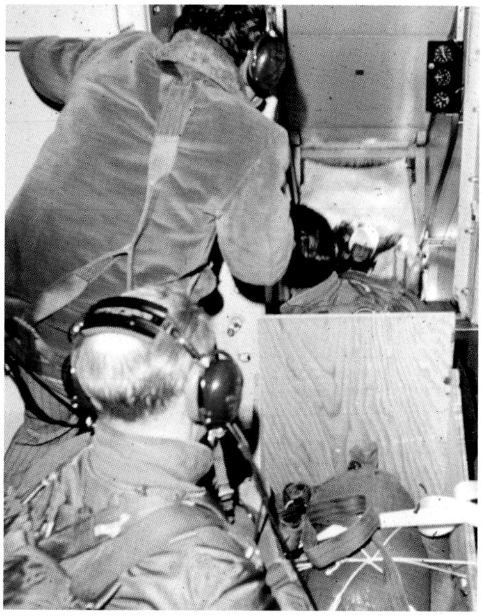

**Figure 8.5**. January 6, 1972: on board Boeing 727, registration N467US, preparation for sled test. *Courtesy of Washington State Historical Society. Image credit: John Detlor, FBI*

The Washington State Historical Society posed to Wally Johnson a most pertinent question:

**Wally Johnson: So when the man left the airplane it was kind of like using a stopwatch[,] so we know exactly where he was at then. One of the reasons there was never a reward offered.**

**WSHS: So, would the cabin pressure of the plane be something that was also measured and recorded by the black box [of Flight 305]?**

**Wally Johnson: Yes, it would.**

Wally Johnson was almost saying that there had been no need for the sled test flight; the "black box" (flight data recorder) of Flight 305 would have revealed the moment when the hijacker departed.

## THE FRAILTY OF MEMORY

In passing: Wally Johnson's testimony provides at least two illustrations of the frailty of human memory.

Firstly, as we noted in chapter 5, Johnson recalled that there was only one "black box" aboard Flight 305: the flight data recorder. But there were two. Flight 305 also had a cockpit voice recorder, which had been mandatory on all jet airliners in the USA since June 30, 1966.

Secondly, Johnson identified Captain Thomas Spangler as one of the Air Force personnel in the group photo from the "sled test." He then reminisced about another flight with Spangler. In his recollection, they had both been aboard a C-141 at 23,000 feet over Oregon when three of the four engines went into reverse. Such an event can make for a bad day. They wrestled the bucking beast, dropping at almost 3,000 feet a minute, down to a safe landing at Baker City Municipal Airport. That incident was real: it occurred in the spring of 1969 and was written up in the Air Force journal *MAC Flyer*, issue of June 1969. Johnson was indeed aboard that flight, but Spangler was not. No doubt, Johnson knew Spangler as a C-141 pilot and conflated him with Captain Earl H. Heal, the pilot in the Baker City incident.

Most probably, on the day of the "sled test" flight, Spangler was the pilot of the C-141 chase plane, and in that capacity appeared in the group photo which survives to this day.

It is quite likely that most of our documents that draw upon decades-old memories—for example Rataczak in 2009, Detlor, Johnson, and Mitchell in 2013, Anderson in 2014—are peppered with events similarly misremembered, confused with others, or heard at second hand.

## THE SLED DROP

John Detlor's recollections of the sled test flight provided a vivid description of what happened:

> **We took that plane up over the ocean and dropped some sandbags out the back. Yep, we figured that the guy [was?] jumping off over Southwestern Washington because of the bump in cabin pressure[,] but nobody was quite sure, so we took the plane up, dropped some sandbags out of the back to simulate somebody jumping. And [we] discovered what happens is with that rear air-stair opens, the air pressure causes it to trail somewhat up. As it gets weights on it, it drops down. When that weight suddenly leaves, the door pops up instantaneously closed, but doesn't stay closed, but that instant closing is enough to cause that bump in cabin pressure. Funny, how we did that.[12]**

On January 10, 1972, Milnes sent film and photographs of the sled test flight to FBI director Hoover with the following comments:

> **A review of the film shows the normal flight, together with a depression of the stairway as the load descends on the steps. . . . Sequential black[-]and[-]white still photos [show] the depression of the rear stairway by the addition of the sled and the reaction of the stairway to the actual departure of the sled, it being noted that the stairway immediately returned to a near closed position when the weight was taken from it.[13]**

On January 14, eight days after the sled test flight, Milnes wrote again to Director Hoover to summarize these findings:

> **The last three rows of seats were removed from the aircraft[,] and special measuring devices were attached to the rear end of the cabin so that it could be determined exactly what happened in the aircraft when the weight was dislodged. Through the assistance of members of the U.S. Air Force, three sleds were made on which were placed sand bag weights, bringing the total weight to approximately 235 pounds, that being the estimated weight of the hijacker, the parachute, and the money. On the morning of January 6, 1972, . . . the 727 ascended to approximately 7,000 feet over the Pacific Ocean west of Hoquiam, Washington. [Redacted] put the aircraft in the same flight configuration as the hijacker had directed.**[14]

Here we must at least lodge an objection. The altitude of Flight 305 between 8:06 and 8:11 p.m. on November 24, 1971, was 10,000 feet above mean sea level, not 7,000 feet. There is a significant difference in pressure between 7,000 feet and 10,000 feet. This difference varies from place to place, between day and night, and according to the season of the year. In the US Standard Atmosphere, which is one of the references for measuring atmospheric conditions, the pressure at 7,000 feet is 1,633 pounds per square foot; the pressure at 10,000 feet is 1,456 pounds per square foot.[15]

It is perhaps reasonable also to wonder whether MSgt Johnson's recollection of 275 to 300 pounds, or Milnes's report of 235 pounds, was the more accurate, and indeed, whether three sleds were dropped (as Milnes's letter of January 14 implied) or only one (as Johnson recalled), and, if only one, whether that was sufficient basis for an investigation that would probably cost millions of dollars.

Regarding the flight configuration, although it is not made explicit in any public document of the FBI, we have to assume that Special Agent Milnes was referring to a flap setting of 15 degrees with landing gear down, which we know was the configuration of Flight 305.

Regarding the indicated airspeed of the "sled test" flight, to match the relevant segment of Flight 305, the closest settings should have been either 160 knots (as recorded on the ARINC transcript between 7:57 and 8:01 p.m.) or 170 knots (as noted by two Northwest observers patched into the ARINC network at 8:00 p.m.). But Milnes did not confirm whether the airspeed was matched or not.

Nevertheless, Milnes was determined to press his case:

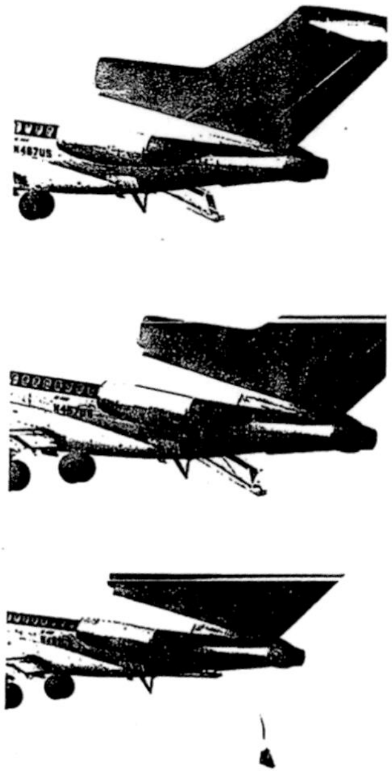

**Figure 8.6**. Pacific Ocean, January 6, 1972: the only image in the public domain purporting to represent the sled test flight of N467US. Landing gear is down and flaps appear to be at 15 degrees. Ventral airstair is lowered but not locked. *Image courtesy of Wayne Walker, n467us.com. Image credit: FBI*

> **At which time Air Force personnel allowed the weighted sled to fall from the end of the stairs. The reaction was instantaneous and was described by [redacted] as being the same reaction that they had in the airplane when they believed the hijacker jumped. As a result, [redacted] has now taken this information, together with some refined data given to him by the Air Force,**

**and has identified an area near Highland, Washington, where it is believed the hijacker jumped.**[16]

Milnes was asking Director Hoover to bet the entire search strategy of the FBI on a single test flight at a different altitude from Flight 305, at an unspecified airspeed, flown over the ocean in the morning rather than over land in the evening, and possibly with a single air drop of undocumented weight and dimensions. In the world of commercial or military testing, any head of flight test operations would have told the pilot to go back and do the flight again, and do it not once but many times. To put it another way: a test flight does not constitute a flight test.

In short, the conduct of the "sled test" flight was extraordinarily superficial. We cannot attribute this to the norms of the 1970s. We can go back as far as 1947 for an example of a careful, meticulous, and ultimately successful flight test program; namely, the tests that led to the first documented supersonic flight of a manned airplane, by Charles E. "Chuck" Yeager in the Bell XS-1. Over a twenty-month period from January 1946 to October 1947, pilots from Bell Aircraft and the US Air Force made seventeen glide flights and thirty-two powered flights at speeds up to Mach 0.997 before the program managers felt confident to push the airplane through the "sound barrier."[17]

A serious flight test for the "oscillation theory" would have incorporated at least the following variations in the parameters:

- indicated airspeeds of 150, 155, 160, 170, and 180 knots (the speeds reported by Flight 305 at various times between 7:46 p.m. and 8:18 p.m. on November 24, 1971)
- altitudes of 10,000 feet (as reported by Flight 305 at 8:00 p.m.) and 11,000 feet (reported at 10:26 p.m.)
- outside air temperatures down to −5 degrees C (as reported at 9:28 p.m.) or below
- weights of the dummy load reflecting a range of body weights between 150 and 190 pounds (as variously reported by eight witnesses)
- and in each case, a full and transparent recording of the airplane's cabin pressure, pitch angle, vertical speed, and other relevant flight parameters, for comparison with the flight data recorder from Flight 305

**Figure 8.7**. January 6, 1972: Boeing 727, registration N467US, on ramp for sled test flight. *Courtesy of Washington State Historical Society. Image credit: John Detlor, FBI*

As far as is known from the public record, none of these variations were tested. Crucially, there is no evidence that the "sled test" flight reproduced Flight 305's actual cruise altitude of 10,000 feet (where the air pressure would have been substantially lower than at 7,000 feet).

We also recall from chapter 2 that on Flight 305, from the moment when Tina Mucklow retreated to the cockpit until the landing in Reno, the cockpit door was closed and locked. Much later, the crew would report a "pressure bump" that, they implied, had been transmitted through the closed cockpit door. On the sled test flight, the cockpit door was apparently open (as figure 8.8 below seems to illustrate), allowing any pressure changes in the cabin to be transmitted into the cockpit without hindrance. This did not reproduce the conditions of Flight 305.

But in our view, the most egregious omission in the "sled test" flight was the failure to recognize that the ventral airstair can be locked in the down position. There is nothing in the public record that states unequivocally that the hijacker of Flight 305 locked (or did not lock) the airstair, but we know that the hydraulic system that operated the airstair was available, and the hijacker had only to operate the same control lever as the cabin crew would use in a normal passenger disembarkation. That done, the stairs would descend fully to the down and locked position. We know (because the Boeing tests of 1963–1964 had demonstrated) that an airspeed of 150 to 180 knots would not impede this deployment.

On the "sled test" flight, it is clear from the chase plane's photographs that the airstair was not locked, since the stair snapped upward after the release of the dummy load. For this to happen, the "sled test" crew must have disabled the hydraulic system (whether by bleeding out the hydraulic fluid, or by pulling a circuit breaker, or by some other means, we do not know).

We reiterate: the "sled test" flight did not replicate Flight 305. Whatever oscillation occurred on the "sled test" flight, it could not have been the same aerodynamic event that produced the oscillation on Flight 305. On the sled test, the stair was disconnected from the hydraulic system and must have fallen free under gravity; on Flight 305, the stair was powered by hydraulics and possibly locked down.

Setting aside all the errors and omissions of the "sled test" flight, we can now correlate Milnes's report of January 14, 1972, with the conception of the trapezoidal "jump zone" in the area of Lake Merwin. As we recounted in chapter 5, Paul Soderlind of Northwest Airlines,

**Figure 8.8**. January 6, 1972: on board Boeing 727, registration N467US, flight deck. Pilot in command (in left hand seat) is Paul Soderlind. Flight engineer (foreground) appears to be Harold E. Anderson. *Courtesy of Washington State Historical Society. Image credit: John Detlor, FBI*

was the author of the memo dated January 9, 1972, that set out the "jump zone" concept. The logic of the "oscillation theory" was as follows:

- The "sled test" flight had, in one shot and flawlessly, reproduced the "oscillation" of Flight 305.
- The "oscillation" (with the benefit of hindsight) was therefore presumed to be the moment when the hijacker took his leave from Flight 305.
- The "oscillation" was considered to be accurately correlated with the time of 8:11 p.m. (plus or minus one minute).
- On the basis of unspecified radar data attributed to an unnamed person at McChord Air Force Base, Flight 305 was considered to have been overhead Highland Washington at 8:11 p.m. (plus or minus 1 nautical mile in the east-west direction).

We can add here only that as the FBI memo of November 29, 1971, records, Northwest Airlines downloaded the data from the flight data recorder of Flight 305, but Northwest has never disclosed its contents. Neither the FBI nor Northwest has ever disclosed (if they ever possessed) the Air Force radar data purporting to represent the tracking of Flight 305. Neither the FBI nor Northwest nor the US Air Force has ever disclosed the technical parameters of the heavily instrumented "sled test" flight. From this author's FOIA requests, we also know that the FAA claims to have retained no civilian radar data pertaining to Flight 305, and that the US Air Force denies any knowledge of the military radar data on which the FBI's search was predicated.

It remained only for the author of the "oscillation theory" to factor in an undocumented 25-knot wind from the southwest, on which the hijacker would drift helplessly from 10,000 feet to the ground, and the Lake Merwin trapezoid was complete.

As history has recorded (and we do not need to elaborate the story here), the FBI searched the trapezoid practically inch by inch and found nothing.

CHAPTER

# 9

# THE DESCENT PATH

We have seen how, within days of the hijacking, Northwest Airlines proposed to the FBI a search area in the region of Lake Merwin, in Washington State. This proposal was based on their belief that an oscillation in cabin pressure had identified the hijacker's time and place of departure from Flight 305.

This first search area appears to have been defined on or before December 6, 1971, as per Farrell's report to Milnes:

> **A facsimile copy of a memo prepared by [redacted][,] which was accompanied by a map, which is also a facsimile, were received at 6:05 PM, 12/4/71, from Minneapolis.**
>
> **The map shows the course of the aircraft from slightly north of the Kelso-Longview area to just south of Battle Ground and sets out the most likely area for the parachute drop according to [redacted] latest calculations as an area described by parallel lines C, D, E, & F. Generally speaking this would be an area between Pidgeon [*sic*] Springs and an area just north and east of Woodland.**
>
> **The above information was furnished on 12/6/71 by ASAC Bibler to SA Manning, at which time SA Manning advised that he is sure that the area now described has already been searched by helicopter and fixed[-]wing aircraft and that much of it has been covered on the ground as well.[1]**

As far as we can determine, this map does not exist anywhere in the public files of the "FBI Vault" and has never been released in the public domain. From Farrell's description, the proposed search area seems to have had the shape of a rectangle or parallelogram. We know that later on, Northwest would obtain radar data from the US Air Force, purporting to

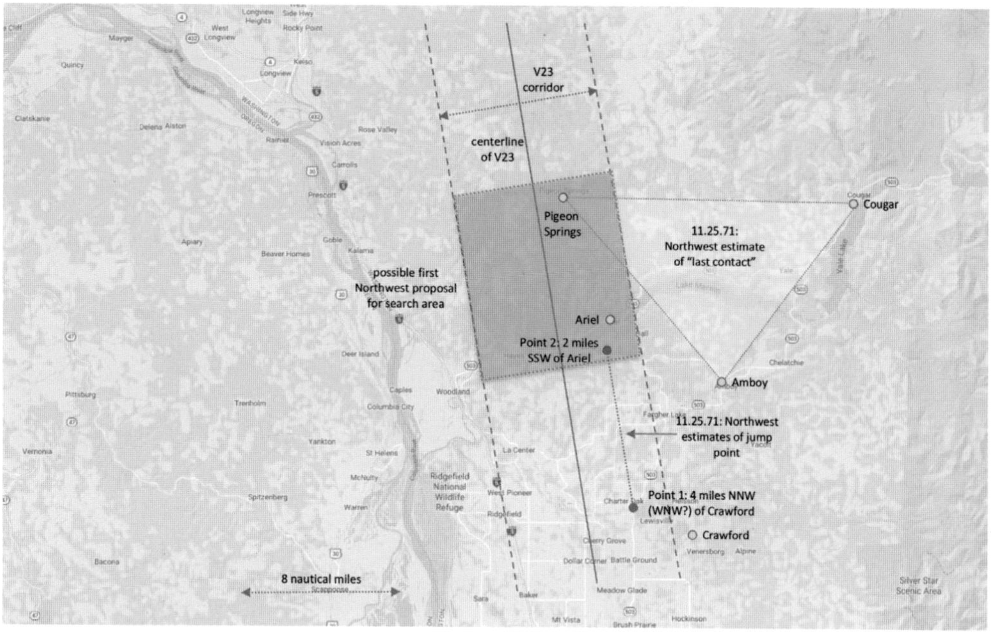


**Figure 9.1**. Reconstruction of Northwest Airlines' first proposal for the search area, as of December 6, 1971. *Base map © 2020 Google Maps; graphics by author*

represent the track of Flight 305, but as of December 6, 1971, they did not possess these data. Their most logical working assumption, in the absence of radar data or position reports, would be that Flight 305 had been within the Victor 23 corridor, which indeed is bounded by parallel lines. From Farrell's references to Pigeon Springs and Woodland, we can approximately reconstruct the parallelogram as shown in figure 9.1 above.

However, as early as December 2, 1971, Northwest were having second thoughts. Farrell reported to Milnes as follows:

> **[redacted] advised that because it was [on] automatic pilot, the crew might not be able to detect a change in the attitude of the flight caused by a 180-pound man parachuting from the back stairway. However, he advised that he is examining the flight recorder with a microscope[,] which he expects will reveal "little bobs" or anomalies where the automatic pilot has mechanically made an adjustment to maintain the level flight of the aircraft.**
>
> **He noted that there was a "little bob" at approximately 8:09 p.m., and based on that finding and the fact that the air stairs had gone down sometime earlier, [redacted] suggested that the search area probably should be extended to the north an additional three miles and to the south as far as the Columbia River. These extensions of the search area would be from the center of the search boundaries previously given to this office.**[2]

The "little bob" on the flight data recorder, at 8:09 p.m., was two minutes earlier than the estimated time when the crew had reported an "oscillation." This would be equivalent to about 6 nautical miles over the ground and would be a reason to extend the search area by about 7 statute miles (not 3 miles) northward.

However, it is not at all evident why Northwest should propose to extend the search area southward to the Columbia River. If they meant a southward extension along Victor 23, this would expand the search area as far as Vancouver, Washington, which is 20 statute miles south of Woodland. That would be equivalent to about seven flying minutes and would imply that Flight 305 had crossed the Columbia at about 8:18 p.m.

This proposal raises a further conundrum. Northwest would have known, from their own notes of the ARINC transmissions, that at 8:18 p.m. Flight 305 had been 23 miles south of Battle Ground, approximately overhead Tualatin, Oregon. If Northwest wanted the FBI to search as far south as the flight point at 8:18 p.m., they should have proposed a search area extending to the south bank of the Columbia River and into Oregon.

Again, there is no illustration of this second proposal in the public domain. From Farrell's report of Northwest's proposal, we have reconstructed it in figure 9.2 below.

For whatever reason, the Columbia River proposal was not pursued. In just over a month, Northwest came up with a revised map, which proposed to shift the whole search area to the southeast, but nowhere near the Columbia.

The first known reference to Northwest's new map appears in a memo dated January 11, 1972, in which Farrell wrote to Milnes as follows:

> **Copies of the revised map of the area to be searched were forwarded the night of 1/10/72 to Sacramento.[3]**

Two days later, Farrell wrote to the SAC in Portland elaborating the genesis of the map, as follows:

> **Enclosed are a memo and a revised map of the probable drop area as prepared by [redacted] Northwest Airlines. These were prepared after an experimental flight conducted by Northwest Airlines on 1/6/72[,] and the calculations are based on a refined radar map provided by the Air Force.[4]**

In both cases, Farrell was referring to the memo and map dated January 9, 1972, from Paul Soderlind of Northwest Airlines, proposing that the hijacker's exit point had been overhead Highland, Washington, and that 8:11 p.m. was the central estimate for the moment of his departure.

Soderlind had elaborated the analysis of the exit point with a map, defining a geographical area within which the hijacker's descent path could be bounded. The map was based on the US Geological Survey map of the *La Center Quadrangle*, at a scale of 1:62500, and was annotated with a hand-drawn sketch of the possible descent paths.

The start of the descent path was delimited by a polygon, roughly in the shape of a parallelogram. The north–south axis of the parallelogram was aligned with the flight path, as derived by Northwest from the Air Force radar data, with the following dimensions:

- a width of 1 mile in the east–west direction (reflecting the assumed east–west uncertainty in the radar plot)
- a length of approximately 6.8 miles in the north–south direction (apparently reflecting the airplane's ground speed of about 3 miles per minute, and the 1-mile north–south uncertainty in the radar plot, and also possibly a two-minute uncertainty in the time of departure).

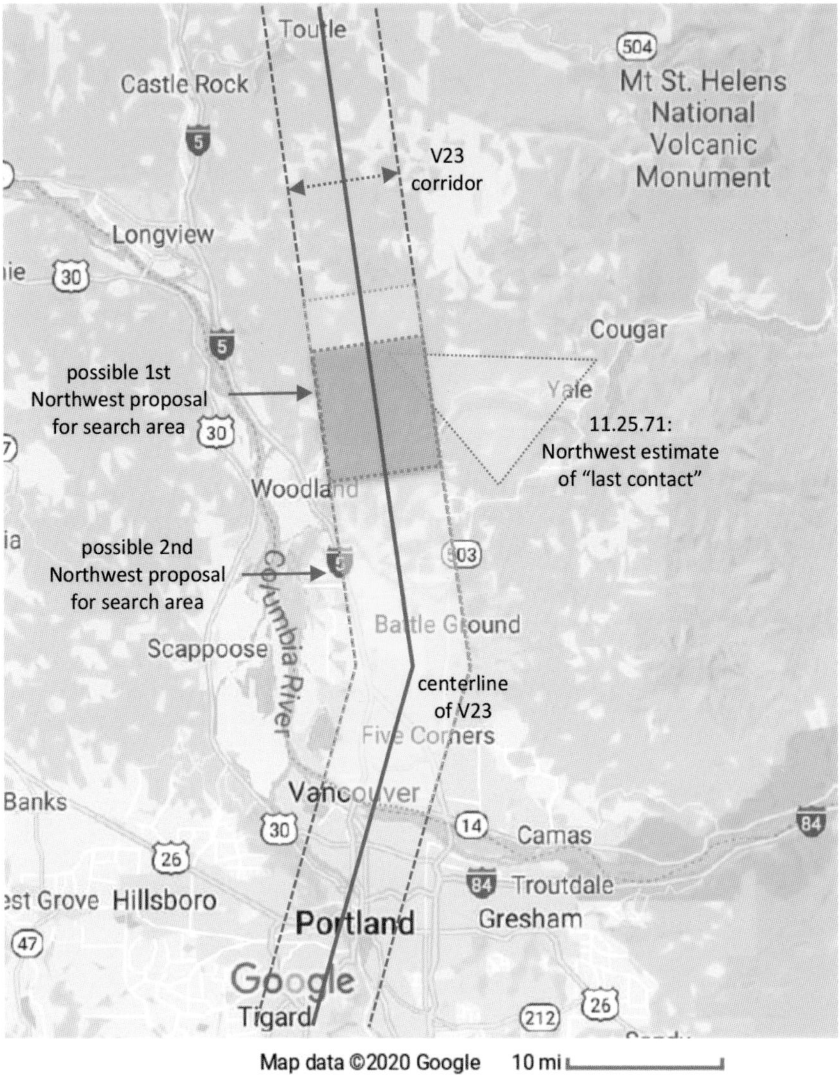


**Figure 9.2.** Comparison of Northwest Airlines' first and second proposals for the search area. *Base map © 2020 Google Maps; graphics by author*

The end points of the descent path rested on a series of assumptions and scenarios, which Soderlind set out as follows:

- that the earliest possible deployment of the parachute was on exit from the airplane (at 10,000 feet AMSL), the latest possible deployment was at 2,500 feet AMSL, and there was a possibility of no deployment (meaning a free fall to the ground and the demise of the hijacker)

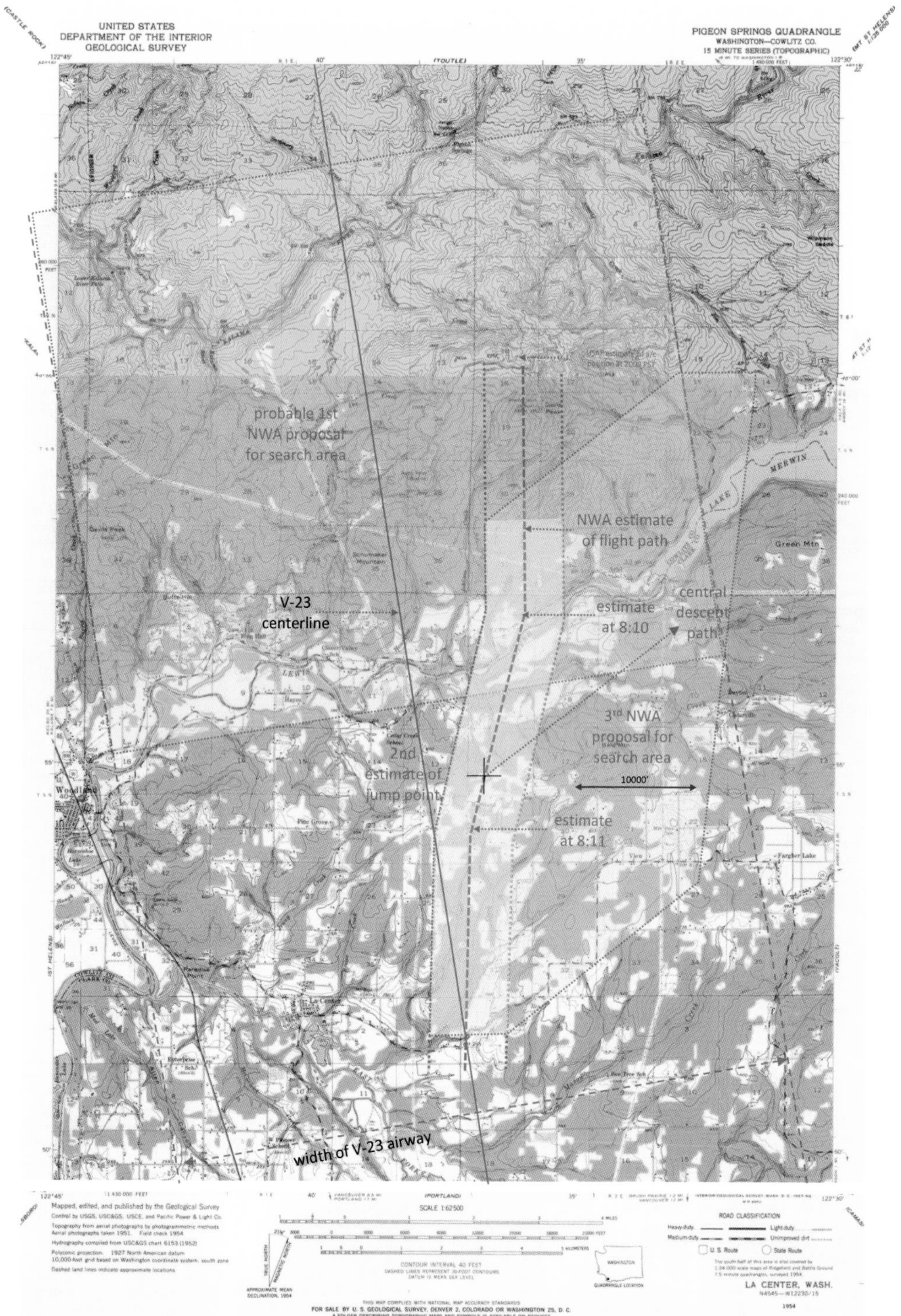


**Figure 9.3**. Reconstruction of Northwest Airlines' first and third proposals for the search area. *Base map from USGS, Pigeon Springs and La Center Quadrangles, scale 1:62500; graphics by author*

- that if the hijacker had not deployed the parachute (in other words, had fallen to his death), his descent path would cover 2,600 feet horizontally in the direction of the airplane's track
- that if the hijacker had deployed the parachute, his descent path would be in a constant direction and at a constant speed, determined by the wind.

A low-resolution copy of this map, evidently photocopied or faxed many times, exists in the public files of the FBI. For ease of understanding the change in Northwest's thinking, we have reconstructed the map in figure 9.3 above.

## THE DIAGONAL ARROW

Soderlind's memo does not specify the assumptions for the wind speed and direction, stating only that, "wind information from 10,000' [A]MSL to the ground [was] as determined by NWA Meteorology Chief [redacted; identified as Dan Sowa]."[5]

However, the accompanying map is marked with a diagonal arrow, which must represent Northwest's central estimate of the descent path. The arrow has a compass bearing of 233 degrees, or approximately from the southwest. The length of the arrow is approximately 20,000 feet, or 3.3 miles.

The hijacker was known to have departed the airplane with a NB-6 or NB-8 military parachute container, which probably held a C-9 canopy.[6] If he had deployed the parachute immediately on exit, his vertical descent rate with this type of canopy would have been a relatively constant 18–20 feet per second.[7] If the landing was at 1,000 feet above sea level (which was the approximate height of the terrain around Highland), his vertical descent would have been 9,000 feet and the descent would have lasted 450–500 seconds. To cover 20,000 feet horizontally in this time, he would have had an average horizontal speed of 40–44 feet per second, or 24–26 knots.

In summary, Northwest Airlines evidently assumed an average wind of 24–26 knots from 233 degrees (8 degrees west of southwest).

The FBI, either working independently or using Northwest's estimates, had apparently estimated the wind at 7,000 feet AMSL over Woodland as 25 knots from 227.5 degrees. This is practically identical to what we see from Northwest's map of the *La Center Quadrangle*. We conclude that this estimate became the central assumption of the FBI's search on the ground.

As we recounted in chapter 6, this assumption could have been cross-checked against independent sources of weather data, but apparently this was never done.

## THE LANDING ZONE

Northwest's assumptions on the exit point, and on the wind speed and direction, together led them to construct a larger, roughly trapezoidal, polygon of putative landing points, 6.8 miles from north to south and 3.5 miles from east to west. They superimposed this trapezoid on the map that they sent to the FBI on January 9, 1972. The "landing zone" was roughly bisected in the east–west direction by the Lewis River. Northwest posited a "most probable" landing point in the wooded hills south of Lake Merwin, about 3 miles east of the town of Ariel, Washington.

## AN AIR FORCE MAP?

An intriguing footnote to the Northwest calculations is evident from a memo filed nearly five months later. On June 8, 1972, Farrell wrote again to Milnes, referring to a map of the descent path apparently prepared not by Northwest but by an Air Force member of the "sled test" crew:

> **On 1/6/72, an experimental flight was conducted by NWA using the actual plane hijacked in this case[,] and on that flight [redacted] U.S. Air Force observed the experiment. After completion of the experiment [redacted] prepared a handwritten map of his calculations concerning the drop and the probable drift of the parachute if it opened.[8]**

The names of some of the Air Force crew on the "sled test" flight are known: Sr. MSgt Wally Johnson, MSgt David A. Saiz, Capt. Thomas Spangler, and Capt. Ron Wilson.[9] As we observed in chapter 8, Capt. Spangler was probably the pilot of the C-141 chase plane. Wally Johnson, in his interview in 2013 for the Washington State Historical Society, made no mention of a map or calculations prepared either by himself or by his colleagues.

A reference to the Air Force calculations appears in a memo to Milnes from Special Agent Robert Newton Nichols, dated November 13, 1972:

> **Northwest Orient Airlines ... [redacted] further advised that [redacted] McChord Air Force Base, also calculated the area into which Unsub [unknown subject] parachuted and would have in his possession radar data concerning the above-mentioned flight.**
>
> **Leads ... At McChord Air Force Base, Washington ... will contact [redacted] and review with him his calculations of the flight path and course of the Norjak airplane in order to determine if there is a possibility of an error in the computation of the search area.[10]**

From the further efforts of Special Agent Nichols in January 1973, it appears to be confirmed that the Air Force calculations and map were were made in collaboration with Northwest Airlines:

> **The search area was calculated by [redacted; probably Soderlind] Northwest Orient Airlines employee and by [redacted; probably Capt. Spangler] McChord Air Force Base, Tacoma, Washington.**
>
> **Attempts are being made to contact [redacted; probably Capt. Spangler] by the Seattle Division to recalculate the search area with him[11]**

However, the Air Force had no intention of handing over the calculations. As we recall from chapter 5, by this time Capt. Spangler (if it was he who was the object of the FBI's attentions) had been transferred to the Far East.

The data and calculations prepared by the Air Force have never been released in the public domain. A FOIA request by this author to the US Air Force eventually yielded the following reply:

> **I am providing you with all table and rules related to radar records within the Air Force Records Information Management System. The longest disposition listed is "destroy 10 years after superseded." Due to the records creation being well over this disposition[,] it is safe to assume that they were destroyed a long time ago.[12]**

## THE FOURTH SEARCH ZONE

It is a matter of record that Northwest's first and third proposed "landing zones" were searched thoroughly, on foot, in vehicles, and by surveillance aircraft. No trace of the hijacker, the briefcase, or the parachutes was found. There the matter might have rested, but Northwest meanwhile was willing (or was asked) to give the calculations another try, and in due course they came up with another landing zone.

On March 2, 1973, Special Agent Nichols attempted to pitch this idea to the acting director of the FBI in Washington (his use of the term "first search area" apparently referring to the third proposal of Northwest Airlines, as we have defined it):

> **In [an] attempt to determine the accuracy of the first search area, the following was learned: The first search area was calculated using a system of plotting known as "GEOREF" (i.e.[,] Geographical Reference)[,] which has a plotting error of plus or minus one mile. A new plotting system using a computer-generated latitude and longitude has a plotting error plus or minus 1/2 mile. Using the new system, [redacted name] Northwest Orient Airlines [redacted position] plotted a new course for the Norjak airplane and a new search area based on the new course. The new search area**

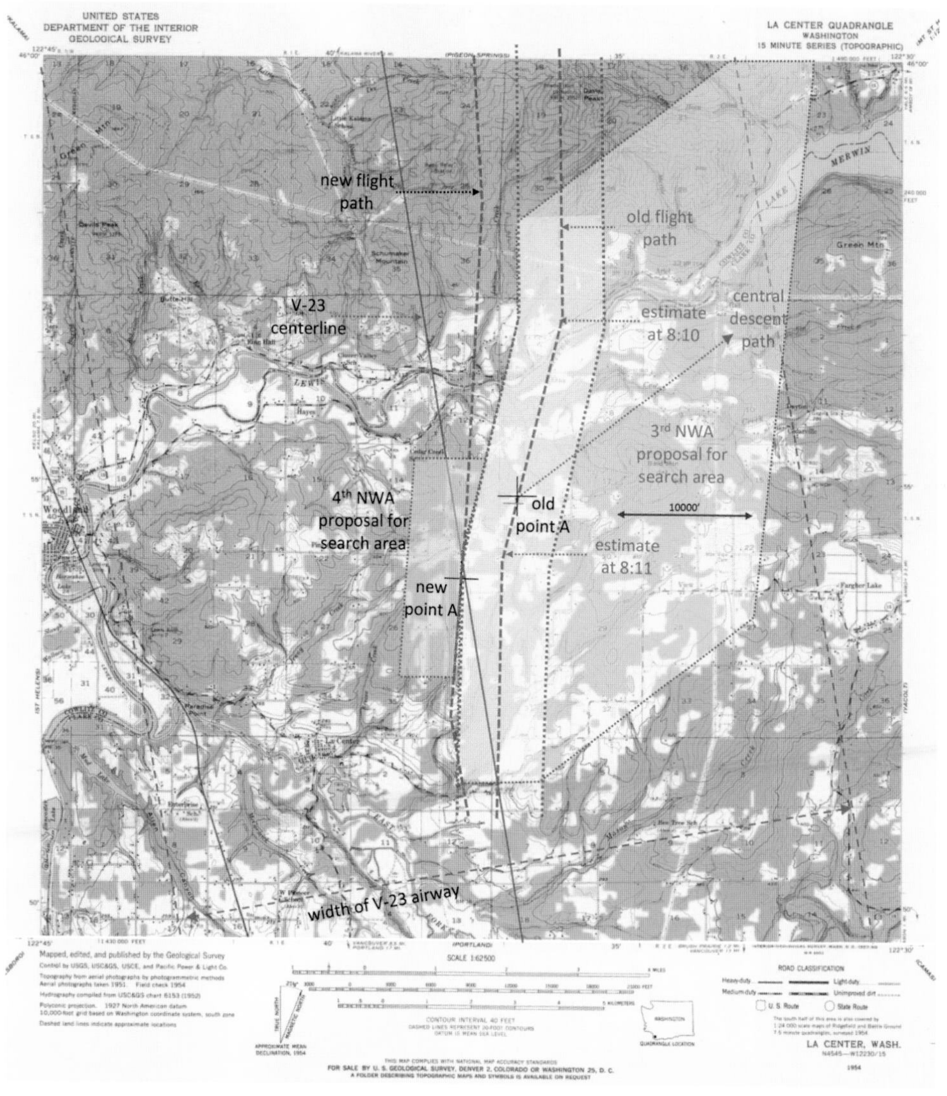


**Figure 9.4.** Reconstruction of Northwest Airlines' third and fourth proposals for the search area. *Base map from USGS,* La Center Quadrangle, *scale 1:62500; graphics by author*

**is partially outside the first area. . . . Seattle Division is currently making arrangements to search that portion of the above described area not previously searched.**[13]

We do not know whether, at this date, Paul Soderlind was still involved in the case of Flight 305. Before his fiftieth birthday in August 1973, he would retire from Northwest with a mild heart condition. Nothing in the archives of the FBI gives a clue as to who in Northwest was still working with them in March 1973.

The map depicting the revised flight path and the proposed additional search area is reconstructed in figure 9.4 below.

As our figure 9.4 shows, the revised flight path was between 3,000 and 6,000 feet west of the previous plot, but still firmly within the Victor 23 corridor. The new "point A" (denoting the central estimate of the hijacker's presumed exit) was almost exactly on the centerline of Victor 23. It was about 7,400 feet southwest of the old "point A," which had been the central point for the search in early 1972. Northwest evidently felt that margins of about 2 miles north or south of this point, and about 4,000 feet east–west, would cover all possible uncertainties. Since the whole area east of the new flight path had already been searched, the new proposal called only for the FBI to return to an area of about 4 square miles on the western side.

However, nothing in the FBI's public files records the outcome of this proposition. Outside the archives of the FBI and perhaps those of Northwest Airlines, nothing is known about whether that additional search was ever undertaken.

## ANOTHER LOOK AT THE WIND

As we recounted in chapter 7, in attempting estimates of the wind on Victor 23 at the hijacker's exit point, the FBI (and apparently also Northwest) used an estimate derived from the winds at Portland and Salem McNary Field. To refer to Portland was understandable, since Portland Airport was 20 nautical miles south of "point A" (the January 1972 version). Salem was not an obvious reference, since it was 63 nautical miles south of "point A." On the other hand, Gray Army Air Field was 70 nautical miles north, and Seattle-Tacoma was 92 miles north, of "point A." Consequently, a more robust estimate for "point A" would have been based on an interpolation between Gray AAF or Seattle-Tacoma in the north, and Portland or Salem/McNary in the south. It would have been a reasonable assumption that the wind speed and direction had changed smoothly between the northerly and southerly points.

The second lacuna in the FBI's and Northwest's estimates was that they used (or could find) data only on winds from the surface up to 7,000 feet. But Flight 305 had been flying at 10,000 feet. There is generally a substantial difference in weather between 7,000 and 10,000 feet: certainly in the air pressure and temperature, and, it would be expected, also in wind speeds and directions.

We would not have expected the FBI to be expert at accessing the meteorological data on which to base these estimates. On the other hand, Northwest were in a business where they had to know meteorology.

In the public record, there is no evidence that either the FBI or Northwest used data from the most authoritative source of all: the NOAA. By 1971, the NOAA had been launching radiosondes (instrumented weather balloons) for over sixty-five years. Data were available for Gray AAF since 1920, for Portland International since 1928, for Seattle-Tacoma International since 1944, and for Salem/McNary since 1956. If the investigators of Flight 305 had looked up these data, the only substantive shortfall that they would have found was that the NOAA had stopped launching radiosondes from Portland in 1956; they would not resume until November 1972.

For our own analysis of the wind, which we summarized in chapter 7, we constructed a mathematical model of the historical radiosonde data for Gray AAF, Seattle-Tacoma, and Salem/McNary for the months of November and December 1971, and for Portland (absent data for 1971) for the months of November and December 1972. For any point on Victor 23, for any altitude from sea level up to 10,000 feet, and for any time of day, we were then able to make an estimate of the wind speed and direction. Every estimate was of course subject to statistical uncertainty, both in the speed and in the direction. But in each case we could establish a central estimate, and a range of outcomes on each side of the central estimate, in the form of a probability distribution.

For the purposes of this chapter, one example may suffice.

Let us use the FBI's assumption that at 8:11 p.m. the hijacker departed Flight 305 at "point A" (the Northwest version of January 9, 1972). The coordinates of this point, as nearly as we can read them from the much-photocopied FBI maps, are 45°54'54"N, 122°36'44"W. We assume that the altitude of the jump was 10,000 feet.

In these circumstances, our central estimate is that the hijacker jumped into a wind of 28 knots from 247 degrees (approximately west-southwest). Once he lost the forward motion imparted by the airplane, and assuming he deployed his parachute immediately, he would start drifting at about 28 knots toward the east-northeast.

So far, so good. Our estimate of the wind is not greatly different from that of FBI and Northwest Airlines: stronger by about 3 knots, and more westerly by about 20 degrees.

However, as the hijacker descended, the wind would change. The FBI and Northwest assumed a constant wind from 10,000 feet down to the ground, and therefore a straight and uniform track from the hijacker's exit point to his landing. Our estimates are that the wind would be backing (turning counterclockwise) and weakening as the altitude wound down. The closer the hijacker came to the ground, the more his drift would become northerly and the slower it would become.

By our central estimates (for this particular point, altitude and time of departure), by the time the hijacker reached 1,000 feet above sea level (which is roughly ground level in the area of Highland, Clark County), he would be carried by a wind of 11 knots from 158 degrees (slightly east of south). He would therefore be traveling not northeast, as the FBI and (no pun intended) Northwest assumed, but slightly west of north.

These estimates are summarized in table 9.1 below.

**Table 9.1. Point A, overhead Highland, Clark County, Washington, latitude 45.92°N, longitude 122.61°W: Author's central estimates of wind speed and direction from 10,000 feet to MSL**

| Altitude<br>Feet AMSL | Wind direction<br>Degrees from N | Wind speed<br>Knots |
|---|---|---|
| 10,000 | 247 | 28 |
| 9,000 | 238 | 26 |
| 8,500 | 233 | 25 |
| 8,000 | 228 | 24 |
| 7,000 | 218 | 22 |
| 6,000 | 208 | 20 |
| 5,000 | 198 | 18 |

**Table 9.1. Point A, overhead Highland, Clark County, Washington, latitude 45.92°N, longitude 122.61°W: Author's central estimates of wind speed and direction from 10,000 feet to MSL**

| | | |
|---|---|---|
| 4,000 | 188 | 16 |
| 3,000 | 178 | 14 |
| 2,000 | 168 | 12 |
| 1,000 | 159 | 11 |
| 0 | 149 | 9 |
| | | |

*Source*: estimates by author

We can now calculate the vertical and horizontal movement of the hijacker, on the following assumptions:

- The weight of the hijacker is assumed to be 180 pounds, which is the highest of the estimates by witnesses. (A lower estimate of his weight will yield a lower vertical velocity, therefore a longer descent time and a larger horizontal distance traveled.)
- The weight of the parachutes is assumed to be 21 pounds.
- The weight of the money is assumed to be 20 pounds.
- The air density is assumed to be 0.0565 pounds per cubic foot at 10,000 feet, increasing to 0.0765 pounds per cubic foot at sea level.
- The coefficient of drag of the parachute is assumed to be 0.75 (a standard value for a parachute without holes or slits cut in the fabric).
- The surface area of the parachute is assumed to be 592 square feet.
- The above assumptions yield estimates, using standard aeronautical formulas, of the hijacker's descent rate in each 1,000-foot vertical segment from 10,000 feet to the surface or sea level (whichever comes first).
- The earliest possible deployment of the parachute is at 10,000 feet (either by immediate pull of the ripcord, or by static line). In this case the hijacker descends at an average of 24.2 feet per second in the first 1,000 feet, decreasing to 20.8 feet per second in the denser air of the final 1,000 feet. (For a hijacker weighing 150 pounds, these estimates become 22.5 and 19.3 feet per second, respectively.)
- In the case of earliest deployment, his total descent time is 451 seconds, and the horizontal distance traveled is 13,825 feet.
- The latest possible deployment of the parachute is at 2,000 feet. In this case, the hijacker falls under gravity to reach terminal velocity of 174 feet per second in 12 seconds; at that point his altitude is 8,500 feet, he remains at terminal velocity from 8,500 feet to 2,000 feet, and he then deploys the parachute and descends at an average of 20.9 feet per second in the final 2,000 feet.
- In the case of latest deployment, his total descent time is 145 seconds, and the horizontal distance traveled is 3,448 feet.

These calculations are summarized in table 9.2 on pages 148–149.

If we now combine the horizontal distances traveled with the wind directions, we obtain a bird's-eye view of the hijacker's descent path. Our central estimates of the descent path, for the cases of earliest and latest deployment, are illustrated in figure 9.5 below. It may be observed that the descent path is predominantly in a northerly direction (rather than toward the northeast, as the FBI was led to assume), and that in the final 2,000 vertical feet of the descent, the hijacker is drifting slightly west of north.

This is by no means the end of the story. Let us not forget that the data from which we constructed our model were weather observations in the Pacific Northwest during the months of November and December. As chapter 7 illustrated, and as one would expect, these observations paint a picture of extreme variability. At any given combination of location, altitude, and time of day, the speed and direction of the wind can be greatly different from one day to the next. The model therefore does not yield a single estimate, but rather a range of estimates defined by probabilities.

In statistical terminology, the uncertainty in any estimate is expressed by the term "standard error of the estimate." We know that the true value is not exactly what we estimated, but the standard error gives us a way to measure our confidence in the estimate. Using the standard error, we expect the probabilities to be approximately as follows:

- With about 68 percent probability, the true value is within one standard error of the estimate; that is, between (estimate minus one standard error) and (estimate plus one standard error).
- With about 16 percent probability, the true value is more than one standard error above the estimate.
- With about 16 percent probability, the true value is more than one standard error below the estimate.

With this context, we may now introduce the standard errors of our estimates, as follows:

- The standard error of the wind speed was 12 knots.
- The standard error of the wind direction was 83 degrees.

In other words, when a moment ago we gave the example of the hijacker jumping into a wind of 28 knots from 247 degrees, it would have been more accurate to say the following:

- With 68 percent probability, the speed of the wind was between 16 (28 minus 12) knots and 40 (28 plus 12) knots.
- With 68 percent probability, the direction of the wind was between 164 (247 minus 83) degrees and 330 (247 plus 83) degrees.

By recognizing the statistical uncertainty of our knowledge, we reach a better position to define the boundaries of the hijacker's descent path and therefore the possible boundaries of his landing zone.

**Table 9.2. Point A, overhead Highland, Clark County, Washington, latitude 45.92°N, longitude 122.61°W: Horizontal and vertical profile of jump from 10,000 feet to MSL**

| | | | Earliest deployment of parachute | | | Latest deployment of parachute | | |
|---|---|---|---|---|---|---|---|---|
| Altitude AMSL | Horizontal wind velocity | Horizontal wind direction | Average vertical velocity | Duration | Horizontal distance | Average vertical velocity | Duration | Horizontal distance |
| feet | fps | deg from N | fps | sec | feet | fps | sec | feet |
| 10,000 | 47 | 247 | 24 | 0 | 0 | 0 | 0 | - |
| 9,000 | 44 | 238 | 24 | 42 | 1,924 | 111 | 9 | 412 |
| 8,500 | 42 | 233 | 24 | 21 | 917 | 167 | 3 | 130 |
| 8,000 | 41 | 228 | 23 | 21 | 889 | 174 | 3 | 120 |
| 7,000 | 38 | 218 | 23 | 43 | 1,699 | 174 | 6 | 225 |
| 6,000 | 34 | 208 | 23 | 44 | 1,580 | 174 | 6 | 206 |
| 5,000 | 31 | 198 | 22 | 45 | 1,457 | 174 | 6 | 187 |
| 4,000 | 28 | 188 | 22 | 45 | 1,330 | 174 | 6 | 168 |
| 3,000 | 24 | 178 | 22 | 46 | 1,198 | 174 | 6 | 149 |
| 2,000 | 21 | 168 | 21 | 47 | 1,062 | 174 | 6 | 130 |
| 1,000 | 18 | 159 | 21 | 47 | 921 | 21 | 47 | 921 |
| 0 | 14 | 149 | 21 | 48 | 776 | 21 | 48 | 776 |
| **Total** | **31** | | **22** | **451** | **13,753** | **69** | **145** | **3,425** |

Source: estimates by author

| No deployment | | | | | | | Earliest deployment | |
|---|---|---|---|---|---|---|---|---|
| Average vertical velocity | Duration | Horizontal distance | Horizontal wind velocity | Horizontal wind direction | Horizontal wind velocity | Horizontal wind direction | cumulative duration | cumulative horizontal distance |
| fps | sec | feet | fps | deg | fps | deg | sec | feet |
| – | 0 | – | 47 | 247 | 47 | 247 | 0 | 0 |
| 111 | 9 | 412 | 44 | 238 | 44 | 238 | 42 | 1,924 |
| 167 | 3 | 130 | 42 | 233 | 42 | 233 | 63 | 2,842 |
| 174 | 3 | 120 | 41 | 228 | 41 | 228 | 85 | 3,731 |
| 174 | 6 | 225 | 38 | 218 | 38 | 218 | 128 | 5,430 |
| 174 | 6 | 206 | 34 | 208 | 34 | 208 | 172 | 7,010 |
| 174 | 6 | 187 | 31 | 198 | 31 | 198 | 217 | 8,467 |
| 174 | 6 | 168 | 28 | 188 | 28 | 188 | 262 | 9,796 |
| 174 | 6 | 149 | 24 | 178 | 24 | 178 | 308 | 10,994 |
| 174 | 6 | 130 | 21 | 168 | 21 | 168 | 355 | 12,056 |
| 174 | 6 | 111 | 18 | 159 | 18 | 159 | 403 | 12,977 |
| 174 | 6 | 93 | 14 | 149 | 14 | 149 | 451 | 13,753 |
| **164** | **61** | **1,932** | **32** | | **24** | | | |

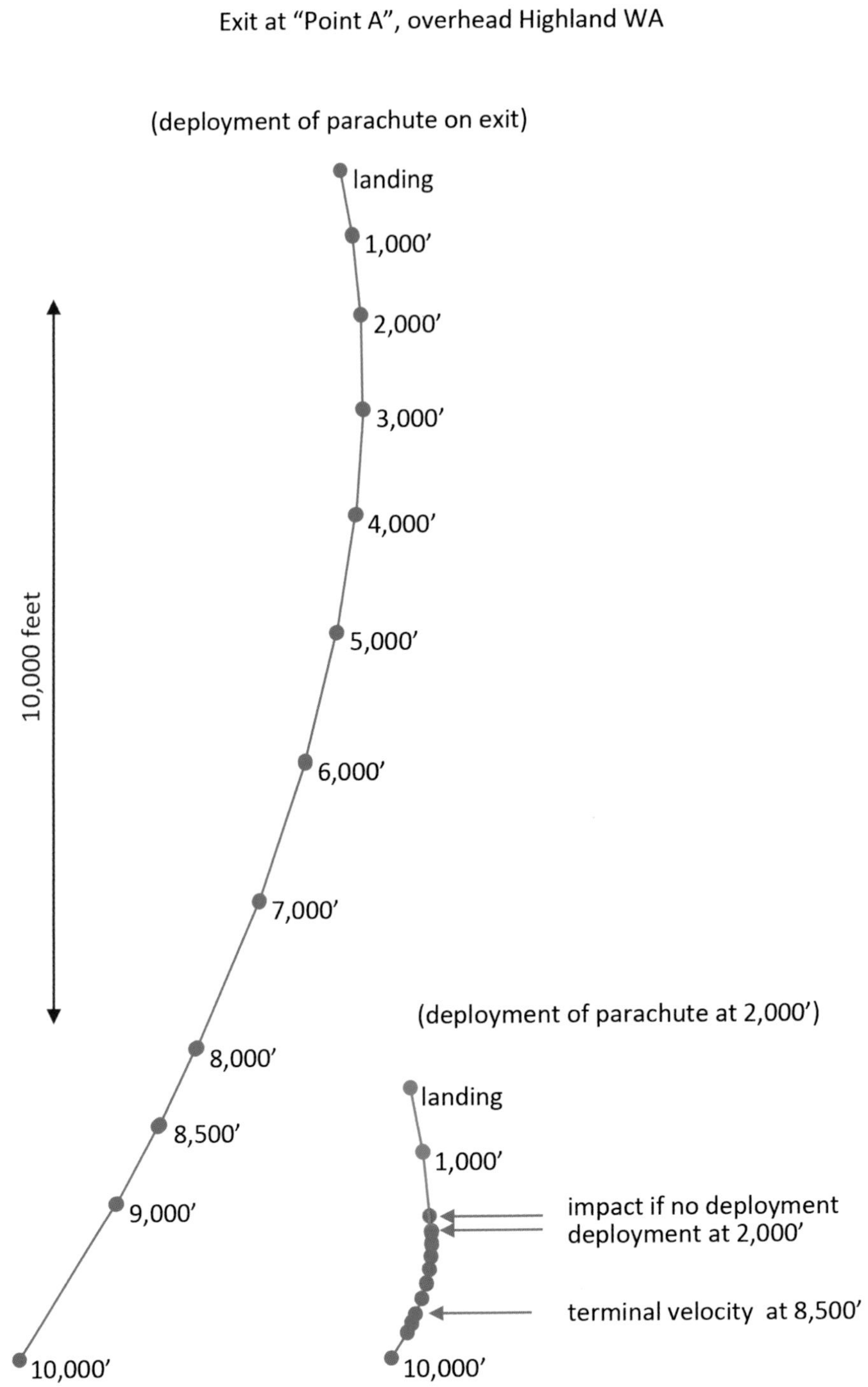


**Figure 9.5**. Point A, overhead Highland, Clark County, Washington: central estimate of the hijacker's descent path assuming (a) earliest (b) latest deployment of parachute. *Source: estimates and graphics by author*

As an example, we may take the central estimate that we illustrated in figure 9.5 above, and for the moment leaving aside the uncertainty in the wind speed, we will consider the range of uncertainty in the wind direction. If we want to see what the 68 percent probability range looks like, we can represent one standard error by rotating the descent path through 83 degrees clockwise, and one standard error in the other direction by rotating the descent path through 83 degrees counterclockwise. Then the descent path, instead of a single line, looks more like a fan, as figure 9.6 illustrates.

The outline of this fan shape is based on our central estimate of the wind speed; that is, 28 knots. If the wind had been slower, he would have landed correspondingly short: in other words, within the fan. If the wind had been faster, the fan would need to be correspondingly larger. Alternatively, if the hijacker had attempted a free fall followed by a late deployment, he could have stayed well within the fan. The probabilities then become impossible to calculate, since we have no way of knowing whether the deployment was early or late. Since this is only an exercise in scenarios, we propose to proceed on the assumption that the fan, as drawn, is something close to the limits of the hijacker's drift range.

If we now superimpose this fan-shaped range of descent paths on the FBI's search zone, we can have an idea of where they might have searched with more success.

If the hijacker had jumped exactly at point A (the January 1972 version), then about 40 percent of his range would have been west of the presumed jump zone; but since the FBI had excluded any form of westerly drift, they did not search in that direction.

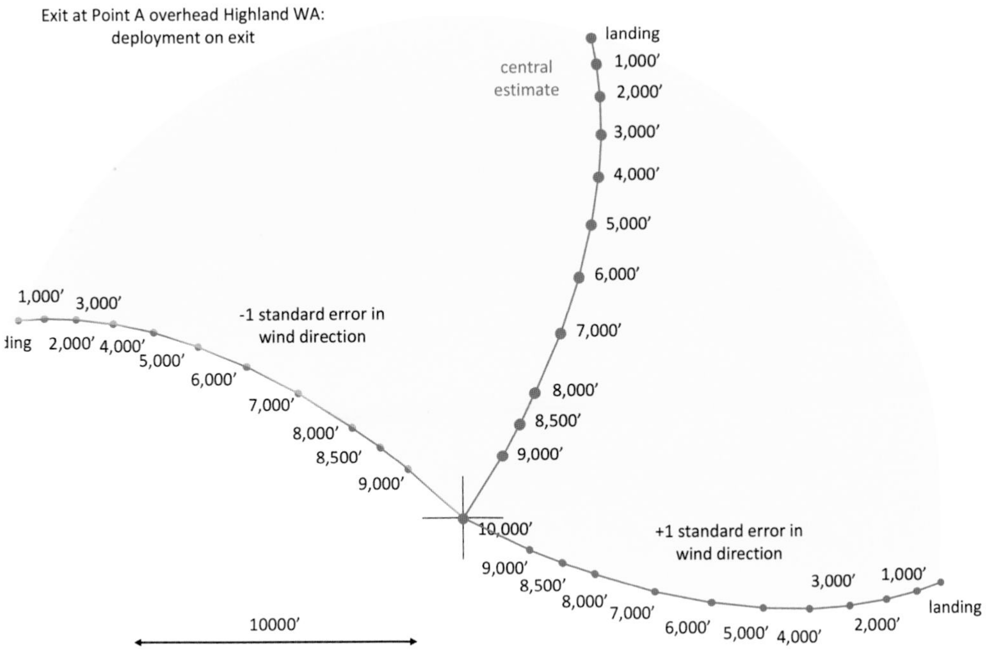


**Figure 9.6.** Point A, 10,000 feet AMSL, November 24, 1971, 8:11 p.m.: an illustration of the uncertainty in the direction of the wind. Shaded area shows 68 percent probability range. *Estimates and graphics by author*

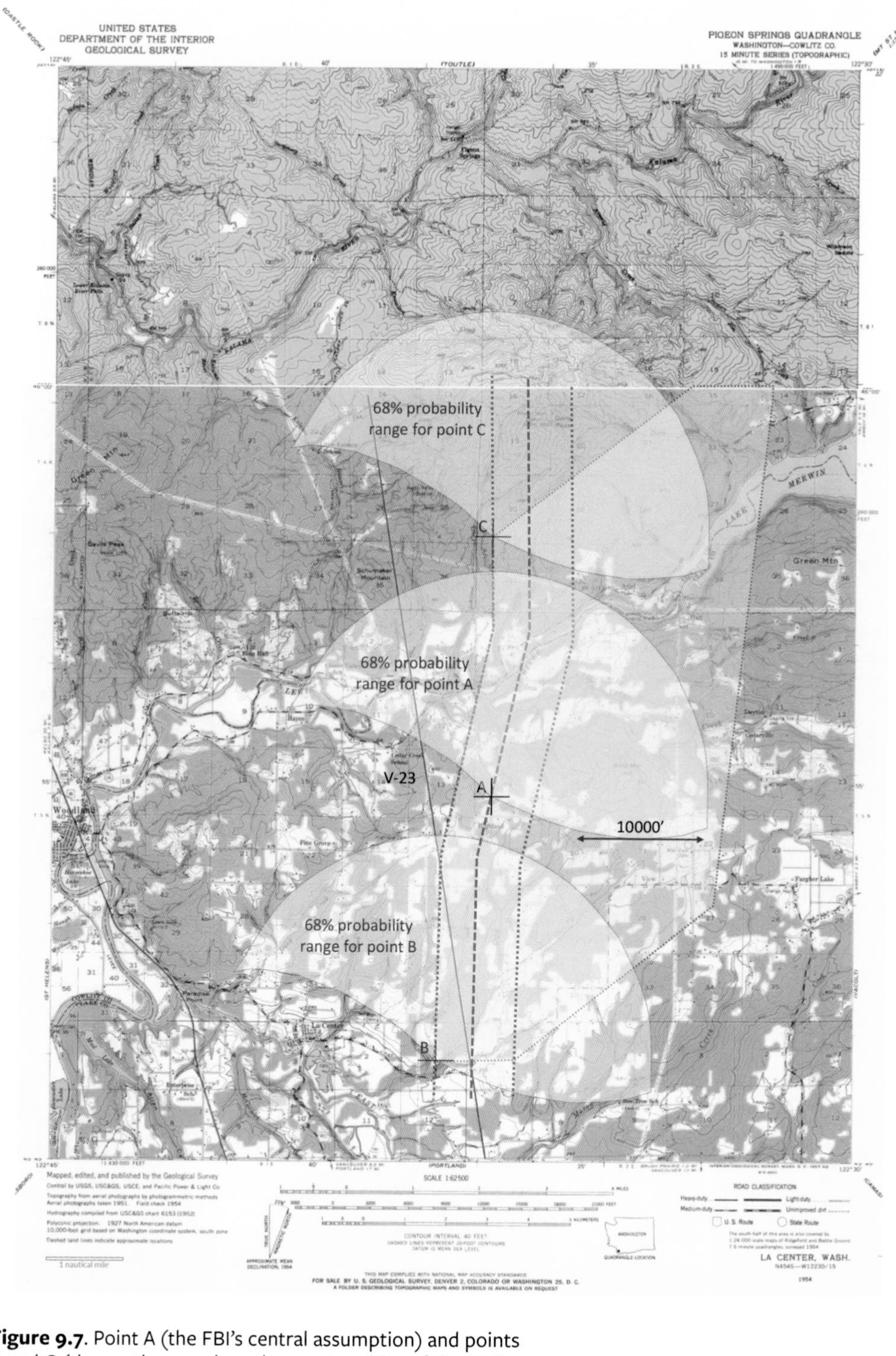


**Figure 9.7**. Point A (the FBI's central assumption) and points B and C (the southern and northern extremities of the FBI's assumed jump zone): estimated probability ranges of the hijacker's descent path. *Base map from USGS*, La Center Quadrangle; *graphics by author*

If he had jumped at the southern extremity of the presumed jump zone (what we have called point B), about 70 percent of his range would have been outside the search area. The FBI had excluded not only a westerly drift but also an easterly; for them, it was northeast or nothing.

If he had jumped at the northern extremity of the jump zone (point C in our illustration), again about 70 percent of his range would have escaped the later attention of the FBI. All of his possible drifts with a mainly northerly or northwesterly component would have taken him out of the search area.

With a jump at any intermediate point between B and C, the hijacker would have had something between a 40 percent and 70 percent chance of landing outside the search area.

In short, even if their point A had been accurate, once the FBI defined their trapezoidal landing zone, they had about a 30 percent chance of finding evidence of the landing.

Regarding the attempts of Northwest Airlines and the US Air Force to define the descent path and the search zone, no doubt sincere but doomed, we propose to let the matter rest here. History records that the FBI found nothing in any of the landing zones proposed by Northwest Airlines. As we recall, some of the ransom money showed up in another, unexpected, location, to which we shall return.

*Spoiler alert*: We do not believe in point A or in the narrative of the leap at 8:11 p.m. A new hypothesis is necessary to account for all the evidence, at least for the evidence that will withstand scrutiny. Our own narrative of the jump location and the descent path will be presented in a later chapter.

CHAPTER

# 10

# THE PLACARD

Almost seven years after the hijacking of Flight 305, an item of possible independent evidence came to light.

We begin the story with the FBI's first report on the discovery:

> On November 8, 1978, Cowlitz County Sheriff's Office, Kelso, Washington, provided a photograph of a portion of a decal found by an individual approximately twelve miles due east of Castle Rock, Washington, in a remote area. This decal, which was made of white plastic with dark red lettering, was torn but read "... URGENCY ... IT HANDLE, AFT AIR STAIR, TO OPERATE, ACCESS DOOR, PULL ON RE ... DOE. LOCK WIRE WILL BRE ... EGN HANDLE IS PULLED." At the bottom were the letters and numbers BAC27DPA.[1]

The object was a square of tough but flexible plastic, about 6 by 6 inches, probably no thicker than a credit card and probably weighing no more than a few ounces. The fragmented lettering clearly associated it with an airplane and with an emergency exit.

On December 1, 1978, the FBI showed a photograph of this object to Northwest Airlines at their headquarters at Minneapolis–St. Paul International Airport. Northwest made an immediate identification:

> The photograph of the decal is identical to Boeing Aircraft Standard Marker Number BAC27DPA-152, The decal states as follows:
>
> Emergency Exit Handle, Aft Airstair to Operate, Open Access Door, Pull on Red Handle. Lock Wire Will Break When Handle Is Pulled.
>
> This decal is located on the outside of the aircraft near the rear door.... the decal came from the same type of aircraft, that is a Boeing 727.[2]

Northwest provided the FBI with a facsimile copy of the BAC27DPA152 decal and what was described as "blueprints depicting location of decal on 727." By means of a FOIA request, this author obtained a copy of these documents. The facsimile is shown in figure 10.3. The "blueprint" is titled "Northwest Airlines Inc, Color Scheme Instl—727 Exterior." Although it does not include a legible diagram that explicitly shows the location of the BAC27DPA152 decal, it does list this decal as one of the exterior items. This document states specifically: "Exposed surfaces are defined as exterior areas when all access doors are in place & control surfaces are in faired position."[3]

There is no doubt, therefore, that the decal, or placard, was on the exterior of the airplane, and not within the stairwell of the ventral airstair. It could not, in any plausible circumstances, have been removed by the hijacker.

Bruce Kitt, a former airframe and power plant mechanic at Northwest, and now president of the Northwest Airlines History Center, recalls:

> **Yes, this placard was affixed to the outside of the fuselage. As my memory recalls, it was located just ahead of the panel that was secured by 2 spring-loaded clips which concealed the emergency handle.[4]**

To this day, part number BAC27DPA-152 is available for sale from airplane parts and accessories suppliers in the USA and China. It is described as a "marker" for Boeing aircraft (not only the 727, but also the 737 series).[5]

Neither the fragment found in 1978 nor the example that Northwest furnished to the FBI has any sign of holes for rivets, screws, or other fixtures. We can assume therefore that the placard is intended to be attached to the plane by an adhesive that will hold it in place at airspeeds up to 519 knots[6] and at temperatures down to –50 degrees C. This is not a placard that can be readily detached by human effort.

The placard found near Castle Rock was clearly linked to an airstair (though not necessarily a ventral airstair, as installed on the 727), and it had an identifiable Boeing part number. Probably on the hypothesis that the placard was from a Boeing 727, and possibly from Flight 305, the discovery of the placard generated a brief flurry of activity.

On December 6, 1978, the FBI had a further interview in Minneapolis, with a Northwest Airlines pilot who had been one of the crew of Flight 305 and had been aboard the same airplane, N467US, on the "sled test" flight back on January 6, 1972. The unnamed respondent was probably Harold Anderson, who had been second officer on Flight 305 and appeared in a group photograph of the "sled test" flight. He recalled that

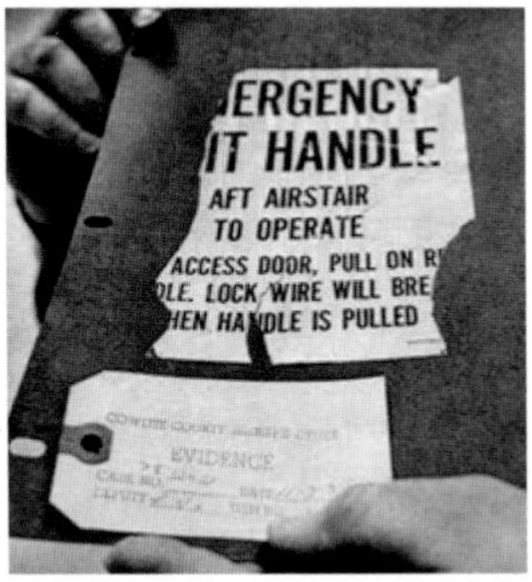


**Figure 10.1.** The airstairs decal found on November 8, 1978, displayed at Cowlitz County Sheriff's Department. *Image credit: AP, seattlepi.com*

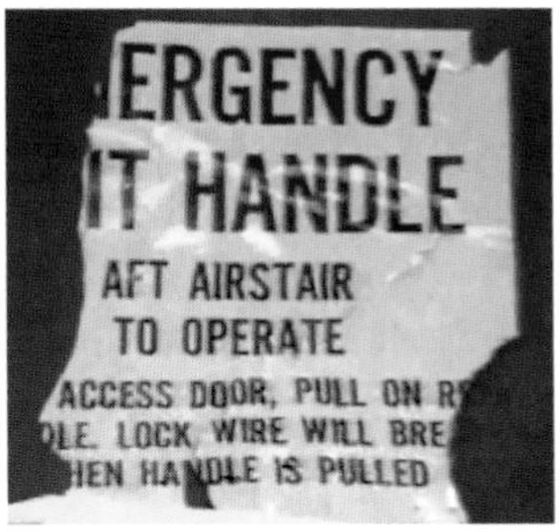


**Figure 10.2.** The airstairs decal found on November 8, 1978, as filmed by KIRO television station, Seattle. *Image credit: KIRO TV*

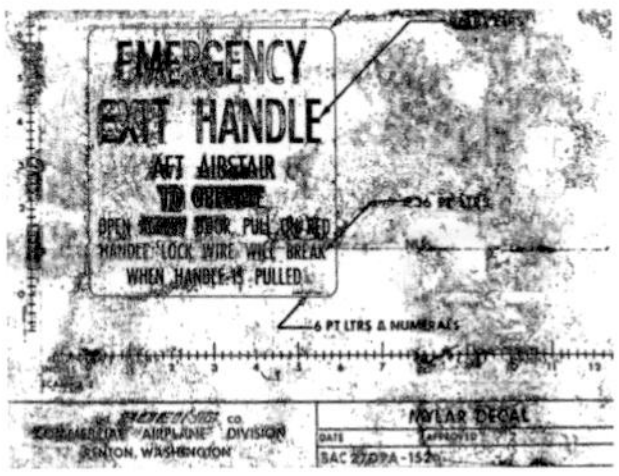


**Figure 10.3.** Boeing decal, part number BAC27DPA152, as furnished by Northwest Airlines to FBI. *Image credit: FBI*

**he and [redacted] took the same aircraft . . . in order to determine whether or not there was a change in pressure at the time [the hijacker] parachuted from the aircraft. [Redacted] recalls that he and [redacted] flew out over the ocean and ran their theory and returned to Seattle, Washington. He noted after returning to Seattle, that decals had come off the aircraft.[7]**

The Northwest Airlines pilot did not say which decals had come off the airplane during the flight over the Pacific, nor did he say (and nor was he asked) whether any decal had detached from the airplane on November 24, 1971, when it was operating as Flight 305. However, FBI spokesperson Ray Mathis would later tell the press that it was only after the "sled test" flight that they were aware that decals were missing from N467US:

**We noticed the decal was missing after that [the sled test flight], but not before.[8]**

This statement seemed to allow the possibility that a decal or decals had fallen from Flight 305 on November 24, 1971, but that their absence was not noticed until January 6, 1972, during which period the airplane must have been flying daily.

Returning to the placard discovery: by January 1979, there had been two new developments. First, the finder had been publicly identified:

**Earlier this week Cowlitz County Sheriff Les Nelson disclosed the discovery of the decal last November by Carroll Hicks, a self-employed welder from Kelso who was elk hunting when he found the bit of debris. . . . The 10-inch square decal [actually 6 inch by 6 inch] has stirred wide interest.[9]**

Second, the FBI was no longer ready to admit to an association between the placard and Flight 305.

**An FBI agent here said this morning that the piece of plastic decal found by a Kelso hunter last November could have dropped from any Boeing 727. . . . The placards, used to give emergency directions for the rear door on 727s, have been known to fall off under normal conditions.[10]**

A Boeing spokesperson supported this comment:

**Those placards have been known to fall off on the runway.[11]**

In backing away from a link between the placard and Flight 305, the FBI agents had a valid argument. They might have already discovered that the placard was an item intended for use on Boeing 737s as well as 727s. They would have been aware from the Northwest blueprints that the placard would have been affixed on the exterior of the airplane and could not have been removed by the hijacker. They would also have known that there were many daily flights between Seattle and Portland, which would generally fly much the same route as Flight 305. Northwest alone had ten such flights per day, counting only those operated by 727s. In the seven years since the hijacking, there had been at least 25,000 flights of Boeing 727s over the vicinity of Castle Rock, and, in principle, any one of them could have lost a placard.

While in public the FBI was downplaying the significance of the placard, in private they continued talking to Northwest Airlines. As of July 1979, at least one person in Northwest was sure, against all statistical probability, that the placard was from Flight 305, and at the same time had doubts about it:

> **[Redacted] Northwest Orient Airlines . . . advised that there is a ninety-nine per cent chance at this decal came from the same aircraft hijacked by D. D. [*sic*] Cooper.**
>
> **[Redacted] noted that the decals placed on the aircraft are bright red in lettering and that the one recovered in Washington and displayed to him appears to be more maroon. . . . This, of course, could be accounted for by the weather conditions. The second thing noted by [redacted] is that the decal does not appear to be as worn as one would think after having been located in the out[-]state area for the past eight years.[12]**

With that, as far as we know, the placard dropped out of the FBI's reckoning. Nothing in the public record indicates that the FBI ever searched the area where the placard was found, or conducted any form of cross-reference of the placard's location with its own presumptions of the trajectory of Flight 305. It fell to private citizens to continue the investigation.

## THE PRIVATE INVESTIGATION

We can imagine several rationales for the continuing private fascination with the airstair placard, including the following:

- Accepting that tens of thousands of flights had passed overhead Castle Rock in the intervening seven years, Flight 305 was certainly the only one that had flown with the airstair down.
- Accepting that the placard had been on the exterior of the airplane, and therefore beyond any plausible reach of the hijacker, the lowered airstair could have generated a turbulent airflow that might have weakened the attachment.
- The airplane that operated Flight 305, tail number N467US, had first flown in 1965. The adhesive that held the placard could have weakened in the six years from then until the hijacking.

In any event, from 1979 until today, much of the effort of private researchers has focused on establishing whether the location of the placard implies an alternative flight path to that depicted by the "FBI map" or "Air Force map."

For at least thirty years, the location was known only from the Cowlitz County Sheriff's Department as "about 12 miles east of Castle Rock." The city of Castle Rock, in Cowlitz County, has coordinates of 46°16'26"N, 122°54'18"W. On the reasonable assumption that the sheriff's report referred to statute miles and not nautical miles, this description would place the placard discovery at about 46°16'26"N, 122°39'4"W.[13] This point is 2.9 nautical miles (about 18,000 feet) east of the centerline of the Victor 23 airway.

Carroll C Hicks, the finder of the placard, died in 1995. Sometime between 2007 and 2010, the Citizen Sleuths team headed by Tom Kaye made contact with Hicks's family and identified the location where Hicks had discovered the placard. The family accompanied Kaye to that location, where with his handheld GPS, he recorded the coordinates as 46.243157°N, 122.683612°W, or 46°14'35.37"N, 122°41'1"W.[14] This point is 1.3 nautical miles (8,130 feet) east of the centerline of the Victor 23 airway. It is about 8 statute miles south of the town of Toutle, Washington, along a dirt track, and about 200 feet north of the track.

In 2018, researcher Robert Blevins published almost identical coordinates on the website of Adventure Books of Seattle: 46.244000°N, 122.683694°W, or 46°14'38.4"N, 122°41'1.3"W.[15] This spot is about 308 feet north of the point reported by Kaye.

In essence we have two distinct points that represent the placard discovery, as shown in the map below.

We may now inquire whether these locations permit any inference about the position of the airplane from which the placard fell.

We shall take Kaye's coordinates as the most reliable estimate of the placard location.

Let us for the moment ignore the "FBI map" and assume that Flight 305 was traveling along the centerline of Victor 23 (as it had been authorized by Seattle air traffic control). Prior to reaching the town of Toutle, Washington, Flight 305 had to pass the waypoint known by the FAA code MALAY, at latitude 46°25'21.99"N, 122°45'39.29"W, 63.55 nautical miles from Seattle-Tacoma.

MALAY has nothing to do with the Malay language or Malaysia; it is just a five-letter code, one of thousands in the FAA system, and one of the few that form a recognizable word.

Prior to reaching MALAY, Flight 305 should have been traveling on the 197° radial from Seattle-Tacoma (that is, 17 degrees west of due south). At MALAY, in order to keep on the

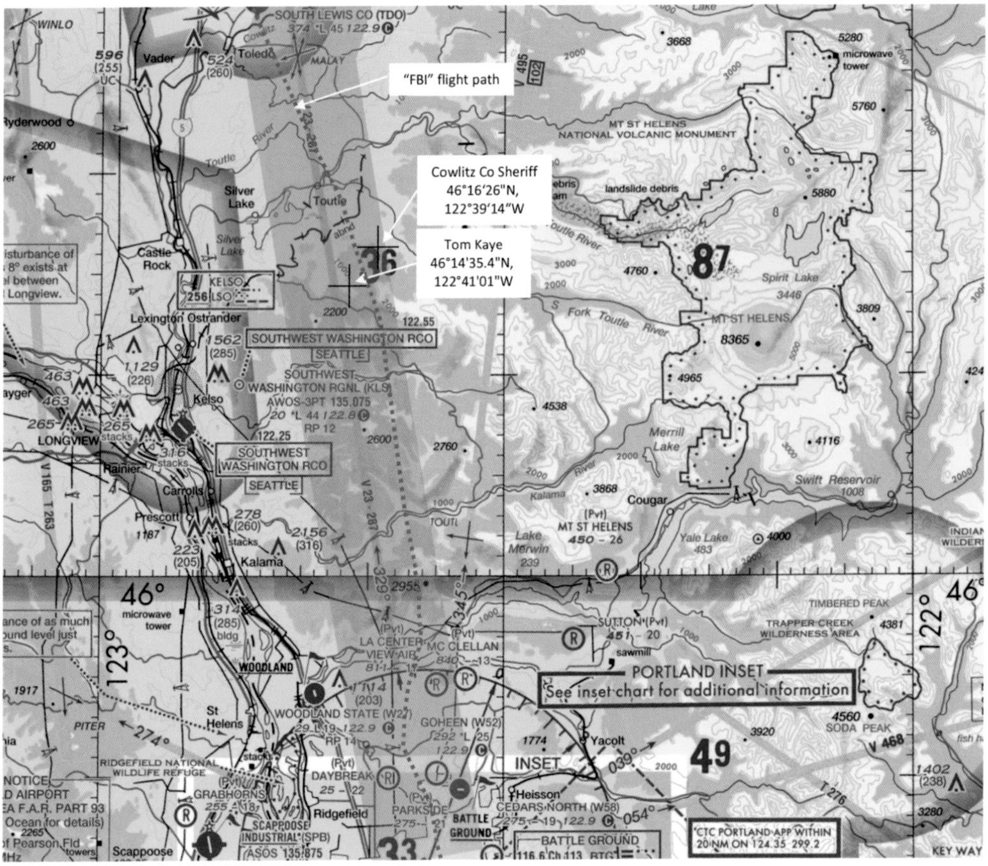


**Figure 10.4.** The two reported locations of the placard discovery, in comparison with Victor 23 airway and the FBI flight path of NWA305. *Base map from FAA Sectional Chart no. 97, Seattle region, scale 1:500,000; graphic by author*

centerline, it would need to turn 27 degrees to port and establish on the 170° radial to Battle Ground. The crew would know that they were on this radial by switching one of their navigation aids to the frequency of the VORTAC at Battle Ground. If they performed this maneuver accurately, after passing MALAY they would be on a track of 170 degrees (10 degrees east of due south) and would remain so when they crossed the latitude of the placard location.

At this moment, as we noted earlier, Flight 305 would be 1.3 nautical miles west of where the placard was found, and 11.25 nm south of MALAY. Adding the 63.55 nm from Seattle-Tacoma to MALAY, Flight 305 would have traveled 74.8 nm since takeoff. We can now attempt to estimate the time at which this occurred. For this, we need to know the ground speed of the airplane.

We estimated in chapter 4 that between Seattle-Tacoma and Tualatin, the average ground speed of the airplane was between 179 and 187 knots.

Returning to the segment from Seattle-Tacoma to Toutle, we have limited means of knowing whether the ground speed was slower or faster than the average. We know that this segment included the climb to 10,000 feet, and that an airplane is normally slower in the climb than in level flight. But by order of the hijacker, Flight 305 had landing gear and flaps down and was limited to an indicated airspeed of about 170 knots even in the cruise. Likewise, we have so little information on the weather conditions in this segment that we do not know whether the wind might have pushed Flight 305 along or slowed it down. So the best we can do is assume that over the first 75 or so nautical miles, Flight 305 was averaging 179 to 187 knots over the ground.

If so, having taken off from Seattle-Tacoma at 7:36 p.m., Flight 305 arrived abeam the placard location after twenty-three to twenty-six minutes; that is, between 7:59 and 8:02 p.m.

We may now refer to the radio communications to see whether we can detect any sign of the loss of a placard.

From the communications with Seattle air traffic control, which were recorded to the nearest second, we know that at 7:44:22 p.m., Flight 305 had temporarily stopped the climb and was holding an altitude of 7,000 feet, and that the aft airstair was down. At 7:50:05 p.m. the controller at position R2 gave Flight 305 the altimeter setting for Toledo (which they did not acknowledge, but from which we know that the flight was still north of Toledo, and therefore north of MALAY). At 7:53:34 p.m., Flight 305 reported leveling off at 10,000 feet; it had taken them seventeen minutes to complete the climb, and a few seconds later they reported their indicated airspeed as around 170 to 180 knots. In the critical period from then until 8:13:14 p.m., the transcript is silent (or has been redacted).

If we turn to the transcript of the communications on the ARINC frequency, our understanding is constrained by uncertainties in the timing. The crew spoke to the company (and to anyone else listening on this frequency) without making references to the time; there was no reason why they should. A teletype operator, probably in Minneapolis, transcribed what he or she heard, in highly abbreviated form, and periodically hit the "send" key, which generated a time stamp. All we know of the timing is that each block of text was bracketed by time stamps. The delay between the voice transmission and the time stamp could be as much as four minutes.

Between the time stamps for 7:57 and 8:01 p.m., the ARINC transcript records a report from the crew that Flight 305 was at 10,000 feet (this agrees with what the crew had told air traffic control at 7:53:34 p.m.) and that it would stay at that altitude until "he" (meaning the hijacker) had left. Between the time stamps for 8:03 and 8:05 p.m., the transcript records that after two attempts by the crew to contact him, the hijacker had spoken on the public address system and had said that everything was "OK."

An unknown observer in Northwest operations made a note at 8:05 p.m.: "last contact with hijacker."[16]

As far as we can determine, between 7:59 and 8:02 p.m. the aft airstair was down (and indeed had been down for at least fifteen minutes), and the hijacker was still in the passenger cabin. If Flight 305 lost a placard during this interval, it must have departed without the intervention of the hijacker.

It remains conceivable that Flight 305 lost a placard a few minutes later and that as the airplane continued southward, the placard drifted northward and eastward to arrive where Carroll Hicks would find it, or one like it, nearly seven years later. To examine this hypothesis, we have to know something about the aerodynamics of lightweight rectangular objects.

In the voluminous archive of internet correspondence and discussion on the airstair placard, we have found just one reference to an empirical study of falling flat plates. This study, identified by courtesy of researcher Robert Nicholson, is titled "Free-Fall Rotation and Aerodynamic Motion of Rectangular Plates."[17] The study reports on a series of experiments conducted by Sandia Laboratories in 1966, in which eighteen rectangular wooden boards were dropped from a stationary helicopter, of which eight boards were dropped at an altitude of 10,000 feet above ground level.

The altitude of these tests is nearly a perfect match for the path of Flight 305, which, if it flew overhead Toutle, would have been about 9,500 feet above terrain. Conversely, the boards used in the Sandia tests had dimensions of 32 × 27 × 0.69 inches and weighed 40 pounds; we would have to think hard about whether their flying qualities would resemble those of a plastic placard weighing a few ounces.

For what it is worth, in the Sandia tests the boards dropped from 10,000 feet covered horizontal distances, from release to impact, of between 1,500 and 6,000 feet; their terminal velocities were between 80 and 86 feet per second, and by our estimates the descent times were between 119 and 126 seconds. The study did not record in which directions the boards traveled between release and impact, or the speed and direction of the wind during the tests. Of the eight boards, five impacted the ground in good condition or with minor damage.

In 2018, James E Brunk, former president of Alpha Research Inc., conducted a research project that more closely approximated the fall of the airstair placard.[18] Brunk's research was aimed at an understanding of the descent characteristics of various aerodynamic objects. In particular, he examined rectangular paper plates with an aspect ratio, or width-to-length ratio, of between 0.17 and 3.0 (the placard was exactly square, with an aspect ratio of 1.0), and he focused on thin plates, with a thickness of 0.1 percent of the length (probably comparable to the placard).

Brunk's experiments showed that thin rectangular plates could achieve steady gliding flight. With regard to the Boeing placard, Brunk told this author that:

> **The maximum possible aerodynamic dispersion by configuration glide angle in autorotative descent would be an angle of 23–34 degrees from vertical. This is due to the inherent lift/drag ratio of an autorotating thin square plate. However, the point of ground impact could be anywhere within the intersection of the described cones. The average descent rate of about 25 fps in auto-rotative descent would allow additional dispersion due to atmospheric wind. This vector could be added separately. Descent rate is average of 10,000 ft. to sea level.**[19]

The cones within which a thin flat object would fall, according to Brunk's research, are illustrated in figure 10.5 below.

The placard was found at a location about 500 feet above sea level. A placard falling from 10,000 feet to the ground in still wind could land up to 6,700 feet horizontally from its departure point and would take about 380 seconds to reach the ground. If there were a horizontal wind of, say, 15 knots or 25 feet per second, the placard would be carried an additional 9,500 feet horizontally in the direction of the wind.

We recall that the placard location, as measured by Tom Kaye, was 8,130 feet east of the centerline of Victor 23. Brunk's experiments showed that a lightweight placard could travel a similar distance horizontally. If Flight 305 had been overhead Toutle between 7:59 and 8:02 p.m., and a placard would take six minutes to reach the ground, this permits the possibility that Flight 305 could have lost the placard between 8:05 and 8:08 p.m. At this time the hijacker was still in the passenger cabin, and the placard, if it fell from Flight 305, could have departed without the hijacker's intervention. Indeed it must have done so if, as Northwest told the FBI, the placard was on the outside of the airplane.

At this point, we may return to the "FBI map," the origin of which remains unknown to this day, even, it is said, to those few FBI agents who are willing to discuss it. In the segment between MALAY and Battle Ground, this map shows a flight path that is mostly to the east of the centerline of Victor 23. Where the flightpath crosses the latitude of the placard location, it is about 4,300 feet east of that location. Compared to the centerline, this would be an even-shorter distance for a lightweight object to travel.

From the Sandia experiments, and from James Brunk's research, we know that between 10,000 feet and the ground, a lightweight flat object can easily travel a mile or more horizontally. We do not know what direction it may take.

Furthermore, we do not know whether the placard found by Hicks came from Flight 305 or from one of tens of thousands of other overflights of the Toutle area.

Finally, we have no evidence to link the hijacker with the placard.

At the end of the day, we can say only that the placard is consistent with any flight by a Boeing 727 (possibly even a Boeing 737) on the Victor 23 airway. The placard discovery is not a challenge to the "FBI map" or a basis for a hypothesis of an alternative path of Flight 305.

The last word must surely rest with Bruce Kitt:

> **I clearly remember replacing worn placards for the airstair during my years as an A&P mechanic at Northwest. We edge[-]sealed all external placards with a 3M product to help delay the airflow from lifting the edges and prematurely fraying them away. Mother nature and airflow always win, it was the best we could do.[20]**

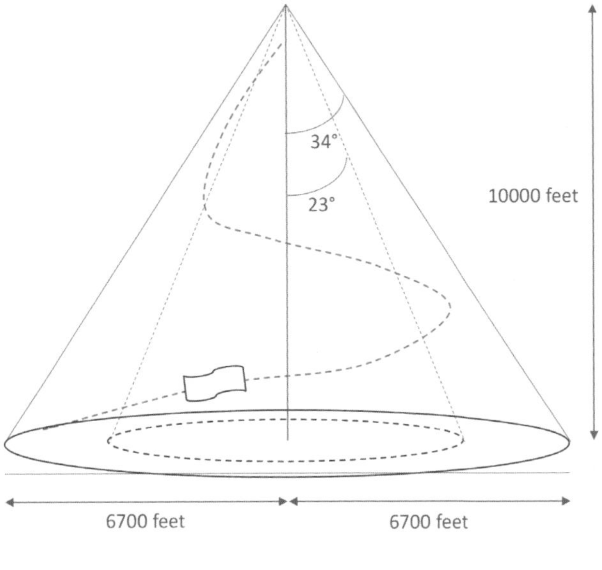


**Figure 10.5.** An illustration of the possible descent paths of a thin flat object falling from 10,000 feet above ground level. *Data by courtesy of James Brunk. Graphics by author*

CHAPTER

11

# TENA BAR

In 1980, a discovery occurred that would permanently change the nature and direction of the case of Flight 305.

The facts that we can set down with certainty or with confidence are simply stated:

- On February 10, 1980, Brian Ingram, aged eight, was on a camping trip with his parents at a beach known as Tena Bar on the Columbia River, in Clark County, Washington. A few inches below the surface of the sand, he found three bundles of decomposed $20 bills, each bundle held together by rubber bands, which were intact but brittle. The bundles contained the remains of 290, or by some accounts 294 identifiable bills, with a total face value of $5,800 or $5,880.
- The FBI cross-referenced every readable serial number against the numbers of the ransom money that Northwest Airlines had handed over to the hijacker of Flight 305 on November 24, 1971. Every number was a match.
- No other bill from the ransom money was ever found.
- In March 2009, the Citizen Sleuths team led by Tom Kaye visited Tena Bar and estimated that the location of Brian Ingram's discovery was latitude 45.717888 N, longitude 122.759500 W.[1]
- In March 2021, researcher Eric Ulis revisited Tena Bar and made a slightly different estimate, that the location of the discovery was latitude 45.718591 N, longitude 122.759434 W. This point was 257 feet north of Kaye's estimate.[2]

- These two points are 6.56 nautical miles west of the centerline of the Victor 23 airway at the same latitude: in other words, 2.56 nautical miles outside the Victor 23 corridor.

We now turn to the public records of the FBI, in an effort to decipher what the bureau made of this discovery.

On February 12, 1980, an FBI agent, accompanied by the sheriff of Clark County, visited Richard Fazio, who with his brother Al owned the beach and the adjoining farmland, and advised Fazio of the FBI's desire to search the area. For this, apparently Fazio gave the FBI his permission.[3]

The public files of the FBI, to this day, have never disclosed exactly what investigation then took place. However, it is known that on February 12 or 13, the FBI called in Dr. Leonard A. Palmer, an associate professor of geology at Portland State University. Accompanied by FBI agents and deputies from the Clark County Sheriff's Department, Dr. Palmer excavated a trench several feet deep in the beach at Tena Bar, and a hole around the spot where Brian Ingram had found the money. On February 15, the FBI left the site.[4] By February 22, the trench and the hole had been filled in.[5] The FBI has never publicly disclosed the dimensions or the geographical coordinates of the trench or the hole.

Dr. Palmer's report to the FBI is known only from an interview dated February 13, 1980,[6] in which his name is redacted. One of his most important observations, and one that came to dominate all subsequent research and discussion regarding the money discovery, was that:

> **US Corps of Engineering records . . . reflect that they dredged the Columbia River at this site in 1974.[7]**

The US Army Corps of Engineers indeed had been dredging the Columbia River for decades. Their report for fiscal year 1974 includes the following reference to navigation work on the Columbia and Lower Willamette Rivers below Vancouver, Washington, and Portland, Oregon:

> **Existing project. Provides for . . . a channel 40 feet deep and 600 feet wide from Vancouver, Wash., river mile 105.5 to mouth of Columbia River, river mile 3.[8]**

This part of the Columbia River project would clearly have included the dredging of the navigable channel at the point where it passes Tena Bar, which is approximately abeam river mile 96.

The FBI's interviews with the Corps of Engineers confirm that the corps had dredged that section of the river in the summer and fall of 1974:

> **[Redacted] . . . advised that the only dredging operation between November 24, 1971[,] and the present in the vicinity of the [redacted; probably Fazio property] was during August 6 through September 18, 1974. Material dredged from the river channel in the Columbia River was placed in several locations on or near the [redacted] as well as one location across the river on the Oregon side. The dredge material deposited at the site where the money was located came from the north half of the ship channel, which is 300 feet wide, between river mile 96 plus 38 feet and river mile 97 plus 17 feet. This material was deposited on the beach area of the [redacted] between August 19 through the 25th, 1974, and consisted of 91,100 cubic yards of fill.[9]**

Since at Tena Bar the Columbia River runs slightly east of north, the reference to the "north half of the ship channel" must mean what a layman would call the western half; that is, the Oregon side of the channel.

The Corps of Engineers also provided the FBI with aerial photographs of Tena Bar from August 1970, September 1974, and September 1979. The photographs from 1974 show clearly where the dredging spoil had been deposited. The dredged material was apparently deposited in two approximately equal piles, each of which, we could assume, contained about 45,000 cubic yards of material. The piles were then bulldozed into approximately circular shapes. If we guess that the two resulting discs of material were about 6 feet thick, they would each have had an area of about 22,500 square yards and a radius of about 85 yards.[10] If they were thicker, the radius would be correspondingly smaller.

The Corps of Engineers did not describe the composition of the fill: whether it was sand, clay, or some other material. Possibly a geographer or hydrologist would know the nature of the riverbed on the Oregon side, between river miles 96 and 97. The composition, location, and dimension of the dredged deposits are relevant to our understanding of the money discovery, for reasons that will become clear.

Returning to the FBI's interview with Dr. Palmer, the transcript of this interview has three themes: the observed stratification of the material in the beach, the observed condition of the money as found, and Dr. Palmer's hypotheses as to how the money could have arrived where it was found.

The stratification of the beach, as reported by Dr. Palmer, was as follows:

- Within the trench that he had excavated, the beach had four distinct layers.
- The top layer consisted of 6 to 8 inches of "reworked" beach sand. The term "reworked" seems to mean that the sand had been repeatedly redistributed by water action. This was the layer in which the money had been found. This layer also contained beverage cans and other debris, which were not severely corroded.
- The layer immediately below was sand, which Dr. Palmer believed had been deposited after the 1974 dredging. This layer contained beverage cans, nails, spikes, and other metallic objects, which were much more corroded.
- The layer below was "a mixture of coarse sand and fragments of organic clay material, ranging from one inch to five inches in size," which in Dr. Palmer's view had been deposited during the dredging. This layer was 2 feet below the surface at the site of the money discovery, and 4 feet below the surface at a distance of 25 yards.
- The lowest layer excavated consisted of sands "which were light in color and uniform in texture" and were assumed to have been deposited prior to the dredging.

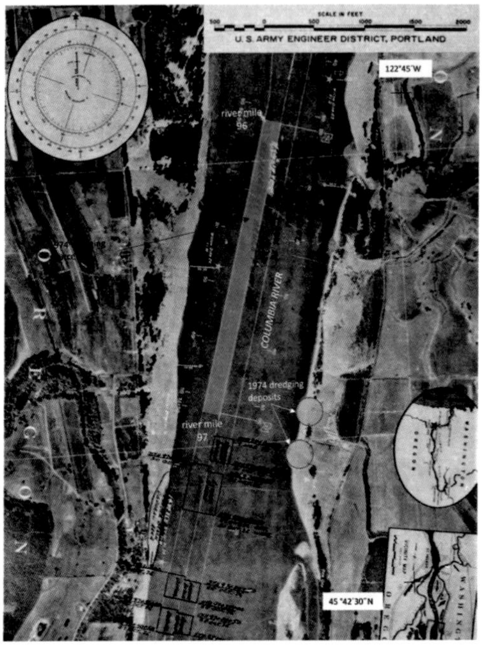


**Figure 11.1.** Tena Bar, Clark County, Washington, August–September 1974: source and destination of dredged material. *Aerial photo by courtesy of US Army Corps of Engineers; graphics by author*

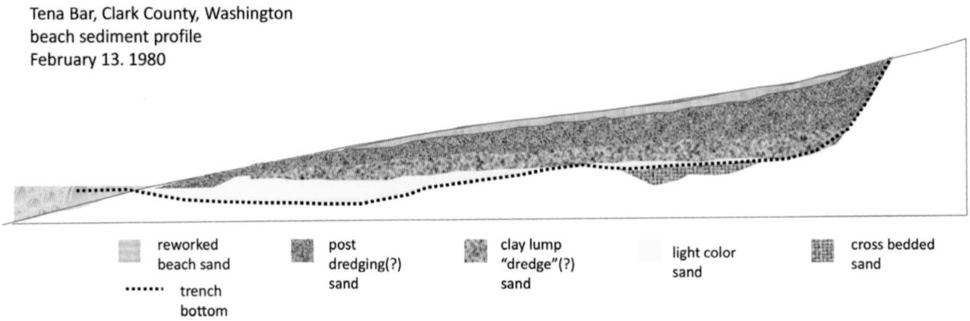


**Figure 11.2**. Tena Bar, Clark County, Washington, February 10, 1980: beach sediment profile. Question marks are from original. No scale was given on the original. *Graphic by author based on FBI, D.B. Cooper Part 43 of 46.pdf, p. 372, document reference SE164-81-8296, footnote DB Cooper-17604, dated February 14, 1980*

Dr. Palmer reported the condition of the money as follows:

- The bills were in much-better condition than he would have expected if they had been exposed to "nature" (which we interpret to mean the open air). Their condition was consistent with prolonged preservation in sterile sand.
- The corners of the bills had become rounded, which Dr. Palmer interpreted to mean that the bills had rolled and become eroded while being transported by water.
- The rubber bands were in place but were badly deteriorated and crumbled upon touch.

The hypotheses that Dr. Palmer advanced for the history of the money were as follows:

> The money had been buried in clean sand for most of the time since it had been "lost."
>
> The money had been deposited on Tena Bar at least four years after the last dredging; that is, after August 1978.
>
> "The money was probably washed into the location where it was found by natural river flow and was probably placed at the location of Tena Bar during the last rise in the Columbia River in the past two or three months." [which we interpret as the period from November 1979 to February 1980]

An enigma must have been immediately apparent to the FBI. If these hypotheses were to be accepted, the money had reached Tena Bar between 1978 and 1980, and more likely later in that period than earlier. If so, its whereabouts at least between 1971 and 1978 had been elsewhere than Tena Bar, and during this period it had been protected against decomposition. But where, and how?

## THE WASHOUGAL WASHDOWN

At this juncture in the interview, Dr. Palmer made an extraordinary and unsolicited claim, which at face value seems entirely out of context with a geological investigation.

> **[Redacted] displayed a U.S. Geological Survey-Topographical Map, Bridal Veil Washington—Oregon Section, which reflected a twelve[-]mile cross section of the drainage basin for the Washougal River. It is from this area [redacted] felt the money likely originated from.**[11]

Until this moment, there had been no mention of the Washougal River. There is no indication that the FBI brought up the subject. The Washougal is the first northern tributary of the Columbia River upstream from Tena Bar. It rises in Skamania County, Washington, crosses westward into Clark County, and joins the Columbia at the town of Washougal, east of Vancouver.

There is no doubt that Dr. Palmer was referring to the USGS topographic map of the *Bridal Veil Quadrangle*, scale 1:62500, which is still available today. This map, in its northwest corner, includes an area of about 10 by 6 statute miles that depicts part of the course of the Washougal River.

However, the center of the *Bridal Veil Quadrangle* is approximately 21 nautical miles east of the centerline of Victor 23 (therefore, about 17 nautical miles outside the Victor 23 corridor).

In order to accept the Washougal hypothesis even as a basis for further investigation, the FBI had to believe the following:

- that Flight 305 had been up to 17 nautical miles outside its authorized air corridor, without informing air traffic control or Northwest Airlines operations
- that the hijacker had landed sufficiently close to the Washougal River either to let slip, or intentionally to discard, three bundles of bills in the river
- that over a period of eight years, the bills had made their way approximately 12 miles downstream to the Columbia River, and approximately 20 miles downstream the Columbia to arrive at Tena Bar

Flight 305, Victor 23 airway and Washougal River

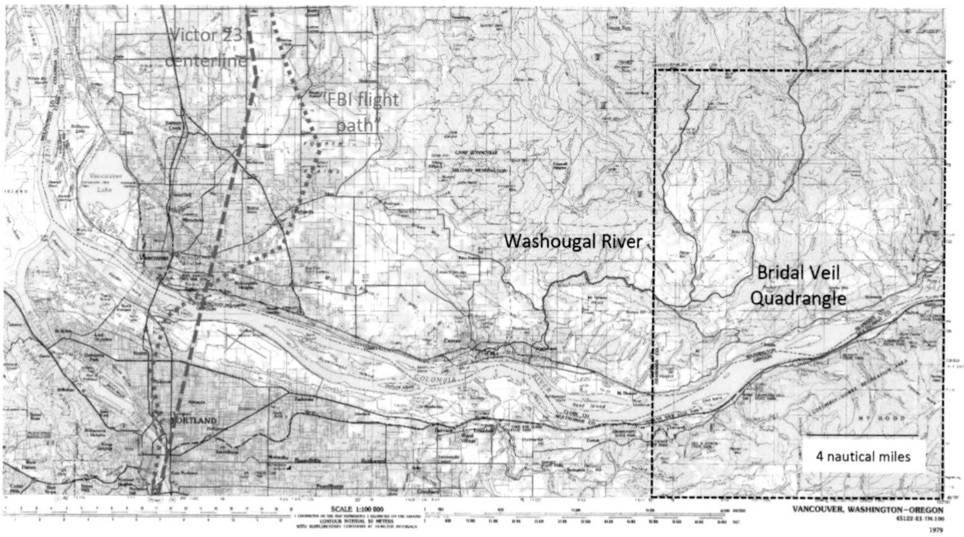


Base map from USGS, Vancouver Quadrangle, scale 1:100,000. Graphics by author.

**Figure 11.3**. Flight 305 track, Victor 23 airway and the Washougal River, Washington. *Base map from USGS,* Vancouver Quadrangle, *scale 1:100,000; graphics by author*

- that during these eight years, the three bundles had remained attached to each other, and the rubber bands had not crumbled away
- that during these eight years, the bills had remained in sufficiently good condition as to resemble bills that had been preserved in sand

Despite the implausibility of this scenario, the "Washougal washdown theory" (as it came to be known) had traction.

Sometime in February 1980, the FBI commissioned a study of the flow patterns of the Columbia River:

**In February 1980, $5,800 in currency identified with this hijacking was recovered from the Tena Bar area of the Columbia River, just south of Vancouver. A flow study commissioned by the FBI at that time determined that the money had likely been naturally deposited in that location and had probably flowed down the Washougal River or one of its tributaries.**[12]

On March 16, 1980, *The Columbian* reported that Christopher J. Fiedler, described as the chief FBI geologist on the case of Flight 305, believed that the hijacker had landed in the Washougal River. By this time, the bills had been sent to the FBI Laboratory in Washington, where they had been tested for fingerprints (negative); for greases, oils, and amino acids (negative); and for sand particles (which were present). Fiedler based his view on the pronounced erosion of the sand particles, on their similarity with sand from the Columbia River and its tributaries, and on the absence of clays.

Despite the headline in *The Columbian*, Fiedler did not specify the Washougal as the sole possibility. What he actually said was this:

**He could have landed in the Columbia River, . . . Or he could have come down in the Washougal. The latter is where training, and instincts, tell me is more likely, based on the data I have available.**[13]

What training and what instincts led him to this inclination, Fiedler did not say.

To compound the confusion, Fiedler's view, which he described as personal, was rejected by his boss, the head of the mineralogy division, and did not form part of the FBI Laboratory's report to the principal investigators in Seattle.

Nothing in the public files of the FBI (at least in the 24,000+ pages released so far) indicates what that report said. We remain in the dark as to what the Seattle team learned from the FBI Laboratory.

Likewise, to this day it has never been explained why either Leonard Palmer or Chris Fiedler, both of them geologists, created a link in their minds between Tena Bar and the Washougal River, some 25 miles away. It is almost as if Sherlock Holmes, sifting particles of sand between his bony fingers on a beach of the Columbia River, had remarked to his friend Dr. Watson that *this sand* could be found in the Washougal, and *nowhere* else.

If we were asked to devise a thought process underlying Palmer's and Fiedler's hypothesis, we would have to guess that both had chosen to step outside the realms of geology and to construct a detective story. Both would have been aware of the FBI narrative, which had prevailed since 1971, that the hijacker of Flight 305 had landed in the region of Lake Merwin, some 25 miles north of the Columbia. Confronted with the money found on the bank of the

Columbia, they had to identify a river that could have carried that money southward. The closest such river was the Washougal.

At this point, our mining of the "FBI Vault" runs out of seams, and we have to turn to other sources. Here we acknowledge our debt to the original research conducted by Tom Kaye and the Citizen Sleuths, which is comprehensively documented at citizensleuths.com.

In March 2009, Kaye's team visited Tena Bar, where by that time the beach was severely eroded and the river was several feet below its level of previous years. The erosion had exposed several layers of clay, which appeared to be of natural origin. The team referred to FBI photographs of the excavations of 1980 and cross-referenced them against their own photographs of the few landmarks that remained. By these means they estimated the GPS location of the money find, thereby rectifying an egregious omission of the FBI.

Kaye's team was also able to locate aerial photographs of Tena Bar from September 6, 1974, and September 29, 1979, probably the same photographs that the Corps of Engineers had furnished to the FBI in February 1980. By September 1979, the dredging deposits were gone, no doubt washed away by the river. When Brian Ingram and his parents arrived in February 1980, they would have found a straight, flat beach.

The Kaye team's crucial insight was that the money discovery was outside the circle where the nearest dredging deposit had been, by a margin of at least 30 feet in a northerly direction.

It remained only for Eric Ulis to return in 2019 and 2021 and relocate the money discovery to a point 257 feet farther north (as shown in figure 11.4).

These two measurements essentially removed Brian Ingram's discovery not only from the physical frame of the dredging but also from its time frame. In other words, it was no longer necessary to assume that the dredging had preceded the arrival of the money on Tena Bar.

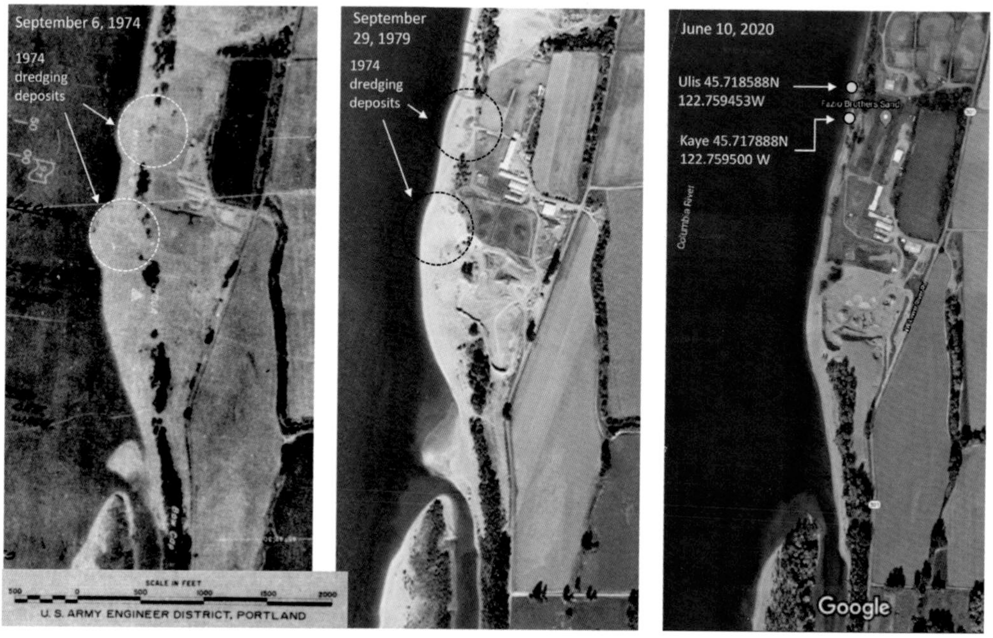


**Figure 11.4**. Tena Bar, Clark County, Washington: aerial photographs from 1974, 1979, and 2020. *Aerial photographs from 1974 and 1979 by courtesy of US Army Corps of Engineers. Kaye's coordinates by courtesy of citizen-sleuths.com, © Tom Kaye. Ulis coordinates by courtesy of thecoopercase.com, © Eric Ulis. Image dated 6.10.2020 © Google Maps. Graphics by author.*

This being the case, it became possible to imagine a scenario in which, from the moment that the hijacker had lost or discarded these three bundles of twenties, the money had traveled expeditiously to its final resting place on Tena Bar, where eight years later Brian Ingram would rediscover it.

When, how, and by what agency the money made this journey are issues that we shall now attempt to address.

## THE MONEY'S JOURNEY

We may first posit, without fear of contradiction, that the 290 or 294 twenties found by Brian Ingram arrived on Tena Bar by air, land, or water.

If the money arrived by air, it must have fallen either from Flight 305 or from another aircraft (in either case, possibly accompanied by the hijacker, or possibly not).

We know without doubt that the money was on board Flight 305 at 7:36 p.m. on November 24, 1971, and was no longer on board at 11:03 p.m. the same evening. For the money to fall from Flight 305 to Tena Bar, we require the airplane to have been at least 6.5 nautical miles from the Victor 23 centerline. For this excursion, there is no documentation, no witness report, and no physical evidence. On the contrary, we have at least two reports from the crew that they were on Victor 23: reports transmitted to their own employer on a private radio frequency. We have the "FBI map," admittedly of unknown authorship, which depicts a flight path entirely within Victor 23. We have the statement of Clifford Ammerman, the air traffic controller at Seattle Center, that Flight 305 was within the Victor 23 corridor throughout the period when it was under his tracking; that is, from near Battle Ground, Washington, to near Eugene, Oregon.

In short, we cannot sustain a hypothesis that the money fell from Flight 305.

If we are to propose a fall from an aircraft other than Flight 305, we require the money to reach the ground elsewhere (again, with or without the hijacker; in other words, intentionally or otherwise). We then require the money to be transferred to another aircraft—this second aircraft to fly over Tena Bar (intentionally or otherwise), and the money to fall or be thrown from the second aircraft to land on the beach at Tena Bar, there to be buried by the waves before anyone notices it. This does not have to happen in November 1971, but it has to happen by around 1978, in order for the money to degrade into the state in which it was found. The scenario is riveting, but the evidence for it is zero.

If the money arrives on Tena Bar by land, we require an agency of its transport. By Occam's razor, this agency has to be human. If human, the agent can be the hijacker, or an accomplice of the hijacker, or a person having no relationship with the hijacker. Here the possibilities become more colorful, since they skirt the realm of conjecture on the hijacker's personality and personal history. But we have vowed not to enter that realm. Therefore we must be content with delineating what must happen for any version of this hypothesis to work:

1. The hijacker lands on November 24, 1971, at a point not less than 6.5 miles away from Tena Bar (the nearest point on the centerline of Victor 23), and possibly over 20 miles away if we give credence to the FBI narrative of a landing near Lake Merwin. Either on that night or at some subsequent time, he travels unremarked to Lower River Road in Clark County, enters the Fazio brothers' property, and walks to the beach at Tena Bar. There he either buries three packs of money or (having come for another purpose entirely) accidentally loses them. An alternative version of this scenario is that he stores this money in another location and later transfers it to Tena Bar. Again, all these events have to happen between November 24, 1971, and around 1978, so that the money can deteriorate. This scenario strongly favors the night of the hijacking itself.

2. The hijacker lands on November 24, 1971, at a location that, in this scenario, is immaterial. At some subsequent time, he transfers three (or more) packs of money to an accomplice. This transfer may or may not be accompanied by instructions to the accomplice. The rest of this scenario is the same as the first, with the accomplice replacing the hijacker.

3. The hijacker lands on November 24, 1971, at a location that, in this scenario also, is immaterial. It is not necessary to assume that he survives the landing. Sometime during his time aboard Flight 305, or during his descent, or on landing, he discards or loses three (or more) packs of money. At some subsequent time, another person finds the three (or more) packs of money. The rest of this scenario is the same as the first and second, with the lucky or unlucky finder replacing the hijacker or his accomplice.

In all three of the "land transport" scenarios, the story is the stuff of screenplay but is based on no evidence whatsoever.

It remains for us to consider the arrival of the money on Tena Bar by the agency of water.

In this scenario, as a certainty we can say that the last stage of the money's journey was by the agency of the Columbia River. We must pose this question: Was this last stage a long or a short one?

For example, we can readily imagine a short journey by water, perhaps of no more than a few hundred feet, beginning when the three (or more) packs of money fall or are thrown from a ship in the Columbia River.

In this case, we have a version of the "land transport" scenario: a human agent is involved. Again, this person could be the hijacker, an accomplice, or an unrelated person; the only

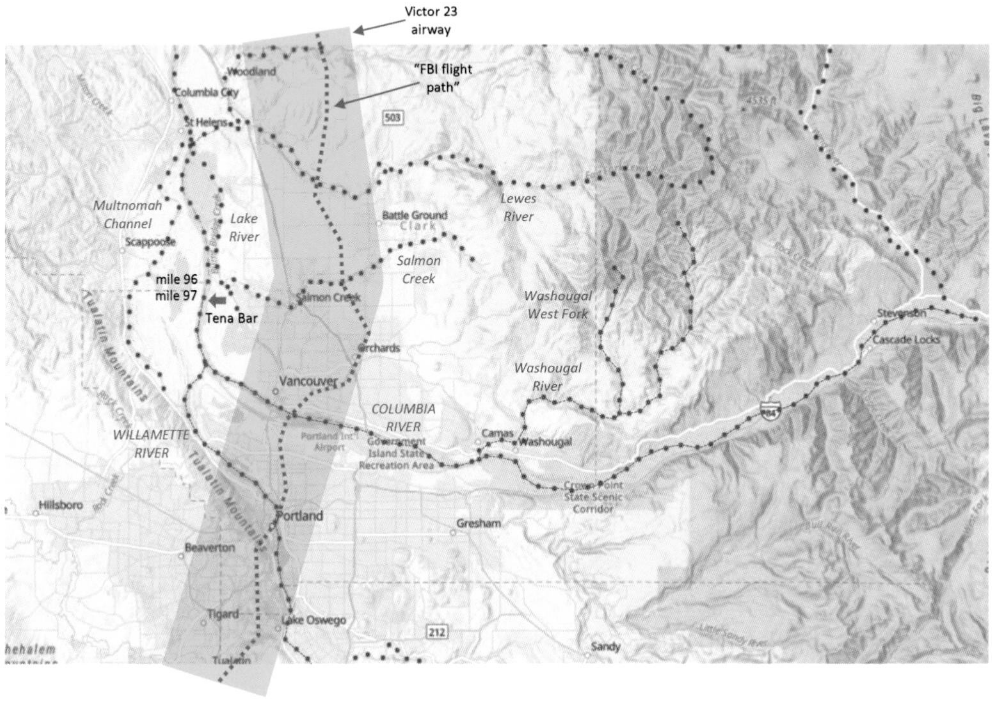


**Figure 11.5.** The Victor 23 airway, the "FBI flight path," and the Columbia River system in the area of Portland, Oregon. *Base map from ESRI; river mile markers from Washington Geospatial Open Data Portal; graphics by author*

difference is that the person is on a marine vessel and not on the beach. The motives and circumstances for the departure of the money have to remain in the realm of speculation. The vessel does not have to be passing Tena Bar; it can be anywhere upstream on the Columbia (may we be forgiven for excluding downstream locations). The time frame is the same; the money has to remain in the water long enough to lose its corners, and for the rubber bands to become brittle but not to break.

If a marine vessel is not involved, then we have to posit a journey in which the money floats down the Columbia to Tena Bar, and possibly, prior to that, in another river that feeds into the Columbia.

Here we can create scenarios with and without a human agency. Like Leonard Palmer and Christopher Fiedler, we can imagine the hijacker losing or intentionally discarding the bills in a river upstream of Tena Bar. We can imagine an accomplice or a third party doing the same. But we can also imagine the money entering the river system, with or without the hijacker, directly from Flight 305.

An examination of the relationship between Victor 23 and the Columbia River system illustrates how this could happen.

As figure 11.5 shows, upstream of Tena Bar there are several rivers that could be candidates for the transport of the three bundles to their final resting place: the Columbia itself, the Willamette, the two forks of the Washougal, and various tributaries farther upstream from the Washougal.

As we argued earlier, the Washougal is too far east of Victor 23 for us to imagine an intentional or even an accidental overflight of this river by Flight 305. The same applies to the tributaries of the Columbia that are farther east. But two rivers upstream of Tena Bar have sections that are directly below the Victor 23 corridor and, for what it is worth, directly below the path of Flight 305 that are central to the FBI narrative. They are the Columbia and the Willamette.

In a later chapter we will examine the circumstances in which the Columbia alone, or the Willamette and the Columbia together, could have transported three bundles of twenties to Tena Bar.

CHAPTER

# 12

# DIATOMS

On August 3, 2020, researchers Thomas G. Kaye and Mark Meltzer reported a remarkable discovery.[1] From a colleague known only by the username "377" on the internet forum dropzone.com, they had gained access to one of the $20 bills found by Brian Ingram at Tena Bar. They had obtained permission to remove four small samples, totaling about 1.5 square centimeters, from the edges of what remained of the bill. They had placed these samples under an electron microscope. They were looking for diatoms.

What we need to know about diatoms is this: They are tiny living creatures, each consisting of a single cell. They belong to a wider community known as phytoplankton, and in turn to the vast family of algae. They live in waterways. Some species form colonies in which groups of cells are attached to each other. The size of each cell is typically comparable to the width of a human hair. An individual cell lives for at most a few days. When a diatom dies, its shell sinks to the bed of the waterway.

On their four samples of the $20 bill, Kaye and Meltzer found approximately forty cells that could be identified as diatoms. About twenty-seven cells, apparently in four or five colonies, belonged to the genus[2] *Asterionella*; four cells, forming a single colony, were of the genus *Fragilaria*; and the other nine were of the genera *Stephanodiscus*, *Cyclotella*, *Cymbella*, or *Melosira*. These genera are common in some of the rivers, streams, and lakes of the Pacific Northwest.

The numbers of cells found by Kaye and Meltzer, and our interpretation of their published data, are summarized below.

**Table 12.1. Diatom cells identified on four samples from a US$20 bill recovered at Tena Bar, Washington, on February 10, 1980**

| Genus | Cells/cm² | Number of cells | Number of colonies |
|---|---|---|---|
| *Asterionella* | 16.1 | 27 | 4 or 5 |
| *Fragilaria* | 2.98 | 4 | 1 |
| *Stephanodiscus* | 1.79 | 3 | – |
| *Cyclotella* | 1.79 | 3 | – |
| *Cymbella* | 1.19 | 2 | – |
| *Melosira* | 0.6 | 1 | 1 |

Source: Cells/cm² from Kaye and Meltzer 2020, table 1; numbers of cells calculated by author; numbers of colonies of *Asterionella* and *Fragilaria* from Thomas G. Kaye (personal communication); others estimated by author

The identification of these diatoms constitutes the first tangible new evidence since 1980 in the case of Flight 305. This evidence opens the door to the possibility of an educated inference as to where the $20 bill had been prior to its discovery.

The first step is to attempt an identification of these diatoms at the species level. Mr. Kaye and Mr. Meltzer published photographs of their specimens of *Asterionella* and *Fragilaria*, which are reproduced below. Mr Kaye kindly provided this author with an unpublished photograph of a *Cymbella* cell. In the case of the sole *Fragilaria* colony, the photograph shows that the four cells were trapped between the sampled $20 bill and a fragment of another, long-disintegrated bill.

From these images, a reasonable inference would be that 3(A) shows four cells of *Asterionella formosa*, which is by far the most common species of *Asterionella* in the waterways of the Pacific Northwest; that 3(B) shows a single cell of *Cymbella tumida* (which this author identifies on the basis of the number of striae[3]); and that 3(C) shows four cells of *Fragilaria crotonensis*, which is one of several common species of *Fragilaria* in that region. This author suggested the identifications of the *Asterionella* and *Fragilaria* species to Mr. Kaye, who concurred, while cautioning that the power of the electron microscope available to him did not permit a definitive identification of the species.[4]

With this provisional inference, we may now embark on a voyage of discovery to find possible places where the diatoms might have encountered the $20 bill on their journey to Tena Bar.

We need first to remark that *Asterionella*, *Cyclotella*, *Cymbella*, *Fragilaria*, *Melosira*, and *Stephanodiscus* have no independent means of movement. They are carried by water currents. We can therefore imagine two possible scenarios in which, sometime between November 1971 and February 1980, a diatom becomes attached to a $20 bill.

In one scenario, the bill is stationary, perhaps still in a bag of some kind, on the bed of a waterway, and the diatom, haphazardly drifting in the current, falls into the bag and thence onto the bill. At the scale of a diatom, irregularities in the surface of the bill might be sufficiently large to trap the diatom.

In the second scenario, the bill is traveling downstream, either on the surface of the water or underwater. Again, perhaps it is in a bag, or perhaps it is traveling among the three bundles of bills, somehow attached to each other, that Brian Ingram will eventually find on Tena Bar.

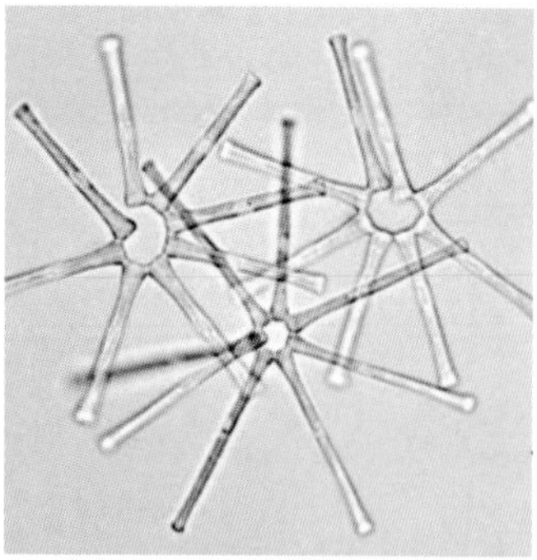

**Figure 12.1**. Two eight-cell colonies and one seven-cell colony of *Asterionella formosa*. *Courtesy of diatoms.org. Image credit: Jan Parmentier*

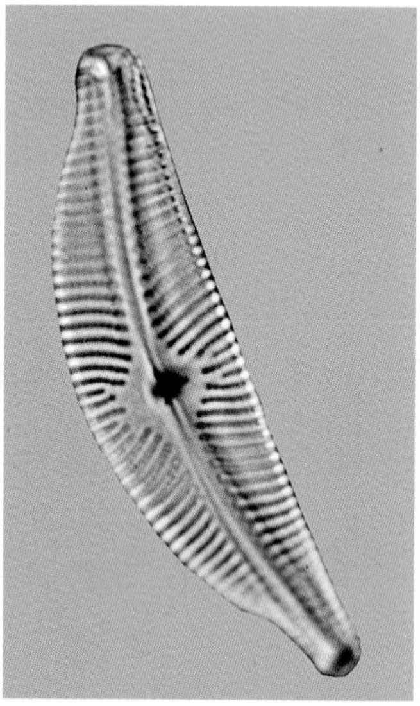

**Figure 12.2**. A single cell of *Cymbella tumida*. *Courtesy of Muséum national d'histoire naturelle. Image credit: D. Milan*

**Figure 12.3**. A six-cell colony of *Fragilaria crotonensis* from North Hills Pond, West Virginia. *Image credit: diatoms.org*

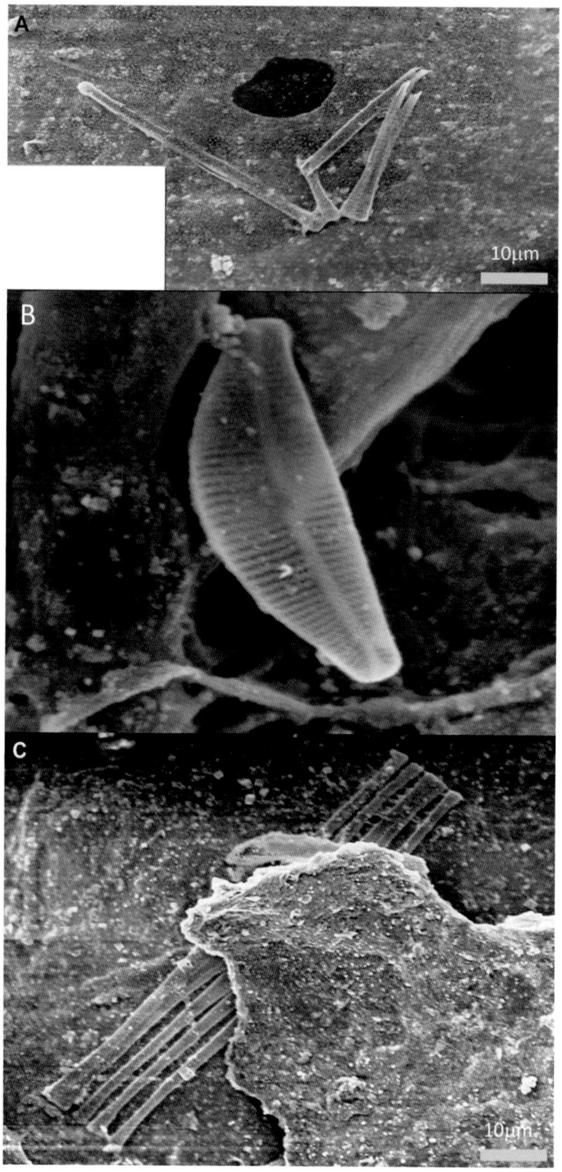


**Figure 12.4**. Examples of diatoms found on a US$20 bill retrieved from Tena Bar, Washington, on February 10, 1980. (A) a fragmented three-cell colony of *Asterionella*, (B) a single cell of *Cymbella*, and (C) a four-cell colony of *Fragilaria*. *Image credit: Thomas G Kaye and Mark Meltzer*

The diatom is traveling in the same channel, and by the chance movements of water, its trajectory converges with that of the bill.

To the layman, either scenario seems plausible, and we have no basis for rating one more probable than the other. We are therefore impelled to look both for stationary bodies of water, such as lakes, sloughs, and reservoirs, and for moving waterways, such as rivers, streams, and canals, in which our diatoms could have begun their brief existence.

Second, we may fruitfully consider the kinds of environment in which diatoms flourish. They are living creatures and need nutrients, which they absorb from water. In any given body of water, the more nutrients there are in the water, the more diatoms will bloom, and other things being equal, the greater the probability that this body of water will be the source of the diatoms on Tena Bar.

In this respect we may refer to diatoms.org for succinct descriptions of the preferred environments of *Asterionella formosa* and *Fragilaria crotonensis*:

> ***Asterionella formosa*** **is common in mesotrophic and eutrophic lakes globally and is one of the most common planktonic diatoms in these lakes in the northern hemisphere. . . . It has been increasing in presence and abundance in oligotrophic alpine lakes. This increase is interpreted as a response to atmospheric nutrient enrichment. . . .** ***Asterionella formosa*** **lives in colonies, joined by mucilage pads. The elongate shape of the frustules and the spiral colonies are resistant to sinking in their planktonic habitat.**[5]
>
> ***Fragilaria crotonensis*** **is a common species in temperate, mesotrophic lakes of North America. Cells can be joined in large ribbon-like colonies. These colonies are resistant to sinking in the water column and help** ***F. crotonensis*** **maintain position in the phytoplankton.** ***Fragilaria crotonensis*****, along with** ***Asterionella formosa*****, is considered a marker that the levels of reactive nitrogen (Nr) have increased above the threshold in oligotrophic lakes of the western United States.**[6]

Here we need to furnish definitions.

Still bodies of water, such as lakes and reservoirs, are often classified on the basis of their trophic state, which is a measure of their nutrient content. In essence, oligotrophic lakes are poor in nutrients (and therefore good sources of drinking water), eutrophic lakes are rich in nutrients (and not safe to drink from), and mesotrophic lakes are intermediate. There is no universal agreement on how to measure the trophic state, and therefore there is no definitive method of classification. For simplicity, we have adapted below a descriptive presentation from the Environmental Protection Agency.

**Table 12.2. Illustration of a trophic classification system based on lake characteristics**

| Indicator | General characteristics | | |
|---|---|---|---|
| | oligotrophic | mesotrophic | eutrophic |
| total production of aquatic plants | low | intermediate | high |
| number of algal species | many | intermediate | few |
| characteristic algal groups | green algae, diatoms | diverse | blue-green algae |
| rooted aquatic plants | sparse | intermediate | abundant |
| oxygen in bottom layer | present | intermediate | absent |

**Table 12.2. Illustration of a trophic classification system based on lake characteristics**

| | | | |
|---|---|---|---|
| characteristic fish | deep-dwelling, coldwater fish | diverse | surface-dwelling, warmwater fish |
| water quality for domestic and industrial use | good | intermediate | poor |
| | | | |

Source: United States Environmental Protection Agency, *Nutrient Criteria Technical Guidance Manual, Lakes and Reservoirs*, 1st ed., table 2.1 (Washington, DC: EPA, April 2000)

We therefore could start looking for the original breeding grounds of *Asterionella formosa* mainly in mesotrophic to eutrophic lakes (that is, lakes with medium to rich nutrients) and for *Fragilaria crotonensis* mainly in mesotrophic lakes (with intermediate nutrient production). In both cases we have to consider the lower probability, but still a possibility, that these diatoms might have originated in clear oligotrophic lakes and reservoirs, even those that provide drinking water to towns and cities in the Pacific Northwest.

Since the majority of the diatoms found on the bill from Tena Bar were *Asterionella*, we are predisposed to search in lakes that are toward the eutrophic (nutrient-rich) end of the spectrum.

Third, wherever the diatoms may have been born, they could have been flushed out of their original habitats and into streams and rivers. This phenomenon is common in the Pacific Northwest and typically results in seasonal blooms of diatoms in the major rivers, especially in the spring and early summer after rain. The abundance of diatoms can increase exponentially as the water flows downstream, which from a layman's viewpoint is as we might expect, considering that the water continuously collects nutrients in the form of runoff from farms and gardens.

Fourth, we recall that the $20 bill was found near river mile 95 of the Columbia River. If the diatoms encountered the bill through water transport and not through any human agency, then they must have originated upstream of river mile 95. In principle, that could include anywhere in the Columbia River and its myriad tributaries, even as far as the source of the Columbia in Canada. In practice, since diatoms live only a few days, we can reasonably confine our search to the basins of the lower Columbia River and the Willamette River.

With that preamble, we may start our search for sightings of *Asterionella* and *Fragilaria*, or identification of their habitats, in the waterways of Washington and Oregon.

It became apparent to us that there was no systematic or continuous monitoring of diatoms in these waterways.

We identified the following sources of data on the absolute or relative abundance of diatoms in Washington and Oregon over the last seventy years:

- the Environmental Protection Agency's *National Lakes Assessment* (NLA), which is normally scheduled to be conducted every five years but, at the time of writing, has been published only in respect of the fieldwork done in 2007 and 2012[7]
- the US Geological Survey's *National Water-Quality Assessment* (NAWQA), which covered the Willamette River basin between 1991 and 1995[8]
- Portland State University's *Atlas Of Oregon Lakes* (1985), which reported diatom measurements made in selected lakes between 1981 and 1982[9]

- the US Geological Survey's *Lakes of Oregon* series, volumes 2, 3, 4, and 5, which reported diatom measurements made in selected lakes in the Willamette River basin between 1971 and 1975[10]
- various ad hoc studies of the Columbia River at various sites between the estuary and the Hanford Reach, conducted between 1949–50 and 1981–82[11, 12]

Taking the last source first, we assembled diatom data for the Hanford Reach, at approximately river mile 377, for 1949–50; for the Columbia River between river miles 276 and 324 for the period 1951 to 1953; and for the Columbia estuary for 1981–82. These data are summarized and illustrated below.

From this illustration we were able to make the following observations:

- The abundance of diatoms in the Columbia River estuary was vastly greater than that in the Hanford Reach, by a factor of nearly 75, but since the respective data were thirty-two years apart, we could not determine whether this was a phenomenon that occurred in space (representing the presumably richer nutrients as the water moved downstream) or in time (representing the increasing industrialization and urbanization of Washington and Oregon between the 1940s and the 1980s).
- The genus *Asterionella* was a common diatom in all the samples. In the samples from the Columbia estuary, *Asterionella formosa* was the single most common species of diatom.

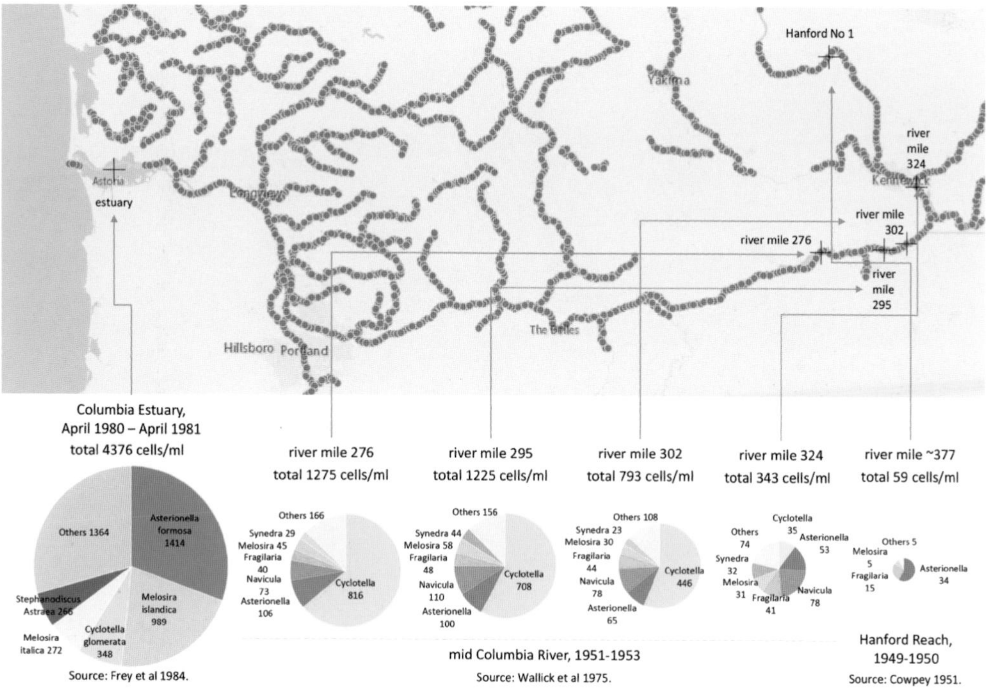


**Figure 12.5**. Counts of diatoms, and principal genera or species recorded, in samples from the Columbia River between the Hanford Reach and the estuary, 1949–50 to 1981–82. Sources as shown. *Graphics by author*

- The genus *Fragilaria* was a common diatom in all the samples from 1949–50 to 1953 but was not identified in the samples from the estuary in 1981–82. It could have been included under "others."
- The genus *Stephanodiscus* (of which Kaye and Meltzer found three cells) was identified only in the samples from the estuary.
- The genus *Cyclotella* (of which Kaye and Meltzer found three cells) was by far the dominant diatom in the samples from river mile 276 to 302 but was much less common in the estuary.
- The samples from the Columbia estuary (dated 1981–82) were the closest in time to the events of Flight 305. However, the estuary is 95 miles downstream of Tena Bar, so the water in the estuary had had ample opportunity to change its composition.

We insert a note of caution from Claudia Tausz of BSA Environmental Services, who wrote her master's thesis on phytoplankton in the lower Columbia River:

> **As for being able to make an inference at where the bills would have been, this is probably going to be very difficult. Planktonic diatoms get advected downstream, and as far as I know[,] no one has tried to determine how far they travel—although I supposed you could calculate the growth rate [and] compare that with the river's flow rate. Both *Asterionella formosa* and *Fragilaria crotonensis* are very common and widespread species within the lower Columbia River . . . [and] even at the same physical collection site, phytoplankton/diatom community composition is highly variable year to year, due to things like flow rate, temperature, precipitation[,] etc.[13]**

We have to remember also that we were comparing an ad hoc sample of about forty cells with previous samplings of hundreds or thousands of cells over periods of months or years. Of the six genera identified on the bills from Tena Bar, at least five are common in the Columbia River. Conversely, of the seven most common genera in large samples from the Columbia, only two (*Navicula* and *Synedra*) were not found on the samples from Tena Bar.

From the available data on the Columbia River, the most that we can say is that the Tena Bar sample yields no surprises; the identified genera are consistent with any location in the Columbia River as far upstream as the Hanford Reach.

We may then turn to the data on diatom counts in the basins of the Willamette and lower Columbia Rivers.

For this purpose, we confined our attention to specific drainage basins delimited by eight-digit hydrologic unit codes (HUC), as defined by the US Geological Survey. These basins are illustrated in the figure below. We excluded basins that drain into the Columbia River downstream of river mile 95.

The sources available to us present their diatom data in a variety of ways, which we may summarize as follows:

- The EPA's *National Lakes Assessment* nearly always records the genus of the diatom, and sometimes (but not always) the species. The absolute numbers of cells in the sample are recorded. It is not clear whether the sample is of a fixed volume; rather, it appears that the bench analyst counts a predetermined number of cells (say, 500) and then stops. The lake is identified by name, HUC-8 code, and latitude and longitude.

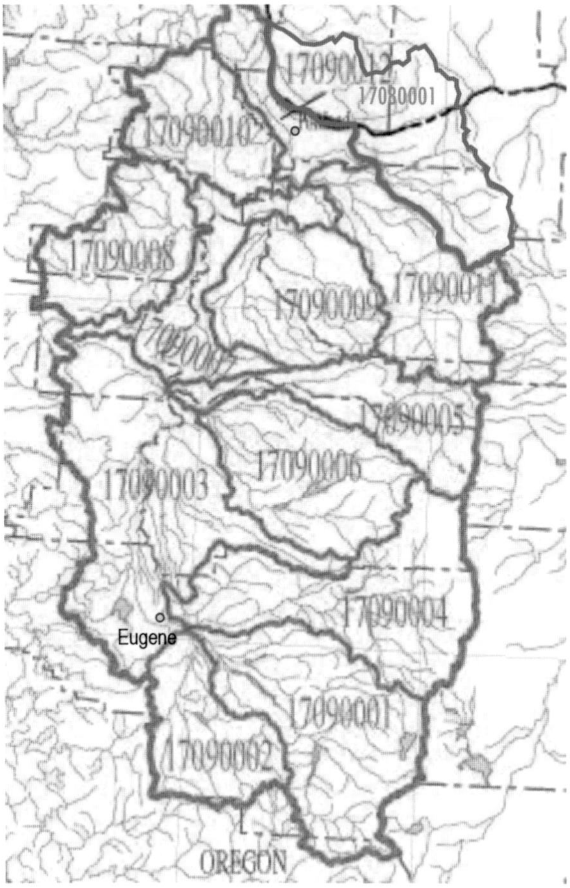


| | |
|---|---|
| HUC-4 basin: 1708 Lower Columbia | |
| 17080001 | Lower Columbia - Sandy |
| HUC-4 basin: 1709 Willamette | |
| 17090001 | Middle Fork Willamette |
| 17090002 | Coast Fork Willamette |
| 17090003 | Upper Willamette |
| 17090004 | Mckenzie |
| 17090005 | North Santiam |
| 17090006 | South Santiam |
| 17090007 | Middle Willamette |
| 17090008 | Yamhill |
| 17090009 | Molalla-Pudding |
| 17090010 | Tualatin |
| 17090011 | Clackamas |
| 17090012 | Lower Willamette |

**Figure 12.6**. Selected hydrological unit codes (HUCs) for assembly of diatom data. *Base maps and HUCs from US Geological Survey. Selection and additional graphics by author*

- Portland State University's *Atlas of Oregon Lakes* generally identifies the genus and species. The diatom abundance is recorded in cells per milliliter. The lake is identified by name and by a unique fourteen-digit code that consists of six digits added to the standard USGS eight-digit code. Each lake is characterized as oligotrophic, mesotrophic, or eutrophic, and in some cases as hyperoligotrophic (practically nutrient free) or hypereutrophic (what we might call nutrient soup).
- The USGS Lakes of Oregon series generally records only the genus of the diatom. This source records, in some cases, the number of cells per milliliter and, in other cases, simply records that the genus was dominant or was present in some samples. The lake is identified by name, latitude, and longitude; this permits a cross-reference to PSU's fourteen-digit code.
- The USGS's NAWQA project covers only rivers and streams and therefore complements the other sources. The NAWQA data invariably record the genus of the diatom and in nearly all cases the species also. The data record the absolute numbers of cells in the sample but not cells per milliliter; it appears that for any given sample, the counting stops after 600 cells have been identified. The site number is identified by an eight-digit code that can be cross-referenced to a site database giving the latitude and longitude.

With this multiplicity of sources and sampling methods, it is evident that we cannot construct a simple hierarchy or ranking of water bodies in Washington and Oregon according to their probability of being the source of the diatoms at Tena Bar. What we can attempt is something less ambitious; namely, to plot the locations where the two principal genera (*Asterionella* and *Fragilaria*) have been found, and to assess whether these locations cluster in any observable way.

First, a summary of the data from these four sources:

- Within our study area, we identified sixty-seven sites in lakes or reservoirs, and forty-three sites in streams or rivers, where diatoms had been sampled by one or more agencies.
- Of the lakes or reservoirs, thirty had been classified by Portland State University according to their perceived trophic state. Of these, three were classified as hyperoligotrophic, four were oligotrophic, eighteen were mesotrophic, four were eutrophic, and one (Oswego Lake) was hypereutrophic. In the other thirty-seven lakes, the USGS had observed mild to heavy blooms of algae, which would be indicative of mesotrophic to eutrophic lakes.
- From the sixty-seven lakes and reservoirs, we assembled quantitative or qualitative data on 354 samples, taken during the period 1971 to 2012, of diatoms of the six genera identified on the bill from Tena Bar.
- Of the lake and reservoir samples, twenty-six recorded the presence of *Asterionella formosa*. The highest counts of *Asterionella* were found in the following bodies of water:
    - In the eutrophic Bybee Lake, which drains into the lower Willamette, in fifteen samples between June and November 1982 there was an average of 148 cells per milliliter (2% of the sample).
    - In the adjacent eutrophic Smith Lake over the same period, there was an average of thirty-nine cells per milliliter (1% of the sample).
    - In the eutrophic Blue Lake, which drains into the lower Willamette, there were 190 cells per milliliter (5% of the sample).
    - In Smith Reservoir, which drains into the McKenzie River, there were 451 cells counted in a sample of 500 cells; 90% of the sample.
- Among the lake and reservoir samples, *Fragilaria* of various species was present in fifty-four samples. The highest counts of *Fragilaria* were found in the following lakes:
    - In Bybee Lake, *Fragilaria construens* was counted at an average of 228 cells per milliliter (5% of the overall sample).
    - In Smith Lake, *Fragilaria construens* averaged 447 cells per milliliter (6% of the overall sample).
    - In Detroit Lake, which drains into the North Santiam River, *Fragilaria crotonensis* was counted on three occasions at between two and fifty-three cells per milliliter (1% to 29% of the respective samples).
- Of the other genera of interest, *Melosira* was present in sixty-eight, *Cyclotella* in forty-five, *Stephanodiscus* in forty-nine, and *Cymbella* in just four (two at Bybee Lake, one at Clear Lake, and one at Smith Reservoir).
- From the forty-three sites in streams and rivers, we assembled quantitative data from twenty samples of *Asterionella formosa* and 190 samples of *Fragilaria* of various species, made during the period 1993 to 2010. The highest counts of *Asterionella formosa*, as measured by biovolumes,[14] were at sites in the drainage basins of the

Tualatin and middle Willamette Rivers. The highest counts of *Fragilaria* were at sites in the drainage basis of the Clackamas and Molalla/Pudding Rivers.

These data reinforced our conclusions that with the exception of *Cymbella*, most of the genera found on the bill from Tena Bar were common and widespread in the Willamette River basin. Within this basin, *Fragilaria* was more widely dispersed than *Asterionella*. We found no samples of either *Asterionella* or *Fragilaria* in the Sandy River basin, which flows into the Columbia upstream from Portland. If we were to look farther upstream the Columbia, we would have to fall back on USGS data from the Yakima River basin, or on seventy-year-old data from river mile 276 to 324. Insofar as the available data permitted us to make inferences, we came to feel that the sources of the Tena Bar diatoms were more probably in the Willamette basin than in the lower Columbia basin.

At this point, we plotted the sites where *Asterionella formosa* or *Fragilaria* had been identified, as well as the rare cases of *Cymbella*, within the Willamette River and Sandy River basins, and on this plot we superimposed the track of Flight 305 on the evening of November 24, 1971, and the centerline of the Victor 23 airway, which was the corridor assigned to Flight 305. The result is shown below.

From this graphic it will be evident that below and alongside the path that Flight 305 took on the night of November 24, 1971, there are many lakes, streams, and rivers where, at one time or another, diatoms of *Asterionella formosa* and *Fragilaria* have been identified.

North of the Columbia, Franz Lake is the only identified site that drains into the Columbia upstream of Tena Bar. South of the Columbia, all the sites are either in the Willamette River or drain eventually into the Willamette, which in turn joins the Columbia at Portland, 6 miles upstream of Tena Bar.

Among the lakes that could be candidates for the original birthplaces of the diatoms, four might merit our particular attention. They are Bybee and Smith Lakes, which drain into the Willamette at river mile 1 in Portland; Blue Lake, which has an outflow into the Columbia near river mile 118; and Oswego Lake, which drains into the Willamette near river mile 21. All four lakes are classified as eutrophic: that is, rich in nutrients that support plants and algae. These lakes are characterized in the *Atlas of Oregon Lakes* as follows:

**Bybee and Smith Lakes: "The lakes are considered to be part of the Columbia Slough hydrologic system. Bybee Lake is connected to the Willamette River via the slough, and a narrow channel connects Smith Lake to Bybee Lake. . . . The phytoplankton in both lakes is usually dominated by species of diatoms, but on occasion green algae are also very abundant. . . . Several of the species of diatoms observed in these two lakes are also common in the Columbia River and probably originate from inflow rather than growth in lakes. The population densities and the dominant species (*Sphaerocystis schroeteri, Oocystis pusilla, Melosira ambigua, Stephanodiscus astrea, Fragilaria construens*) indicate eutrophic conditions. . . . Smith and Bybee Lakes are strongly eutrophic due to their shallowness and the rich supply of nutrients."[15]**

**Blue Lake: "A dike (along which Marine Drive runs) now extends along the south shore of the Columbia, blocking any surface connection with the river. . . . The outflow . . . runs eastward through a short creek into a drainage ditch along the Columbia dike. From here it is pumped back over the dike into the Columbia. . . . Transparency of the water is decreased during the summer months due to an abundance of microscopic planktonic algal growth dominated by diatoms and blue-green algae."[16]**

**Oswego Lake: "The water quality in Lake Oswego is poor[,] and by all indications it is a hypereutrophic lake. When sampled on 9/21/82, the hypolimnion[17] was anoxic**

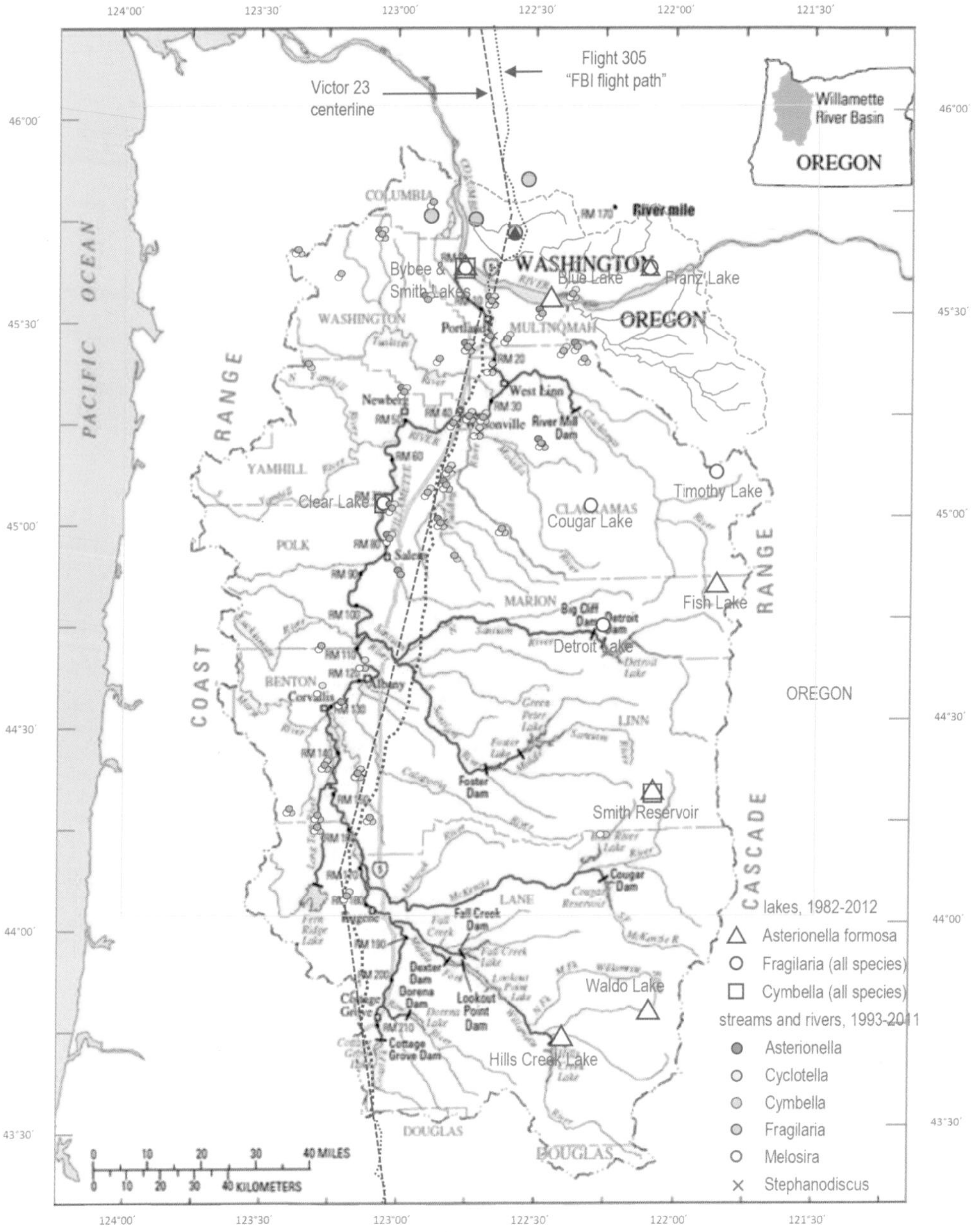


Base map modified from USGS and other digital data sets (1:2,000,000, 1:100,000).
Projection converted by author from Oregon Lambert Conformal Conic to Mercator

**Figure 12.7**. Flight 305, Victor 23 airway, and identified sites of *Asterionella formosa*, *Fragilaria*, and *Cymbella* diatoms in the Willamette River basin. *Base maps from US Geological Survey. Data for diatom sites from Environmental Protection Agency, Portland State University, and US Geological Survey. Graphics by author*

**(oxygen-depleted) below 22 feet (7 meters), the transparency was low (Secchi disk depth[18] = 4.6 feet; 1.4 meters), and the concentrations of total phosphorus and phytoplankton were very high, as were nitrogen values. . . . There is very little existing biological and chemical data on Lake Oswego, partially because it is a private lake without public access."[19]**

We may add here that Bybee Lake is just over 4 nautical miles from the centerline of Victor 23, and just over 2 nautical miles from the path of Flight 305, and is the only lake in the Willamette or Sandy River basins where all six of the genera *Asterionella*, *Cyclotella*, *Cymbella*, *Fragilaria*, *Melosira*, and *Stephanodiscus* have been recorded.

Accordingly, without necessarily forming any view about where the money from Flight 305 first entered the water, it is possible to imagine that some of the money picked up diatoms in one of three stretches of waterway:

- from the outflow of Bybee and Smith Lakes, a 1-mile stretch of the Willamette from river mile 1 to the junction with the Columbia, followed by a 6-mile stretch of the Columbia from river mile 101 to river mile 95
- or from the outflow of Blue Lake, a 23-mile stretch of the Columbia from river mile 118 to river mile 95
- or from Oswego Creek, a 21-mile stretch of the Willamette to the Columbia, followed by the 6 miles of the Columbia between river miles 101 and 95.[20]

These plausible trajectories are illustrated in the figure below.

On that note, with regard to the origins of the diatoms and their journey to Tena Bar, we have perhaps made all the educated inferences that are permitted by the available data.

It remains for us to consider whether the data permit any reasonable hypothesis about the timing of the encounter between the money and the diatoms. We therefore conclude this chapter with a discussion of the seasonality of the diatom bloom.

## *ASTERIONELLA* AND *FRAGILARIA*: SEASONALITY

We are fortunate to have access to four studies that document the seasonal patterns of the blooms of diatoms in the Columbia and Willamette Rivers. Three were mentioned above (those for the Hanford Reach, the middle Columbia, and the Columbia estuary), each covering at least one full year of monthly diatom sampling. The fourth is Daphne Clifton's study of Bybee and Smith Lakes from June to November 1982, for the US Geological Survey.[21]

From these four studies, we assembled the data for *Asterionella formosa* and for *Fragilaria* (all species) on a monthly basis for a complete calendar year, or for as much of a calendar year as the data covered. We converted the monthly counts to percentages of the annual totals, in order that, irrespective of the heaviness or lightness of the bloom, we could more clearly see the seasonality. The results are illustrated below.

These graphs allow us to make the following observations:

- *Asterionella formosa* is a creature of the late spring and early summer. Its peak bloom is between May and July. Between 40 and 65 percent of its annual population can be expected to live and die in this three-month period.
- *Fragilaria*, with a few exceptions, flourishes in the summer and early fall. Its peak is between June and September. During this period, between 30 and 45 percent of its annual population will be alive.

**Figure 12.8**. The diatoms' journey to Tena Bar: three plausible trajectories. *Base map from Washington Geospatial Open Data Portal, WAECY River Miles. Legend and graphics by author*

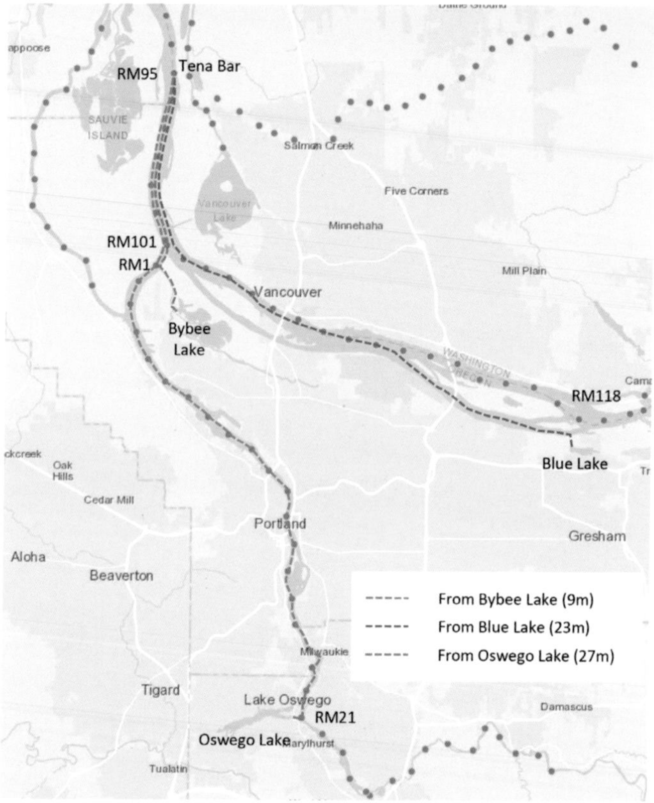


- Both *Asterionella formosa* and *Fragilaria* are relatively rare in November and December. Less than 5 percent of the annual population will be alive in December.

In relation to the diatoms found on the bill from Tena Bar, Kaye and Meltzer made a similar observation:

> **Several examples [of] *Asterionella* were found on the Cooper bills[,] and this diatom is nearly absent in November[,] when the jump occurred. There is however a very large bloom of *Asterionella* in early summer during the months of May and June. The other diatoms identified on the Cooper bill such as *Stephanodiscus* are also more prevalent in the summer season. . . . The mix of genera, abundance[,] and elemental signatures suggests the Cooper bills did not get submerged during the November event but more closely aligns with a May–June time frame.**[22]

We concur that, with a high probability, the $20 bill from Tena Bar collected most of its diatoms during a spring or a summer. We know that this bill departed from Flight 305 on November 24, 1971. In February 1980, Brian Ingram would dig up the bill on the beach at Tena Bar. We have to assume that he, his parents, the FBI, and the subsequent owners of the bill, during their decades of custody, did not wash the bills with river water or with any water that contained diatoms (even tap water, which in Portland comes from Bull Run Lake). If that assumption is correct, the encounter between the bill and the diatoms could not have been earlier than the spring of 1972 or later than the summer of 1979. In which year that encounter occurred, we think that the data do not permit us to say.

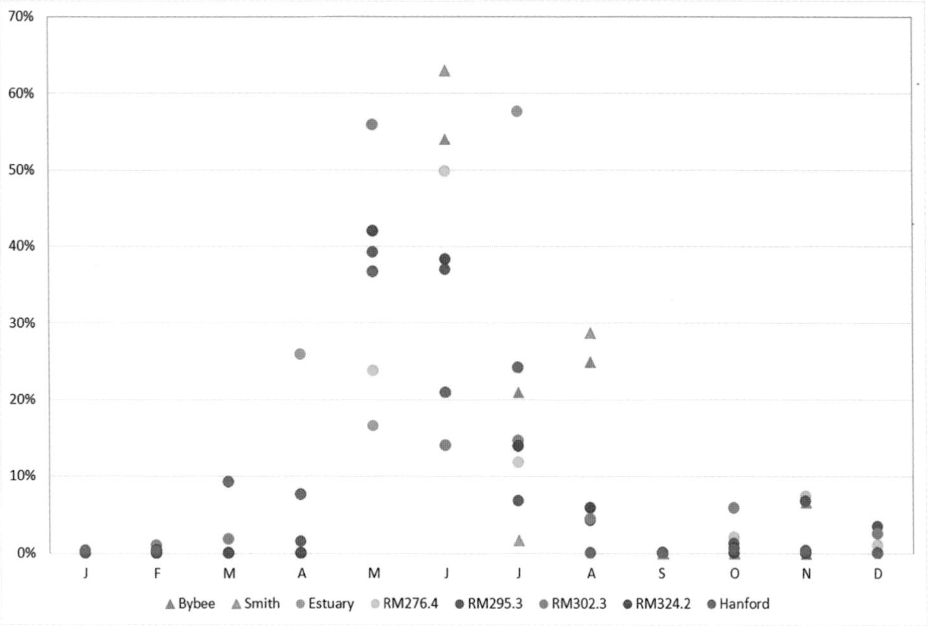


**Figure 12.9**. *Asterionella formosa*: monthly counts as percentages of annual totals, at eight sites in Columbia River and Willamette River basin, 1949–50 to 1982. Data from Cowpey 1951, Wallick et al. 1975, Frey et al. 1984, and Clifton 1983 (June–November 1982 only). *Graphics by author*

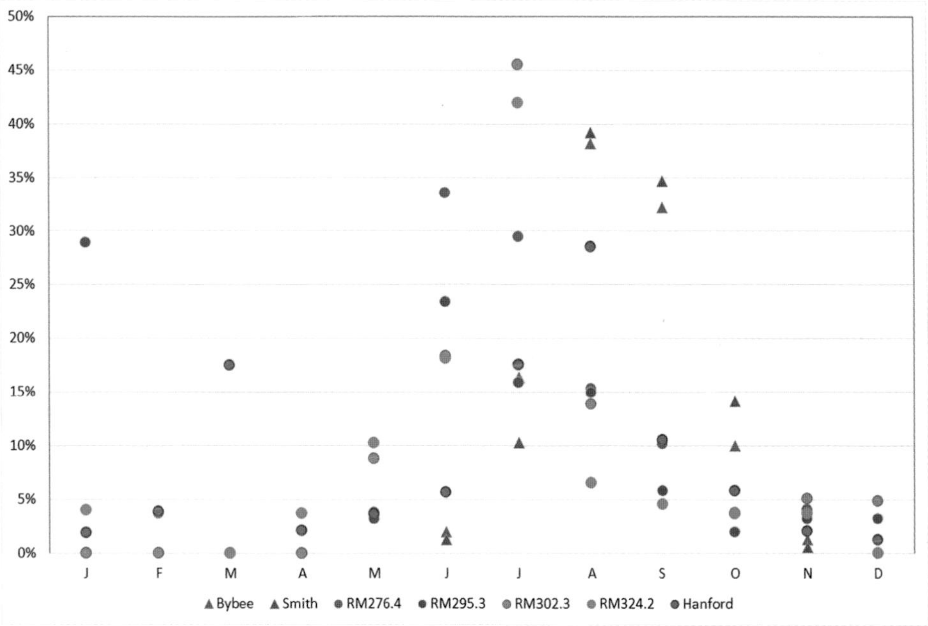


**Figure 12.10**. *Fragilaria* (all species): monthly counts as percentages of annual totals, at eight sites in Columbia River and Willamette River basin, 1949–50 to 1982. Data from Cowpey 1951, Wallick et al. 1975, Frey et al. 1984, and Clifton 1983 (June–November 1982 only). *Graphics by author*

CHAPTER

# 13

# THE TIE

From chapter 1, we recall that fourteen witnesses offered the FBI their personal observations of the hijacker. Of the fourteen, eleven had seen him in person, either up close or from a distance no greater than the length of the passenger cabin. Six of the witnesses (cabin crew members Tina Mucklow, Florence Schaffner, and Alice Hancock, and passengers Cord Spreckel, William Mitchell, and Robert Gregory) reported that the hijacker had worn a tie. Four of them remembered the tie as black or dark; two of them recalled it as "thin" or "skinny." Not one of them noticed whether he had a tie clip. But something about the hijacker's apparel, or maybe the tie, was not right.

- **overall impression of laboring-type man as opposed to office worker.**[1]
- **white shirt, skinny little tie, you know, suit, and he didn't look like, an executive . . . I mean it looked like, it was a skinny little tie you know, it was 1970s and that didn't look very hip**[2]

We restate these observations because we are now about to encounter the hijacker's tie again, or if not that tie, one very much like it.

The FBI introduces the story.

At 11:25 p.m., on November 24, 1971, at Reno Municipal Airport, FBI special agents Marvin T. Bell, Harold E. Newpher, Francis J. Schmidt, and Norman M. Stone boarded the now-abandoned Boeing 727 that had started the day as Flight 305. As we recounted earlier, they found a complete parachute and the dismembered remains of another. On seat 18-E, which had been occupied by the hijacker, they made another discovery:

**On the seat numbered 18E[,] a black clip-on tie was observed. This black tie contained a tie clasp, yellow gold in color: with a white pearl circular stone in the center. The label on this tie indicated it to be a "Towncraft™" tie and bore the store name of JC Penney number 3. It further bore a label showing it to be a "Snapper" patent[-]type tie.[3]**

Did we just read Penney's Store Number 3? Was the place of purchase of the tie hiding in plain sight? Regrettably, no. Agent Schmidt followed up on December 1 by talking to JC Penney store number 44 in Las Vegas, which was not entirely logical since the tie had presumably traveled from Portland. However, at store number 44 Schmidt learned that Number 3 was merely a price code, signifying that the tie sold for $1.50.

The tie was an extraordinary discovery, but over two months passed before the principal investigators in Seattle reacted. Only on February 8, 1972, did the Seattle office set in motion a search for the origins of the tie:

**Las Vegas [is] requested to send to Portland the black snap[-]on tie with a tie pin in it bearing Towncraft label. . . . These items should be sent via registered mail and handled as evidence, being careful to preserve the chain of evidence. Portland [should,] on receipt of the tie and the tie pin, contact Penney's at Portland and make every effort to determine if possible, the source of these items. In contacting Penney's[,] explore all possibility of checking with their purchasing department, etc. to narrow down, again, if possible, where these items might have been purchased.[4]**

Las Vegas dispatched the tie and tie pin on February 9, and by February 10 the Portland division had started talking to JC Penney's stores in Portland. By February 24, they had made some progress:

**Investigation at Portland concerning tie found on aircraft, determined it is type of tie which has not been sold for several years. Tie is being forwarded by Portland to laboratory for examination.[5]**

**Enclosures have been displayed to J.C. Penney Co., store personnel at Las Vegas, Nevada, and Portland, Oregon. All personnel contacted uniformly agree that the tie, which bore the "Towncraft" label, exclusive with Penney's, could not have been sold at any time in the recent past. At Las Vegas, the most recent sales of such ties were estimated at one and one-half years ago, and at Portland, three years ago.[6]**

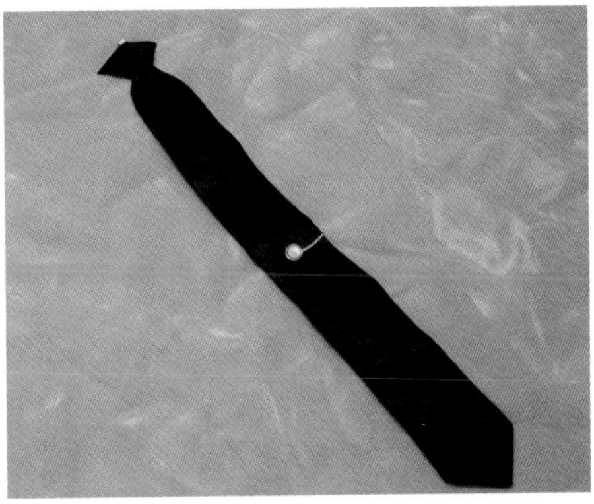

**Figure 13.1.** The tie and tie clip found on seat 18-E of aircraft N467US at Reno Municipal Airport on November 24, 1971. *Image credit: FBI*

The tie and the tie clip were shipped forthwith to the director of the FBI (at that time, none other than J. Edgar Hoover) for the attention of the FBI Laboratory in Washington, DC. Portland's request was only to search the exhibits for human body residues such as fluids and hairs. The laboratory's response was prompt and entirely unproductive.

**Q40 Tie Q41 Tie clip**

**Result of examination: No stains having the appearance of body fluids were found**

**on Q40 or Q41. No hairs or foreign textile fibers were found on Q40 or Q41. No identifying marks were found on Q41 that would indicate either the owner or the manufacturer of this item.**[7]

This negative response cannot be excused by the technology of the 1970s. The FBI Laboratory did what the Portland division asked, but nothing more. Their response suggests that they did a cursory inspection with an optical microscope. They could have done, or they could have offered to do, much more. The laboratory had had the capability for metallurgical analysis since 1939, and it had had electron microscopes since at least 1949.[8] They could have offered Portland a spectral analysis of the tie clip to determine its chemical composition. By electron microscopy, they could have offered to identify organic or inorganic particles too small to be detected by optical instruments. At best, the laboratory's response reads like a job that received the lowest of priorities.

In addition, we do not know what unit of the laboratory performed the examination. The Portland office had addressed its request to the director of the FBI (office code 164-2111), and the reply came from the same office code, further identified only as "Lab. No. PC-5141 MC GX."

By the 1990s, the FBI Laboratory had at least three divisions concerned with examinations of materials: the Materials Analysis Unit (MAU), the Chemistry Toxicology Unit (CTU), and the Explosives Unit (EU). If these same divisions existed in the 1970s, the logical division to handle Portland's exhibits would have been the Explosives Unit. It seems more likely, however, that the tie and tie clip went to the Materials Analysis Unit; if so, an opportunity was missed. Director Hoover had to be aware that the NORJAK case involved a bomb (whether real or simulated). It would be an extraordinary lapse to receive exhibits thought to have been handled by the hijacker, and not direct them to be tested for explosive residues.

However, even if the tie and tie clip had been delivered to the Explosives Unit, the outcome might have been equally unproductive. From 1995 to 1997, the Department of Justice conducted an investigation into allegations of scientific misconduct at the FBI Laboratory. In the department's report, authored by Michael Bromwich, the Explosives Unit came under specific criticism for its use of law enforcement personnel without adequate scientific knowledge:

**The EU should be reorganized and reconstituted. The EU unit chief and EU examiners should have scientific backgrounds in addition to experience and training in bomb reconstruction.**[9]

In any event, Portland did not complain about the laboratory's curt reply. By April 12, 1972, Director Hoover was able to inform the FBI office in Salt Lake City (where there had been a copycat hijacking) that the two exhibits had been returned to the Las Vegas office, where they were retained as evidence.[10]

At least two agents, probably in the Seattle office, were unwilling to give up on the investigation of the tie. On May 30, 1972, they wrote to the special agent in charge at Seattle to the following effect:

**An examination of the tie by the writers revealed noticeable amounts of dust lodged in the inner knot area. . . . It is recommended that the Lab be requested to examine this tie, particularly, the dust particles lodged in the inner knot area, to determine if it is possible to determine what area of the country this tie has been in.**[11]

This recommendation was turned down. Charles Farrell, the special agent in charge at Seattle, wrote on June 30, 1972, to the acting director of the FBI, quoting the original response of the FBI Laboratory and adding

> **In view of the above, the tie and clip will not again be forwarded to the laboratory, uacb [unless advised to the contrary by the bureau].[12]**

The same two agents were evidently convinced that the tie, at least, had been manufactured overseas. They urged a further dialogue with the foreign buying department of JC Penney:

> **In addition to the markings "3 Penneys," two other labels were found as follows: "Snapper Pat. 2972750. It's a snap to snap on"; and "100% Dacron Polyester Washable RN16484 ... RN number is a manufacturer's code. Penneys headquarters will be able to determine where the tie was manufactured, when imported[,] and which stores sold this tie.[13]**

The agents were correct that RN16484 was a manufacturer code. Today, according to the Federal Trade Commission, RN16484 is the registered identification number of the Remington Apparel Company, Inc., 1217 South 13th Street, Wilmington, North Carolina.[14] This company was incorporated in 1984; it is conceivable that in 1971, the same code was allocated to another company. For our purposes it does not matter, since the identification cannot lead to any plausible avenue of investigation.

To this day, vintage ties bearing the code RN16484 are offered for sale on eBay and are proudly displayed on forums for lovers of 1960s and 1970s menswear. But the tie was not necessarily an import. At least some of the ties made by RN16484 were labeled "Made in USA" or "Made in USA from imported fabric."

In any event, there is no evidence in the public domain that the FBI continued the conversation with JC Penney. Today, no one outside JC Penney and the FBI knows where the Towncraft RN16484 tie was first sold at retail. Even less is known of the tie clip, which was not necessarily sold with the tie; its manufacturer and its retailers have never been identified.

The FBI's public files have an intriguing postscript, with no evidence or attribution, that suggests that the hijacker either was, or wished to appear, a person of limited means and skills. On June 27, 1972, the acting director of the FBI wrote to the SAC Seattle as follows:

> **Investigation at Las Vegas indicated that this type sold for about a dollar and a half, ... and it was a favorite item for individuals such as waiters, busboys, and bartenders.[15]**

With that, as far as anyone knows, the FBI lost interest in the tie and the tie clip. The two items were stored under unknown conditions, probably at the FBI office in Las Vegas, being the jurisdiction where they were first discovered. Nearly thirty years would pass before they would resurface.

**Figure 13.2**. Mid-1960s silk tie, made by manufacturer number RN16484 for Sears. *Image credit*: *The Fedora Lounge*

## THE DNA SAMPLE

By 1985, thanks to the work of Professor Alec Jeffries, DNA profiling was a viable forensic technology. In 1987, DNA-based evidence was used for the first time in a criminal case in the United States. In 1994, via the DNA Identification Act, the FBI received the authority to establish a database of individual DNA profiles.[16] During 2001, the Seattle office of the FBI came to believe that the tie might still have traces of DNA from whoever had handled it:

> **During 2001, advancements in sensitivity of DNA PCR/STR testing reached a point that resubmission of an item believed handled and worn by the UNSUB in this case was deemed worthwhile.[17]**

On August 23, 2001, Seattle retrieved the tie, the tie clip, and the airline ticket from storage and resubmitted them to the FBI Laboratory, this time with a specific request for DNA analysis.[18]

The tests took more than nine months to be completed. On April 2, 2002, the laboratory reported on their examinations of the samples from the tie and the tie clip (which they had combined for the purposes of analysis):

> **The STR [short tandem repeat] typing results . . . indicate the presence of DNA from more than one individual. The typing results from the amelogenin locus indicate the presence of male DNA. . . . No other DNA examinations were conducted.[19]**

In short, more than one person had handled the tie or the tie clip (or both), and at least one of these persons was male. The airline ticket apparently was not, or could not, be tested.

Internally, the FBI would eventually come to the conclusion that, in any case, the DNA samples were too degraded to yield a positive identification of the hijacker:

> **In 2006, the Laboratory Division determined [that] the degraded DNA sample could only be used to exclude individuals as possible donors.[20]**

The FBI would not disclose the existence of these tests for over five years. On December 31, 2007, at the instigation of Special Agent Larry Carr, the FBI posted an article on its website under the heading "Help Us Solve the Enduring Mystery." In this article the FBI published, for the first time, photographs of various physical items of evidence (including the tie with its tie clip), and a map of unknown provenance, purporting to be the flight path of Flight 305. By this means, the FBI invited the general public to come forward with leads, suggestions, or suspects. Buried in the article was this cryptic phrase:

> **[W]e lifted a DNA sample from Cooper's tie in 2001.[21]**

Four years after the publication of this article, "Cooper's tie" was no longer "Cooper's tie." In an interview with ABC News in August 2011, in the context of a flurry of attention over a new suspect, FBI special agent Fred Gutt tabled the following reservations:

> **It's possible that the DNA sample taken off the tie was not from the hijacker. There are questions about the tie. It may have been borrowed, or purchased used. The DNA may**

**be from someone else. . . . The tie had two small DNA samples, and one large sample lifted off in 2000–2001. It's difficult to draw firm conclusions from these samples.[22]**

The "questions" to which Agent Gutt referred have never been disclosed. The FBI has never directly alluded to possible contamination of the tie within its premises, or to any specific reason why the tie might have had a previous wearer other than the hijacker. The results of the DNA test have not been published. This author's FOIA request for the results, even without any information relating to an individual, was denied.

## CITIZEN SLEUTHS

During 2007, Special Agent Larry Carr persuaded the FBI to share some of the physical evidence with selected private parties. Carr's intention was apparently to continue research and analysis of the documents and evidence without consuming FBI funds and resources.

The team to whom Carr turned for help with the physical evidence was headed by Tom Kaye, of the Burke Museum in Seattle. Kaye was supported by Alan Stone, president of Aston Metallurgical Services Co., Inc., and Carol Abraczinskas of the University of Michigan. This team began a three-year investigation, during which time Agent Carr named them the "Citizen Sleuths."

The team's investigation of the NORJAK case centered on the tie that had been found on seat 18-E some thirty-six years earlier, which evidently was released from storage a second time for this purpose. By this date, the tie and tie clip were in the custody of the Seattle office of the FBI, where the Citizen Sleuths had physical access to the two exhibits.

The Sleuths' investigations focused on the extraction and analysis of microscopic particles from the tie. These investigations were conducted in at least two phases: the first in 2010 and the second in August 2011, for which the team brought particle collection and imaging equipment to the FBI office in Seattle. In all, the team collected and manually analyzed approximately 800 individual particles from the tie.[23]

The Sleuths' analysis, discussions, and inferences are comprehensively documented on their website at www.citizensleuths.com. For our current purposes, we have attempted to summarize the principal findings of their analysis as follows:

- The tie had at least twelve localized stains. The stains were composed of chemical elements in the same proportions that were found in match heads from paper book matches. The tie had no stains that could be attributed to food or drink.[24]
- The tie contained no pollen that could be associated with a specific geographical area. The tie contained spores from common club moss (*Lycopodium clavatum*).[25]
- The tie contained particles with the chemical signature of titanium.[26] The Citizen Sleuths website describes the source as titanium metal; however, our communications with Mr. Kaye indicate that the particles were titanium oxide ($TiO_2$),[27] a widely used component of food coloring, paints and pigments, and sunscreen.

## MCCRONE LABORATORIES

As far as the public record shows, the FBI never took action on the basis of the work performed by the Citizen Sleuths. It is possible that, as Agent Gutt seemed to attest, the FBI was no longer confident that the tie and the hijacker were connected by more than the duration of the flight. After the Sleuths completed their analysis, there the matter rested, until sometime in 2016.

On January 11, 2017, the Travel Channel aired episode 3.7 of the television series *Expedition Unknown*, hosted by Josh Gates, under the title "Cracking the D. B. Cooper Case." The episode did not—and did not intend to—crack the case but included an interview with Tom Kaye, from which we transcribed the following extract:

> **Josh Gates: "We've assisted D. B. Cooper investigator Tom Kaye in securing the technology needed to scan particles left on the discarded necktie."**
>
> **Tom Kaye: "So we have representations here and these little lines. . . . So this is cerium. It's a rare-earth element. And lanthanum is another one. This is yttrium. And this one is mercury. . . . We start with the most unusual of those, which is the rare-earth element yttrium. . . . What's the most common use for yttrium in 1971? It turns out it's the red phosphor in TV screens. Twenty-three out of the twenty-six particles we found are related to production of CRT tubes . . . it's the cathode ray tube that's used in televisions. But it's also used in other things, like in the military. They would use it for radar screens and instruments. They would use it for like an oscilloscope screen. So these cathode ray tubes are found in lots of different products.[28]**

On the Citizen Sleuths website, Kaye explains how this third phase of particle investigations came about. In 2016, in preparation for episode 3.7, the producers of *Expedition Unknown* provided funding for the McCrone Group, of Westmont, Illinois, to conduct a more comprehensive analysis of the particles collected by the Sleuths. McCrone received twenty stubs of adhesive tape, bearing particles from the tie, and used an automated scanning electron microscope to identify, image, and analyze over 100,000 of these particles.

A summary of McCrone's results from nineteen samples is published on the Citizen Sleuths website. The samples are numbered 559, 560, 566, 644 through 647, and 664 through 675; we presume that these numbers correspond to nineteen of the adhesive tape stubs that were provided to McCrone. For each sample, the number of particles was recorded in each of thirty-three classes, on the basis of the predominating chemical element or compound. Among the thirty-three classes, twenty-four had a single predominating chemical element, three referred to a chemical compound, two referred to mixtures or alloys, and four were unclassified.

We felt that it would be productive to examine these particle counts in relation to the abundance of the respective elements or compounds in the material world. For this purpose, we assumed that the tie had been manufactured in the United States. We therefore assumed that for any given element or compound, the total annual consumption of that product in the United States, in the late 1960s, would be a reasonable benchmark against which to assess whether the respective particle count was normal or abnormal.

Thanks to the archives of the United States Geological Survey, statistics are available on the consumption of almost every one of the elements and compounds listed in the McCrone analysis. These archives go back, in most cases, to the 1920s; for our purposes we used the statistics for 1969, as the most probable year when the tie was first sold at retail. It would make little difference if we had chosen 1968 or 1970; US consumption of most major materials did not change much from year to year.

Our comparison of the particle counts with US domestic consumption is summarized below. We highlighted the classes of particle for which the counts were unusually high (that is, higher than we would expect from the abundance of the respective element or compound). It should be noted that in the raw data, we found no references to cerium, lanthanum, or yttrium, all of which were mentioned in the interview with *Expedition Unknown*.

**Table 13.1. Necktie Analysis: comparison of McCrone particle counts, 2016, with relative abundance of respective elements, compounds and mixtures in the US economy, 1969**

| Particle class | Total of tie samples 559–566, 644–675 | | US consumption, 1969 | | | tie vs US consumption |
|---|---|---|---|---|---|---|
| | **Number** | **%** | **metric tons** | ***note*** | % | |
| A | B | C | D | | E | C/E |
| aluminum-rich | 3515 | 3.3% | 3,710,000 | | 2.0% | 2 |
| antimony-rich | 343 | 0.3% | 16,200 | | 0.0% | 38 |
| bromine-rich | 2 | 0.0% | 150,000 | | 0.1% | 0 |
| calcium-rich | 29748 | 28.2% | *13,221,950* | *1* | 7.1% | 4 |
| chlorine-rich | 326 | 0.3% | *26,027,850* | *2* | 13.9% | 0 |
| chromium-rich | 52 | 0.0% | 619,000 | | 0.3% | 0 |
| copper-rich | 790 | 0.8% | 2,060,000 | | 1.1% | 1 |
| fluorine-rich | 0 | - | 1,240,000 | | 0.7% | 0 |
| gold | 263 | 0.2% | 312 | | 0.0% | 1494 |
| iron-rich | 9225 | 8.8% | 86,900,000 | | 46.6% | 0 |
| magnesium-rich | 2085 | 2.0% | 94,000 | | 0.1% | 39 |
| molybdenum-rich | 88 | 0.1% | 21,500 | | 0.0% | 7 |
| nickel-rich | 112 | 0.1% | 129,000 | | 0.1% | 2 |
| phosphorus-rich | 1077 | 1.0% | 23,200,000 | *3* | 12.4% | 0 |
| platinum-rich | 0 | - | 89 | | 0.0% | 0 |
| silicon-rich | 38843 | 36.9% | 433,000 | | 0.2% | 159 |
| sodium-rich | 15 | 0.0% | *16,472,150* | *4* | 8.8% | 0 |
| sulfur-rich | 751 | 0.7% | 9,320,000 | | 5.0% | 0 |
| tin-rich | 473 | 0.4% | 74,200 | | 0.0% | 11 |
| titanium-rich | 3178 | 3.0% | 18,300 | | 0.0% | 308 |
| tungsten-rich | 7 | 0.0% | 9,390 | | 0.0% | 1 |
| zinc-rich | 2751 | 2.6% | 1,260,000 | | 0.7% | 4 |
| zirconium-rich | 78 | 0.1% | 145,000 | | 0.1% | 1 |
| barium sulfate | 566 | 0.5% | 1,540,000 | *5* | 0.8% | 1 |
| bismuth chloride | 495 | 0.5% | 1,150 | *6* | 0.0% | 763 |
| salts | 2125 | 2.0% | – | | – | – |

**Table 13.1. Necktie Analysis: comparison of McCrone particle counts, 2016, with relative abundance of respective elements, compounds and mixtures in the US economy, 1969**

| | | | | | | |
|---|---|---|---|---|---|---|
| brass (copper-zinc) | 175 | 0.2% | – | | – | – |
| calcium-phosphorus | 1330 | 1.3% | – | | – | – |
| sodium, sulfur-rich | 139 | 0.1% | – | | – | – |
| 300 series s.s. | 339 | 0.3% | – | | – | – |
| 400 series s.s. | 107 | 0.1% | – | | – | – |
| corrosion | 6 | 0.0% | – | | – | – |
| unclassified | 6314 | 6.0% | – | | – | – |
| total | 105318 | 100.0% | *186,663,091* | | 100.0% | |
| | | | | | | |

*Source*: particle counts from https://citizensleuths.com/mccrone1.html; US annual consumption from United States Geological Survey, National Minerals Information Center, *Historical Statistics for Minerals and Material Commodities in the United States*, https://www.usgs.gov/centers/nmic/historical-statistics-mineral-and-material-commodities-united-states

1. estimated as calcium content of lime consumption; 2. estimated as chlorine content of salt consumption; 3. phosphorus rock; 4. estimated as sodium content of salt consumption; 5. barium metal; 6. bismuth metal

If we take this comparison at face value, six elements stand out as unusually prevalent in the particle counts, in comparison with their abundance in the United States economy. They are gold, bismuth, titanium, silicon, magnesium, and antimony.

In our correspondence with Mr. Kaye, he suggested the following interpretations:

- The gold particles could have come from the tie clip.
- The titanium signature came from titanium oxide, which is a common material.
- The excess silicon probably came from the residues of match heads.
- Magnesium is found in sand.
- Antimony was an outlier for which there was no ready explanation.[29]

In summary, we found little in the published analysis of the particles that would manifestly lead to a focused avenue of investigation. Titanium, which at one time suggested an exposure of the tie to an environment within the aerospace industry, eventually appeared to be no more than a marker for, most probably, paints and pigments. The correlation of the stains and the particles to paper match heads told us that the previous wearer or wearers of the tie had been smokers, but in 1971, 44 percent of American males were smokers. Signatures for gold required only exposure to gold jewelry. The most common use of antimony is in flame retardants, which are widespread in furniture, textiles, and insulation. References to cerium, lanthanum, and yttrium were not corroborated by the data that have been published, so we have no way of knowing whether these elements were present in unusual concentrations.

## WHAT WE KNOW

In the public domain, the substantive documents relating to the tie and tie clip record their discovery, the FBI's unproductive inquiries to JC Penney as to the origins of the tie, and the cursory examination of the two items at the FBI Laboratory (all within the period from November 24, 1971, to March 8, 1972), as well as a thirty-eight-year period of storage in unknown conditions, the examinations by the Citizen Sleuths in 2010 and 2011, and the intensive, but to our minds inconclusive, testing by the McCrone Group in 2016.

It remains to inquire whether any of these documents, in principle, could serve to elucidate the NORJAK case.

Mr. Kaye writes—we suppose from personal conversations with FBI employees—that the FBI is unprepared officially to accept a connection between the tie and the hijacker:

**The position of the FBI is that "we don't know if it's his [the hijacker's] tie."[30]**

On the Citizen Sleuths website, Mr. Kaye presents estimates of the probabilities that the tie had been worn by a passenger or crew member on a previous flight, or by another passenger on Flight 305, and concludes that with overwhelming probability, the tie discovered on seat 18-E was the tie that at least six witnesses saw on the hijacker's person. We have no difficulty accepting this argument.

We think it is legitimate to pose another question: Had the hijacker worn the tie prior to buying his ticket for Flight 305?

We acknowledge at the outset that this question cannot be answered on the basis of any data or document. The first witness to remember a tie was Florence Schaffner, who received the "bomb" note. Prior to that, ticket agent Dennis Lysne could not recall a tie. Prior to that, sometime in November 1971 a parking-lot attendant at Portland Airport encountered a man who she thought was identical to the FBI artist's impression of the hijacker; she made no report of a tie.[31]

We do not propose to invent a personality or a personal history for the hijacker. It can only be said, as a matter of due diligence, that his planning for this mission could have included the purchase of new or secondhand clothing, accessories, and tools for single use only. Special Agent Gutt's 2011 interview with ABC News voiced this possibility. If this were the case, the tie and the tie clip would not bear witness to the prior life of the hijacker, and all analysis of the tie and the clip would be in vain.

This leads to a corollary question: Did the hijacker leave the tie intentionally?

Again, only by working backward from a preconceived narrative of the hijacker's personality could we attempt to answer this question. No data exist that could cast light on the question. We can conceive of at least three possibilities:

- The hijacker left the tie unintentionally, having systematically retrieved all other items that could be used to identify him, but overlooking this one item.
- The hijacker left the tie intentionally, believing or assuming that it held no evidence that could identify him.
- The hijacker left the tie intentionally, intending it to be discovered and believing that it would mislead efforts to identify him.

None of these possibilities can be quantified.

At the end of the day, we do not know the significance of the tie, and it presents us with no productive avenue of investigation.

CHAPTER

# 14

# HOWEVER IMPROBABLE

Sherlock Holmes is said to have remarked on more than one occasion to his friend Dr. Watson to the effect that "when you have eliminated the impossible, then whatever remains, however improbable, must be the truth."[1]

It is in practice impossible to eliminate the impossible, since the number of impossibilities is infinite. In this book we have a more modest aim: to eliminate the more improbable and thereby arrive at the least improbable.

The case of Flight 305 abounds with improbabilities, of which, if we draw upon the official narrative, we may enumerate just a handful:

- A mild-mannered, middle-aged man, armed with no more than a cheap briefcase containing six red cylinders and what looks like a battery, holds the lives of thirty-six passengers and six crew to ransom.
- The hijacker knows that it is practicable and safe to parachute from a Boeing 727 at 10,000 feet.
- The crew do not transmit the hijacking code on the transponder.
- The hijacker executes his leap to freedom wearing a business suit and loafers, in the dark, above the clouds, and, by all accounts, with densely timbered wilderness below.
- The hijacker jumps with two parachutes, one of which, unknown to him, is a dummy.
- Having otherwise given every appearance of meticulous planning and the removal of evidence, the hijacker leaves a necktie on the airplane.

- The flight path of the airplane is never established. The crew never tell air traffic control where they are, and air traffic control never asks. No civilian radar data are retained. Military radar data disappear. The flight data and cockpit voice recordings disappear.
- Eight years later, some of the money is discovered on a riverbank upwind, and upstream, of where the hijacker could have lost or discarded it.

And we could continue . . .

The improbabilities that could be constructed on the basis of the hijacker's character, personality, and personal history, we shall leave aside. Sherlock Holmes also said that "life is infinitely stranger than anything which the mind of man could invent."[2] We shall not attempt to construct the hijacker's story. We are obliged to accept that he had the skills, the experience, and the qualities necessary to pull off his mission.

Insofar as we can hope to advance our understanding of Flight 305, it can be only by a reconciliation of the documentation and the physical evidence, at least of those elements that, after scrutiny, can be deemed accurate and relevant to the case.

From our study of the documents and evidence assembled and presented in the foregoing chapters, this is what we think we know with certainty or with reasonable confidence:

- The hijacker was on board the airplane at 8:05 p.m. on November 24, 1971, and was not on board when the airplane landed at Reno at 11:03 p.m.
- The crew sent six position reports to Northwest Airlines. The third report, at a time reliably recorded as 8:18 p.m., said that they were 23 nautical miles south of the Battle Ground VORTAC: that is, approximately overhead Tualatin, Oregon.
- From Seattle-Tacoma to Tualatin, the airplane's average ground speed had been about 180 knots (approximately 3 nautical miles or 3.5 statute miles per minute).
- A hand-drawn map exists that purports to be based on military radar data and to represent part of the flight path between Seattle and the Oregon-California border. This part of the flight path, as depicted, is entirely within the Victor 23 corridor. The authorship of this map is a secret. The underlying data are unknown. However, there is no evidence that the map is wrong.
- It is possible that the hijacker departed the airplane with two parachutes. One of them might have been inoperative as delivered; conceivably he could have made it operative, and conceivably he could have discarded it from the airstair. It is not known whether he deployed a parachute on exit, or at the last moment, or not at all.
- It is practically certain that the hijacker departed with all or most of the money on his person.
- It is practically certain that the hijacker jumped at an altitude of 10,000 feet above sea level.
- Data on wind speeds and directions from the surface to 10,000 feet along Victor 23 are known from NOAA radiosondes that were launched from Seattle-Tacoma Airport, Gray AAF, and Salem/McNary Airport, several times per day on most days in November and December 1971.
- At or shortly before 8.11 p.m., the crew of Flight 305 reported a fluctuation in the cabin rate-of-climb indicator. At some subsequent moment, the crew had a physiological sensation of a "pressure bump"
- The "sled test" flight on January 6, 1972, attempted to replicate the conditions of Flight 305 and of the hijacker's departure. By the normal standards of flight testing, it failed

to do so: notably by setting a lower altitude than that of Flight 305, by conducting a single drop test rather than multiple tests, and by dropping the sled with the airstairs apparently unlocked.

- Accordingly, it cannot be determined with reasonable probability that the oscillation in cabin pressure signified the departure of the hijacker.
- The airstairs placard found near Toutle, Washington, in 1978 cannot be determined with reasonable probability to have fallen from Flight 305.
- The necktie found on seat 18-E at Reno can reasonably be assumed to be the tie that the hijacker was wearing upon boarding Flight 305. In 2001 it yielded two partial samples of DNA, which have never been matched with any person alive or dead. In 2016, electron microscopy revealed unusual concentrations of antimony, gold, magnesium, silicon, and titanium, of which all but antimony have mundane explanations It cannot be determined with reasonable probability that the hijacker had ever worn the tie prior to Flight 305.
- The two parachutes that the hijacker left on the airplane are not known to have yielded any evidence of the hijacker's identity or of his place or time of departure from Flight 305.
- The money found in 1980 on Tena Bar, on the Columbia River, is undoubtedly from Flight 305. There is no evidence that Flight 305 was ever overhead or upwind (west or southwest) of Tena Bar. It is reasonably certain that the money was not deposited there by the dredging in 1974. It is a reasonable probability that it arrived by water, via some stretch of the Columbia River. It is possible that it entered the Columbia from a tributary, for which the only plausible candidate is the Willamette. With regard to the "Washougal washdown" hypothesis, there is no evidence that Flight 305 was ever sufficiently close to the Washougal River for the money or the hijacker (or both) to land in its basin.
- There is no need to assume a human agency for the arrival of the money at Tena Bar, except insofar as a person may have lost or discarded it when it first entered the water.
- The diatoms found on a $20 bill recovered from Tena Bar are of genera (and probably species) that are common in the Pacific Northwest but are typically found in slow-flowing eutrophic lakes which have high concentrations of nutrients. Within or near the Victor 23 corridor, there are several such lakes that drain into the Columbia or the Willamette River upstream of Tena Bar.
- No other physical evidence is known to exist, and no document exists in the public domain, that would further elucidate the hijacker's points of exit and landing.

Here we propose to begin eliminating the improbabilities.

First we posit that, for our purposes, the "FBI map" of the flight path is sufficiently accurate. To be more precise, we are willing to accept the hand-drawn points on the map, which look as though they were radar-based coordinates taken at one-minute intervals. We are willing to consider these points as accurate within plus or minus half a nautical mile in the east–west direction. We are not too much worried about errors in the north–south direction, since these would be outweighed by errors in the timing of the airplane's flight. At a ground speed of about 3 nautical miles a minute in a southerly direction, an error of half a minute would translate into one and a half nautical miles.

Our position implies that between Seattle and the Oregon-California border, Flight 305 never left the Victor 23 corridor; in other words, it was never more than 4 nautical miles from the centerline.

By taking this position, we eliminate the following improbabilities:

- that Flight 305 passed overhead or to the west of Tena Bar, which is 6.5 nautical miles west of the centerline
- that Flight 305 passed within parachuting distance of the Washougal River, which, at the latitude of Tena Bar, is 18.8 nautical miles east of the centerline

Second, we propose that the hijacker did not depart Flight 305 at Northwest Airlines' "point A" overhead Highland, Washington (neither the 1972 version nor the 1973 version), whatever the time that the airplane may have crossed that point, nor at any location north of that point, and that he departed at least as far south as Battle Ground (on which proposition, we will elaborate).

Let us accept for the moment that there was an oscillation in cabin pressure between 8:09 p.m. and 8:11 p.m. Let us recall that Flight 305 was timed at 8:18 p.m. at a position 23 miles south of the Battle Ground VORTAC (BTG). Traveling at 3 miles a minute over the ground, Flight 305 had to have crossed the following points at the following times:

| | | |
|---|---|---|
| 8:09 p.m. | 4 nm north of BTG | 6 nm south of point A |
| 8:11 p.m. | 2 nm south of BTG | 12 nm south of point A |
| 8:18 p.m. | 23 nm south of BTG | 33 nm south of point A |

The oscillation was therefore not at point A, but between 6 and 12 miles to the south. By taking this position, we eliminate the following improbabilities:

- that the hijacker jumped within the C-D-E-F parallelogram bounded by Pigeon Springs, Woodland, and the Victor 23 boundaries (as we have interpreted Northwest's proposal to the FBI immediately after the hijacking)
- that the hijacker jumped anywhere within the trapezoidal "jump zone" centered on Highland, as proposed by Northwest in January 1972, which became the scene of the intensive and futile search effort in and around Lake Merwin
- that the hijacker jumped within the additional search area proposed by Northwest in May 1973.

We thereby reiterate our view that the "jump zone" was a lost cause. The FBI and their ancillaries did not find anything, because there was nothing to find.

If this were all the evidence available to us, we would be tempted to place the hijacker's leap in the region of Battle Ground. If we were inclined to speculate, we would have to say that this location made much more sense than Lake Merwin: with wide-open country, mostly flat with a few low hills, and a grid of perfectly straight country roads leading south to Vancouver or west to the Interstate 5. The centerline of Victor 23 passes 2 miles west of the city center of Battle Ground. The lights of the city might have been visible through the clouds.

However, our task is not finished until we reconcile the jump and the landing point with the money at Tena Bar. There is no conceivable weather condition that could carry the hijacker and the money, together or separately, a distance of over 7 miles on a track of 255 degrees, against the prevailing wind. Unless we invent accomplices, decoys, and false trails, there is no plausible scenario whereby the hijacker lands near Battle Ground and some part of the money arrives at Tena Bar. By the principle of Occam's razor, we have to exclude Battle Ground. We are now obliged to look farther south.

If challenged to reconcile a southerly jump point with the reported pressure oscillation, we are willing to hypothesize (more accurately, to speculate) that the hijacker did indeed descend the airstair at 8:09 p.m. or 8:11 p.m. but that he did not jump. We can conceive that he tested the airstair. Certainly he must have discarded the briefcase prior to his jump; this might have been the moment. Possibly, having found one of the chest parachutes to be unusable, he jettisoned this parachute in its container. He could not use the other chest parachute because he had severed the shroud lines. In that event, he would have decided to jump with only a backpack chute. If so, perhaps one day the remains of the briefcase and the chest parachute will be discovered a few miles southwest of Battle Ground. We can conceive that the hijacker then retreated to the passenger cabin, to prepare for the jump itself.

We may now consider what scenario, consistent with the above assumptions and eliminations, can transport three bundles of money to Tena Bar.

We are as certain as is possible that at 8:05 p.m. on November 24, 1971, the hijacker was in possession of the whole of the $200,000. We have read Tina Mucklow's testimony that at one point the hijacker offered her one bundle of the ransom money, and that she might have briefly handled it and then returned it to him. We have read Florence Schaffner's testimony that the hijacker offered tips to her and the other cabin crew, in single bills from his pocket, which they also declined. Therefore the entire ransom was attached to him during the minutes preceding the jump.

Equally, we are certain that at some subsequent time the hijacker became separated from at least three bundles of money. It is conceivable that he became separated from all of the money, of which only three bundles (and hundreds of fragments) have been discovered. For convenience, we will refer to this money as the "lost money" (in all cases recognizing that the loss could have occurred by accident or by design).

We may attempt to enumerate the possibilities:

- The lost money fell from the airplane prior to the hijacker's jump. In this case, the lost money reached the ground at a position to the north of his landing or impact point. The horizontal separation on the ground could be measured in miles.
- The lost money separated from the hijacker during the descent (which could include the moment of exit, or the moment of deployment of the parachute if different, or any subsequent moment). Again, the money reached the ground roughly to the north of the hijacker. The money and the hijacker were separated horizontally by a distance measured in thousands of feet.
- The lost money separated from the hijacker at the moment of his landing or impact.
- The lost money became separated from the hijacker at some subsequent time or date. In this case there is no necessary relationship between the hijacker's landing or impact point and the point of discovery of the money.

Again we propose to apply Occam's razor to exclude the more improbable scenarios.

We propose that an intentional loss of the money requires complex assumptions and is improbable. We think that an accidental loss of the money from the airstair, in a relatively benign physical environment, is improbable. We think that an accidental loss during a stable descent is improbable. We suggest that the least improbable scenario involves an accidental loss of the money as a consequence of an abrupt physical movement—in other words, a deceleration.

In a parachute jump, the first deceleration occurs when the canopy is deployed. In a typical "soft opening," the jumper will experience between 2 g and 3 g (two to three times the force of gravity) for about five seconds. In a "hard opening," the jumper may experience between 2 g and 6 g for about two seconds.[3] The hardness of the opening depends on the model of the canopy and the quality of the packing. We do know the model of the hijacker's canopy (a military C-9), but we do not know how it was packed. The evidence favors a relatively hard opening.

The second deceleration occurs on landing. At this point, assuming a fully deployed and stable C-9 canopy, the jumper has a descent rate of about 20 feet per second, which reduces abruptly to zero on landing. A normal landing will cause a peak deceleration of the spine averaging 5.8 g, depending on the parachute, for a fraction of a second.[4]

If we were to postulate the loss of the money on deployment of the parachute, it would follow that the money fell freely from that point in the direction of the prevailing wind. Given that some of the money was found on Tena Bar, we would require Flight 305 to have been upwind of Tena Bar. But we have already eliminated that flight path. Therefore we have to eliminate the scenario of separation of the money on deployment.

In the wake of our eliminations, what remains as the least improbable scenario is the loss of the money at the moment of the hijacker's landing or impact.

In order then to account for the money at Tena Bar, we require the hijacker to have landed, or to have fallen in the water, upstream of Tena Bar.

We do not need to make an assumption as to whether the hijacker survived. This scenario allows him to lose his life on impact, or to drown, or to swim to the shore. It requires only that he land with a deceleration sufficient to detach some or all of the money from his person.

We can first conceive that he loses all the money, together with the bag that Tina Mucklow thought she saw him trying to attach to his waist. Then to account for the money at Tena Bar, we require only that the bag and its contents traveled downstream to its destination. Over the next eight years, either the bag disintegrates on the beach and all but three bundles of the money are washed away, or the bag disgorges three bundles near Tena Bar and continues downstream, possibly to the Pacific. Experts on river flows, or on the properties of materials, could no doubt elaborate this scenario.

An alternative scenario is that the hijacker loses only the three bundles on landing or impact. This requires a mechanism to keep the bundles together until they reach Tena Bar. This mechanism may be no more complex than an additional rubber band, which survives the journey to Tena Bar but is long gone when Brian Ingram goes camping in 1980.

We may now finally propose a jump zone that conforms to all the reliable evidence.

We reiterate that, absent evidence to the contrary, we are prepared to accept the flight path as depicted on the "FBI map." Shortly after 8:05 p.m. on November 24, 1971, this flight path crossed two waterways upstream from Tena Bar: the Columbia River and the Willamette River. We estimate that Flight 305 crossed the Columbia at about 8:13 p.m. and the Willamette at about 8:14 p.m. The points of crossing are shown in figure 13.1 below.

We can now introduce the drift ranges that we calculated in chapter 8 and thereby outline the circumstances whereby the hijacker lands or falls in the water.

## THE COLUMBIA RIVER

The time is 8:13 p.m. The hijacker has been in an unpressurized cabin for thirty-seven minutes. The temperature is around –5 degrees centigrade. Flight 305 approaches the Columbia on a southwesterly track, possibly attempting to rejoin the centerline of Victor 23, or to avoid overflying Portland International Airport, or to rendezvous with Air Force chase planes that have been vectored west of Portland. The airplane passes over the eastern end of Pearson Field airstrip in Vancouver. It crosses the Columbia, passes overhead Tomahawk Island, picks up Interstate 5, and makes a 45-degree turn to port, to follow the freeway.

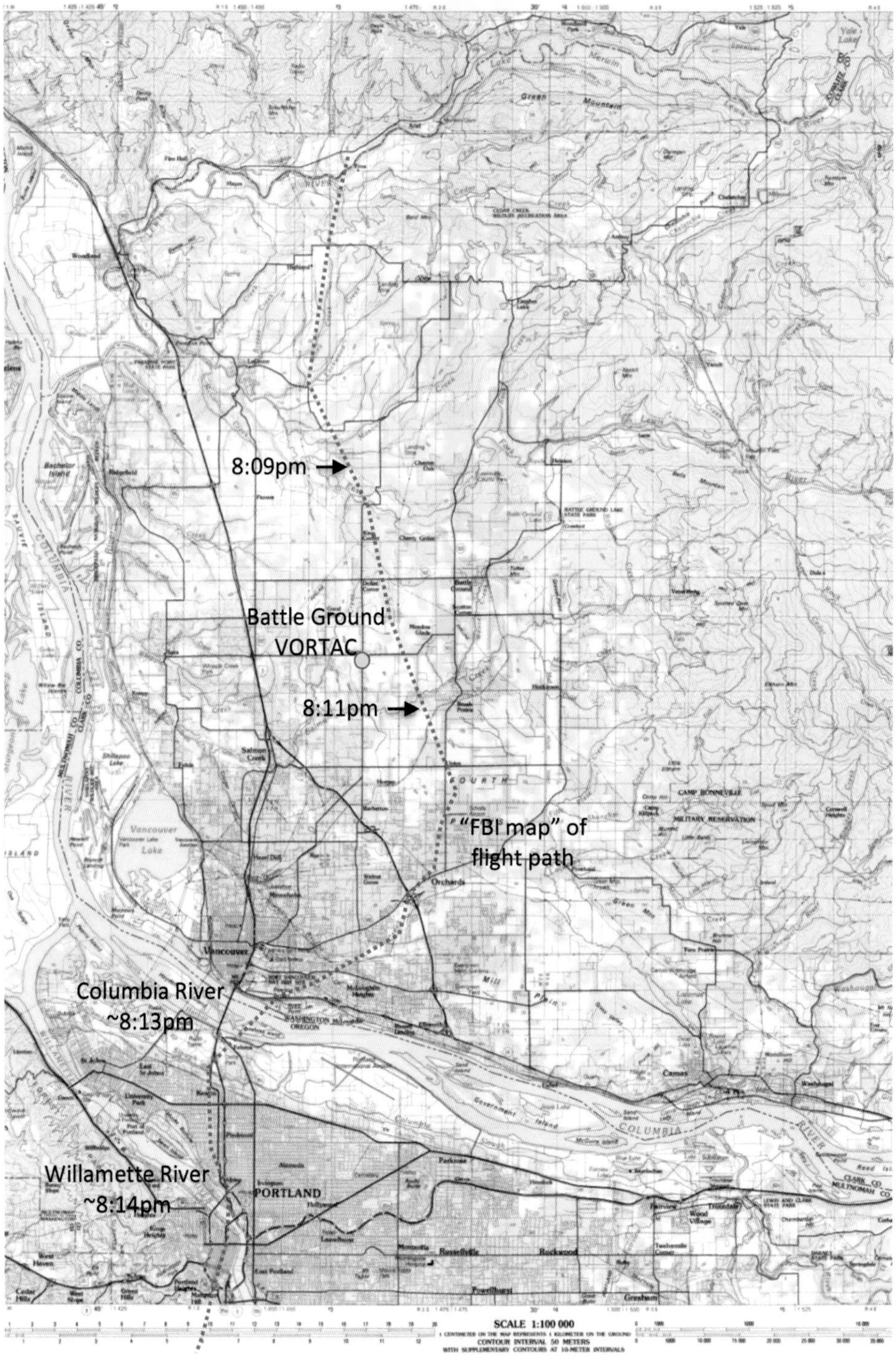


**Figure 14.1**. The "FBI map" of the flight path, and the estimated crossings of the Columbia and Willamette Rivers. *Base map from USGS*, Vancouver Quadrangle; *graphics by author*

The hijacker is on the airstair. At the moment of the turn to port, if there is a gap in the clouds, the runway lights of Portland International Airport will be visible, about 3 miles east. Within the next twenty seconds, the hijacker jumps. He is at an altitude of 10,000 feet, approximately overhead North Portland Boulevard.

Whether by accident or design, if the hijacker deploys the chute immediately, he is heading for the Columbia River.

The Columbia at this point is a few feet above sea level. The hijacker takes seven and a half minutes to reach the surface, traveling in a predominantly northerly direction, and covers a horizontal distance of 13,000 feet. About half of his landing arc is in the Columbia, between Hayden Island on the west and Broughton Beach in the east. His probability of landing in the Columbia is about 30 percent.

This is of course not the only possibility. The hijacker can free-fall till the last possible moment, say at 2,000 feet of altitude, in which case his descent time is 160 seconds and the horizontal distance is 3,400 feet. In this case, an exit over North Portland Harbor, in the channel between Hayden Island and the mainland, gives him a 60 percent probability of a water landing.

For any intermediate time of deployment, there is a corresponding exit point on the flight path that will lead to a water landing.

Finally, there is the possibility that the back parachute fails to open. In this context, we may recall that the chest pack was possibly unusable, and possibly the hijacker is not even wearing it. In this case, his descent time to impact is sixty-one seconds and the horizontal distance is about 1,800 feet. Where Flight 305 passes overhead the Columbia, the crossing from Tomahawk Bar to Tomahawk Island measures 3,200 feet. Somewhere on the crossing, the hijacker may have met his end in the freezing water.

## THE WILLAMETTE RIVER

The second scenario that can account for the money at Tena Bar is a landing or impact in the Willamette River.

At approximately 8:14 p.m., less than two minutes after crossing the Columbia, Flight 305 crosses the Willamette. As nearly as we can tell from the hand-drawn markings on the "FBI map," the crossing point is about 2,000 feet south of the Fremont Bridge. In this area, the Willamette runs roughly southeast to northwest and is generally between 1,000 and 2,000 feet wide. To the south of the bridge, the river is flowing approximately from south to north; north of the bridge, it angles to the northwest.

From approximately 8:15 p.m. to 8:18 p.m., there is a window in which the hijacker is at risk of landing in the Willamette. Very early in the window, a drift to the west will take the hijacker into the water; after the bridge crossing, at most points in this window, the drift path that ends in the Willamette will have a primarily northeasterly direction. The standard error of our estimates is such that any of these drifts is possible.

At any given moment, a landing in the Willamette is a relatively small risk, since the airplane is flying nearly parallel with the river, and the river does not present a large target. It would be like making the basket from the sideline. But over a three-minute window, in which the airplane covers 9 nautical miles, the probabilities add up.

## OSWEGO LAKE

The third scenario is a landing or impact in Oswego Lake.

Shortly before 8:18 p.m., Flight 305 passes over the western tip of the lake. We recall that at 8:18 p.m., the crew will report via the company radio that they are 23 nautical miles south of the Battle Ground VORTAC. That point is abeam Tualatin, a small town just south of Oswego Lake. The lake flows from west to east, with the outflow draining through Oswego Creek and into the Willamette River. Between 8:18 p.m. and 8:19 p.m., there is a window of less than a minute during which the hijacker, if he deploys the parachute on exit, could land in the lake. Although the time window is short, the lake is a big target, with a surface area of 395 acres and an axis running perpendicular to the flight path.

What makes this scenario a long shot is not so much the chances of landing or impact in the lake, but the necessity that the money, or part of it, find its way to the Willamette and thence to the Columbia. This journey could occur only via Oswego Creek.

Today, below the dam at the east end of the lake, Oswego Creek is usually barely more than a streambed with a trickle of water. For the above scenario to work, there had to have been a moment sometime between November 1971 and February 1980 when the dam was opened sufficiently for a money bag, or three bundles of bills somehow attached to each other, to begin the journey to Tena Bar.

Since 1971, Oswego Lake has been partially drained for sewage works at least three times: in 1979, again sometime in the 1980s, and in 2010–2011.[5] In the course of the works in 2010, the level of the lake was lowered by a level reported variously as 16 to 20, 22, or 24 feet, and the western and eastern ends of the lake bed were exposed. The works resulted in the discharge of up to 350 million cubic feet of lake water into Oswego Creek.[6] Canoe enthusiasts took advantage of the rare opportunity to paddle down Oswego Creek from Oswego Lake to the Willamette.

In previous drainage projects, smaller volumes of lake water were released, but probably on each occasion the volume was hundreds of millions of cubic feet. In the 1979 drawdown, perhaps the water discharged from Oswego Lake carried the money that would be found in February 1980 at Tena Bar.

As for traces of the hijacker's landing, on the last three occasions when the lake was drained, nothing connected to Flight 305 was reported to the newspapers. Perhaps the center of the lake, which was never drained and where the depth of water in some places is over 50 feet, is still a repository of secrets.

## WILSONVILLE AND SOUTHWARD

The fourth scenario for a water landing takes place in the vicinity of the Boone Bridge in Wilsonville, Oregon.

By our estimates, Flight 305 passes overhead Wilsonville, probably slightly north of the Boone Bridge, at about 8:20 p.m. It is possible that the city lights of Wilsonville are visible from the air, and even that the crew of Flight 305 are using the Boone Bridge for navigation. Here the Willamette flows

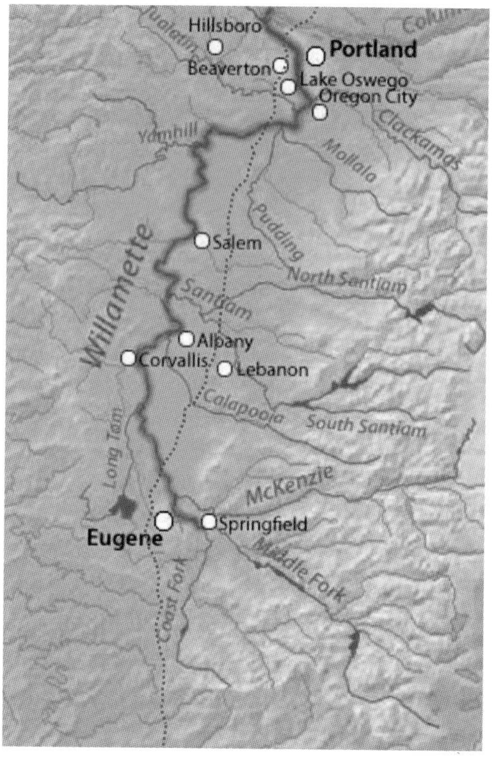


**Figure 14.2.** Flight 305 track and the Willamette River basin. *Base map from Wikipedia Commons; graphics by author*

from west to east, and the width of the river is about 1,000 feet. There is a window of about one minute when the hijacker could have the misfortune to land in this stretch of the river. It is perpendicular to his most probable drift path, and a wide range of wind conditions could put him in the water. In this scenario as in the others, we assume that he loses all or part of the money, which eventually makes its way between 36 and 42 miles downstream to the Columbia River, and another 3 miles down the Columbia to Tena Bar.

On its journey southward, Flight 305 will make at least four further crossings of the Willamette River system. The southernmost crossings are the North Santiam River south of Marion, Oregon; the South Santiam River west of Crabtree, Oregon; the Calapoola River near Halsey, Oregon; and finally the Willamette itself for the third and last time, northwest of Eugene, Oregon.

South of Eugene, as illustrated in figure 14.2, Flight 305 is outside the Willamette River basin, and there is no landing point from which any part of the ransom money could arrive by natural means on a bank of the Columbia.

## ELIMINATING THE IMPROBABLE

We are inclined to rank the probabilities, or the improbabilities, of a water landing as follows:

- An earlier time of exit is more probable than a later time (since the hijacker is exposed to the thin air, and to temperatures well below freezing).
- An early deployment of the parachute is more probable than a late deployment (since there is at least partial cloud cover below, the height above terrain may be difficult to estimate, and a prolonged descent gives more opportunity to use whatever steering is available).
- The parachute is far more likely to deploy than to fail (since the container and canopy are models of known reliability).
- A landing in the Columbia is more probable than a landing in the Willamette (since the Columbia is wider, and its east-west orientation presents a bigger target).

In figure 14.3 below, we illustrate this scenario.

In summary, we believe that the least improbable scenario that is consistent with all the reliable evidence is as follows:

- that Flight 305 crossed the Columbia River with the hijacker still on board
- that within a minute of the crossing, the hijacker departed from the ventral airstair
- that the hijacker successfully deployed the back parachute
- that a drift course averaging between northeasterly and northwesterly took him to a landing point in the Columbia
- that on landing, the money bag or some part of the money became separated and was transported downstream, eventually to arrive at Tena Bar and to be concealed by a shallow layer of sand.

We do not know whether the hijacker survived the landing or died. What we surmise is that somewhere on the bed of the Columbia River, within a mile or two east of Hayden Island, a search may uncover the rusted metallic components of an old Navy parachute pack, possibly some shreds of a C-9 canopy, and conceivably the mortal remains of the man who came to be known as D. B. Cooper.

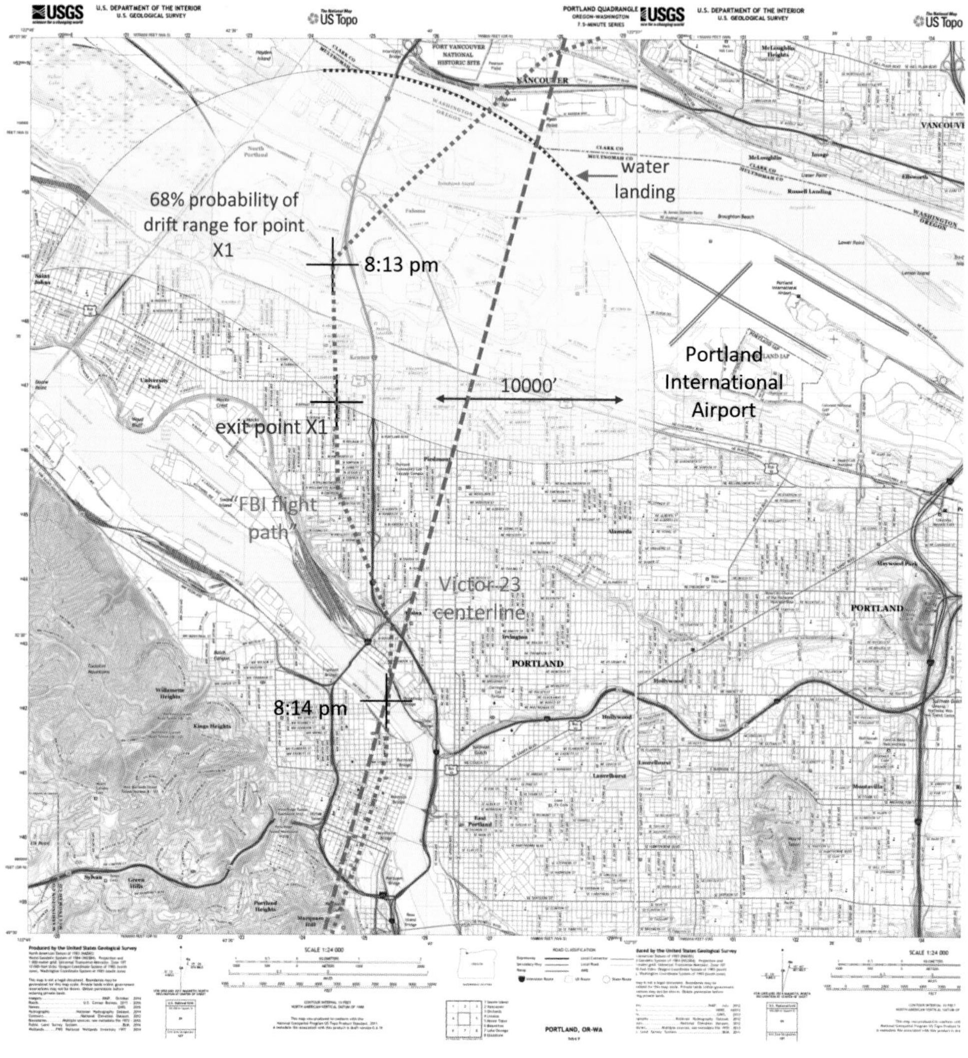


**Figure 14.3.** Illustrative scenario of the hijacker's departure after crossing the Columbia River, followed by immediate deployment of the parachute and landing in the Columbia. *Base maps from USGS, Portland and Mount Tabor Quadrangles; graphics by author*

# EPILOGUE

This epilogue is addressed—and is an invitation—to the following parties in no particular order:

- the Federal Bureau of Investigation
- the sheriff's departments of Clark County in Washington, and Clackamas. Multnomah, and Washington Counties in Oregon
- the police departments of Portland, Oregon, and Vancouver, Washington
- the Washington State Historical Society
- the Northwest Airlines History Association
- any private citizen with a metal detector and a spirit of inquiry

In this story we have set out a scenario for the events of November 24, 1971, that we believe is consistent with all the reliable documentation and physical evidence in the public domain. This scenario can be tested by searching on land and underwater, by anyone who feels impelled to do so. To this end, we propose five locations.

The first is the location of the briefcase in which the hijacker stored the contraption that he described as a bomb. The briefcase was described by witnesses as cheap looking and black or dark brown, and measuring about 12 by 18 inches. The contents of the briefcase were a bundle of six or eight reddish-colored sticks, with no labels or inscriptions, each about 6 or 8 inches long, possibly taped together; two or more wires attached to the bundle, with red insulation; and a cylindrical object, about 8 inches long and 2½ inches in diameter, with terminals resembling those of a battery.

We have proposed that the hijacker jettisoned this briefcase from the airstair a few minutes prior to his jump. It would have fallen 10,000 feet and, judging by tests on similar objects, might have survived the fall relatively intact.

We think it possible that at the same time, the hijacker may have discarded the chest parachute pack, which the FBI described as the "number 1 pack." The "number 2 pack" was found later in the airplane. The "number 1 pack," as delivered to the hijacker, was said to be unusable. It had an inscription that the FBI has redacted from its reports (probably a person's name; possibly "Johnson"). The contents of the packs were described as "chest chutes, twenty-four feet in diameter, all white nylon, model T-7A, white shrouds, about fourteen feet long" (although the canopy and shrouds would not be visible without opening the pack). The pack, if jettisoned, might also have survived the fall.

From our analysis, we surmised that the hijacker discarded the briefcase, and possibly the number one chest pack, at the time that the crew noticed an oscillation in the cabin pressure: that is, between 8:09 p.m. and 8:11 p.m. At 8:09 p.m., by our estimates, the airplane was 4 nautical miles north of the radio beacon now known as the Battle Ground VORTAC; at 8:11 p.m., it was about 2 nautical miles south of the beacon. As shown on our figure 15.1, the VORTAC is located at 7799 NE 174th Street, Vancouver, 98662; this is where the search can begin.

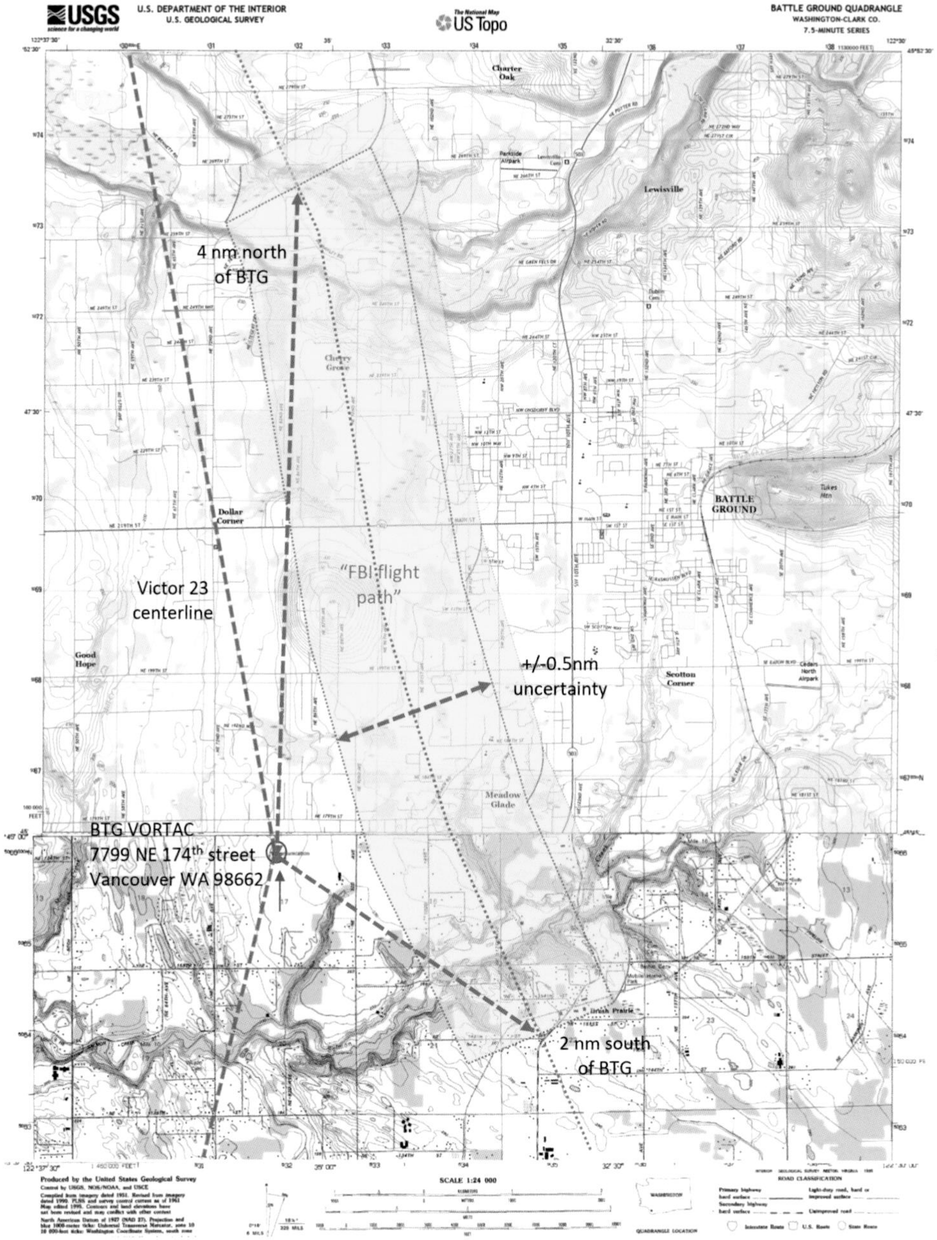


**Figure 15.1.** Battle Ground, Washington: proposed search area for the hijacker's briefcase and chest parachute. *Base maps from USGS,* Battle Ground *and* Orchards Quadrangles*; graphics by author*

The second search area is the possible landing or impact point of the hijacker in the Columbia River. We related that Flight 305 had to cross the Columbia; the "FBI map" places the crossing point just east of the interstate bridge. We estimated the time at about 8:13 p.m.

Once the airplane was about 13,000 feet south of the Columbia, a jump with immediate deployment would have taken the hijacker back toward the river. At the winds that we have estimated,

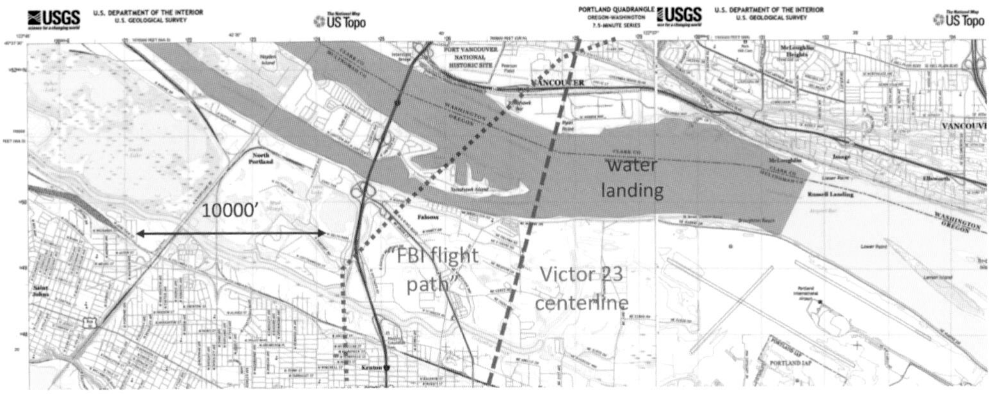


**Figure 15.2.** Columbia River between river miles 106 and 110: proposed search area for traces of the hijacker's landing. *Base maps from USGS, Portland and Mount Tabor Quadrangles; graphics by author*

with between a 30 percent and a 60 percent probability the hijacker would have overshot the Oregon shore, missed Hayden Island and Tomahawk Island, and landed either in the channel south of the islands or in the main river channel. Here we surmise that he would have lost the money, or some of it; if he freed himself of the backpack, some parts of it would have probably sunk to the riverbed, and if he was unlucky, he would have lost his life. The area that could be searched for the parachute harness, and possibly the hijacker's remains, is shown in figure 15.2 above.

The third search area, corresponding to an exit between 8:15 p.m. and 8:18 p.m., is the possible scene of the landing or impact of the hijacker in the stretch of the Willamette River that passes through Portland on its way to the Columbia.

The target stretch of the river is from river mile 8, 3 statute miles north of the Fremont Bridge, to river mile 21, abeam Oswego Creek, as shown in figure 15.3 below.

The fourth search area, corresponding to an exit between 8:18 p.m. and 8:19 p.m., is Oswego Lake itself.

Oswego Lake is a hypereutrophic lake:[1] that is, a lake that is very rich in nutrients that support algal growth, and in which, consequently, the water is opaque. Any object on the lake bed, even a few feet down, will not be visible from the surface, and any object buried in the deep soft sediments of the lake bed will not be visible at all.

A map of the proposed search area is shown in figure 15.4 below.

The fifth search area corresponds to the hijacker's exit during the window between 8:20 p.m. and 8:21 p.m. This area is the east–west stretch of the Willamette River, between river mile 35 and river mile 42, centered approximately on the Boone Bridge on Interstate 5 in Wilsonville, Oregon.

As we recounted in chapter 14, on its journey southward Flight 305 made at least four further crossings of the Willamette River system, which offer remote possibilities for anyone contemplating a search for traces of the hijacker.

It remains for an adventurous soul to search for the shattered fragments of a briefcase, and possibly a chest parachute, around Battle Ground; or the rusted remnants of a Navy backpack harness on the banks or the riverbed of the Columbia or the Willamette, or in the muddy sediments of Oswego Lake; or conceivably the mortal remains of the quiet man who hijacked Flight 305 on November 24, 1971. Whoever finds a trace of his passage may solve a mystery that has endured for fifty years.

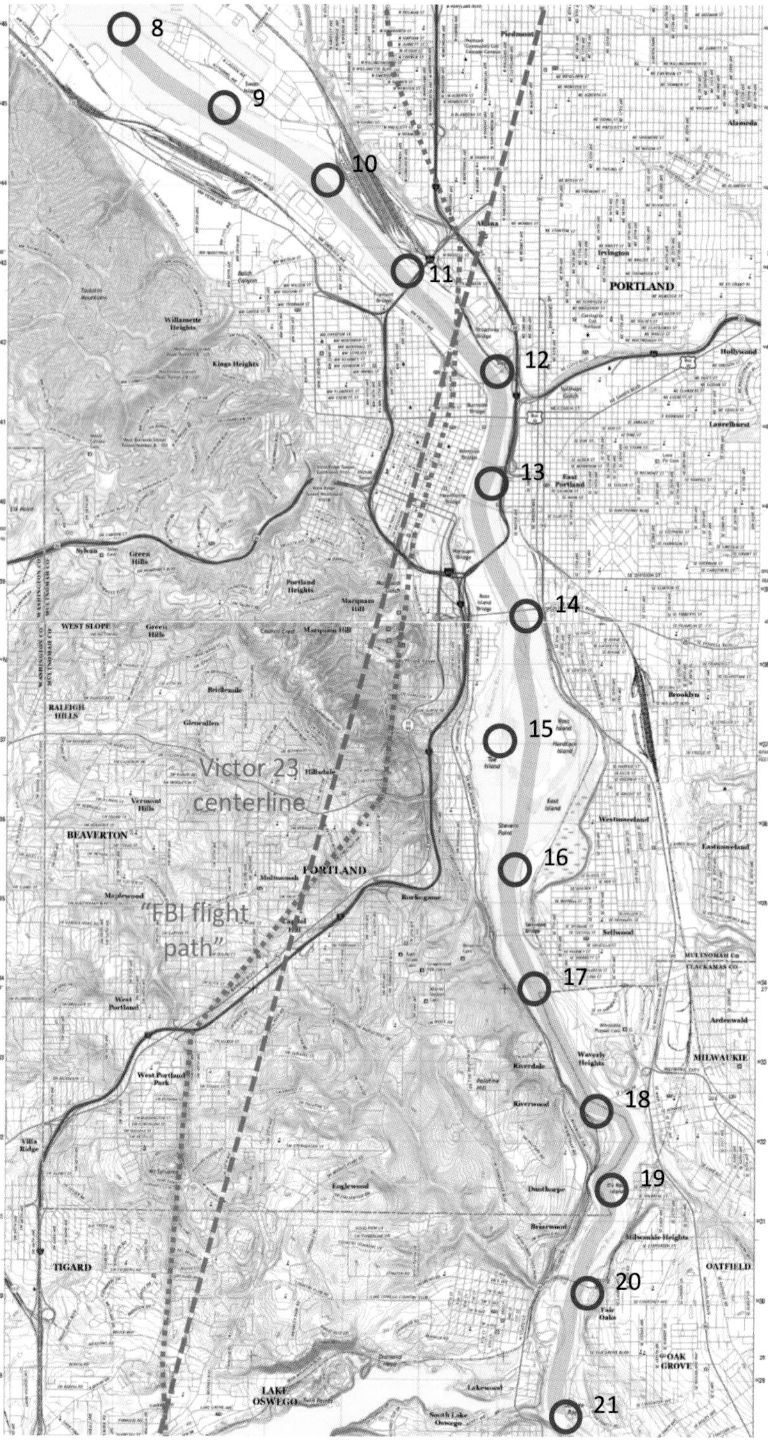


**Figure 15.3.** Willamette River between river miles 8 and 21, Oregon: proposed search area for traces of the hijacker's landing. *Base maps from USGS, Portland and Lake Oswego Quadrangles; river mile markers from Washington Geospatial Open Data Portal, WAECY–River Miles; graphics by author*

**Figure 15.4**. Lake Oswego, Oregon: proposed search area. The search area is primarily the area within the 20-foot isobath (for traces of the landing), plus Oswego Creek (for traces of money). *Base map of Lake Oswego from* Atlas of Oregon Lakes *© Portland State University; base map of Oswego Creek © 2020 Google Maps; graphics by author*

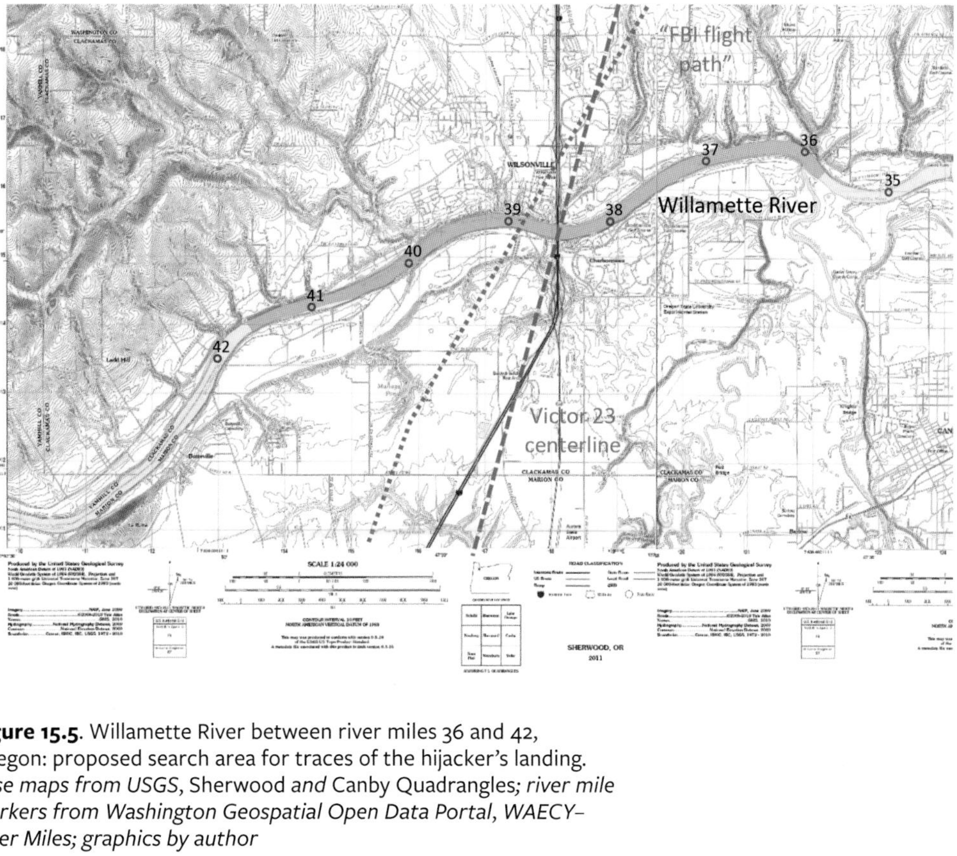


**Figure 15.5**. Willamette River between river miles 36 and 42, Oregon: proposed search area for traces of the hijacker's landing. *Base maps from USGS,* Sherwood *and* Canby Quadrangles*; river mile markers from Washington Geospatial Open Data Portal, WAECY–River Miles; graphics by author*

# AFTERWORD

## *The Usual Suspects*

In our prologue, we promised that it was not our objective to identify the hijacker of Flight 305. That task, we happily delegate to our readers. To conclude this narrative of Flight 305, we will simply dwell for a moment on the probability that any given person, alive or dead, could be a suspect in the case.

The FBI has only this to say:

> **By the five-year anniversary of the hijacking, we'd considered more than 800 suspects and eliminated all but two dozen from consideration.**[1]

On July 8, 2016, the FBI suspended the investigation, having publicly identified only three persons who had at one time been considered as suspects.

A quick search on internet forums will yield at least sixteen names of persons who have been discussed publicly as candidates for the hijacker of Flight 305. Of these, one was an actual (copycat) hijacker, four (including a transgender woman) personally claimed to have been the hijacker, two were proposed by relatives, five were proposed by researchers, and four were known to have been investigated and eliminated by the FBI. In every case, there is no evidence in the public domain that links the person to the case of Flight 305.

As an example of the futility of the best-intentioned leads, we selected a story from an attorney in Holden, Maine, who wrote a six-page letter to the FBI in Seattle on April 5, 2003, regarding a person, probably the husband of a female client, named only as "X."[2] The attorney's story, in its essence, was as follows:

- "X" looked somewhat like the FBI sketches; he had been in his thirties in 1971, but most people thought he was older; he was balding but could have worn a toupee.
- "X" was calm, self-disciplined, and methodical; had stable employment in a professional capacity; often traveled by air; and was also a keen outdoor sportsman.
- "X" had served in the US Air Force at Travis Air Base near San Francisco and had a private pilot's license and a civilian parachute rating.
- Around 1971, "X" needed money, but afterward the money problems disappeared.
- "X" was interested in, even obsessed by, the "D. B. Cooper" case and on one occasion took the attorney's client on an impromptu tour of Portland Airport.

The attorney followed up with a photograph, a social security number, and a copy of "X"'s military record. The FBI agent was not convinced. Finally, the attorney submitted a DNA profile of "X," covertly obtained.

The FBI marked the file "Cooper was not balding; eliminate"; and that was that.

It would not serve our purpose here to discuss the individuals who are mentioned, by name or otherwise, in the FBI files, and the reasons why they could or could not be the hijacker of Flight 305. Instead, we propose to end this story on a note of fun with statistics. Let us see how many persons could have been consistent with what we know, or what we believe with reasonable confidence, about the hijacker.

By all accounts, the hijacker was American. Nothing in his appearance, his accent, or his behavior gave reason to think otherwise. He was white or Hispanic or possibly Native American. By most accounts, he was between forty and fifty years old, stood between 5 foot 10 and 6 foot 1 tall, and weighed between 170 and 190 pounds; he was relatively thin, for his height.

The 1970 census of the United States enumerated 11,223,000 males aged thirty-five to forty-four and 11,101,000 males aged forty-five to fifty-four.[3] We could reasonably estimate the male forty-to-forty-nine age group at about 11.2 million.

In 1970, the census categories for ethnic groups were white (apparently including Hispanic Americans), Negro, and other (including Native Americans). In the thirty-five-to-fifty-four age group, 91 percent of the population was white or other. So we can further estimate that there were about 10.1 million white or other Americans aged forty to forty-nine.

In the period 1976 to 1980, among American males aged thirty-five to fifty-four, 31.5 percent were between 5 foot 10 and 6 foot 1, and 26.2 percent weighed between 170 and 190 pounds.[4] We could reasonably assume that the percentages were similar in 1971. If so, on November 24, 1971, about 3.2 million American men would have matched the hijacker's race, age group, and height, and about 2.6 million would have matched his race, age group, and weight.

In short, on the basis of the little that we know, 2.6 million to 3.2 million American males could have fit the hijacker's physical description.

If we were challenged to address the artists' sketches that were circulated by the FBI, we could respond that every one of the sixteen favorite suspects has been claimed to resemble one or more of those images. Yet, the sixteen suspects are visibly greatly different from each other. Not one of them has been shown to have the distinctive "turkey neck" remarked by William Mitchell. In some cases, their resemblance to the FBI's drawings requires a toupee, colored contact lenses, dark makeup, aging by fifteen years or more, or even a change of sex.

To approach the profiling from another angle, we would surely not invite contradiction if we allowed the hijacker at least some prior experience of parachuting. In that case, we should refer to the numbers of persons who were registered as sport parachutists or had had jump training with the US armed forces.

The United States Parachuting Association describes the evolution of the sport from the 1960s onward as follows:

> **Around 1970 . . . the old men on the drop zone were typically in their 40s . . . the average age for all jumpers [in 1967 was] 24.86 years. . . . From the late '60s . . . membership hovered around 10,000 to 15,000.[5]**

If the hijacker had been a registered sport parachutist in 1971, he would have been one of a community of up to 15,000 persons, although he would have been conspicuously older than the average.

Alternatively, he might never have joined a parachuting club. He might have been one of a generation of former paratroopers and other jump-trained servicemen. During the Second World War, the US Army had five airborne divisions: the 11th, 13th, 17th, 82nd, and 101st.

In the Korean War the US had only one airborne unit, the 187th Regiment of the 101st Division. An army division typically has 10,000 to 15,000 soldiers; a regiment has 1,000 to 2,000. In 1971, depending on how many airborne unit soldiers had survived the two wars, there might have been up to 77,000 Army veterans with parachute training. To these we would need to add the jump-trained veterans of the Navy, Air Force, Marines, and National Guard.

In short, on November 24, 1971, there could have been up to 92,000, and possibly many more, Americans who were capable of jumping from a Boeing 727.

We could try one final elaboration of these numbers. Let us suppose that the jump-trained Americans were physically more-or-less representative of the male American population of their age group. In that case, about 30,000 of them were between 5 foot 10 and 6 foot 1, and about 25,000 of them weighed 170 to 190 pounds.

The FBI's 800 suspects were just the tip of the iceberg.

At the end of the day, we have had some fun with statistics, but they could never lead us to the identity of the hijacker. There were simply too many men who could have done the job. No amount of leads, suggestions, claims, or denunciations, well intentioned or otherwise, could have given the FBI a viable strategy for tracking down their quarry.

On this note, we conclude our story. We did not set out to unmask the man who hijacked Flight 305, but we believe that somewhere in the Pacific Northwest, the traces of his mission are there to be found. To advance our hopes of resolving the mystery of Flight 305, we invite our readers to visit the tracts of Washington and Oregon that we have identified, and to search for themselves.

## POSTSCRIPT: THE LOADMASTER

Sometime in the early 1950s, a young man from a small town in Oregon enlisted in the US Air Force. They trained him and sent him to fight in the Korean War.

It was a step into the unknown. His family had no tradition of military service. His father owned a drugstore and his mother worked in the store. He himself, in high school, had had the ambition to be a "psychologist" (he had put the word in quotes). In the school yearbook, he had written that his greatest regret was "putting the first coin in the slot."

We do not know the details of his service history. Later, he would tell his friends that he had been a loadmaster on cargo airplanes.

That designation was formally created by the Air Force only after the Korean era. But in the early 1950s, there was only one airplane that used this term as an air crew description: the Douglas C-124 Globemaster II.

The Air Force took the first deliveries of the C-124 in May 1950. In some of the early missions, personnel from the Douglas factory were assigned to the crew of these heavy-lift airplanes, and were listed as the "Douglas Loadmaster."[6] It seems that the Douglas Aircraft Company invented this job title and the Air Force liked it. At some point, the Air Force started assigning enlisted cargo specialists to the air crew of the C-124, and designated them as "loadmasters."[7]

The young man's basic training may have started something like this:

> **I was first stationed at McChord and went through "Boot Camp" there ... After BC Training, we were asked if some of us would be willing to volunteer for an unidentified assignment. I did and was given some tests to determine my math skills, and "passed" so the result was going to Loadmaster training for a new airplane soon to begin arriving. All of us were the first class to be trained. This was in 1950, and after graduating, I**

**became a Loadmaster on a C-124, with tail number 50105 [probably operated by the 7th Troop Carrier Squadron, Heavy]. There was no slide[-]rule at that time for this aircraft loading weight and balance computations, also no hand[-]held calculators![8]**

The young man's duty as a loadmaster would include distributing and securing loads within the airplane, and as necessary, managing air drops of cargo and personnel. To prepare him for this job, he was probably sent to the survival, escape and evasion school at the 3904th Training Squadron at Camp Carson, Colorado. Today, parachute and land or water survival training is mandatory for all Air Force loadmasters; every loadmaster has access to a parachute, knows how to use it, and knows how to survive after landing.

A loadmaster would know the airspeeds and flap settings at which air drops could safely be made: something a paratrooper would not need to know. He would know how to operate the innovative load handling equipment on the C-124, such as the cargo elevator, internal hoists and clamshell doors. He would also know how to jettison cargo in an emergency. Here's a loadmaster who had over 5,000 hours on the C-124 in the 1950s:

**The cargo elevator platform can be jettisoned and cargo can be jettisoned out the opening. ... If you have oversized items, they go down with you and the aircraft. We did carry parachutes if we needed them.[9]**

In June 1950, North Korea invaded the South.

The story of the many advances and reverses of the opposing parties to the Korean War has been told elsewhere. For our purposes, it suffices to say that by the spring of 1951, the US Air Force was looking for more airlift capacity. Gen. John P. Henebry, commander of the 315th Air Division (Combat Cargo), asked for bigger airplanes. In response to his request, the Air Force ordered test flights of the C-124 between Japan and Korea, starting on 27 September 1951. The flights were a success, and from May 1952, the 374th Troop Carrier Wing at Tachikawa Air Base began the conversion to the C-124.[10]

Aviation historian Nicholas M Williams has a summary of the C-124's involvement in Korea:

**... MATS [Military Air Transport Service] C-124s played an increasingly important part in supplying allied forces in Korea, although not directly.**

**... as more MATS C-124 squadrons became operational from 1951 onwards, they took up an increasing part of the Pacific shuttle flights, carrying personnel and supplies westward into Japan ... and returning eastward with war casualties.**

**Combat Cargo would take over the actual delivery into the Korean war zone ... the Combat Cargo Command began its first operational flights from Japan to Korea with the C-124A in July 1952.[11]**

If the young man from Oregon flew the C-124 into the war zone, he would have been attached to one of six units: the 4th, 6th, 15th, 22nd, or 53rd Troop Carrier Squadrons (Heavy) or the 61st Troop Carrier Group (Heavy), as they were then designated. These were the only C-124 units that earned campaign streamers in the Korean theater.[12] If so, he could have been based at Ashiya, Johnson or Tachikawa air base in Japan, or at Larson or McChord AFB in Washington state, the latter cases involving transpacific operations. A veteran of the 22nd remembers how a squadron had to earn its streamer:

**Chanute in 1954, then to Tachikawa Japan. ... 22nd TCH. We operated thru out the far east. We had to do a remote field ops from Pyontec [Pyeongtaek] in Korea to prove we were a combat cargo Sqdn.[13]**

At mid-1953, as the war drew to a close, the Air Force had 260 C-124s in its inventory. There were 227 trained C-124 crews on hand, with 2,261 personnel.[14] At that time, the Air Force authorized an air crew of seven in the heavy troop carrier squadrons and six in the logistics and strategic support squadrons; that meant that a C-124 would have one loadmaster or two. On completion of his Far East tour, the young man from Oregon would have been one of around 350 loadmasters who had experienced the war.

After the Korean War, he was posted back to the USA. In 1955, he married his high school sweetheart in a small town in northern Oregon. On the marriage license, he gave his occupation as "US Air Force." If he was still working on C-124s, he must have been stationed at Larson or McChord, the only bases on the West Coast hosting C-124 operations at that time. If so, he would probably have been assigned to one of the squadrons of the 61st or 62nd Troop Carrier Groups at Larson or the 1705th Air Transport Group at McChord.[15]

One imagines that commuting from Larson or McChord to northern Oregon did not work for too long. He left the Air Force in 1956. With the GI Bill, he enrolled in a state college. He and his wife lived off-campus in the college town. He was a quiet and industrious student. He was not sociable. He graduated with a degree in business and technology.

The year 1962 was not a good one for him. In the summer, his mother died. A few days after Christmas, his wife brought a charge of cruelty against him: on what grounds, we do not know. Several years later, they were divorced. He had no siblings and he was alone.

In 1963 and 1964, at Larson Field, the Boeing Airplane Company conducted its tests of the 727 with the airstair lowered in flight.

On November 24, 1971, the loadmaster was nearly forty years old. Of his whereabouts on that day, we know nothing.

We fast-forward to the early 1980s. He had settled in a small town in Washington state. He had a job with a high-tech industrial facility, and as far as we can tell, he worked there until his retirement. He married again. He loved golf and was a churchgoing man. A few years prior to this writing, he passed peacefully away.

In 2020, the FBI released several new batches of files on the case of Flight 305. Among them was a letter, dated 1997, from a US Army veteran then living in Washington state. It was a thoughtful and diligent missive. The author wanted to share a story that had been on his mind for over a quarter century. In the late 1950s he had attended a state college in Oregon. He had had a classmate with whom he had sometimes shared course notes but otherwise had not known well. The classmate had said he was from Portland and had been a loadmaster in the US Air Force during the Korean War. After graduation, they had lost touch. But on reading the newspapers after Flight 305, the author said, he had been astounded by the resemblance of the FBI sketches to his former classmate. He mentioned the "shape of his head, protruding jaw, small mouth and ears."

The names of the author and his classmate, and the year of their graduation, were redacted as per FBI policy. However, this author was able to identify the year; to retrieve the yearbook from the college archives; and by analysis of the redacted spaces in the FBI files, to work out the names of the two men. Both are now deceased. The resemblance of the classmate to the FBI sketches was indeed intriguing; although, to this author's eye, he did not look Hispanic. The story of the loadmaster, which we narrated above, is the story of the classmate, to the extent that we could reconstruct it.

An FBI agent wrote on the letter "No connection to subj[ect]. No action." This author's FOIA request confirmed that the FBI did not follow up on the letter.

Was the FBI right to round-file the letter? They had chased many, flimsier, leads. Perhaps after twenty-six years they were tired of claims and confessions. Perhaps they suspected that the sketches did not greatly resemble the hijacker, and that anyone who merely resembled the sketches was probably not their man. Perhaps there were thousands of stories out there, that would fit the evidence just as well.

For what it is worth, we are prepared to advance the hypothesis that the single most likely prior occupation of the hijacker would have been loadmaster in the US Air Force, and that all or part of his service would have been in the Korean War. In that event, he would have most probably flown on the C-124, which its surviving crew still remember fondly as "Old Shakey." The Douglas Aircraft Company built 448 of these hulking airplanes; each had one or two loadmasters; thereby as many as 896 young Americans could have acquired the necessary skills to hijack Flight 305.

The service records of all Americans who fought in Korea are now in the public domain. They are held at the National Personnel Records Center in St. Louis, Missouri. At the time of this writing, the Center is closed indefinitely. Someday it will reopen, and when it does, the USPS will deliver this author's SF180 form requesting the service history of the loadmaster from the small town in Oregon. Likewise, perhaps it would not be a waste of time for the FBI to dig out the records of the airmen who worked as loadmasters on the C-124. Otherwise, we invite our readers to make of this story what they will.

# APPENDIXES

**Appendix 1. Victor 23 airway: Southbound waypoints from Seattle-Tacoma, Washington, to Red Bluff, California**

| Waypoint | Navigation aid | Latitude N | | | Longitude W | | | Radial southbound | Segment distance | | Cumulative distance | |
|---|---|---|---|---|---|---|---|---|---|---|---|---|
| | | deg | min | sec | deg | min | sec | degrees from N | km | nm | km | nm |
| Seattle-Tacoma, WA | VORTAC | 47 | 26 | 07 | 122 | 18 | 35 | – | 0.0 | 0.0 | 0.0 | 0.0 |
| MALAY intersection | – | 46 | 25 | 22 | 122 | 45 | 39 | 197 | 117.7 | 63.6 | 117.7 | 63.6 |
| Battle Ground, WA | VORTAC | 45 | 44 | 52 | 122 | 35 | 29 | 170 | 76.2 | 41.1 | 193.9 | 104.7 |
| CANBY intersection | – | 45 | 18 | 38 | 122 | 45 | 53 | 195 | 50.5 | 27.3 | 244.4 | 131.9 |
| Eugene, OR | VORTAC | 44 | 07 | 15 | 123 | 13 | 22 | 195 | 137.1 | 74.0 | 381.5 | 206.0 |
| Rogue Valley, OR | VORTAC | 42 | 28 | 46 | 122 | 54 | 47 | 172 | 184.2 | 99.5 | 565.7 | 305.4 |
| Fort Jones, CA | VOR-DME | 41 | 26 | 59 | 122 | 48 | 23 | 175 | 114.9 | 62.0 | 680.6 | 367.5 |
| Red Bluff, CA | VORTAC | 40 | 05 | 56 | 122 | 14 | 11 | 162 | 157.7 | 85.2 | 838.3 | 452.6 |

Sources: waypoints from FAA, Order JO 7400.11D—Airspace Designations and Reporting Points; navigation aids from airnav.com; radials and distances calculated by author

**Appendix 2. Flight 305 position reports as recorded by ARINC, air traffic control, and FBI, between Seattle-Tacoma International Airport and Oregon-California border**

| Source | Time PST h:mm | Altitude feet AMSL | IAS kt | TAS kt | DME from KSEA nm | OAT deg C | Altimeter in Hg |
|---|---|---|---|---|---|---|---|
| ATC | before 7:41 | | | | | | 29.91 |
| FBI. | 7:36 p.m. | 0 | | | 0 | | |
| ATC | 7:40:06 p.m. | 6,500 | | | | | |
| GH/C | 7:40 p.m. | 7,000 | | | 14 | | |
| GH/D | 7:40 p.m. | 7,000 | | | 14 | | |
| FBI | 7:40 p.m. | 7,000 | | | 14 | | |

**Appendix 2. Flight 305 position reports as recorded by ARINC, air traffic control, and FBI, between Seattle-Tacoma International Airport and Oregon-California border**

| | | | | | | | |
|---|---|---|---|---|---|---|---|
| ATC | 7:40:37 p.m. | 7,000 | 160 | 180 | | | |
| ARINC | | 7,000 | | | 19 | | |
| GH/C | 7:44 p.m. | 7,000 | | | 19 | | |
| GH/D | 7:44 p.m. | 7,000 | | | 19 | | |
| FBI | 7:43 PM | 7000 | | | 19 | | |
| ATC | 7:44:22 p.m. | 7,000 | | | | | |
| FBI | 7:45 p.m. | 7,000 | 160 | 180 | | | |
| ARINC | | 7,000 | 160 | 180 | | | |
| GH/C | 7:47 p.m. | | 160 | 180 | | | |
| GH/D | 7:47 p.m. | | 160 | 180 | | | |
| GH/D | 7:47 p.m. | | 170 | | | | |
| GH/D | 7:47 p.m. | 7,000 | 150 | 170 | | | |
| GH/C | 7:49 p.m. | | 155 | 175 | | | |
| GH/D | 7:49 p.m. | | 155 | 175 | | | |
| ATC | 7:50:05 p.m. | | | | | | 29.98 |
| ATC | 7:51:31 p.m. | 9,000 | | | | | |
| ATC | 7:53:34 p.m. | 10,000 | | | | | |
| ATC | 7:53:40 p.m. | | 170–180 | 208 | | | |
| ARINC | | 10,000 | 160 | 190 | | | |
| GH/C | 8:00 p.m. | 10,000 | 170 | 200 | | | |
| GH/D | 8:00 p.m. | 10,000 | 170 | 200 | | | |
| ARINC | 8:02 p.m. | | | | | -7 | |
| GH/C | 8:02 p.m. | | | | | -7 | |
| GH/D | 8:02 p.m. | | | | | -7 | |
| FBI | 8:10 p.m. | 10,000 | 170 | 200 | | -7 | |
| ATC | 8:13:14 p.m. | 10000 | | | | | |
| ATC | 8:15:52 p.m. | | | | | | 30.03 |
| ATC | 8:15:52 p.m. | | | | | | 30.03 |
| GH/F | 8:18 p.m. | 10,000 | 165 | 195 | 127.7 | | |
| GH/F | 8:18 p.m. | 10,000 | 165 | 195 | | | |
| GH/C | 8:22 p.m. | 10,000 | 165 | 195 | 127.7 | | |
| GH/D | 8:22 p.m. | 10,000 | 165 | 195 | 127.7 | | |
| FBI | 8:22 p.m. | 10,000 | 165 | 195 | 127.7 | | |
| ATC | 8:33:51 p.m. | 10,000 | | | | | |

**Appendix 2. Flight 305 position reports as recorded by ARINC, air traffic control, and FBI, between Seattle-Tacoma International Airport and Oregon-California border**

| | | | | | | | |
|---|---|---|---|---|---|---|---|
| GH/F | 8:50 p.m. | 10,000 | | | 206 | | |
| GH/D | 9:30 p.m. | 10,000 | 170 | | 305.4 | -5 | |
| GH/C | 9:30 p.m. | 10,000 | 170 | | 305.4 | -5 | |
| GH/C | 9:54 p.m. | 11,000 | | | 367.5 | | |
| GH/D | 9:54 p.m. | 11,000 | | | 367.5 | | |
| GH/F | 9:52 p.m. | | | | 367.5 | | |
| | | | | | | | |

ARINC: Transcript of ARINC teletype held by Washington State Historical Society

GH: George Harrison's notes held by Washington State Historical Society (letter following GH/ denotes code for original author of notes)

ATC: Transcripts of radio communications between ATC and NWA305

FBI: FBI notes dated 11.25.1971 based on ARINC and ATC

**Appendix 3: Transcripts and interpretations of radio communications between Flight 305 and Northwest Airlines Flight Operations, and between Flight 305 and air traffic control, from 7:36 p.m. to 8:34 p.m. PST on November 24, 1971**

| Source | Time PST h:mm | Raw transcript | Interpretation |
|---|---|---|---|
| FBI | 7:36 p.m. | Airplane OFF at SEA | NWA305 takes off from Seattle |
| ARINC | | MSP FLT OPS | MSP Flight Operations: [no text] |
| GH/A | 7:38 p.m. | 0338 OFF GROUND | NWA305 leaves Ground Control frequency. |
| GH/D | 7:38 p.m. | 0338 Over to Dep. Con. on 120.2 | NWA305 changes to Departure Control frequency on 120.2 kHz |
| ARINC | | 305 OUT SEA 14 MILES ON V23 OUT SEA | NWA305: [We are] out of Seattle at 14 [nautical] miles [DME] on [airway] V-23 out of Seattle. He [hijacker] is trying to get the [aft] door down. The stewardess is with us. He cannot get the [aft] stairs down. We now have an aft stair light on. |
| ARINC | | HE IS TRYING TO GET THE DOOR DOWN | |
| ARINC | | STEW IS WITH US HE CANNOT GET THE STAIRS DOWN | |
| ARINC | | WE NOW HAVE AN AFT STAIR LITE ON | |
| ARINC | | MSP FLT OPS R | MSP Flight Operations: Roger. |
| ATC | 7:40:06 p.m. | NW305: Three oh five through sixty five hundred ah trying to get the steps down back there ah | NWA305 reports passing 6,500 feet AMSL and [that hijacker is] trying to lower aft stairs |

**Appendix 3: Transcripts and interpretations of radio communications between Flight 305 and Northwest Airlines Flight Operations, and between Flight 305 and air traffic control, from 7:36 p.m. to 8:34 p.m. PST on November 24, 1971**

| | | | |
|---|---|---|---|
| GH/C | 7:40 p.m. | 0340 - 7000' 14DME V23 | NWA305 is at 7000 feet AMSL, 14 nautical miles from Seattle on airway V-23 |
| GH/D | 7:40 p.m. | 0340 7000 14DME V23 | NWA305 is at 7000 feet AMSL, 14 nautical miles from Seattle on airway V-23 |
| GH/D | 7:40 p.m. | Slowing to marked bug | NWA305 is slowing to the recommended airspeed. |
| GH/D | 7:40 p.m. | Cockpit door closed. Stew in cockpit. | The cockpit door is closed. The stewardess is in the cockpit. |
| GH/D | 7:40 p.m. | No contact. Aft stair light on. | The crew have no contact [with the hijacker]. The aft stair light is on [in the cockpit]. |
| FBI | 7:40 p.m. | 14 DME S SEA VOR at 7,000 feet, gear DOWN, flaps extending to 30° | 14 nautical miles south of Seattle VORTAC at 7,000 feet AMSL, undercarriage down, flaps at 30 degrees |
| ATC | 7:40:37 p.m. | NW305: One oh five ah three oh five we're gonna level off here for a while at seven thousand he wants the steps down and ah we're gonna have er about down to a hundred and sixty knots | NWA305 reports in level flight at 7,000 feet AMSL, [hijacker] wants to lower aft stairs, and indicated airspeed is about 160 knots |
| ARINC | 7:42 p.m. | KC0342CK | Time stamp 03:42 GMT |
| ARINC | | 11/25Φ↓ | Date stamp 11.25.1971 GMT |
| ARINC | | 305 STILL AT 7THSD FT 19 DME S V23 | NWA305: We are still at 7000 feet [AMSL] at 19 [nautical miles] DME south [of Seattle VORTAC] on [airway] V-23. Don't know, we have no communications with him [hijacker] but we have an aft stair light [illuminated in the cockpit]. |
| ARINC | | DUNNO NO COMMS WITH HIM BUT HAVE | |
| ARINC | | AN AFT STAIR LITE | |
| GH/C | 7:44 p.m. | 0344 – 7000' 19DME V23 | NWA305 is at 7,000 feet AMSL,19 nautical miles from Seattle on airway V-23 |
| GH/D | 7:44 p.m. | 0344 7000 19 DME V23 air stair light | NWA305 is at 7000 feet AMSL, 19 nautical miles from Seattle on airway V-23. The aft stair light is on [in the cockpit]. |
| FBI | 7:43 p.m. | Airplane now 19 DME S SEA VOR on V23, with gear DOWN, flaps at 30°, and at APPROACH speed. | NWA305 is 19 nautical miles south of Seattle VORTAC on airway V-23, with undercarriage down, flaps at 30 degrees, and indicated airspeed set for [landing] approach [probably 160 knots] |
| ARINC | | MSP FLT OPNS AFTR WHILE SOMEONE WIL HAVE | MSP Flight Operations: After a while someone will have to take a look in back to see if he [hijacker] is out of the aircraft. |
| ARINC | | TO TAKE A LOOK BACK TO SEE IF HE IS OUT OF | |
| ARINC | | ACFT | |

**Appendix 3: Transcripts and interpretations of radio communications between Flight 305 and Northwest Airlines Flight Operations, and between Flight 305 and air traffic control, from 7:36 p.m. to 8:34 p.m. PST on November 24, 1971**

| | | | |
|---|---|---|---|
| ARINC | | 305 R | NWA305: Roger. |
| ARINC | | MSP IF HAVE CONT ANY DISTANCE IN THAT | MSP: If [you] have contemplated[?] [flying] any distance in that configuration, 170 [knots] is your indicated optimum [air] speed. |
| ARINC | | CONFIG 170 IS UR INDCTD OPTIMUM SPEED | |
| ARINC | | 305 R | NWA305: Roger. |
| ATC | 7:44:22 p.m. | NWA305: Okay we'll hold at seven here we got the back steps down now and ah it looks like we aren't gonna be able to climb anymore ah we'll hold seven thousand | NWA305 reports leveling off at 7,000 feet AMSL and [the hijacker] has lowered the aft stairs |
| ARINC | 7:45 p.m. | KC0345CK | Time stamp 03:45 GMT |
| ARINC | | 11/25Φ↓ | Date stamp 11.25.1971 GMT |
| FBI | 7:45 p.m. | Flight at 7,000 feet, 160KIAS, fuel flow (FF) 4500°/engine, flaps 30° gear DOWN | NWA305 is at 7,000 feet AMSL, indicated airspeed is 160 knots, fuel flow is 4500 [lb/hr?] per engine, flaps are 30 degrees, undercarriage is down |
| ARINC | | MSP FLT OPNS HAVE PDX REDFBLUFF AND MEF XXX | MSP Flight Operations: You have Portland, Red Bluff, and Medford as your alternate [airports]. |
| ARINC | | MEDFORD AS ALTNTS | |
| ARINC | | 305 R | NWA305: Roger. |
| ARINC | | SEADD R HAVE THE WEA HERE. | SEADD: Roger. We have the weather here. |
| ARINC | | MSP FLT OPNS IS IT GENRLLY GOOD | MSP Flight Operations: Is it generally good? |
| ARINC | | SEADD ITS FOG AND HAZE | SEADD: It's fog and haze. |
| ARINC | | MSP FLT OPNS WIL GET IT HERE | MSP Flight Operations: We will get it [weather] here. |
| ARINC | 7:46 p.m. | KC0346CK | Time stamp 03:46 GMT |
| ARINC | | 11/25Φ↓ | Date stamp 11.25.1971 GMT |
| ARINC | | 305 HLDG 160 INDCTD WHICH IS APPROX 5 KTS | NWA305: We are holding 160 [knots] indicated [airspeed] which is approximately 5 knots above the bug [= stall speed?]. Holding 7000 feet [altitude AMSL]. Fuel flow is 4,500 [lb./hour for each engine]. |
| ARINC | | ABV THE BUG HLDG 7THSD FT INDCTD 160 | |
| ARINC | | FUEL FLO IS 4TXXX RIXXX RTHNDXXXK 45HND | |
| ARINC | | MSP FLT OPKS OK U WILL NOT BE ABLE TO GET | MSP Flight Operations: OK. You will not be able to get to Reno in that configuration unless he [hijacker] is gone. |

**Appendix 3: Transcripts and interpretations of radio communications between Flight 305 and Northwest Airlines Flight Operations, and between Flight 305 and air traffic control, from 7:36 p.m. to 8:34 p.m. PST on November 24, 1971**

| | | | |
|---|---|---|---|
| ARINC | | 70 RENO IN THAT CONFIG UNLESS HE IS GONE | |
| ARINC | | 305 R | NWA305: Roger. |
| ARINC | | MSP R 170 KTS INDCTD AND HIER THE CABIN IS | MSP: Roger. [You need] 170 knots indicated [airspeed] and higher. The cabin [air?] is the better if you guys have [oxygen] masks on. |
| ARINC | | THE BETTER IF U GUYS HAVE MASKS ON | |
| ARINC | | 305 R | NWA305: Roger. |
| GH/C | 7:47 p.m. | 0347 – 160K IAS → 160 K IAS ↗ 10000 | NWA305 has indicated airspeed of 160 knots, climbing to 10,000 feet AMSL |
| GH/D | 7:47 p.m. | 0347 160 IAS 5 ab flap bug FF 4500 ea | NWA305 has indicated airspeed of 160 knots, 5 knots above the recommended speed for the flap setting. The fuel flow is 4,500 lb/hour for each engine. |
| GH/D | 7:47 p.m. | going to 170k 2 of 3 on $O_2$ | NWA305 is going to 170 knots [indicated airspeed]. Two of the three [air crew?] are using oxygen. |
| GH/D | 7:47 p.m. | leaving 7000 for 10000 150 IAS slow | NWA305 is leaving 7000 feet to climb to 10000 feet AMSL at an indicated airspeed of 150 knots. This is a slow climb. |
| GH/D | 7:47 p.m. | climb | |
| ARINC | 7:48 p.m. | KC0348CK | Time stamp 03:48 GMT |
| ARINC | | 11/25Φ↓ | Date stamp 11.25.1971 GMT |
| ARINC | | 305 GG TO 15DEG AND BEGINNING OUR CLIMB | NWA305: Going to 15 degrees [flap?] and beginning our climb. |
| ARINC | | MSP R | MSP: Roger. |
| ARINC | 7:48 p.m. | KC0348CK | Time stamp 03:48 GMT |
| GH/C | 7:49 p.m. | 0349 - 155 IAS | NWA305 has indicated airspeed of 155 knots |
| ARINC | between 7:48 and 7:54 | 11/25Φ↓ | Date stamp 11.25.1971 GMT |
| ARINC | | 91 LWT 0336 350 MLP 0410 | Appears to refer to another flight |
| ARINC | | ETA SEA 0455 | |
| ARINC | | NEED 0M30 FORMS | |
| GH/D | 7:49 p.m. | 0349 going to 15° flaps 155 IAS | NWA305 reports setting flaps at 15 degrees and indicated airspeed at 155 knots. |
| ARINC | | 11/25Φ↓ | Date stamp 11.25.1971 GMT |
| ARINC | | MSP FLT OPS AS SOON AS REASONBLY SURE THE MAN | MSP Flight Operations: As soon as you are reasonably sure that the man [hijacker] has left, the quicker you can land. |

**Appendix 3: Transcripts and interpretations of radio communications between Flight 305 and Northwest Airlines Flight Operations, and between Flight 305 and air traffic control, from 7:36 p.m. to 8:34 p.m. PST on November 24, 1971**

| | | | |
|---|---|---|---|
| ARINC | | HAS LEFT THE QUICKER U CAN LAND | |
| ARINC | | 305 R MISS MUCKLOW SAID HE APPARENTLY | NWA305: [Cabin crew] Miss Mucklow said that he apparently has the knapsack around him and she thinks that he will attempt a jump. |
| ARINC | | HAS THE KNAPSACK AROUND HIM AND THINKS HE | |
| ARINC | | WILL ATTEMPT A JUMP | |
| ARINC | | MSP FLT OPS R AFTR LVG THIS FREQ GO TO | MSP Flight Operations: Roger. After leaving this frequency, go to 131.8 [kHz]. We have a direct phone patch there. |
| ARINC | | 131.8 WE HAVE DIRECT PHONE PATCH THERE | |
| ARINC | | 305 R | NWA305: Roger. |
| ATC | 7:50:05 p.m. | SEA R2: Northwest three zero five Toledo altimeter two niner niner eight | Seattle ARTCC controller R2 advises NWA305 that altimeter setting for Toledo VORTAC is 29.98 inches |
| ATC | 7:51:31 p.m. | NWA305: Center Northwest three oh five ah we're gonna climb out climbing up ah to ten thousand and ah we're through nine now | NWA305 reports passing 9000 feet AMSL and climbing to 10,000 feet AMSL |
| ATC | 7:53:34 p.m. | NWA305: Northwest three oh five we're leveling at ten thousand | NWA305 reports leveling off at 10000 feet AMSL |
| ATC | 7:53:40 p.m. | NWA305: Airspeed in the vicinity of one seventy one eighty | NWA305 reports indicated airspeed around 170–180 knots |
| ARINC | 7:54 p.m. | KC0354CK | Time stamp 03:54 GMT |
| ARINC | | 11/25Φ↓ | Date stamp 11.25.1971 GMT |
| ARINC | | MSP FLT OPS HAVE STEW DESCRIBE TO U | MSP Flight Operations: Have the stewardess describe to you the briefcase contents. We understand that there are red dynamite sticks, wire and a battery. |
| ARINC | | THE BRIEF CASE CONTENTS UNDERSTAND | |
| ARINC | | RED DYNAMITE STICKS WIRE AND BATTERY | |
| ARINC | | 305 STEW IN BRF CASE LEFT CORNER HAD 8 | NWA305: Stewardess [says that] the left corner of the briefcase had 8 sticks of dynamite, about 6 inches long and 1 inch in diameter, two rows of them, then a wire out of there, then a battery like a flashlight battery, only "as thick as my arm" and 8 inches long. |
| ARINC | | STICKES OF KXXK DYNAMITE ABT 6 INCHES LONG | |

**Appendix 3: Transcripts and interpretations of radio communications between Flight 305 and Northwest Airlines Flight Operations, and between Flight 305 and air traffic control, from 7:36 p.m. to 8:34 p.m. PST on November 24, 1971**

| | | | |
|---|---|---|---|
| ARINC | | AND 1 INCH IN DIAMTR TWO ROWS OF THEM | |
| ARINC | | THEN A WIRE OUT OF THERE THEN A BATT LITE | |
| ARINC | | A FLASKLITE BATT ONLY AS STHIK AS MY ARM | |
| ARINC | | AND 8 INCHES LONG | |
| ARINC | | MSP R | MSP: Roger. |
| ARINC | 7:57 p.m. | KC0357CK | Time stamp 03:57 GMT |
| ARINC | | 11/25Φ↓ | Date stamp 11.25.1971 GMT |
| ARINC | | MSP FLT OPS WHT IS ALTDE | MSP Flight Operations: What is your altitude? |
| ARINC | 7:58 PM | 305 NOW AT 15THSD INDCTD 160 FUEL FLOW | NWA305: We are now at 15,000 [?] [feet AMSL]. Indicated [airspeed is] 160 [knots]. Fuel flow is 4000 [lb/hour, each engine]. 15 degrees of flap, gear down configuration. Will stay at 10,000 [feet AMSL] until he [hijacker] has left. |
| ARINC | | 4,000 15 DEG FLAP GEAR DOWN CON WILL STAY | |
| ARINC | | AT IXX TEN THSD TIL HE HAS LEFT | |
| ARINC | | MSP FLT OPS R | MSP Flight Operations: Roger. |
| GH/C | 8:00 p.m. | 0400–10,000 LEVEL 170 IAS | NWA305 is level at 10,000 feet AMSL, indicated airspeed is 170 knots |
| GH/D | 8:00 p.m. | 0400 10,000 level 170 IAS FF 4000 ea | NWA305 is level at 10,000 feet AMSL, indicated airspeed is 170 knots, fuel flow is 4000 lb/hour each engine. Flap setting is 15 degrees, undercarriage is down. |
| GH/D | 8:00 p.m. | 15° Flaps, gear down. | |
| GH/F | 8:00 p.m. | 0400 100/ FF 4000# Qh per eng gear down flaps 15 | NWA305 is at 10,000 feet AMSL, fuel flow is 4,000 lb/hour for each engine, undercarriage is down, flap setting is 15 degrees. |
| ARINC | 8:01 p.m. | KC0401CK | Time stamp 04:01 GMT |
| ARINC | | 11/25Φ↓ | Date stamp 11.25.1971 GMT |
| ARINC | | MSP FLT OPNS NO TERRAIN XCEES 8THSD ON THAT | MSP Flight Operations: There is no terrain exceeding 8,000 [feet AMSL] on that route. Then you have to go to 10,500 or 11,000 [feet AMSL] between Red Bluff and Reno, if you have to go that far. |
| ARINC | | RTE THER HAVE TO GO TO TEN FIVE OR ELEVEN BTWN | |

**Appendix 3: Transcripts and interpretations of radio communications between Flight 305 and Northwest Airlines Flight Operations, and between Flight 305 and air traffic control, from 7:36 p.m. to 8:34 p.m. PST on November 24, 1971**

| | | | |
|---|---|---|---|
| ARINC | | RED BLUFF AND RENO IF U HAVE TO GO THAT FAR | |
| ARINC | | 305 R | NWA305: Roger. |
| ARINC | 8:02 p.m. | KC0402CK | Time stamp 04:02 GMT |
| ARINC | | 11/25Φ↓ | Date stamp 11.25.1971 GMT |
| ARINC | | 305 TTL AIR TEMP MINUS 7 DEG MACH METER | NWA305: total air temperature is minus 7 degrees [C]. The Mach meter has no indication. |
| ARINC | | NO- INDCTN | |
| GH/C | 8:02 p.m. | 0402 - NO MACH IND. TAT -7°C | NWA305 has no indication on the Mach meter. The Total Air Temperature is minus 7 degrees C. |
| GH/D | 8:02 p.m. | 0402 No Mach. TAT -7°C | NWA305 has no indication on the Mach meter. The Total Air Temperature is minus 7 degrees C. |
| ARINC | | MSP FLT OPNS OX THE MACH METER WOND INDTE TIL | MSP Flight Operations: OK. The Mach meter won't indicate until you get higher. |
| ARINC | | U GET HIER | |
| ARINC | | 305 R | NWA305: Roger. |
| ARINC | B:03 | KCO403CK | Time stamp 04:03 GMT |
| GH/D | Between 7:54 and 8:05 | 11/25Φ↓ | Date stamp 11.25.1971 GMT |
| GH/D | | 91 HAS MR REIFF THE ALP FLIGHT | Appears to refer to another flight |
| GH/D | | SECURITY COORDINATOR AND IS INBOUND | |
| GH/D | | TO SEA ON THEIR FLIGHT. RQST THE FAA | |
| GH/D | | BE CONTACTED 905↓3 ↓9EE | |
| GH/D | | ON THE HOT LINE | |
| ARINC | | 11/25Φ↓ | Date stamp 11.25.1971 GMT |
| ARINC | | 305 HAVE ATTMPTD 2 OCCNS TO MAKE CTC | NWA305: We have attempted on two occasions to make contact with the individual [hijacker]. He did not reply. Then [he came on] the Public Address system and he said that everything is OK. |
| ARINC | | WITH INDVDL HE DID NOT APXXX EPLY | |
| ARINC | | DID NOT REPLY THEN P A SYSTEM AND HE | |
| ARINC | | AID EVRYTHING IS OK | |

**Appendix 3: Transcripts and interpretations of radio communications between Flight 305 and Northwest Airlines Flight Operations, and between Flight 305 and air traffic control, from 7:36 p.m. to 8:34 p.m. PST on November 24, 1971**

| | | | |
|---|---|---|---|
| ARINC | | MSP FLT OPS OK [PORTLAND] | MSP Flight Operations: OK. [Portland annotated by hand] |
| ARINC | 8:05 p.m. | KC0405CK | Time stamp 04:05 GMT |
| ARINC | | 11/25Φ↓ | Date stamp 11.25.1971 GMT |
| GH/C | 8:05 p.m. | 0405 - LAST CONTACT WITH HIJACKER | NWA305 crew have last contact with the hijacker. |
| ARINC | | MSP FLT OPNS MEDFORD IS BEST CHOICE SHORT | MSP Flight Operations: Medford [airport] is your best choice short of Reno. And [landing at] Reno may become a bit tight. |
| ARINC | | OF RENO AND RENO MAY ECOME A IT TITE | |
| ARINC | | 305 R | NWA305: Roger. |
| ARINC | 8:06 p.m. | KCO406CK | Time stamp 04:06 GMT |
| ARINC | | 11/25Φ↓ | Date stamp 11.25.1971 GMT |
| ARINC | | 305 CHK MANUALS DONT HAVE MEDFORD APRCHP | NWA305: [Can you] check the manuals. We don't have the Medford [airport] approach plates. |
| ARINC | | PLATES | |
| ARINC | | MSP R WILHV IT FOR U IF WE HAVE A COMM | MSP: Roger. Will have it for you. If we have a communication problem, the tower will guide [you] through it. |
| ARINC | | PROBLEM THE TWR WILL GUIDE IT THRU IT | |
| ARINC | | 305 R | NWA305: Roger. |
| ARINC | 8:09 p.m. | KCO409CK | Time stamp: 08:09 GMT |
| ARINC | | SEADD EXXX WE GAVE HIME PLATES FOR ALL OF IT | SEADD: We gave him [approach] plates for all of it. |
| ARINC | | 305 R FOUND IT | NWA305: Roger. We found it. |
| ARINC | | 11/25Φ↓ | Date stamp 11.25.1971 GMT |
| ARINC | | MSP FLT OPS RENO LOLKS BETTER AS TIME | MSP Flight Operations: Reno [weather] looks better as time goes by. It has 25 [percent?] overcast. 12 [nautical] miles [visibility?]. North wind, 15 knots, gusty. |
| ARINC | | GOES BY HAS 25T OVC 12 MILES N WIND 15 | |
| ARINC | | GUSTY | |
| ARINC | | 305 R | NWA305: Roger. |
| FBI | 8:10 p.m. | Airplane now at 10,000 feet, 170K, gear DOWN, flaps 15°, FF 4000#/hour/engine, TAT −7°C. | NWA305 is at 10,000 feet AMSL, indicated airspeed is 170 knots, undercarriage is down, flaps are set to 15 degrees, fuel flow is 4,000 lb/hour per engine, outside air temperature is minus 7 degrees C. |

**Appendix 3: Transcripts and interpretations of radio communications between Flight 305 and Northwest Airlines Flight Operations, and between Flight 305 and air traffic control, from 7:36 p.m. to 8:34 p.m. PST on November 24, 1971**

| | | | |
|---|---|---|---|
| ARINC | 8:10 p.m. | KC0410CK | Time stamp 04:10 GMT |
| ARINC | | 11/25Φ↓ | Date stamp 11.25.1971 GMT |
| ARINC | | 305 GETTING SOME OSCLLTNS IN THE CABIN | NWA305: We are getting some oscillations in the cabin. [The hijacker] must be doing something with the [aft] air stairs. |
| ARINC | | MUS BE DOING SOMETHING WITH AIR STAIRS | |
| ARINC | | MSP FLT OPS R | MSP Flight Operations: Roger. |
| GH/C | 8:11 p.m. | 0411 - CABIN FLUCTUATING xA | NWA305 crew experience fluctuation in cabin [pressure?] |
| ARINC | 8:12 p.m. | KC0412CK | Time stamp 04:12 GMT |
| ARINC | | 11/25Φ↓ | Date stamp 11.25.1971 GMT |
| ARINC | | 305 CALLED | NWA305: called [no text?] |
| ARINC | | MSP FLT OPNS GO TO 131.8 | MSP Flight Operations: Go to [frequency] 131.8 [kHz]. |
| ARINC | | SEADD HE IS ALREADY ON THAT FREQ | SEADD: He [NWA305] is already on that frequency. |
| ARINC | | MSP R WE ON HE PHONE WND WILL BE TALING | MSP: Roger. We are on the phone and will be talking to him [NWA305] shortly. |
| ARINC | | JO HIM SHORTLY | |
| ARINC | | SEADD R | SEADD: Roger. |
| ATC | 8:13:14 p.m. | NWA305: Center four oh five (unintelligible) twenty point nine ten thousand | NWA305 reports that [altimeter setting?] is 20.9? and altitude is 10000 feet AMSL |
| ATC | 8:15:52 p.m. | SEA R5: Northwest three zero five the Portland altimeter three zero zero five | Seattle ARTCC controller R5 advises that altimeter setting for Battle Ground VORTAC is 30.05 inches |
| ATC | 8:15:52 p.m. | NWA305: zero zero three | NWA305 reports that altimeter setting is 30.03 inches |
| GH/F | 8:18 p.m. | 0418 23 DME PDX 100/ | NWA305 is 23 nautical miles south of Battle Ground VORTAC; altitude is 10,000 feet; 40,000 lb fuel on board, fuel flow is 4,000 lb/hour for each engine; indicated airspeed is 165 knots. [NO CORRESPONDING ARINC MESSAGE} |
| GH/F | 8:18 p.m. | FOB 40000# FF 4000# 165 | |
| ARINC | 8:20 p.m. | KC0420CK | Time stamp 04:20 GMT |
| ARINC | | 11/25Φ↓ | Date stamp 11.25.1971 GMT |
| ARINC | | 57 BY BIL 0413/350 OAT -58 C-S | Appears to refer to another flight |
| ARINC | | BER GEG 0530 SHIP 377 NO MNTNC | Appears to refer to another flight |

**Appendix 3: Transcripts and interpretations of radio communications between Flight 305 and Northwest Airlines Flight Operations, and between Flight 305 and air traffic control, from 7:36 p.m. to 8:34 p.m. PST on November 24, 1971**

| | | | |
|---|---|---|---|
| ARINC | | MSP GAVE 0400Z OBS | MSP: gave [weather] observations for 0400Z [0400 GMT = 2000 PST] |
| GH/C | 8:22 p.m. | 0422 23 DME S of PDX (DME 10,000) 165 IAS | NWA305 is 23 nautical miles south of Battle Ground VORTAC, at 10,000 feet, Indicated airspeed is 165 knots. [NO CORRESPONDING ARINC MESSAGE} |
| GH/D | 8:22 p.m. | 23 DME S. of PDX 10,000 F.O.B 40,000# FF 4000 165 IAS | NWA305 is 23 nautical miles south of Battle Ground VORTAC, at 10,000 feet, fuel on board is 40,000 lb, fuel flow is 4,000lb/hr for each engine, indicated airspeed is 165 knots. [NO CORRESPONDING ARINC MESSAGE] |
| FBI | 8:22 p.m. | Flight now 23 DME S PDX at 10,000', 40,000# fuel aboard, 165KIAS, FF and configuration remained the same. | NWA305 is 23 nautical miles south of Battle Ground VORTAC, at 10,000 feet AMSL, indicated airspeed 165 knots, fuel flow and configuration same as before. [NO CORRESPONDING ARINC MESSAGE} |
| ARINC | 8:24 p.m. | KD0424KN | Time stamp 04:24 GMT |
| ATC | 8:33:51 p.m. | NWA305: Seattle Center Northwest three zero five ten thousand | NWA305 reports altitude 10,000 feet AMSL |
| | | | |

ARINC: Transcript of ARINC teletype held by Washington State Historical Society

GH: George Harrison's notes held by Washington State Historical Society (letter after GH/ denotes original author)

ATC: Transcripts of radio communications between ATC and NWA305

FBI: FBI notes dated 11.25.1971 based on ARINC and ATC

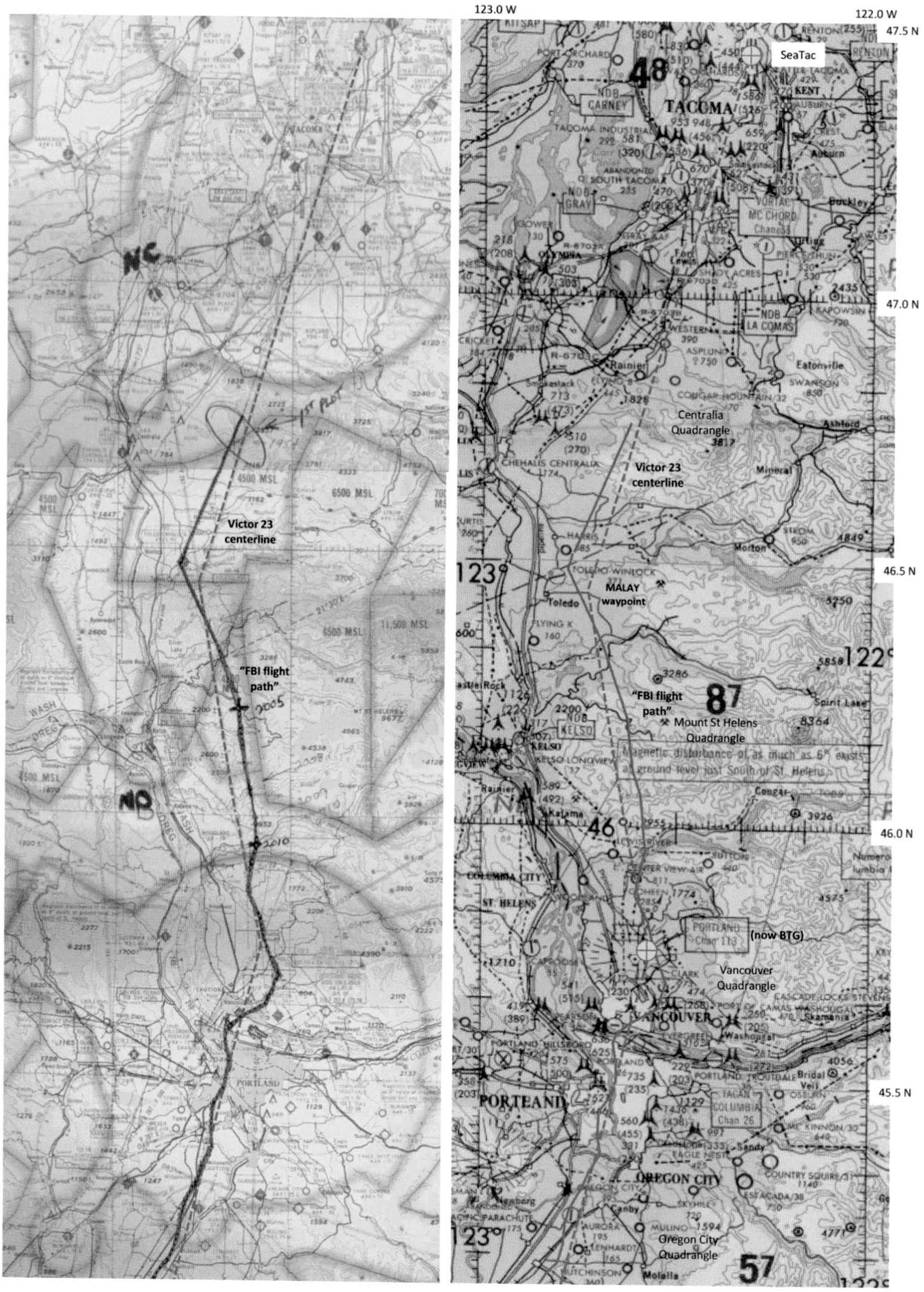


**Appendix 4**. Flight 305, Victor 23, and "FBI map," part 1: *Tacoma Quadrangle to Oregon City Quadrangle. Base maps from FBI (courtesy of Washington State Historical Society) and US Air Force Operational Navigation Chart F-16, 1982 edition (courtesy of University of Texas at Austin). Graphics by author*

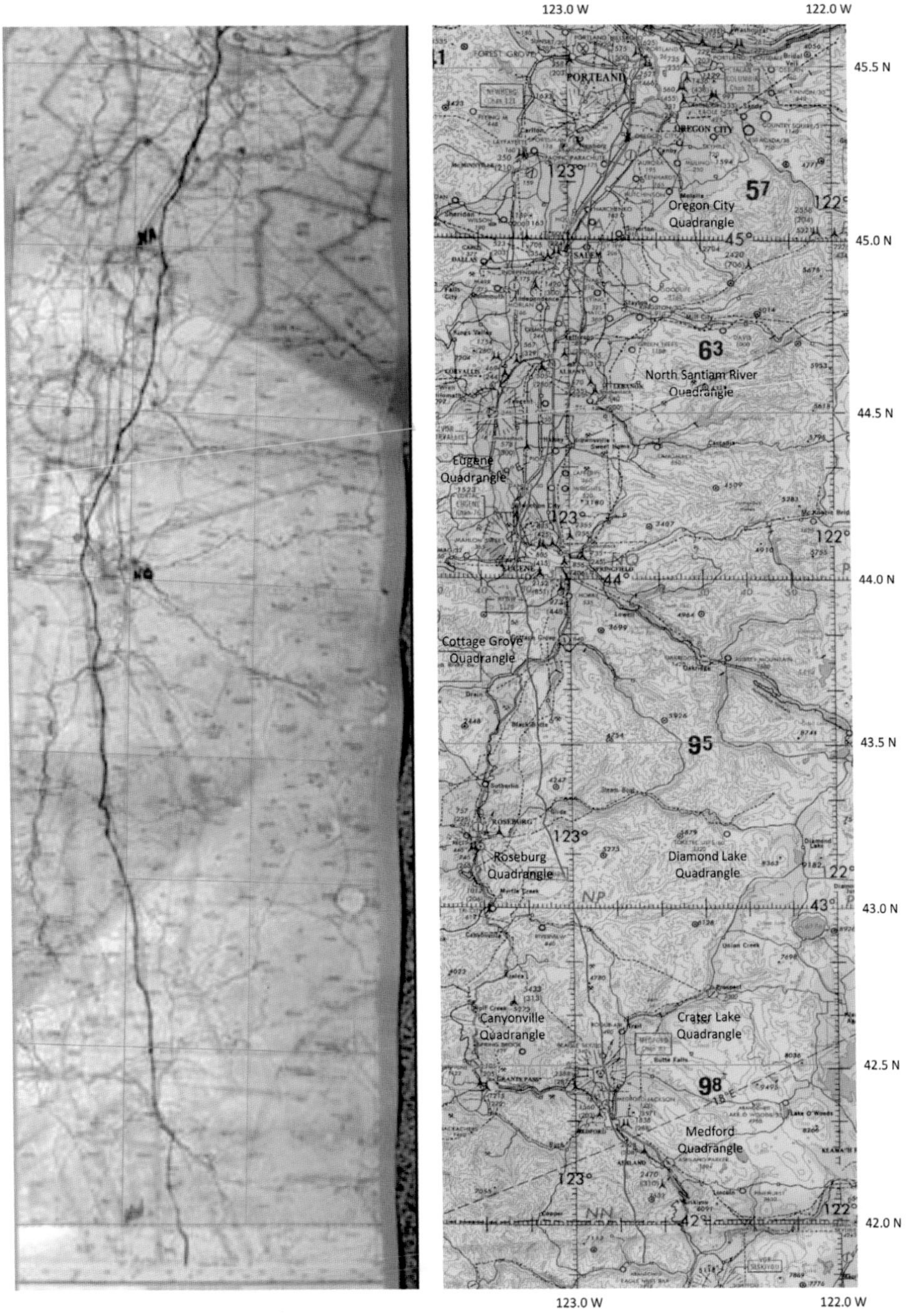


**Appendix 5**. Flight 305, Victor 23, and "FBI map," part 2: *Oregon City Quadrangle* to *Medford Quadrangle. Base maps from FBI and US Air Force Operational Navigation Chart F-16, 1982 edition (courtesy of University of Texas at Austin). Graphics by author*

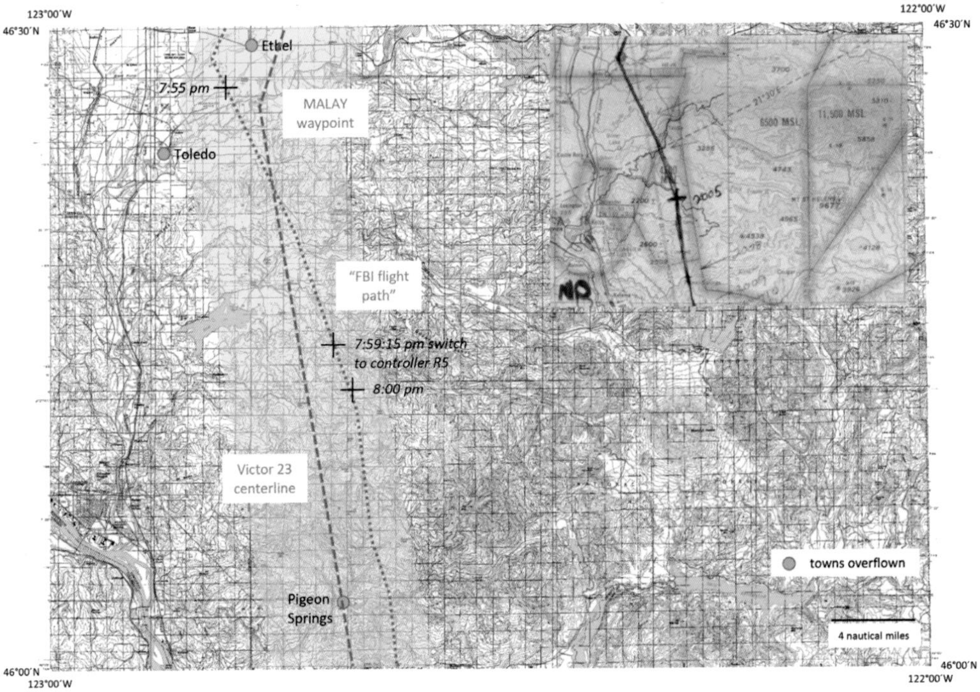


**Appendix 6**. Flight 305, Victor 23 airway, and *Mount Saint Helens Quadrangle. Base map from USGS, scale 1:100,000; inset "FBI map"; graphics and time estimates by author*

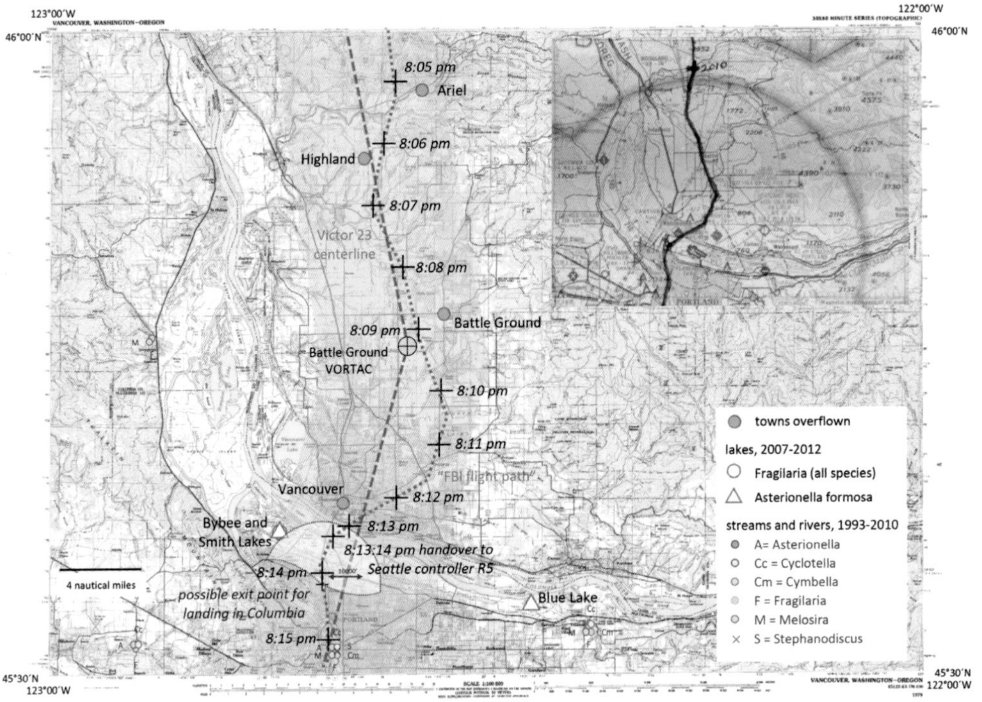


**Appendix 7**. Flight 305, Victor 23 airway, and *Vancouver Quadrangle. Base map from USGS, scale 1:100,000; inset "FBI map"; graphics and time estimates by author*

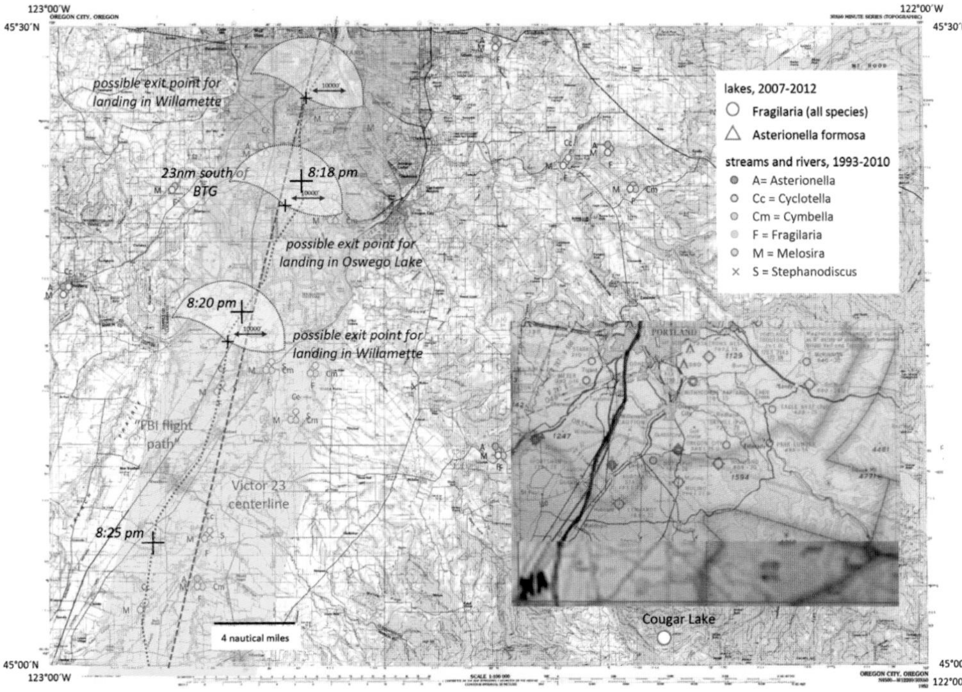


**Appendix 8**. Flight 305, Victor 23 airway, and *Oregon City Quadrangle. Base map from USGS, scale 1:100,000; inset "FBI map"; graphics and time estimates by author*

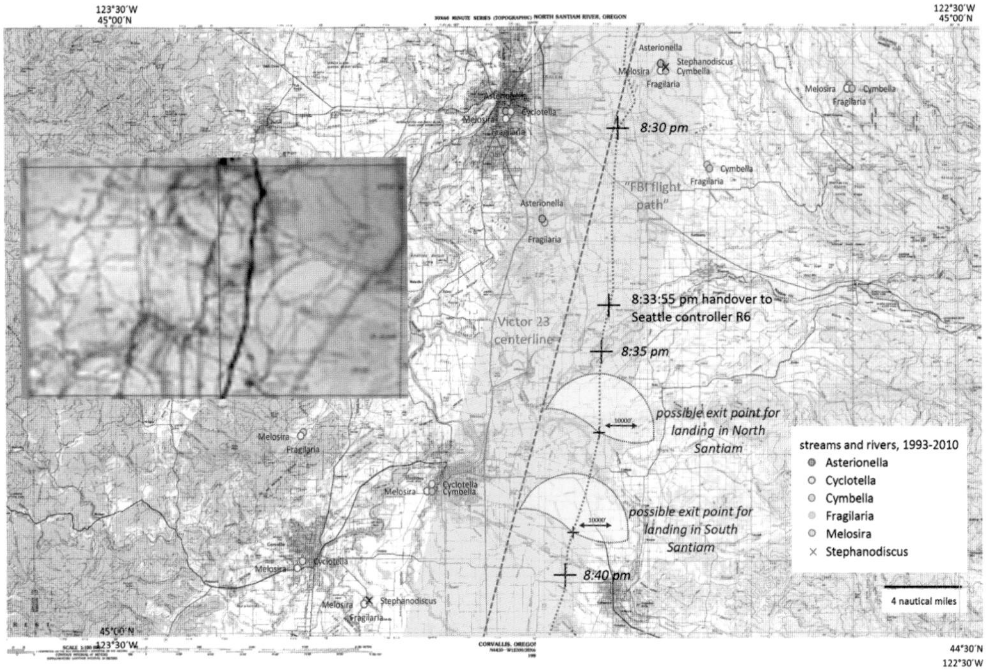


**Appendix 9**. Flight 305, Victor 23 airway, and *Corvallis/North Santiam River Quadrangles. Base map from USGS, scale 1:100,000; inset "FBI map"; graphics and time estimates by author*

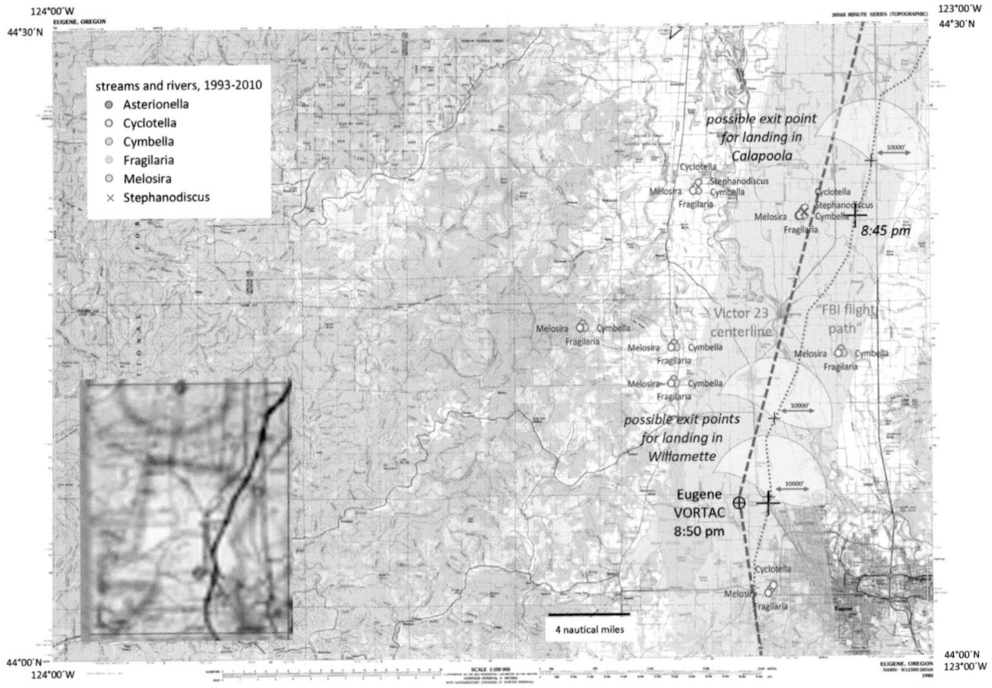


**Appendix 10**. Flight 305, Victor 23 airway, and *Eugene Quadrangle. Base map from USGS, scale 1:100,000; inset "FBI map"; graphics and time estimates by author*

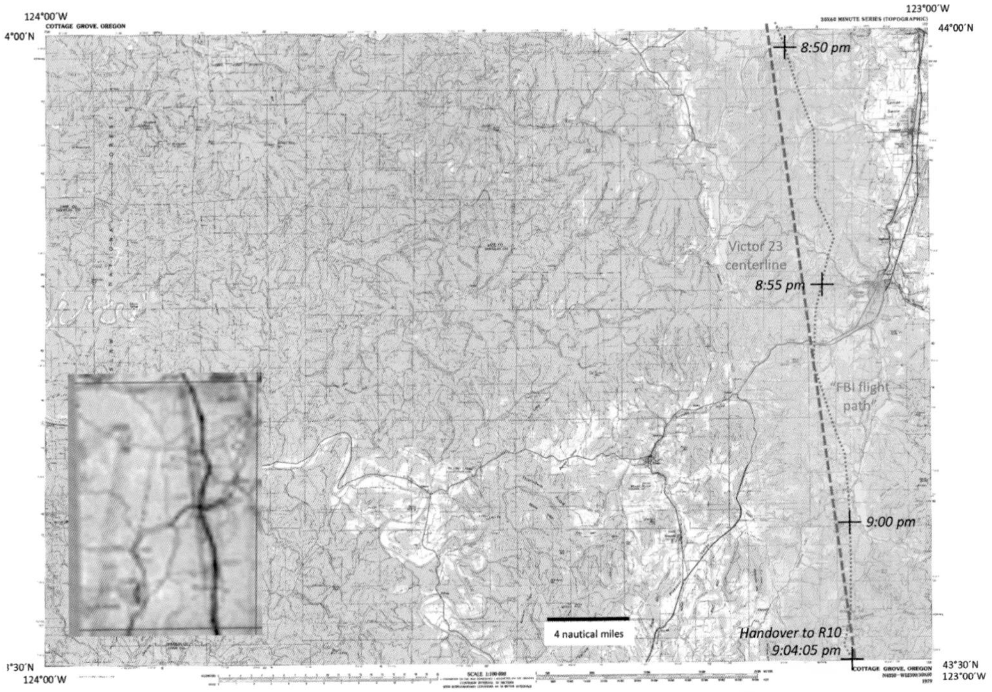


**Appendix 11**. Flight 305, Victor 23 airway, and *Cottage Grove Quadrangle. Base map from USGS, scale 1:100,000; inset "FBI map"; graphics and time estimates by author*

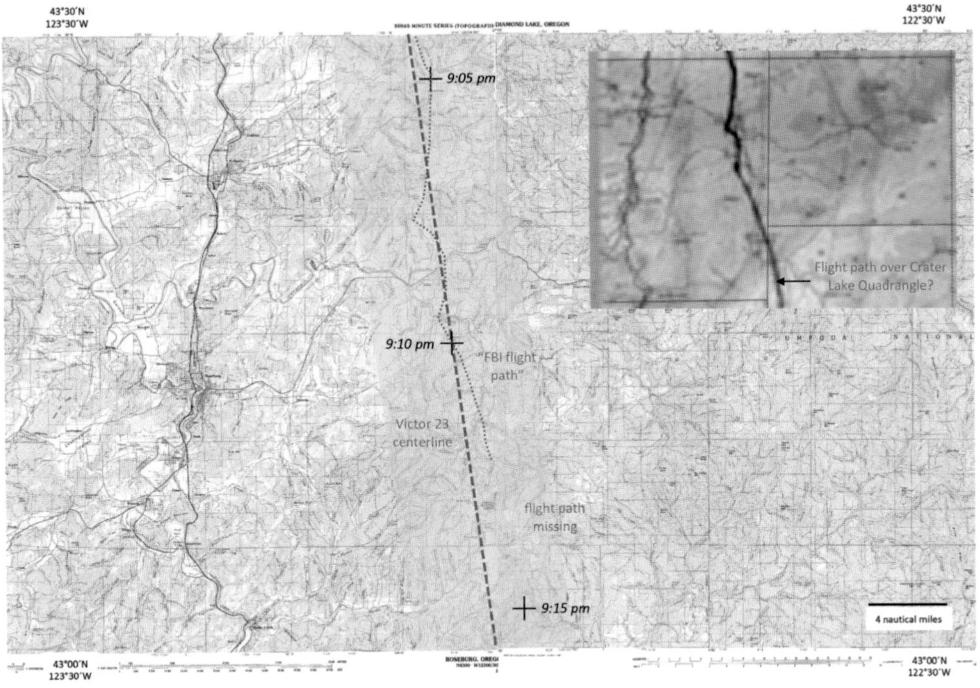


**Appendix 12**. Flight 305, Victor 23 airway, and *Roseburg/Diamond Lake Quadrangles. Base map from USGS, scale 1:100,000; inset "FBI map"; graphics and time estimates by author*

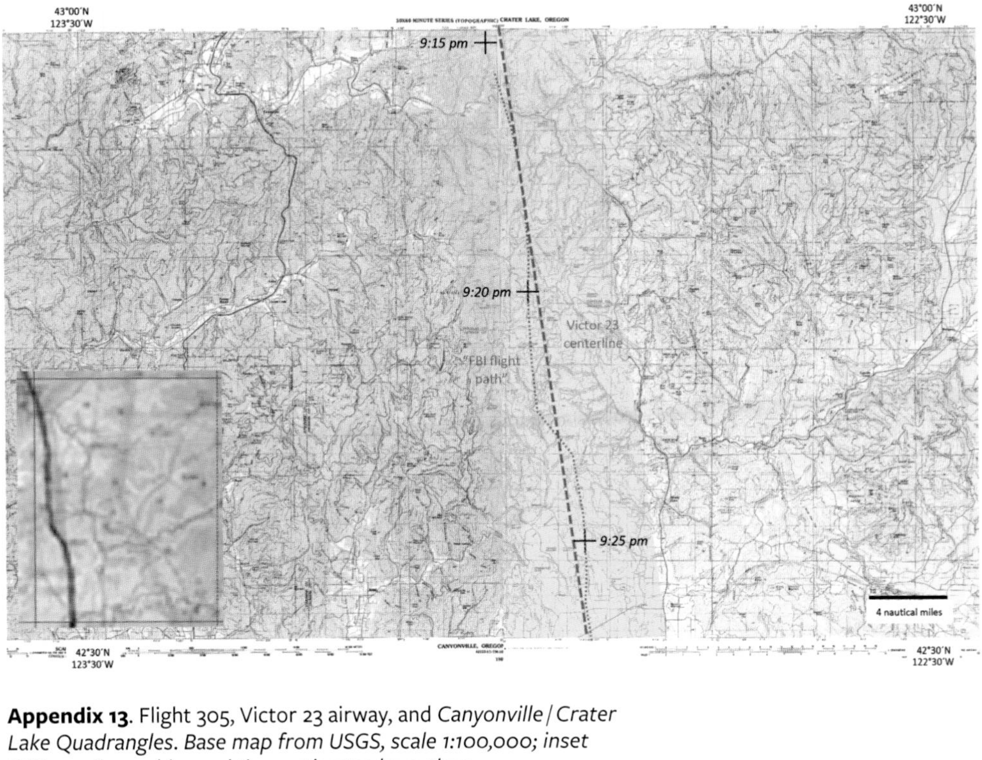


**Appendix 13**. Flight 305, Victor 23 airway, and *Canyonville/Crater Lake Quadrangles. Base map from USGS, scale 1:100,000; inset "FBI map"; graphics and time estimates by author*

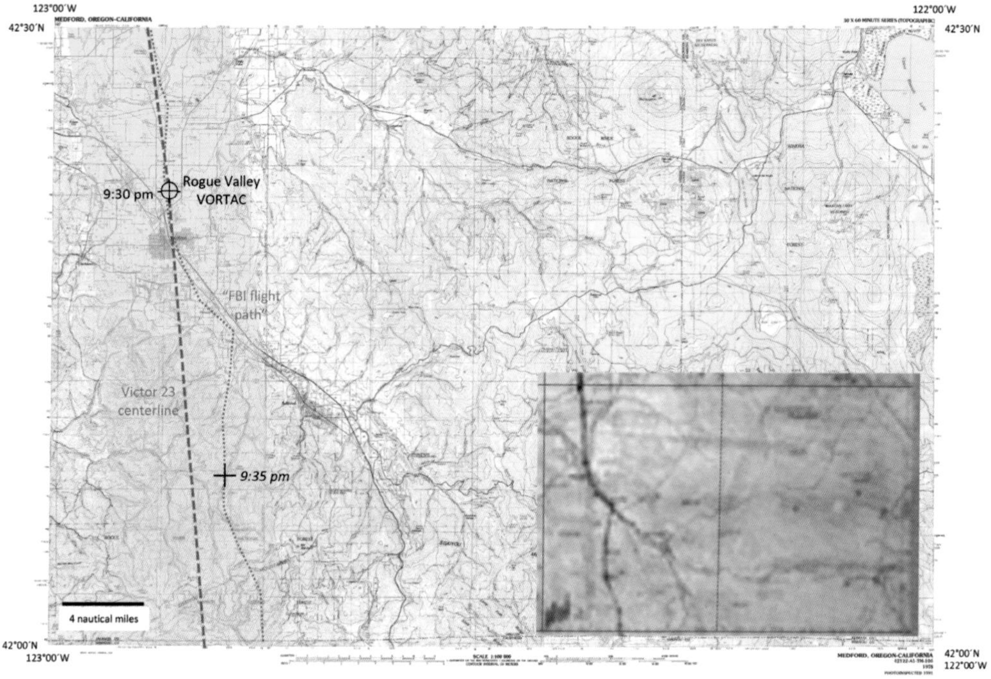


**Appendix 14**. Flight 305, Victor 23 airway, and *Medford Quadrangle. Base map from USGS, scale 1:100,000; inset "FBI map"; graphics and time estimates by author*

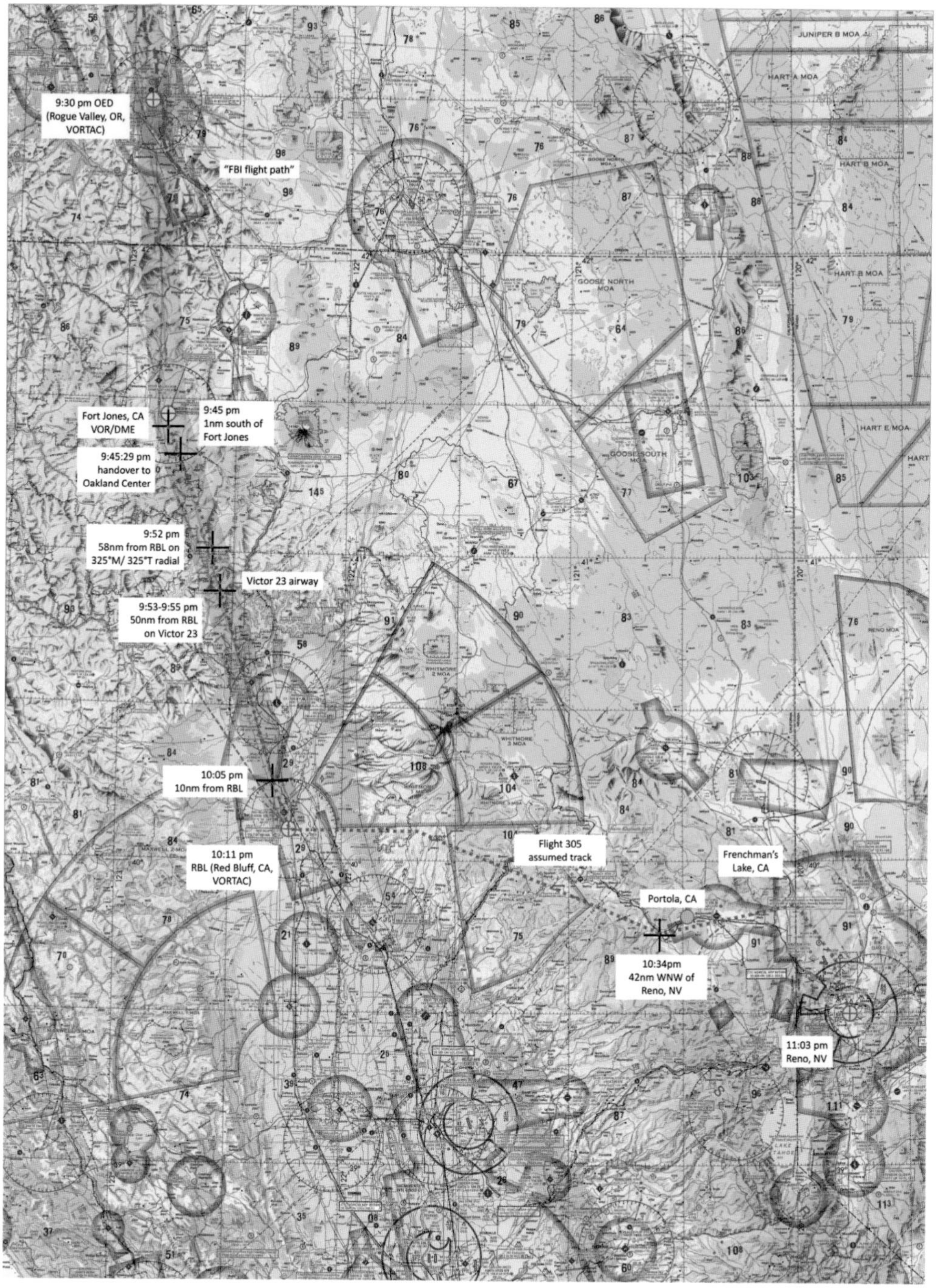


**Appendix 15**. Flight 305, assumed track from Medford to Reno. *Base map from FAA sectional charts for Klamath Falls and San Francisco; graphics by author*

**Appendix 16.1: Lakes and reservoirs in Oregon and Washington, HUCs 17080001 and 1709: Sites where *Asterionella*, *Cyclotella*, *Cymbella*, *Fragilaria*, *Melosira*, or *Stephanodiscus* genera have been identified, 1971–2014**

| HUC-8 drainage basin and HUC-14 site code | County | Name | lat N ° | Long E ° |
|---|---|---|---|---|
| | | | | |
| HUC 17080001: Lower Columbia–Sandy | | | | |
| 17080001017626 | Clackamas, OR | Bull Run Lake | 45.46 | –121.84 |
| n.a. | Skamania, WA | Franz Lake Slough | 45.61 | –122.08 |
| HUC 17090001: Middle Fork Willamette | | | | |
| 17090001005308 | Lane, OR | Hills Creek Lake | 43.69 | –122.43 |
| 17090001020920 | Lane, OR | Waldo Lake | 43.77 | –122.05 |
| HUC 17090003: Upper Willamette | | | | |
| 17090003017645 | Lane, OR | Fern Ridge Lake | 44.12 | –123.30 |
| HUC 17090004: McKenzie | | | | |
| n.a. | Linn, OR | Smith Reservoir | 44.32 | –122.05 |
| HUC 17090005: North Santiam | | | | |
| 17090005012370 | Marion/Linn, OR | Detroit Lake | 44.72 | –122.25 |
| 17090005000775 | Linn, OR | Marion Lake | 44.56 | –121.87 |
| HUC 17090007: Middle Willamette | | | | |
| n.a. | Marion, OR | Clear Lake | 45.04 | –123.03 |
| n.a. | Marion, OR | Walling Lake | 44.92 | –123.02 |
| HUC 17090009: Molalla/Pudding | | | | |
| n.a. | Clackamas, OR | Cougar Lake | 45.04 | –122.27 |
| HUC 17090011: Clackamas | | | | |
| n.a. | Marion, OR | Fish Lake | 44.83 | –121.81 |
| 17090011000850 | Clackamas, OR | Timothy Lake | 45.12 | –121.81 |
| HUC 17090012: Lower Willamette | | | | |
| 17090012000361 | Multnomah, OR | Blue Lake | 45.55 | –122.44 |
| 17090012006624 | Multnomah, OR | Bybee Lake | 45.62 | –122.74 |
| n.a. | Multnomah, OR | Johnson Lake | 45.57 | –122.56 |
| 17090012006623 | Multnomah, OR | Smith Lake | 45.61 | –122.73 |
| | | | | |

Sources: Environmental Protection Agency, *National Lakes Assessment* (2007 and 2012); Portland State University, *Atlas of Oregon Lakes* (1985); C. E. Tausz 2015; US Geological Survey, Lakes of Oregon series (1972–1976); and Clifton 1983

| | Elevation feet | area, 1970s acres | area, 2020 acres | Trophic status |
|---|---|---|---|---|
| | | | | |
| | | | | |
| | 3,175 | 450 | 434 | oligotrophic |
| | | | | |
| | | | | |
| | 1,543 | 2,735 | 2,591 | mesotrophic |
| | 5,414 | 6,298 | 6,062 | ultra-oligotrophic |
| | | | | |
| | 374 | 9,360 | 6,361 | mesotrophic |
| | | | | |
| | 2,609 | | 157 | |
| | | | | |
| | 1,569 | 3,580 | 3,591 | mesotrophic |
| | 4,130 | 261 | 352 | mesotrophic |
| | | | | |
| | 110 | 25 | | |
| | 180 | 8 | | |
| | | | | |
| | 4,070 | | 7 | |
| | | | | |
| | 4,264 | | 36 | |
| | 3,227 | 1,400 | 1,400 | mesotrophic |
| | | | | |
| | 14 | 61 | 66 | eutrophic |
| | 9 | 250 | 232 | eutrophic |
| | 8 | | 15 | |
| | 9 | 600 | 509 | eutrophic |
| | | | | |
| | | | | |

**Appendix 16.2. Rivers and streams in Oregon, HUCs 17080001 and 1709: Sites where *Asterionella, Cyclotella, Cymbella, Fragilaria, Melosira or Stephanodiscus* genera have been identified, 1993–2011**

| HUC-8 | Drainage basin | Lat N | Long E | Site name | Nearest city |
|---|---|---|---|---|---|
| HUC-12 code | site number | ° | ° | | |
| 17080001 | Lower Columbia–Sandy | | | | |
| 170800010703 | 453205122223701 | 45.53 | −122.38 | Beaver Creek | Troutdale, OR |
| 17090001 | Middle Fork Willamette | | | | |
| 170900010702 | 435212122483300 | 43.87 | −122.81 | Lost Creek | Dexter, OR |
| 17090002 | Coast Fork Willamette | | | | |
| 170900020306 | 434745123040200 | 43.80 | −123.07 | Silk Creek | Cottage Grove, OR |
| 17090003 | Upper Willamette | | | | |
| 170900030106 | 440257123103200 | 44.05 | −123.18 | Amazon Creek near Danebo Road | Eugene, OR |
| 170900030109 | 441307123171003 | 44.22 | −123.29 | Bear Creek at Territorial Highway | Junction City, OR |
| 170900030110 | 441549123232503 | 44.26 | −123.39 | Ferguson Creek at Ferguson Road | Junction City, OR |
| 170900030110 | 441451123170903 | 44.25 | −123.29 | Ferguson Creek at Territorial Highway | Junction City, OR |
| 170900030110 | 442223123153703 | 44.37 | −123.26 | Long Tom River at Bundy Bridge | Monroe, OR |
| 170900030509 | 444002123163603 | 44.67 | −123.28 | Soap Creek | Corvallis, OR |
| 170900030606 | 442107123082903 | 44.35 | −123.14 | Muddy Creek at Nixon Road | Halsey, OR |
| 170900030606 | 441430123054803 | 44.24 | −123.10 | Muddy Creek at Weatherford Lane | Harrisburg, OR |
| 170900030607 | 442108123082403 | 44.35 | −123.14 | Little Muddy Creek at Nixon Road | Halsey, OR |
| 170900030608 | 443138123120901 | 44.53 | −123.20 | Muddy Creek near Peoria Road | Corvallis, OR |
| 17090007 | Middle Willamette | | | | |
| 170900070203 | 445029122592600 | 44.84 | −122.99 | Battle Creek | Turner, OR |
| 170900070301 | 445551123015800 | 44.93 | −123.03 | Pringle Creek | Salem, OR |
| 170900070303 | 450022123012400 | 45.01 | −123.02 | Claggett Creek | Keizer, OR |
| 170900070306 | 451734122585400 | 45.29 | −122.98 | Chehalem Creek | Newberg, OR |
| 17090008 | Yamhill | | | | |
| 170900080602 | 452149123194900 | 45.36 | −123.33 | North Yamhill Creek | Yamhill, OR |
| 17090009 | Molalla/Pudding | | | | |

**Appendix 16.2. Rivers and streams in Oregon, HUCs 17080001 and 1709: Sites where *Asterionella, Cyclotella, Cymbella, Fragilaria, Melosira or Stephanodiscus* genera have been identified, 1993–2011**

| | | | | | |
|---|---|---|---|---|---|
| 170900090101 | 445814122505602 | 44.97 | −122.85 | Pudding River at Kaufman Road | Pratum, OR |
| 170900090105 | 14200400 | 44.96 | −122.63 | Little Abiqua Creek | Scotts Mills, OR |
| 170900090109 | 450241122534102 | 45.04 | −122.90 | Little Pudding River near Rambler Drive | Labish Center, OR |
| 170900090110 | 14201000 | 45.06 | −122.83 | Pudding River near Saratoga Drive NE | Mount Angel, OR |
| 170900090204 | 14201300 | 45.10 | −122.82 | Zollner Creek | Mount Angel, OR |
| 170900090501 | 451259122481902 | 45.22 | −122.81 | Senecal Creek at Donald Road | Donald, OR |
| 170900090502 | 14202000 | 45.23 | −122.75 | Pudding River near Liberty St NE | Aurora, OR |
| 170900090603 | 450955122291200 | 45.17 | −122.49 | Milk Creek at Camp Adams | Cedardale, OR |
| 170900090603 | 14199710 | 45.17 | −122.49 | Nate Creek | Colton, OR |
| 170900090607 | 451350122415603 | 45.23 | −122.70 | Gribble Creek | Canby, OR |
| 17090010 | Tualatin | | | | |
| 170900100101 | 14203750 | 45.64 | −123.37 | Gales Creek | Glenwood, OR |
| 170900100102 | 453506123125700 | 45.58 | −123.22 | Iler Creek | Forest Grove, OR |
| 170900100305 | 14205400 | 45.68 | −123.07 | Rock Creek at Quatama Road | Hillsboro, OR |
| 170900100401 | 14206435 | 45.52 | −122.90 | Beaverton Creek at SW 216th Ave | Orenco, OR |
| 170900100501 | 14206750 | 45.37 | −122.86 | Chicken Creek | Sherwood, OR |
| 170900100502 | 14206950 | 45.40 | −122.75 | Fanno Creek | Durham, OR |
| 17090011 | Clackamas | | | | |
| 170900110604 | 452231122200000 | 45.38 | −122.33 | Deep Creek | Sandy, OR |
| 170900110604 | 452414122213200 | 45.40 | −122.36 | Tickle Creek | Boring, OR |
| 170900110605 | 452337122243500 | 45.39 | −122.41 | North Fork Deep Creek | Barton, OR |
| 17090012 | Lower Willamette | | | | |
| 170900120101 | 452912122291200 | 45.49 | −122.49 | Johnson Creek at Circle Ave | Portland, OR |
| 170900120102 | 452526122364400 | 45.42 | −122.61 | Kellogg Creek | Milwaukie, OR |
| 170900120104 | 14211315 | 45.43 | −122.67 | Tryon Creek | Lake Oswego, OR |
| 170900120202 | 14211720 | 45.52 | −122.67 | Willamette River | Portland, OR |
| 170900120301 | 454543122524900 | 45.76 | −122.88 | South Scappoose Creek | Scappoose, OR |
| | | | | | |

Source: US Geological Survey, BioData Data Sets at http://aquatic.biodata.usgs.gov, downloaded on 2020.08.11.0552, file: 20200811.0552.AlgSamp

# ABBREVIATIONS

| | |
|---|---|
| [ ] | author's note |
| [*sic*] | quoted exactly as in original |
| AAF | Army Air Field |
| AFB | Air Force Base |
| AFEHRI | Air Force Enlisted Heritage Research Institute |
| AFHRA | Air Force Historical Research Agency |
| AMSL | above mean sea level |
| AP | Associated Press |
| ARINC | Aeronautical Radio, Inc. |
| ARTCC | Air Route Traffic Control Center |
| ASAC | assistant special agent in charge |
| BAC | British Aircraft Corporation |
| BC | boot camp |
| BTG | Battle Ground, Washington, navigational beacon |
| C-124 | Douglas C-124 Globemaster II |
| CA | California |
| CAB | Civil Aeronautics Board |
| Capt | captain |
| CAT | Civil Air Transport |
| cf. | comparable with |
| CIA | Central Intelligence Agency |
| CJ | Cave Junction, Oregon |
| CRAF | Civil Reserve Air Fleet Program |
| CTU | Chemistry Toxicology Unit, FBI Laboratory |
| DC | District of Columbia |
| DME | distance-measuring equipment |
| EAM | Eduardo Antonio Morales |
| EPA | Environmental Protection Agency |
| EU | Explosives Unit, FBI Laboratory |
| EUG | Eugene, Oregon, navigational beacon |
| EWU | Eastern Washington University |
| ex | excluding |
| *F.* | *Fragilaria* (genus) |
| FAA | Federal Aviation Administration |
| FBI | Federal Bureau of Investigation |
| FL | Florida |
| FOIA | Freedom of Information Act |
| GC | Ground Control |
| GEOREF | World Geographic Reference System |
| GI | "Government Issue" |
| GMT | Greenwich Mean Time (Zulu time) |
| GPS | global positioning system |
| HJ | hijacker |
| HUC | hydrological unit code |
| IAS | indicated airspeed |
| ICAO | International Civil Aviation Organization |
| IGRA2 | Integrated Global Radiosonde Archive, data set 2 |
| IL | Illinois |
| J-5 | Jet 5 airway |
| JCS | Joint Chiefs of Staff |
| JFK | John Fitzgerald Kennedy |
| knot | speed of 1 nautical mile per hour |
| KPDX | Portland International Airport |
| KSEA | Seattle-Tacoma International Airport |
| lat N | latitude north |
| LGA | La Guardia Airport, New York |
| long E | longitude east (negative number indicates west) |
| MA | Massachusetts |
| MAC | Military Airlift Command |
| MALAY | FAA code for intersection of Battle Ground 350° and Seattle 197° radials |
| MATS | Military Air Transport Service |
| MAU | Materials Analysis Unit, FBI Laboratory |
| ME | Maine |
| MHz | megahertz |
| MI | Michigan |
| mm | micrometers (microns) |
| MN | Minnesota |
| MO | Missouri |
| Mo | Monday |
| MSgt | master sergeant |
| MSL | mean sea level |
| MSO | Missoula, Montana |
| MSP | Minneapolis–Saint Paul, Minnesota |
| N | north |
| N467US | tail number of the airplane that operated Flight 305 |
| NASA | National Aeronautics and Space Administration |
| NAWQA | National Water Quality Assessment |

| | |
|---|---|
| NB-6 | Navy Backpack 6 |
| NB-8 | Navy Backpack 8 |
| NCEI | National Centers for Environmental Information |
| NE | northeast |
| NH | New Hampshire |
| NJ | New Jersey |
| NLA | *National Lakes Assessment* |
| nm | nautical mile (6076.12 feet) |
| NOAA | National Oceanic and Atmospheric Administration |
| NORJAK | Northwest hijack (FBI code) |
| Nr | reactive nitrogen |
| NW | northwest |
| NWA | Northwest Airlines |
| NWO | Northwest Orient Airlines |
| NY | New York |
| OAT | outside air temperature |
| OED | Rogue Valley, Oregon, navigational beacon |
| OH | Ohio |
| OPS | Operations |
| OR | Oregon |
| ORD | Chicago O'Hare Airport |
| PCR | polymerase chain reaction |
| PDAS | Public Domain Aeronautical Software |
| PDX | Battle Ground, Washington, VORTAC in 1971 |
| PST | Pacific Standard Time |
| PSU | Portland State University |
| RDD | Redding, California |
| RM | river mile |
| RN 16484 | code for Remington Apparel Company, Inc. |
| SA | special agent |
| Sa | Saturday |
| SAC | special agent in charge |
| SAGE | Semi-automatic Ground Environment (radar system) |
| SAT | Southern Air Transport |
| SEA | Seattle-Tacoma, Washington, navigational beacon |
| SF180 | Standard Form 180, Request Pertaining to Military Records |
| sp. | species undetermined |
| spp. | species (plural) undetermined |
| sq. cm | square centimeters |
| Sqdn | Squadron |
| Sr. MSgt | senior master sergeant |
| SSS | Seattle Sky Sports |
| STR | short tandem repeat |
| Su | Sunday |
| TAS | true airspeed |
| TAT | total air temperature |
| TCH | Troop Carrier Squadron, Heavy |
| UNSUB | unidentified subject |
| USA | United States of America |
| USAF | United States Air Force |
| USGS | United States Geological Survey |
| USPA | United States Parachute Association |
| USPS | United States Postal Service |
| V-23 | Victor 23 airway |
| var. | variety (in biological classification) |
| VHF | very high frequency (30 to 300 megahertz) |
| VOR | VHF omnidirectional range beacon |
| VORTAC | VHF omnidirectional range beacon and tactical air navigation system |
| W | west |
| WA | Washington |
| WAECY | Washington State Department of Ecology |
| WI | Wisconsin |
| WSHS | Washington State Historical Society |
| ZSE | Seattle Air Route Traffic Control Center |

# ENDNOTES

**Prologue**

1. The Boeing Company, "727 Commercial Transport: Historical Snapshot," www.boeing.com/history/products/727 page.

2. Skydive Perris, Douglas DC9-21, https://skydive-perris.com/experienced/facilities.

3. William Kneale and Martha Kneale, *The Development of Logic* (London: Oxford University Press, 1962), p. 243.

4. Sir Arthur Conan Doyle, *The Sign of the Four*, chapter 6 (London: Spencer Blackett, 1890), p. 111.

**Chapter 1**

1. The redacted source documents for the crew's interviews with the FBI are as follows (all extracted from the public files of the FBI at vault.fbi.gov):

Tina Ann Mucklow: 1322460-0-164-LV-60-Section 6, Serial 139, and 1322460-0-164-PH-133-Section 6, Serial 1.

Florence Schaffner and Alice Hancock: 1322460-0-164-SE-81-Section 6, Serial 1.

William Rataczak: 1322460-0-164-LV-60-Section 6, Serial 138.

Harold Anderson: 1322460-0-164-LV-60-Section 6, Serial 137.

William Scott: 1322460-0-164-LV-60-Section 6, Serial 150-1.

The unredacted source documents for the crew's and passengers' interviews (which are identical to those published by the FBI, except that they disclose the names and addresses of the respondents and the names of other persons mentioned) are all from https://true.ink, a defunct web magazine.

2. Press reports in 1973 and 1981 referred to another person, Harold (Hal) Williams, a gate agent, who claimed to have observed the hijacker in Portland International Airport. No reference to this person can be identified in the public files of the FBI.

3. All times in this narrative are Pacific Standard Time (PST).

4. A Dennis E. Lysne, born July 4, 1923, in North Dakota, died in Portland, Oregon, on September 12, 2000. If he is the same man, his two-page testimony to the FBI is the sole record of this encounter.

5. Skipp Porteous, telephone interview with William J. Rataczak, c.2009, posted at https://www.dropzone.com/forums/topic/56036-db-cooper/page/1990/?tab=comments#comment-4290349.

6. Washington State Historical Society, Document 2013.5.22.2, "Bill Mitchell Interview on October 3, 2013, by telephone with Fred Poyner IV and Gwen Whiting," document dated October 18, 2013.

7. Brian Rose, interview with FBI Agent Roy Rose, dated March 24, 2012, transcribed by author. Of the three cabin crew members on board Flight 305, the FBI has never identified the two who met Agent Rose. It could reasonably be assumed that they were Mucklow and Schaffner.

8. Washington State Historical Society, Document 2013.5.22.2, p. 8.

9. Kristofer Noceda, "Livermore Man Recaps Encounter with D. B. Cooper," *Patch*, Livermore, CA, August 5, 2011, https://patch.com/california/livermore/livermore-man-recaps-encounter-with-db-cooper.

10. This narrative is woven together from the testimonies of the eleven witnesses, as recorded and transcribed by the FBI, as well as the ARINC teletype records of radio transmissions between Flight 305 and Northwest ground stations on the private company frequency. As nearly as possible, we have established a chronological order of events that is consistent with the transcripts of the interviews and transmissions. There may remain some small uncertainties in the order of events.

11. The source document for all the ARINC teletype messages is document 2013.5.15.5 held by the Washington State Historical Society.

12. The teletype messages were all transcribed in upper case, without punctuation. The first few characters of each message identified the sender, which in most cases was 305 (Northwest Orient Flight 305), "MSP OPS" (Northwest Orient operations in Minneapolis, Minnesota, or SEADD (apparently Northwest Orient operations in Seattle). The messages were highly abbreviated and contained many errors of spelling. The backspace or erase functions did not exist in teletype, so the transmitter corrected an error by typing a sequence of Xs, followed by the intended word or phrase. Our presentation of the teletype messages is our own interpretation in plain English, with obvious errors removed and punctuation inserted, and editorial insertions in square brackets [ ].

13. The transcript of ARINC teletype messages contains time stamps at irregular intervals, expressed in PST and also Zulu time. These time stamps were triggered each time that the transmitter pressed the "send" key. We have no way of knowing how much time elapsed between the message and the time stamp. So, in all our references to teletype messages, the term "at time x" means strictly "at or before time x, but after the preceding time stamp." In other words, the time stamps bracket the messages. The time stamps are generally spaced at intervals of a few minutes.

14. FBI, D. B. Cooper Part 10 of 48.pdf, p. 306, document reference 164-81-1, footnote DB Cooper 1533, dated 25-Nov-71, downloaded from vault.fbi.gov.

15. FBI, D. B. Cooper Part 13 of 48.pdf, p. 13, document reference 164-81-519, footnote DB Cooper 2797, dated 30-Nov-71, downloaded from vault.fbi.gov.

16. Skipp Porteous, telephone interview with William J. Rataczak, ca. 2009, posted at https://www.dropzone.com/forums/topic/56036-db-cooper/page/1990/?tab=comments#comment-4290349.

**Chapter 2**

1. Skipp Porteous, telephone interview with William J. Rataczak, ca. 2009, posted at https://www.dropzone.com/forums/topic/56036-db-cooper/page/1990/?tab=comments#comment-4290349.

2. FBI, D. B. Cooper Part 04 of 48.pdf, p. 307, footnote DB Cooper-1534, undated, downloaded from vault.fbi.gov; bullet points added for clarity.

3. FBI, undated document, file number SE 164-81, author's initials JSD:klb (probably John S. Detlor), pp. 227–228; downloaded from true.ink.

4. We have reinserted part of the text that was redacted.

5. The FBI's numbering of the chest packs and backpacks follows Harrison's statement but appears to be arbitrary; that is, there is no reason to suppose that the packs were physically marked no. 1 and no. 2.

6 The meaning of the term "burp sack" is unknown.

7. FBI, D. B. Cooper Part 51 of 51.pdf, p. 376, document 164A-81-(pending)4977, footnote DB Cooper21560, August 22, 2001, downloaded from vault.fbi.gov.

8. SSS undoubtedly refers to Seattle Sky Sports of Issaquah, Washington, which supplied the two chest packs to Northwest Airlines. The backpacks were supplied by Hayden Manufacturing Company of Renton, Washington. COSS is possibly a reference to Earl Cossey, who worked for Seattle Sky Sports and rigged (assembled) the two backpacks.

9. FBI, D. B. Cooper Part 14 of 48.pdf, pp. 67–71, footnotes DB Cooper-3376 to DB Cooper-3380, downloaded from vault.fbi.gov.

10. The source document reads "1000," but this must be a typo and should read 10,000 (i.e., 7192 licensed Class C plus 3094 Class D, plus unknown numbers of "Class I" and military).

11. As of February 2020, a USPA Class C license requires 200 jumps plus proficiency in a number of maneuvers. D license holders must have logged 500 jumps and are permitted to perform demonstration and exhibition maneuvers. "Class I" is not a USPA license and appears to refer to instructors.

12. FBI, D. B. Cooper Part 53 of 53.pdf, pp. 121–122, footnotes DB Cooper22459, 22460, dated November 25, 1971, downloaded from vault.fbi.gov.

13. FAA, *Statistical Yearbook of Aviation: 1969*, table 5-13; *Statistical Yearbook of Aviation: 1972*, table 5-13, pp. 120–121, and table 5-13a, p. 122.

14. We have paraphrased this and all other ARINC messages into plain English; the originals are highly abbreviated.

15. The meaning of ERTL is unknown. ER possibly stands for en route; TL possibly stands for takeoff/landing.

16. Skipp Porteous, telephone interview with William J. Rataczak, ca. 2009, posted at https://www.dropzone.com/forums/topic/56036-db-cooper/page/1990/?tab=comments#comment-4290349.

17. Ibid.

18. an aeronautical engineer familiar with 727 documentation (name withheld), personal communication, January 7, 2021

19. Robert (Bob) Bogash, former Director of Quality Assurance, Boeing Commercial Airplane Group, personal communication, January 23, 2021.

20. Washington State Historical Society, document 2013.5.15.5. Transcripts of communications between Flight 305 and air traffic control are verbatim, including pauses and misstatements.

21. Distance measuring equipment; meaning that they are 14 nautical miles from the VORTAC navigation beacon at Sea-Tac.

22. David T. Smith, personal communication, December 20, 2020.

23. aerospace engineer (name withheld), personal communication, January 5, 2021.

24. aerospace engineer (name withheld), personal communication, January 5, 2021.

25. The D. B. Cooper Forum, members "georger" and "hominid" (names withheld), telephone interview with Harold E. Anderson, January 28, 2014, posted at https://www.thedbcooperforum.com/db-cooper/flight-path-and-related-issues/msg37962/#msg37962.

26. Mark Logan, personal communication, December 23, 2020.

27. FBI, D. B. Cooper Part 41 of 48.pdf, p. 32, document reference 164-81, footnote DB Cooper-11400, dated May 30, 1973.

28. The D. B. Cooper Forum, members "georger" and "hominid," post at https://www.thedbcooperforum.com/db-cooper/flight-path-and-related-issues/msg37962/#msg37962

29. Skipp Porteous, telephone interview with William J. Rataczak, ca. 2009, posted at https://www.dropzone.com/forums/topic/56036-db-cooper/page/1990/?tab=comments#comment-4290349.

30. Boeing Airplane Company, Boeing Airliner magazine, March/April 1967, p. 10.

31. Boeing-727.com (unknown author, not associated with Boeing Airplane Company), System Descriptions, Pressurisation, July 18, 2001, p73, https://www.boeing-727.com/Data/systems/infopress.html.

32. Skipp Porteous, telephone interview with William J. Rataczak, ca. 2009, posted at https://www.dropzone.com/forums/topic/56036-db-cooper/page/1990/?tab=comments#comment-4290349.

33. aerospace engineer (name withheld by request), personal communication, January 7, 2021.

34. FBI, D. B. Cooper Part 20 of 48.pdf, p. 242, document 164-81-2087, footnote DB Cooper-6199, November 30, 1971, downloaded from vault.fbi.gov.

35. Mark Logan, personal communication, December 19, 2020.

36. FAA, Order JO 7110.66F National Beacon Code Allocation Plan (NBCAP), effective date June 3, 2019, p. 8.

37. FAA, *Airman's Information Manual*, AIP/GEN/SAR RAC/COM 1/AGA 3, May 1976, pp. 1–82: "Effective September 9, 1976, the ATC hijack code will be changed from 3100 to 7500."

38. FBI, document FD302, file number SE164-81, p. 193, no document number, no footnote number; dated January 5, 1972, released by FOIA request of Robert Nicholson, downloaded from https://website.thedbcooper-forum.com.

39. Washington State Historical Society, document 2013.5.15.5, Seattle Approach Control/NWA-305, reel 1, pp. 144–146.

40. Washington State Historical Society, document 2013.5.15.5, Seattle Approach Control/NWA-305, reel 1, p. 147.

**Chapter 3**

1. Dr. Joe F. Leeker, *The History of Air America*, 2nd ed., 24 August 2015, www.utdallas.edu/library/specialcollections/hac/cataam/Leeker/history/.

2. Dr. Joe F. Leeker, *CAT, Air Asia, Air America—the Company on Taiwan I: Structure and Development*, updated on August 24, 2015, p. 79.

3. CIA, "Memorandum to: Marvin L. Evans, Assistant General Counsel, from [redacted] Managing Director," 7 November 1962, document 196207.pdf, pp 1–2, downloaded from www.cia.gov/library/readingroom/document/5200379f993294098d5171fe.

4. Ibid.

5. Book 1, *Foreign and Military Intelligence*, Final Report of the Senate Intelligence Committee, April 26, 1976, pp. 225, 226, 240, 241; quoted in Aviation Regulatory Reform (95–40) Part II, Hearings before the Subcommittee on Aviation of the Committee on Public Works and Transportation, House of Representatives, 95th Congress, 1st Session on H.R.8813, pp. 1,778–1,779 (Washington, DC: US Government Printing Office, 1978).

6. Dr. Joe F. Leeker, *Air America: Cooperation with Other Airlines*, updated on August 24, 2015, p. 4.

7. As for note 5 [Senate Intelligence Committee].

8. Dr. Joe F. Leeker, *Air America: Boeing 727s*, updated on August 24, 2015, pp. 1, 3, 4; www.utdallas.edu/library/specialcollections/hac/cataam/Leeker/aircraft/jets.pdf.

9. As for note 5 [Senate Intelligence Committee].

10. FBI, D. B. Cooper Part 25 of 48.pdf, p. 307, document reference 164-81-3378, footnote DB Cooper-8376, dated 1 June 1972, downloaded from vault.fbi.gov.

11. Dwight G. Shaw (a.k.a. Bob Sailshaw), post to The D. B. Cooper Forum, September 16, 2016, https://www.thedbcooperforum.com/db-cooper/two-back-packs-two-front-chutes/msg12828/#msg12828

12. FBI Agent Larry Carr, post on dropzone.com, June 10, 2008.

13. FBI, D. B. Cooper Part 26 of 48.pdf, p. 307, document reference 164-81-3481, footnote DB Cooper-8567, dated 8 June 1972, downloaded from vault.fbi.gov.

14. FBI, D. B. Cooper Part 27 of 48.pdf, pp. 29–120, document references 164-81-3695 to 3738, footnotes DB Cooper-9003 to 9096, dated 8 June 1972, downloaded from vault.fbi.gov.

15. FBI, D. B. Cooper Part 25 of 48.pdf, p. 307, document reference 164-81-3378, footnote DB Cooper-8376, dated 1 June 1972, downloaded from vault.fbi.gov.

16. FBI, D. B. Cooper Part 27 of 48.pdf, pp. 29–120, document reference 164-81-3738, footnote DB Cooper-9087, dated 8 June 1972, downloaded from vault.fbi.gov.

17. FBI, D. B. Cooper Part 27 of 48.pdf, pp. 29–120, document reference 164-81-3738, footnote DB Cooper-9095, dated 8 June 1972, downloaded from vault.fbi.gov.

18 Michelle Evans, "The X-15 Rocket Plane: Flying the First Wings into Space—Flight Log," Mach 25 Media, 2013.

19. FBI, D. B. Cooper Part 27 of 48.pdf, pp. 29–120, document reference 164-81-3738, footnote DB Cooper-9096, dated 8 June 1972, downloaded from vault.fbi.gov.

20. FBI, D. B. Cooper Part 27 of 48.pdf, pp. 29–120, document reference 164-81-3738, footnote DB Cooper-9088, dated 8 June 1972, downloaded from vault.fbi.gov.

21. Tom Wolfe, *The Right Stuff* (New York: Farrar, Straus and Giroux, 1979).

22. FBI, D. B. Cooper Part 27 of 48.pdf, pp. 29–120, document reference 164-81-3738, footnote DB Cooper-9096, dated 8 June 1972, downloaded from vault.fbi.gov.

23. CIA, "Memorandum for: Deputy Director for Support, Subject: Southern Air Transport Inc.," dated November 29, 1971, downloaded on February 16 2020, from www.cia.gov/library/readingroom/docs/197109.pdf.

24 Apart from N5055 and N5092, which were leased, and N5093, which was owned, Southern may have leased a fourth 727 (registration number N695WA). Source: Dr. Joe F Leeker, *Air America: Boeing 727s*, August 24, 2015, downloaded on February 16, 2020 from www.utdallas.edu/library/specialcollections/hac/cataam/Leeker/aircraft/jets.pdf.

25. John Wilheim Productions, *Flying Men, Flying Machines*, held at Texas Tech University, the Vietnam Center, and Sam Johnson Vietnam Archive, Item# 1171VI1078, Brian Johnson Collection (Air America Association), downloaded on February 17, 2020 from https://vva.vietnam.ttu.edu/repositories/2/digital_objects/129880.

26. CIA, Request For Records Disposition Authority, Job Number N1-263-00-1, dated January 16, 2003, p. 7.

27. Professor William Leary, document B43F5, provided by courtesy of Dr. Joe F. Leeker.

28. National Smokejumper Association, *Smokejumper Magazine*, January 2014: 28 (copyright 2013, the *Northport Gazette*, Northport, AL); retrieved from Eastern Washington University, EWU Digital Commons.

29. Smoke jumpers' designations include the following: CJ (Cave Junction, Oregon), MSO (Missoula, Montana), and RDD (Redding, California).

30. Quoted by Chuck Sheley, "The Selected Few and 'The List,'" *Smokejumper Magazine*, July 2015:. 5.

31. John Prados, *Safe for Democracy*: *The Secret Wars of the CIA* (Lanham, MD: Rowman & Littlefield, 2006), 170.

32. National Smokejumper Association, *Smokejumper Magazine*, July 2007: 30.

33. John P. Kirkley, personal communications, February 22, 2020, and May 25, 2020, reproduced by permission.

34. John P. Kirkley, personal communication, May 25, 2020, reproduced by permission.

35. John P. Kirkley, personal communications, February 22, 2020, and May 25, 2020, reproduced by permission.

36. John P. Kirkley, personal communication, May 25, 2020, reproduced by permission.

37. John P. Kirkley, personal communications, February 22, 2020, and May 25, 2020, reproduced by permission.

38. CIA, "1971-04-30 Southern Air Transport, Inc. Personnel and Facilities, Personnel," file name 197111.pdf, downloaded from www.cia.gov.

39. FBI, D. B. Cooper Part 36 of 48.pdf, pp. 116–117, document reference 164-81-6605, footnotes DB Cooper 13664–13665, downloaded from vault.fbi.gov.

40. Albert Weinberg, *Dan Cooper 8—Le Secret de Dan Cooper* (Brussels: Lombard/Dargaud, 1965).

**Chapter 4**

1. Washington State Historical Society, Document 2013.5.15.5, p. 99.

2. FAA, *FAA Statistical Handbook of Aviation 1976*, table 5-8: "Aircraft in Operation by Certificated Route Air Carriers by Make and Model."

3. FAA, *Code of Federal Regulations, Part 25 Airworthiness Standards: Transport Category Airplanes, Subpart D—Design and Construction*, Sec. 25.809, issued on November 24, 1972, https://rgl.faa.gov/Regulatory_and_Guidance_Library/rgFAR.nsf/0/42B6073445F438F28525667200519C29?OpenDocument.

4. Washington State Historical Society, Document 2013.5.15.5, p. 100. Our paraphrase, in plain English, of the highly abbreviated transcription of the ARINC teletype.

5. Dr. Joe F. Leeker, *Air America: Boeing 727s*, August 24, 2015, p. 5; and Dr. Joe F. Leeker, *Missions to Tibet*, January 10, 2018, p. 23.

6. Personal communications with Bjorn Larsson, David Keller, and eBay seller airtimes; and based on American, Braniff, Continental, Delta, National, Northeast, Northwest, Trans World, United, and Western system timetables as of October 31, 1971, and Eastern system timetable as of September 8, 1971.

7. Northeast Airlines, System Timetable, October 31, 1971.

8. Northwest Orient, System Timetable Effective October 31, 1971, published by Executive Offices, Northwest Airlines, Minneapolis–St. Paul International Airport, Minneapolis, 55111.

**Chapter 5**

1. Most of this information comes from the following three sources held by the Washington State Historical Society:

- document 2013.5.23.1: "Digitized notes from Northwest Airlines executive George Harrison, who was present at Seattle-Tacoma International Airport during the hijacking of Northwest Airlines flight 305," www.washingtonhistory.org/collections/item.aspx?irn=122775&record=1.
- document 2013.5.15.5: "Digital document, transcript of radio communication between Northwest Orient Airlines flight 305 and Seattle-Tacoma International Airport, Reno International Airport," www.washingtonhistory.org/collections/item.aspx?irn=121548&record=1. The communications referred to are with both Seattle-Tacoma air traffic control and with Northwest Airlines operations at Seattle-Tacoma.
- document 2013.5.23.4: "Curator report for examination of Aeronautical Radio, Incorporated (ARINC) teletypewriter printout documenting communications between the flight crew of Northwest Airlines 305 and Seattle-Tacoma International Airport," www.washingtonhistory.org/collections/item.aspx?irn=123776&record=1. The communications referred to are with Northwest Airlines operations at Seattle-Tacoma and also apparently at Minneapolis, not with Air Traffic Control, since ATC transcripts have no record of these communications.

2. All ARINC messages reproduced here are our paraphrase of the messages as keyed, which are abbreviated and often contain corrections.

3. FBI, "United States Government Memorandum, Optional Form No. 10," dated 12/3/71, footnotes DB Cooper3376 through DB Cooper3380, downloaded from vault.fbi.gov.

4. Washington State Historical Society, document 2013.5.15.5, pp. 183, 192.

5. In all aviation communications, altitudes are expressed in feet above mean sea level (AMSL).

6. Probably a typo for GC (Ground Control).

7. The transponder setting of 3100 denoted a hijack. In the mid-1970s, the USA changed the hijack code to 7500.

8. Victor 23 is currently defined by FAA, Joint Order 7400.11D—Airspace Designations and Reporting Points, August 8, 2019. The relevant portion of V-23 (in the reverse direction to that taken by N467US) is "Sacramento, California; intersection of Sacramento, California, 346° and Red Bluff, California, 158° radials; Red Bluff, California; 58 miles, 95[00 feet] MSL, Fort Jones, California; Rogue Valley, Oregon; Eugene, Oregon; Battle Ground, Washington; intersection of Battle Ground 350° and Seattle, Washington, 197° radials; 21 miles, 45[00 feet] MSL, Seattle, Washington." All radials are from true north.

9. FAA, *FAA Historical Chronology, 1926–1996*, p. 56, www.faa.gov/about/history/chronolog_history/media/bchron.pdf.

10. Alan Billings, FOIA business analyst, Federal Aviation Administration AFN-400, personal communication to author dated September 15, 2020, and attachment. The attached extract from the Federal Register states "§ 71.5 Extent of Federal airways. (a) Each Federal airway is based on a centerline that extends from one navigational aid or intersection to another navigational aid (or through several navigational aids or intersections) specified for that airway. (b) Unless otherwise specified in Subpart B or C of this part (1) Each Federal airway includes the airspace within parallel boundary lines 4 miles each side of the centerline. . . . § 71.19 . . . b) . . . mileages for Federal airways are stated as nautical miles."

11. Unless otherwise specified, all references to "miles" refer to nautical miles, which are the standard units of distance in aviation. One nautical mile is 1.852 kilometers or about 1.15 statute miles.

12. Washington State Historical Society, document 2013.5.23.1, p. 3.

13. Washington State Historical Society, document 2013.5.23.1, p. 3. The same information appears on the teletype transcription, p. 103, just prior to the time stamp 7:42 p.m. We assume that the note recorded by Flight Operations is accurate.

14. Washington State Historical Society, document 2013.5.23.1, p. 3.

15. Ibid.

16. Ibid., 21. Two other observers on the ARINC network recorded the same position at 8:22 p.m.; the difference is probably attributable to the time taken by the ARINC operator to retransmit the original radio message.

17. *The Columbian*, July 3, 2017, www.columbian.com/news/2017/jul/03/readers-get-birds-eye-view-of-mystery-battle-ground-building/.

18. By Pythagoras's law.

19. US Department of Defense and US Department of Transportation, *2001 Federal Radionavigation Systems*, Section 3.2.4, pp. 3–25.

20. Personal correspondence with user Emeritus (retired 727 pilot), Professional Pilots Rumour Network, pprune.org.

21. Personal correspondence with user OvertHawk, Professional Pilots Rumour Network, pprune.org.

22. Calculations by author. The distance from SEA to BTG via the MALAY waypoint, along the centerline of Victor 23, is 104.67 nm (source: FAA). The uncertainty relates to the possibility that the DME (distance measuring equipment) recorded only whole miles.

23. Washington State Historical Society, document 2013.5.21.2: "Interview recorded September 12, 2013, at the Washington State History Museum in Tacoma, Washington, by curators Fred Poyner IV and Gwen Whiting."

24. FBI, D. B. Cooper Part 10 of 48.pdf, p. 417, document reference 1648135, footnote DB Cooper-1650, dated 26-Nov-71, downloaded from vault.fbi.gov.

25. FBI, https://archives.fbi.gov/archives/news/stories/2007/december/image/map.

26. Adjacent to the line are the following handwritten letters, each of which is in the lower left-hand corner of a corresponding GEOREF quadrangle, as follows:

"NC" (quadrangle DKNC)
"NB" (quadrangle DKNB)
"NA" (quadrangle DKNA)
"NQ" (quadrangle DJNQ)

It appears, therefore, that the underlying radar data (presumably expressed in nautical miles and degrees from north) were converted to latitudes and longitudes, and cross-referenced against the relevant GEOREF maps.

27. FBI, D. B. Cooper Part 10 of 48.pdf, p. 331, document reference 164813, footnote DB Cooper-1558, dated 25-Nov-71, downloaded from vault.fbi.gov.

28. FBI, D. B. Cooper Part 11 of 48.pdf, p. 133, document reference 16481211, footnote DB Cooper-1036, dated 25-Nov-71, downloaded from vault.fbi.gov.

29. FBI, D. B. Cooper Part 11 of 48.pdf, p. 90, document reference 16481190, footnote DB Cooper-1993, dated 26-Nov-71, downloaded from vault.fbi.gov.

30. FBI, D. B. Cooper Part 11 of 48.pdf, p. 345, document reference 16481121, footnote DB Cooper1820, dated 27-Nov-71, downloaded from vault.fbi.gov.

31. FBI, D. B. Cooper Part 11 of 48.pdf, p. 329, document reference 16481116, footnote DB Cooper1804, dated 26-Nov-71, downloaded from vault.fbi.gov.

32. FBI, D. B. Cooper Part 12 of 48.pdf, pp. 22, 23, document reference 16481465, footnote DB Cooper2658, dated 02-Dec-71, downloaded from vault.fbi.gov.

33. FBI, "D. B. Cooper, Part 13 of 48.pdf, p. 105, document reference 16481558, footnote DB Cooper2908, dated 03-Dec-71, downloaded from vault.fbi.gov.

34. FBI, D. B. Cooper Part 13 of 48.pdf, p. 124, document reference 16481569, footnote DB Cooper2931, dated 03-Dec-71, downloaded from vault.fbi.gov.

35. FBI, D. B. Cooper Part 13 of 48.pdf, p. 234, document reference 164816166, footnote DB Cooper3073, dated 03-Dec-71, downloaded from vault.fbi.gov.

36. FBI, D. B. Cooper Part 22 of 48.pdf, p. 233, document reference 164812283, footnote DB Cooper6574, dated 17-Feb-72, downloaded from vault.fbi.gov.

37. FBI, D. B. Cooper Part 22 of 48.pdf, p. 342, document reference 164812337, footnote DB Cooper6692, dated 24-Feb-72, downloaded from vault.fbi.gov

38. FBI, D. B. Cooper Part 13 of 48.pdf, p. 310, document reference 16481652, footnote DB Cooper3170, dated 06-Dec-71, downloaded from vault.fbi.gov.

39. FBI, D. B. Cooper Part 17 of 48.pdf, p. 194, document reference 164811508, footnote DB Cooper5024, dated 23-Dec-71, downloaded from vault.fbi.gov.

40. FBI, D. B. Cooper Part 17 of 48.pdf, p. 337, document reference 164811567, footnote DB Cooper5171, dated 27-Dec-71, downloaded from vault.fbi.gov.

41. FBI, D. B. Cooper Part 18 of 48.pdf, p. 318, document reference 164811800, footnote DB Cooper5651, dated 06-Jan-72, downloaded from vault.fbi.gov.

42. FBI, D. B. Cooper Part 18 of 48.pdf, p. 414, document reference 164811853, footnote DB Cooper5745, dated 09-Jan-72, downloaded from vault.fbi.gov.

43. n467us.com, https://web.archive.org/web/20101212230144im_/http://n467us.com/Photo%20Evidence_files/image126.jpg.

44. Department of the Air Force, 62d Operations Support Squadron (AMC), No Records Certification, FOIA Request 2020-00061-A, dated March 2, 2020, personal communication to author.

45. FBI, D. B. Cooper Part 29 of 48.pdf, p. 378, document reference 164814352, footnote DB Cooper10471, dated 23-Jan-73, downloaded from vault.fbi.gov.

46. FBI, D. B. Cooper Part 29 of 48.pdf, p. 452, document reference 164814394, footnote DB Cooper10571, dated 01-Feb-73, downloaded from vault.fbi.gov.

47. FBI, D. B. Cooper Part 11 of 48.pdf, p. 4, document reference 16481151, footnote DB Cooper-1897, dated 28-Nov-71, downloaded from vault.fbi.gov.

48. Clifford A. Ammerman, personal communication, September 10, 2020.

49. FAA, Mission Support Services, Freedom of Information Act (FOIA) Request 2019-010567WS, October 11, 2019 (personal communication).

50. FAA, Mission Support Services, Freedom of Information Act (FOIA) Request 2020-008209WS, September 18, 2020 (personal communication).

51. Washington State Historical Society, document 2013.5.15.5, p. 60.

52. Washington State Historical Society, document 2013.5.23.1, p. 23.

53. Washington State Historical Society, document 2013.5.23.1, p. 14.

**Chapter 6**

1. Technically, Flight 305 terminated at Seattle-Tacoma. After the airplane's departure from Seattle-Tacoma, both air traffic control and the flight crew continued to refer to it as 305, but it was no longer a scheduled flight. More accurately, it was an unscheduled flight of airplane N467US with three crew and one (uninvited) passenger.

2. All miles mentioned in this book are nautical miles. One nautical mile is 1.151 statute miles or 1.852 kilometers.

3. PST = Pacific Standard Time.

4. Many IAS-TAS calculators are available on the internet; for example, at http://indoavis.co.id/main/tas.html.

5. Source: Washington State Historical Society, document 2013.5.23.1, p. 3 and document 2013.5.15.5, pp. 15–16. One knot = 1 nautical mile per hour.

6. A speed of 211 knots if reporting point 3 was reached at 8:18 p.m. (probable); 193 knots if reporting point 3 was reached at 8:22 p.m. (improbable).

7. Washington State Historical Society, document 2013.5.23.1.

8. We have grouped the notes as follows:

- author A—p. 1: unknown author; period 4:07 to 11:03 p.m.
- author B—p. 2: the name Robinson appears on the page; no time period is given.
- author C—p. 3: unknown author, period 7:36 to 11:00 p.m.
- author D—pp. 4–17: the name Bob Lowenthal (then a captain with Northwest Airlines) appears on the first page; period 3:44 to 11:28 p.m.
- author E—p. 18: unknown author; period 3:15 to 5:10 p.m.
- author F—pp. 19–23: unknown author; period 5:30 to 10:19 p.m.

9. Washington State Historical Society, document 2013.5.15.5, pp. 68–74.

10. The correspondence between the raw ATC transcript and our translation is detailed in Appendix 3.

11. Washington State Historical Society, document 2013.5.15.5, pp. 1–18.

12. The correspondence between the raw ARINC transcript and our translation is detailed in Appendix 3.

13. This document, or part of it, bearing the page numbers 272–273, is reproduced on the archived website n467us.com.

14. Minnesota Aviation Hall of Fame, http://www.mnaviationhalloffame.org/inductees/s.html

15. AFB = Air Force Base.

16. Washington State Historical Society, document 2013.5.15.5, p. 69 (p. 195 in the original).

17. Washington State Historical Society, document 2013.5.15.5, p. 18 (p. 106 in the original)

18. FBI, D. B. Cooper Part 41 of 48.pdf, p. 32, case reference SE164-81, footnote DB Cooper-1140, dated May 30, 1971, downloaded from vault.fbi.gov.

**Chapter 7**

1. FBI, D. B. Cooper Part 15 of 48.pdf, p. 332, document reference 164-81-1104, footnote DB Cooper 4221, dated 30-Nov-71, downloaded from vault.fbi.gov.

2. FBI, D. B. Cooper Part 22 of 48.pdf, p. 206, document reference 164-81-2269, footnote DB Cooper 6547, dated 29-Nov-71, downloaded from vault.fbi.gov.

3. FBI, D. B. Cooper Part 15 of 48.pdf, p. 335, document reference 164-81-1105, footnote DB Cooper 4224, dated 30-Nov-71, downloaded from vault.fbi.gov.

4. FBI, D. B. Cooper Part 13 of 48.pdf, p. 86, document reference 164-81-552, footnote DB Cooper 2889, dated 03-Dec-71, downloaded from vault.fbi.gov.

5. FBI, D. B. Cooper Part 20 of 48.pdf, p. 241, document reference 164-81-2086, footnote DB Cooper 6198, dated 09-Dec-71, downloaded from vault.fbi.gov.

6. FBI, D. B. Cooper Part 13 of 48.pdf, pp. 306, 308, document reference 164-81-651, footnotes DB Cooper 3166, 3168, dated 04-Dec-71, downloaded from vault.fbi.gov.

7. FBI, D. B. Cooper Part 39 of 48.pdf, p. 228, document reference 164-81-7398, footnote DB Cooper 15413, dated 01-Mar-77, downloaded from vault.fbi.gov.

8. FBI, D. B. Cooper Part 39 of 48.pdf, p. 330, document reference 164-81-7449, footnote DB Cooper 15518, dated 08-Apr-77, downloaded from vault.fbi.gov.

9. Continental Airlines, October 31, 1971, System Timetable, www.departedflights.com/CO103171p24.html and www.departedflights.com/CO103171p28.html.

10. This calculation can be done online at a variety of sites; for example, at https://e6bx.com/e6b/ or www.luizmonteiro.com.

11. Based on online calculation at www.luizmonteiro.com.

12. Ibid.

13. NOAA/NCEI, Weather Balloon Data, www.ncdc.noaa.gov/data-access/weather-balloon-data.

14. NOAA/NCEI, IGRA2 Station List, www1.ncdc.noaa.gov/pub/data/igra/igra2-station-list.txt.

15. William Brown, meteorologist, NOAA/NCEI, personal communication, August 19, 2019.

16. For the mathematically minded, the best-fitting regression equations, with the coefficients and standard errors of each explanatory variable and the intercept, as well as the regression coefficient, are summarized as follows:

- The relatively low regression coefficients reflect the uncertainty of the estimates.
- Endogenous variables: WSPDkt = measured wind speed (knots); WDIRS = measured wind direction (degrees from due south)
- Explanatory variables: LAT° = latitude of IGRA station (degrees north); LON° = longitude of IGRA station (degrees west); HRPST = Hour of sounding (PST) (00.00-24.00); GPHf = geopotential height (feet AMSL)
- Best-fitting equation for wind speed (standard errors of coefficients in parentheses)
- WSPDkt = -2075.59(429.89) + 2.87(0.82)* LAT° + 15.92(3.21)* LON° + 0.0020(0.0001)*GPHf
- R squared = 24.50%
- Best fitting equation for wind direction (standard errors of coefficients in parentheses)

- WDIRS = -7049.64(3247.54) + 13.79(5.74)* LAT° + 52.20(24.47)* LON° + 0.0099(0.0005)*GPHf 0.75(0.29)*HRPST

- R squared = 14.67%.

**Chapter 8**

1. Washington State Historical Society, interview with John Detlor, retired FBI agent assigned to the NORJAK case, recorded November 16, 2012, by curator Fred Poyner IV, document reference 2013.37.1.2.2, p. 2. Punctuation added for clarity.

2. FBI, "D. B. Cooper." Part 10 of 48.pdf, p. 422, document reference 164-81-38, footnote DB Cooper-1644, dated November 26, 1971.

3. FBI, D. B. Cooper Part 11 of 48.pdf, p. 93, document reference 164-81-192, footnote DB Cooper-1996, dated November 26, 1971.

4. FBI, D. B. Cooper Part 12 of 48.pdf, p. 181, document reference 164-81-329, footnote DB Cooper-2317, dated November 30, 1971.

5. FBI, D. B. Cooper Part 13 of 48.pdf, p. 14, document reference 164-81-519, footnote DB Cooper-2798, dated November 30, 1971.

6. FBI, D. B. Cooper Part 17 of 48.pdf, p. 9, document reference 164-81-1403, footnote DB Cooper-4832, dated December 17, 1971.

7. FBI, D. B. Cooper Part 18 of 48.pdf, p. 154, document reference 164-81-1715, footnote DB Cooper-5487, dated December 29, 1971.

8. Bud May, *Daily News* (Longview, WA), February 13, 1980, reproduced in FBI, D. B. Cooper Part 18 of 48.pdf, p. 392, document reference 164-81-8241, footnote DB Cooper-17422, dated February 21, 1980.

9. Washington State Historical Society, document 2013.37.1.2.2, interview with John Detlor, retired FBI agent assigned to the NORJAK case, recorded November 16, 2012, by Fred Poyner IV, p. 2.

10. FBI, D. B. Cooper Part 18 of 48.pdf, p. 317, document reference 164-81-1800, footnote DB Cooper-5650, dated January 6, 1972.

11. Washington State Historical Society, document 2013.5.21.2, interview with Wally Johnson, retired Sr. MSgt (USAF), recorded September 12, 2013, at the Washington State History Museum in Tacoma, Washington, by Fred Poyner IV and Gwen Whiting.

12. Washington State Historical Society, document 2013.37.1.2.2, interview with John Detlor, retired FBI agent assigned to the NORJAK case, recorded November 16, 2012, by Fred Poyner IV, p. 4. Punctuation added for clarity.

13. FBI, D. B. Cooper Part 18 of 48.pdf, p. 392, document reference 164-81-1841, footnote DB Cooper-5724, dated January 10, 1972.

14. FBI, D. B. Cooper Part 19 of 48.pdf, p. 16, document reference 164-81-1905, footnote DB Cooper-5852, dated January 14, 1972.

15. Public Domain Aeronautical Software (PDAS), Sample Atmosphere Table (US units), July 9, 2017, www.pdas.com/atmosTable2US.html.

16. FBI, D. B. Cooper Part 19 of 48.pdf, p. 17, document reference 164-81-1905, footnote DB Cooper-5853, dated January 14, 1972.

17. NASA, "NASA-Dryden History—Historic Aircraft—X-1 Flight Summary," www.nasa.gov/centers/dryden/history/HistoricAircraft/X-1/fltsummary.html.

**Chapter 9**

1. FBI, D. B. Cooper Part 13 of 48.pdf, p. 310, document reference 164-81-652, footnote DB Cooper-3170, dated December 6, 1971.

2. FBI, D. B. Cooper Part 13 of 48.pdf, p. 28, document reference 164-81-524, footnote DB Cooper-2822, dated December 2, 1971.

3. FBI, D. B. Cooper Part 18 of 48.pdf, p. 413, document reference 164-81-1853, footnote DB Cooper-5745, dated January 11, 1972.

4. FBI, D. B. Cooper Part 19 of 48.pdf, p. 61, document reference 164-81-1927, footnote DB Cooper-5916, dated January 13, 1972.

5. FBI, D. B. Cooper Part 18 of 48.pdf, p. 414, document reference 164-81-1853, footnotes DB Cooper-5746, dated January 11, 1972.

6. Mark Em, Oldschool Skydiving group, personal communication.

7. Dave Huget, Oldschool Skydiving group, personal communication.

8. FBI, D. B. Cooper Part 26 of 48.pdf, p. 166, document reference 164-81-3477, footnote DB Cooper-8562, dated June 8, 1972.

9. Washington State Historical Society, interview with retired Sr. MSgt Wally Johnson, recorded September 12, 2013, at the Washington State History Museum in Tacoma, Washington, by Fred Poyner IV and Gwen Whiting.

10. FBI, D. B. Cooper Part 28 of 48.pdf, p. 381, document reference 164-81-4095, footnote DB Cooper-9946, dated November 13, 1972.

11. FBI, D. B. Cooper Part 29 of 48.pdf, p. 378, document reference 164-81-4352, footnote DB Cooper-10471, dated January 23, 1973.

12. Sr. A. Isiah D. Shortte, USAF, Base Privacy Manager, 627th Communications Squadron, Joint Base Lewis-McChord, Washington, personal communication, March 12, 2020.

13. FBI, D. B. Cooper Part 30 of 48.pdf, p. 156, document reference 164-81-4477, footnote DB Cooper-10800, dated March 2, 1973.

**Chapter 10**

1. FBI, D. B. Cooper Part 43 of 48.pdf, p. 18, document reference 164-81-8163, dated November 9, 1978, footnote DB Cooper-17196, downloaded from vault.fbi.gov.

2. FBI, D. B. Cooper Part 42 of 48.pdf, p. 178, document reference 164-81-8038, dated December 6, 1978, footnote DB Cooper-16888, downloaded from vault.fbi.gov.

3. "Northwest Airlines Inc., Color Scheme Instl—727 Exterior," Project 35459, Revision J, document number 4011-33176, p. 2 and unnumbered page, last dated September 19, 1969, provided by personal communication from FBI to the author, FBI reference 164-81-10a(666).

4. Source, Bruce Kitt, personal communication, October 6, 2020.

5. For example OzTech Industrial, www.ozindustrial.com/?page_id=817&paged=427.

6. Equivalent to Mach 0.9.

7. FBI, D. B. Cooper Part 42 of 48.pdf, p. 180, document reference 164-81-8039, dated December 6, 1978, footnote DB Cooper-16890, downloaded from vault.fbi.gov.

8. *Register Guard* (Eugene, OR), January 19, 1979: 18A.

9. *Columbian* staff, AP, "No Hunt Set for Skyjacker," *The Columbian* (Vancouver, WA, January 19, 1979: 1, reproduced in FBI, D. B. Cooper Part 42 of 48.pdf, p. 330, document reference 164-81-8113, dated February 1979, footnote DB Cooper-17060, downloaded from vault.fbi.gov.

10. *The Columbian* (Vancouver, WA), January 19, 1979: 1.

11. AP, "Decal's Link to Hijacker Discounted," *Register Guard* (Eugene, OR), January 19, 1979: 18A.

12. FBI, D. B. Cooper Part 42 of 48.pdf, p. 415, document reference 164-81-8148, dated July 31, 1979, footnote DB Cooper-17155, and p. 417, document reference 164-81-8149, dated August 3, 1979, footnote DB Cooper-17158, downloaded from vault.fbi.gov.

13. Calculation generated by www.movable-type.co.uk/scripts/latlong-nomodule.html.

14. Robert Nicholson, personal communication, May 21, 2020.

15. Robert M Blevins, "Exact Location of the Instruction Placard from NWA Flight 305," April 3, 2018, https://thedbcooperhijacking.wordpress.com/2018/04/03/exact-location-of-the-plastic-placard-from-nwa-flight-305/.

16. Washington State Historical Society, document 2013.5.23.1: digitized notes from Northwest Airlines executive George Harrison, who was present at Seattle-Tacoma International Airport during the hijacking of Northwest Airlines flight 305, p. 3, document created October 18, 2013.

17. A. C. Bustamante, 9513, and Aerospace Nuclear Safety Department 9510, "Free-Fall Rotation and Aerodynamic Motion of Rectangular Plates," Sandia Laboratories, document reference SC-RR -68-132, August 1968.

18. James E. Brunk, "Free-Flight Aerodynamics of Non-rotating Low-Aspect-Ratio Ultra-thin Rectangular Plates and Open-End Circular Cylinders at Low Reynolds Numbers (Experimental Results)," published by author, September 2018.

19. James E. Brunk, June 9, 2020, personal communication.

20. Bruce Kitt, personal communication, October 5, 2020.

**Chapter 11**

1. "Citizen Sleuths, the Hunt for D. B. Cooper, www.citizensleuths.com.

2. Eric Ulis, The DB Cooper Forum, Tena Bar Money Find, Post# 6101, April 1, 2021, https://www.thedbcooperforum.com/db-cooper/tina-bar-money-find/6101

3. FBI, D. B. Cooper Part 43 of 48.pdf, p. 184, document reference SE164-81-8228, footnote DB Cooper-17389, dated February 27, 1980, downloaded from vault.fbi.gov. The name of the respondent is redacted; he is identified as Richard Fazio by Eric Ulis (https://thecoopercase.com/pages/tena-bar-money-find-spot). Fazio recalled the date as February 11, 1980.

4. Richard Fazio, quoted in the *Daily News* (Longview, WA), February 22, 1980: B1.

5. *Daily News* (Longview, WA), February 22, 1980: B1.

6. FBI, D. B. Cooper Part 43 of 48.pdf, pp. 369–371, document reference SE164-81-8296, footnotes DB Cooper-17601 to -17603, dated February 14, 1980, downloaded from vault.fbi.gov.

7. FBI, D. B. Cooper Part 43 of 48.pdf, p. 369, document reference SE164-81-8296, footnote DB Cooper-17601, dated February 14, 1980, downloaded from vault.fbi.gov.

8. US Army Corps of Engineers, *Report of the Chief of Engineers* (Washington, DC: US Army, 1974), 37-3.

9. FBI, D. B. Cooper Part 43 of 48.pdf, p. 374, document reference SE164818297, footnote DB Cooper-17609, dated February 13, 1980, downloaded from vault.fbi.gov.

10. From the formula area = $\pi$ * radius squared.

11. FBI, D. B. Cooper Part 43 of 48.pdf, p. 370, document reference SE164-81-8296, footnote DB Cooper-17602, dated February 14, 1980, downloaded from vault.fbi.gov.

12. FBI, D. B. Cooper Part 51 of 51.pdf, p. 375, document reference SE164A81(pending)9377, footnote DB Cooper-21599, dated August 22, 2001, downloaded from vault.fbi.gov.

13. "FBI Geologist Favors Washougal Landing for D. B.," *The Columbian* (Vancouver, WA), March 16, 1980: 15.

**Chapter 12**

1. Thomas G. Kaye and Mark Meltzer, "Diatoms Constrain Forensic Burial Timelines: Case Study with DB Cooper Money," *Scientific Reports* 10 (2020):13036, https://doi.org/10.1038/s41598-020-70015-z.

2. Genus (plural: genera) is a category for classifying living creatures. It is the next level up from species. By convention, the name of the genus is capitalized and in italics, and the name of the species is in lower case and in italics.

3. The striae are the lateral ridges. Among the most common species of *Cymbella* in North America, the number of striae is closely correlated with the length of the cell. This specimen has approximately forty-six striae, and on that basis we estimate its length at 42 mm and its width at 16 mm, which is more consistent with *Cymbella tumida* than with any other species of *Cymbella*.

4. Thomas G Kaye, personal communications, August 8 and 13, 2020.

5. "*Asterionella formosa*, Hassall 1850: Autoecology," at https://diatoms.org/species/asterionella_formosa.

6. "*Fragilaria crotonensis*, Kitton 1869: Autoecology," at https://diatoms.org/species/fragilaria_crotonensis.

7. US Environmental Protection Agency, National Aquatic Resource Surveys: *National Lakes Assessment*, at www.epa.gov/national-aquatic-resource-surveys/nla. These studies do not cover all major lakes but are based on a sample that is periodically modified. The NLA of 2007 included six lakes in Oregon; the NLA of 2012 included seventeen.

8. US Geological Survey, National Water-Quality Assessment (NAWQA): 1991–2012, at www.usgs.gov/mission-areas/water-resources/science/national-water-quality-assessment-nawqa-1991-2012. The NAWQA project also covered the Yakima River basin in 1999–2000 and the central Columbia River plateau in 1992–1995, but we judged these study units to be too far upstream from our area of research.

9. Mark Sytsma, *Atlas of Oregon Lakes* (Portland, OR: Portland State University, 1985), https://oregonlakes-atlas.org/map.

10. M. V. Shulters, *Lakes of Oregon*, vol. 2, *Benton, Lincoln, and Polk Counties* (Portland, OR: US Geological Survey, 1974), https://pubs.usgs.gov/unnumbered/70199339/report.pdf; M. V. Shulters, *Lakes of Oregon*, vol. 3, *Hood River, Multnomah, Washington, and Yamhill Counties* (Portland, OR: US Geological Survey, 1975), https://pubs.usgs.gov/unnumbered/70199341/report.pdf; M. V. Shulters, *Lakes of Oregon*, vol. 4, *Clackamas County* (Portland, OR: US Geological Survey, 1976), https://pubs.usgs.gov/unnumbered/70199342/report.pdf; and Joseph F. Rinella, *Lakes of Oregon*, vol. 5, *Marion County* (Portland, OR: US Geological Survey, 1977), https://pubs.er.usgs.gov/publication/70199343.

11. Columbia estuary: Bruce E. Frey, Ruben Lara-Lara, and Lawrence F. Small, *Final Report on the Water Column Primary Production Work Unit of the Columbia River Estuary Data Development Program* (Corvallis, OR: Columbia River Estuary Data Development Program [CREDDP], February 1984); Columbia River, river miles 276 to 324: Lorna Wallick, Ronald Campbell, Vicki Morris, and Richard S. LeGore, *Interim Report: Study Area Vi–C, Columbia River* (Seattle, WA: Parametrix, January 31, 1975); and Hanford Reach: R. W. Cowpey, *Radioactive Plankton from the Columbia River* (Richland, WA: General Electric, March 29, 1951).

12. Additional source identified: Claudia E. Tausz, "Phytoplankton Dynamics in Off-Channel Habitats of the Lower Columbia River Estuary" (MA thesis, Institute of Environmental Health and Oregon Health & Science University, December 2015).

13. Claudia E Tausz, personal communications, August 20 and 21, 2020.

14. Biovolume is the physical volume of the sampled cells, measured in cubic micrometers per milliliter.

15. Mark Sytsma, "Bybee Lake," in *Atlas of Oregon Lakes* (Portland, OR: Portland State University, 1985), https://oregonlakesatlas.org/lake/17090012006624.

16. Mark Sytsma, "Blue Lake (Multnomah County)," in *Atlas of Oregon Lakes* (Portland, OR: Portland State University, 1985), https://oregonlakesatlas.org/lake/17090012000361.

17. The hypolimnion is the bottom layer of the body of water.

18. A Secchi disk is a device for measuring the transparency of water. In this instance, at a depth of 4.6 feet the disk could no longer be seen.

19. Mark Sytsma, "Lake Oswego," in *Atlas of Oregon Lakes* (Portland, OR: Portland State University, 1985), https://oregonlakesatlas.org/lake/17090012000369. My requests to the Lake Oswego Corporation and to the Oswego Lake Watershed Council (OLWC) for data on diatoms in Oswego Lake received no response.

20. This author's requests to the Lake Oswego Corporation and to The Oswego Lake Watershed Council (OLWC), for data on diatoms in Oswego Lake, received no response.

21. Daphne G. Clifton, *Water-Quality Data for Smith and Bybee Lakes, June to November 1982*, Open-File Report 83-204 (Portland, OR: US Geological Survey, 1983), https://pubs.usgs.gov/of/1983/0204/report.pdf.

22. Kaye and Meltzer, "Diatoms Constrain Forensic Burial Timelines," 5, 7.

**Chapter 13**

1. Dennis Lysne, Northwest Airlines ticket clerk, quoted in FBI, D. B. Cooper Part 10 of 48.pdf, pp. 443–444, document reference 164-81-52, dated November 26, 1971, footnotes DB Cooper-1676 and 1677, downloaded from vault.fbi.gov.

2. William M Mitchell, passenger in seat 18-A of Flight 305, quoted in Washington State Historical Society, document 2013.5.22.2, "Bill Mitchell Interview on October 3, 2013, by telephone with Fred Poyner IV and Gwen Whiting," p. 4, dated October 18, 2013.

3. FBI, D. B. Cooper Part 17 of 48.pdf, p. 125, document reference 164-81-1465, dated November 26, 1971, footnote DB Cooper-4951, downloaded from vault.fbi.gov.

4. FBI, D. B. Cooper Part 22 of 48.pdf, p. 91, document reference 164-81-2205, dated February 8, 1971, footnote DB Cooper-6433, downloaded from vault.fbi.gov.

5. FBI, D. B. Cooper Part 22 of 48.pdf, p. 342, document reference 164-81-2337, dated February 24, 1971, footnote DB Cooper-6692, downloaded from vault.fbi.gov.

6. FBI, D. B. Cooper Part 22 of 48.pdf, p. 355, document reference 164-81-2349, dated February 24, 1971, footnote DB Cooper-6706, downloaded from vault.fbi.gov.

7. FBI, D. B. Cooper Part 23 of 48.pdf, p. 165, document reference 164-81-2454, dated March 8, 1971, footnote DB Cooper-7317, downloaded from vault.fbi.gov.

8. FBI, *FBI Law Enforcement Bulletin*, May 1949: 2–6.

9. Michael R Bromwich, *The FBI Laboratory: An Investigation into Laboratory Practices and Alleged Misconduct in Explosives-Related and Other Cases* (Darby, PA: Diane, 1998), 488.

10. FBI, D. B. Cooper Part 24 of 48.pdf, pp. 325–327, document reference 164-81-2673, dated April 12, 1972, footnotes DB Cooper-7725 to 7727, downloaded from vault.fbi.gov.

11. FBI, D. B. Cooper Part 26 of 48.pdf, pp. 174–175, document reference 164-81-3483, dated May 30, 1972, footnotes DB Cooper-8570, 8571, downloaded from vault.fbi.gov.

12. FBI, D. B. Cooper Part 26 of 48.pdf, p. 363, document reference 164-81-3572, dated June 30, 1972, footnote DB Cooper-8769, downloaded from vault.fbi.gov.

13. FBI, D. B. Cooper Part 26 of 48.pdf, p. 174, document reference 164-81-3483, dated May 30, 1972, footnote DB Cooper-8570, downloaded from vault.fbi.gov.

14. Federal Trade Commission, rn.ftc.gov/Account/BasicSearch.

15. FBI, D. B. Cooper Part 26 of 48.pdf, p. 473, document reference 164-81-3483, dated May 30, 1972, footnote DB Cooper-8883, downloaded from vault.fbi.gov.

16. FBI, "The FBI and DNA, Part 1: A Look at the Nationwide System That Helps Solve Crimes," November 23, 2011, www.fbi.gov/news/stories/the-fbi-and-dna-part-1.

17. FBI, D. B. Cooper Part 52 of 52.pdf, p. 39, footnote DB Cooper-21641, downloaded from vault.fbi.gov.

18. FBI, D. B. Cooper Part 52 of 52.pdf, p. 2, footnote DB Cooper-21601, downloaded from vault.fbi.gov.

19. FBI, D. B. Cooper Part 52 of 52.pdf, p. 24, footnote DB Cooper-21625, downloaded from vault.fbi.gov.

20. FBI, D. B. Cooper," Part 52 of 52.pdf, p. 284, footnote DB Cooper-21966, downloaded from vault.fbi.gov.

21. FBI, "D. B. Cooper Redux: Help Us Solve the Enduring Mystery," https://archives.fbi.gov/archives/news/stories/2007/december/dbcooper_123107.

22. Jack Cloherty, "D. B. Cooper DNA Results: 'Not A Match,' Another Inconclusive Lead in Decades-Long Investigation," ABC News, August 8, 2011, https://abcnews.go.com/US/db-cooper-dna-results-match/story?id=14258726.

23. Citizen Sleuths, "McCrone Labs Analysis 2017," https://citizensleuths.com/mccrone1.html.

24. Citizen Sleuths, "Imaging and Identification of Tie Particles," https://citizensleuths.com/uv-imaging-of-tie.html.

25. Citizen Sleuths, "Pollen," https://citizensleuths.com/pollen.html. These spores are highly flammable and are used for this purpose in explosives, fireworks, and video special effects; they are also used as coatings for medical tablets, and as stabilizers for ice cream.

26. Citizen Sleuths, "Titanium Particles from Cooper's Tie," https://citizensleuths.com/titaniumparticles.html.

27. Tom Kaye, personal communication, May 31, 2020.

28. Josh Gates and Tom Kaye, *Expedition Unknown*, episode 3.7, Travel Channel, January 11, 2017. Transcript by author.

29. Tom Kaye, personal communication, May 31, 2020.

30. Citizen Sleuths, "Did the Tie Belong to Cooper?," https://citizensleuths.com/coopers-tie.html.

31. FBI, D. B. Cooper Part 15 of 48.pdf, p. 99, document reference 164-81-958, dated December 9, 1971, footnote DB Cooper-3004, downloaded from vault.fbi.gov.

**Chapter 14**

1. Sir Arthur Conan Doyle, *The Sign of the Four*, chap. 1 (London: Spencer Blackett, 1890), 92, and similar expressions in other stories.

2. Sir Arthur Conan Doyle, *The Adventures of Sherlock Holmes*, chap. 3 (London: George Newnes, 1892), 190.

3. Dr. Jean Potvin and Gary Peek, "Skydiving Canopy Opening G-Forces," Parks College Parachute Research Group, August 2013, www.pcprg.com/g-forces.htm.

4. C. F. Murray-Leslie, D. J. Lintott, and V. Wright, "The Spine in Sport and Veteran Military Parachutists," *Annals of the Rheumatic Diseases* 36, no. 4 (1977): 332–342.

5. Yuxing Zheng, "Oswego Lake Set to Begin Slowly Draining on September 5 for Sewer Project Work," *The Oregonian*, August 27, 2010, www.oregonlive.com/lake-oswego/2010/08/oswego_lake_set_to_begin_slowly_draining_on_sept_5.html.

6. Our estimate based on maximum reported drawdown, assuming 30 percent of the lake area was exposed (277 acres × 43,560 square feet/acre × 24 feet plus 118 acres × 43,560 square feet/acre × 12 feet).

**Epilogue**

1. Mark Sytsma, *Atlas of Oregon Lakes* (Portland, OR: Portland State University, 1985), 115, https://oregonlakesatlas.org/map.

**Afterword: The Usual Suspects**

1. FBI, "D. B. Cooper Hijacking," www.fbi.gov/history/famous-cases/db-cooper-hijacking.

2. FBI, D. B. Cooper Part 52 of 52.pdf, pp. 85–105, footnotes DB Cooper-21698 to 21720, November 2020, downloaded from vault.fbi.gov.

3. US Bureau of the Census, *1971 US Census Report*, section 1, "Population," table 21 (Washington, DC: US Bureau of the Census, 1971), 23, www2.census.gov/prod2/statcomp/documents/1971-02.pdf.

4. U.S. Department of Health and Human Services, Public Health Service, National Center for Health Statistics, Anthropometric Reference Data and Prevalence of Overweight, United States, 1976–80, tables 23, 25; https://www.cdc.gov/nchs/data/series/sr_11/sr11_238.pdf.

5. Paul Sitter, "Skydiving Then and Now: 50 Years of Change," *Parachutist*, July 2019, https://uspa.org/p/Article/skydiving-then-and-now50-years-of-change.

6. MSgt. Karl Hinkamp, Background Paper on the Establishment of the Loadmaster Crew Position/Career Field (Maxwell-Gunter AFB, AL: Air Force Enlisted Heritage Research Institute, AFEHRI File 100.107), August 18, 1992.

7. Sam McGowan, "Loadmaster Evolution," *Air Force Magazine*, December 1, 2011, https://www.airforcemag.com/article/1211evolution/.

8. Roland S. Weber, post on aviastar.com, October 29, 2010.

9. Ernest Gonzalez, post on Aviation Stack Exchange, March 23, 2018, https://aviation.stackexchange.com/questions/24471/how-can-cargo-be-jettisoned-from-a-c-124-in-flight.

10. Robert F. Futrell, *The United States Air Force in Korea 1950–1953*, Revised Edition (Washington, DC: US Air Force, Office of Air Force History, 1983), p. 563.

11. Nicholas M. Williams, *Aircraft of the United States' Military Air Transport Service* (Midland Publishing, Leicester, UK, 1999, ISBN 1-85780-087-7) p. 143.

12. Author's analysis based on Air Force Historical Research Agency, Organizational Records, Squadrons and Flights, https://www.afhra.af.mil/Information/Organizational-Records/Squadrons-and-Flights/.

13. Fred Watkins, post on aviastar.com, January 14, 2014.

14. USAF, *United States Air Force Statistical Digest, Fiscal Year 1953* (Washington, DC: Department of the Air Force, 1953), tables 121, 185, 188.

15. McChord Air Museum, Douglas C-124C Globemaster II, History, http://www.mcchordairmuseum.org/rev%20b%20mam%20collection%20c-124%20border.htm.

# SOURCES


**Books**

Bromwich, Michael R. *The FBI Laboratory: An Investigation into Laboratory Practices and Alleged Misconduct in Explosives-Related and Other Cases*. Darby, PA: Diane, 1997.

Doyle, Sir Arthur Conan. *The Adventures of Sherlock Holmes*. London: George Newnes, 1892. www.gutenberg.org/ebooks/1661.

Doyle, Sir Arthur Conan. *The Sign of the Four*. London: Spencer Blackett, 1890. www.gutenberg.org/ebooks/2097.

Kneale, William, and Martha Kneale. *The Development of Logic*. London: Oxford University Press, 1962.

Prados, John. *Safe for Democracy: The Secret Wars of the CIA*. Chicago: Ivan R. Dee, 2006.

Tausz, Claudia E. "*Phytoplankton Dynamics in Off-Channel Habitats of the Lower Columbia River Estuary*." MA thesis, Institute of Environmental Health and Oregon Health & Science University, 2015.

Weinberg, Albert. *Dan Cooper 8—Le Secret de Dan Cooper*. Brussels: Lombard/Dargaud, 1965.

Williams, Nicholas. M. *Aircraft of the United States' Military Air Transport Service* (Leicester: Midland, 1999).

**Brochures**

Northeast Airlines. "System Timetable, October 31, 1971." Boston: Northeast Airlines, October 31, 1971.

Northwest Airlines. "Northwest Orient, System Timetable Effective October 31, 1971." Minneapolis: Northwest Airlines, October 31, 1971.

**Digital files**

"georger" and "hominid." Telephone interview with Harold E. Anderson (The DB Cooper Forum, 28-Jan-2014). https://www.thedbcooperforum.com/db-cooper/flight-path-and-related-issues/msg37962/#msg37962.

ARINC. Document 2013.5.15.5: "Digital document, transcript of radio communication between Northwest Orient Airlines flight 305 and Seattle-Tacoma International Airport, Reno International Airport." Washington State Historical Society, 2012. https://wshs-collections.s3.us-west-2.amazonaws.com/2013.5.15.5.pdf.

ARINC. Document 2013.5.23.4 [examination report of teletype from hijacking of Northwest Airlines flight 305]. Washington State Historical Society, 12-Jan-14. https://wshs-collections.s3.us-west-2.amazonaws.com/2013.5.23.4.pdf.

Blevins, Robert M. *Exact Location of the Instruction Placard from NWA Flight* 305. Adventure Books of Seattle, 3-Apr-18. https://thedbcooperhijacking.wordpress.com/2018/04/03/exact-location-of-the-plastic-placard-from-nwa-flight-305/.

Boeing Company. *727 Commercial Transport: Historical Snapshot*. Boeing Company, 2020. www.boeing.com/history/products/727.page.

Boeing-727.com. System Descriptions, Pressurisation (Boeing-727.com, 18-Jul-2001). https://www.boeing-727.com/Data/systems/infopress.html.

CIA; 19710430 Southern Air Transport, Inc. Personnel and Fa.cilities, Personnel, file name 197111.pdf. CIA, 30-Apr-71. www.cia.gov/library/reading-room/document/5200379f993294098d517202.

CIA. Memorandum for: Deputy Director for Support, Subject: Southern Air Transport. Inc. CIA, 29-Nov-71. www.cia.gov/library/readingroom/docs/197109.pdf.

CIA. Memorandum to Marvin L. Evans, assistant general counsel, from managing director, document 196207.pdf. CIA, 07-Nov-62. www.cia.gov/library/readingroom/document/5200379f993294098d5171fe.

CIA. Request for Records Disposition Authority, Job Number N1263001. CIA, 16-Jan-03. www.archives.gov/files/records-mgmt/rcs/schedules/independent-agencies/rg-0263/n1-263-00-001_sf115.pdf.

Citizen Sleuths. Did the Tie Belong to Cooper? Citizen Sleuths, 2017. https://citizensleuths.com/coopers-tie.html.

Citizen Sleuths. Imaging and Identification of Tie Particles. Citizen Sleuths, 2017. https://citizensleuths.com/uvimagingoftie.html.

Citizen Sleuths. McCrone Labs Analysis 2017. Citizen Sleuths, 2017. https://citizensleuths.com/mccrone1.html.

Citizen Sleuths. Pollen. Citizen Sleuths, 2017. https://citizensleuths.com/pollen.html.

Citizen Sleuths. The Hunt for D. B. Cooper. Citizen Sleuths, 2020. www.citizensleuths.com.

Citizen Sleuths. Titanium Particles from Cooper's Tie. Citizen Sleuths, 2017. https://citizensleuths.com/titaniumparticles.html.

Clifton, Daphne G. *Water-Quality Data for Smith and Bybee Lakes, June to November 1982.*

Open-File Report 83-204. US Geological Survey, 1983. https://pubs.usgs.gov/of/1983/0204/report.pdf.

Continental Airlines; October 31, 1971, System Timetable. Continental Airlines, 31-Oct-71. www.departedflights.com/CO103171p28.html.

Continental Airlines. October 31, 1971, System Timetable. Continental Airlines, 31-Oct-71. www.departedflights.com/CO103171p24.html.

diatoms.org. *Asterionella formosa*, Hassal 1850: Autoecology. diatoms.org, 2020. https://diatoms.org/species/asterionella_formosa.

diatoms.org. *Fragilaria crotonensis*, Kitton 1869: Autoecology. diatoms.org, 2020. https://diatoms.org/species/fragilaria_crotonensis.

Evans, Michelle. The X-15 Rocket Plane: Flying the First Wings into Space—Flight Log. Mach 25 Media, 2013. www.mach25media.com/Resources/X15FlightLog.pdf.

FAA. Aircraft Hijackings and Other Criminal Acts against Civil Aviation. Statistical and Narrative Reports. Updated to January 1, 1983 (US Government Printing Office, May-1983). https://www.ncjrs.gov/App/Publications/abstract.aspx?ID=91941.

FAA. *Airman's Information Manual*. AIP/GEN/SAR RAC/COM 1/AGA 3. US Government Printing Office, May-76. https://books.google.com.

FAA. *Code of Federal Regulations*. Part 25, Airworthiness Standards: Transport Category Airplanes, Subpart D—Design and Construction, Sec. 25.809. US Government Printing Office, 24-Nov-72. https://rgl.faa.gov/Regulatory_and_Guidance_Library/rgFAR.nsf/0/42B6073445F438F28525667200519C29?OpenDocument.

FAA. *FAA Statistical Handbook of Aviation: 1969*. US Government Printing Office, 31-Dec-69. https://books.google.com.

FAA. *FAA Statistical Handbook of Aviation: 1972*. US Government Printing Office, 31-Dec-72. https://books.google.com.

FAA. Order JO 7110.66F National Beacon Code Allocation Plan (NBCAP). US Government Printing Office, 2019. www.faa.gov/regulations_policies/orders_notices/index.cfm/go/document.information/documentid/1035828.

FAA. Order JO 7400.11D Airspace Designations and Reporting Points. US Government Printing Office, 08-Aug-19. www.faa.gov/regulations_policies/orders_notices/index.cfm/go/document.information/documentID/1036608.

FBI. "D. B. Cooper." Part 04 of 48.pdf. FBI, 08-Nov-11. https://vault.fbi.gov/D-B-Cooper /D.B. Cooper Part 04 of 48/view.

FBI. "D. B. Cooper." Part 10 of 48.pdf. FBI, 31-Mar-17. https://vault.fbi.gov/D-B-Cooper /D.B. Cooper Part 10 of 48/view.

FBI. "D. B. Cooper." Part 11 of 48.pdf. FBI, 03-May-17. https://vault.fbi.gov/D-B-Cooper /D.B. Cooper Part 11 of 48/view.

FBI. "D. B. Cooper." Part 12 of 48.pdf. FBI, 02-Jun-17. https://vault.fbi.gov/D-B-Cooper /D.B. Cooper Part 12 of 48/view.

FBI. "D. B. Cooper." Part 13 of 48.pdf. FBI, 30-Jun-17. https://vault.fbi.gov/D-B-Cooper /D.B. Cooper Part 13 of 48/view.

FBI. "D. .B. Cooper." Part 14 of 48.pdf. FBI, 10-Aug-17; https://vault.fbi.gov/D-B-Cooper /D.B. Cooper Part 14 of 48/view.

FBI. "D. B. Cooper." Part 15 of 48.pdf. FBI, 01-Sep-17. https://vault.fbi.gov/D-B-Cooper /D.B. Cooper Part 15 of 48/view.

FBI. "D. B. Cooper." Part 17 of 48.pdf. FBI, 27-Oct-17. https://vault.fbi.gov/D-B-Cooper /D.B. Cooper Part 17 of 48/view.

FBI. "D. B. Cooper." Part 18 of 48.pdf. FBI, 29-Nov-17. https://vault.fbi.gov/D-B-Cooper /D.B. Cooper Part 18 of 48/view.

FBI. "D. B. Cooper." Part 19 of 48.pdf. FBI, 26-Dec-17. https://vault.fbi.gov/D-B-Cooper /D.B. Cooper Part 19 of 48/view.

FBI. "D. B. Cooper." Part 20 of 48.pdf. FBI, 26-Dec-17. https://vault.fbi.gov/D-B-Cooper /D.B. Cooper Part 20 of 48/view.

FBI. "D. B. Cooper." Part 22 of 48.pdf. FBI, 25-Jan-18. https://vault.fbi.gov/D-B-Cooper /D.B. Cooper Part 22 of 48/view.

FBI. "D. B. Cooper." Part 23 of 48.pdf. FBI, 27-Feb-18. https://vault.fbi.gov/D-B-Cooper /D.B. Cooper Part 23 of 48/view.

FBI. "D. B. Cooper." Part 24 of 48.pdf. FBI, 28-Mar-18. https://vault.fbi.gov/D-B-Cooper /D.B. Cooper Part 24 of 48/view.

FBI. "D. B. Cooper." Part 25 of 48.pdf. FBI, 30-Apr-18. https://vault.fbi.gov/D-B-Cooper /D.B. Cooper Part 25 of 48/view.

FBI. "D. B. Cooper." Part 26 of 48.pdf. FBI, 30-May-18. https://vault.fbi.gov/D-B-Cooper /D.B. Cooper Part 26 of 48/view.

FBI. "D. B. Cooper." Part 27 of 48.pdf. FBI, 25-Jun-18. https://vault.fbi.gov/D-B-Cooper /D.B. Cooper Part 27 of 48/view.

FBI. "D. B. Cooper." Part 28 of 48.pdf. FBI, 25-Jul-18. https://vault.fbi.gov/D-B-Cooper /D.B. Cooper Part 28 of 48/view.

FBI. "D. B. Cooper." Part 29 of 48.pdf. FBI, 30-Aug-18. https://vault.fbi.gov/D-B-Cooper /D.B. Cooper Part 29 of 48/view.

FBI. "D. B. Cooper." Part 30 of 48.pdf. FBI, 27-Sep-19. https://vault.fbi.gov/D-B-Cooper /D.B. Cooper Part 30 of 48/view.

FBI. "D. B. Cooper." Part 36 of 48.pdf. FBI, 01-May-19. https://vault.fbi.gov/D-B-Cooper /D.B. Cooper Part 36 of 48/view.

FBI. "D. B. Cooper." Part 39 of 48.pdf. FBI, 31-Jul-19. https://vault.fbi.gov/D-B-Cooper /d.b.-cooper-part-39-of-48/view.

FBI. "D. B. Cooper." Part 41 of 48.pdf. FBI, 01-Oct-19. https://vault.fbi.gov/D-B-Cooper /d.b.-cooper-part-41-of-48/view.

FBI. "D. B. Cooper." Part 42 of 48.pdf; FBI,

30-Oct-19. https://vault.fbi.gov/D-B-Cooper /d.b.-cooper-part-42-of-48/view.

FBI. "D. B. Cooper." Part 43 of 48.pdf. FBI, 29-Nov-19. https://vault.fbi.gov/D-B-Cooper /d.b.-cooper-part-43-of-48/view.

FBI. "D. B. Cooper Redux: Help Us Solve the Enduring Mystery." FBI, 31-Dec-07. https://archives.fbi.gov/archives/news/stories/2007/december/dbcooper_123107.

FBI. Document FD302, file number SE16481. FBI, 01-May-72. https://website.thedbcooperforum.com.

FBI. *FBI Law Enforcement Bulletin*. FBI, May-49. https://leb.fbi.gov/file-repository/archives/may-1949.pdf.

Futrell, Robert R. *The United States Air Force in Korea, 1950–1953*. Rev. ed. USAF Office Of Air Force History, 1983. https://media.defense.gov/2010/Dec/02/2001329903/-1/-1/0/AFD-101202-022.pdf.

Gates, Josh, and Tom Kaye. *Expedition Unknown*, episode 3.7. The Travel Channel, 11-Jan-17. www.youtube.com/watch?v=6pXlQiLkcbY.

Harrison, George (estate of). Document 2013.5.23.1: "Digitized notes from Northwest Airlines executive George Harrison, who was present at Seattle-Tacoma International Airport during the hijacking of Northwest Airlines flight 305." Washington State Historical Society, 18-Oct-2013. https://wshs-collections.s3.us-west-2.amazonaws.com/2013.5.23.1.pdf.

Hinkamp, MSgt Karl. Background Paper on the Establishment of the Loadmaster Crew Position/Career Field. Air Force Enlisted Heritage Research Institute, 18-Aug-1992. http://afehri.maxwell.af.mil/Documents/pdf/estldmst.pdf.

House of Representatives, 95th Congress. Aviation Regulatory Reform (95–40). Part II, Hearings before the Subcommittee on Aviation of the Committee on Public Works and Transportation. US Government Printing Office, 1978. https://books.google.com.

John Wilheim Productions. *Flying Men, Flying Machines*. John Wilheim Productions, 1970? https://vva.vietnam.ttu.edu/repositories/2/digital_objects/129880.

KIRO TV. "D. B. Cooper, Where Are You?" KIRO TV, 27-Nov-80. www.youtube.com/watch?v=eiuYyfG7-P0.

Leary, Prof. William. Document B43F5. University of Texas at Dallas, received 2006.

Leeker, Prof. Dr. Joachim F. *Air America—Cooperation with Other Airlines*. University of Texas at Dallas, 24-Aug-15. www.utdallas.edu/library/specialcollections/hac/cataam/Leeker/history/Cooperation.pdf.

Leeker, Prof. Dr. Joachim F. *Air America: Boeing 727s*. University of Texas at Dallas, 24-Aug-15. www.utdallas.edu/library/specialcollections/hac/cataam/Leeker/aircraft/jets.pdf.

Leeker, Prof. Dr. Joachim F. *CAT, Air Asia, Air America—the Company on Taiwan I: Structure and Development*. University of Texas at Dallas, 24-Aug-15. www.utdallas.edu/library/specialcollections/hac/cataam/Leeker/history/Taiwan1.pdf.

Leeker, Prof. Dr. Joachim F. *Missions to Tibet*. University of Texas at Dallas, 10-Jan-18. www.utdallas.edu/library/specialcollections/hac/cataam/Leeker/history/Tibet.pdf.

Leeker, Prof. Dr. Joachim F. *The History of Air America*. 2nd ed. University of Texas at Dallas, 24-Aug-15. www.utdallas.edu/library/specialcollections/hac/cataam/Leeker/history/.

Moles, Charles, and Violet Wimbush. *FAA Statistical Handbook of Aviation 1976*. US Government Printing Office, 31-Dec-76. https://books.google.com.

n.a. Course of the Willamette River. Wikipedia, 2020. https://en.wikipedia.org/wiki/Course_of_the_Willamette_River.

n.a. Douglas DC9-21. Skydive Perris, 2020. https://skydiveperris.com/experienced/facilities.

NASA. NASA-Dryden History—Historic Aircraft—X-1 Flight Summary. NASA, 2020. www.nasa.gov/centers/dryden/history/HistoricAircraft/X-1/fltsummary.html.

National Smokejumper Association. *Smokejumper Magazine*. Eastern Washington University, Jan-14. https://dc.ewu.edu/cgi/viewcontent.cgi?article=1085&context=smokejumper_mag.

National Smokejumper Association. *Smokejumper Magazine*. Eastern Washington University, Jul-15. https://dc.ewu.edu/cgi/viewcontent.cgi?article=1091&context=smokejumper_mag.

National Smokejumper Association. *Smokejumper Magazine*. Eastern Washington University, Jul-07. https://dc.ewu.edu/cgi/viewcontent.cgi?article=1055&context=smokejumper_mag.

NOAA/NCEI. IGRA2 Station List. NOAA/NCEI, 2020. www1.ncdc.noaa.gov/pub/data/igra/igra2-station-list.txt.

NOAA/NCEI. Weather Balloon Data. NOAA/NCEI, 2020. www.ncdc.noaa.gov/data-access/weather-balloon-data.

Northwest Orient Airlines. Boeing 727-51/251, Maintenance Training Manual (avialogs.com, ca. 1963). https://www.avialogs.com/aircraft-b/boeing/item/3733-2851northwestorientairlinesboeing727-51251maintenancetrainingmanual-chapter211.

PDAS. A Sample Atmosphere Table (US units). PDAS, 9-Jul-17. www.pdas.com/atmosTable2US.html.

Porteous, Skipp. Telephone interview with William J. Rataczak. Dropzone.com, ca. 2009. https://www.dropzone.com/forums/topic/56036-db-cooper/page/1990/?tab=comments#comment-4290349.

Potvin, Dr. Jean, and Gary Peek. "Skydiving Canopy Opening G-Forces." Parks College Parachute Research Group, Aug-13. www.pcprg.com/g-forces.htm.

Poyner, Fred, IV. Document 2013.37.1.2: interview with John Detlor, retired FBI agent assigned to the NORJAK case. Washington State Historical Society, 16-Nov-12. https://wshs-collections.s3.us-west-2.amazonaws.com/2013.37.1.2.2.pdf.

Poyner, Fred, IV, and Gwen Whiting. Document 2013.5.21.2: interview with Wally Johnson, retired Sr. MSgt (USAF). Washington State Historical Society, 12-Sep-13. https://wshs-collections.s3.us-west-2.amazonaws.com/2013.5.21.2.pdf.

Poyner, Fred, IV, and Gwen Whiting. Document 2013.5.22.2: Bill Mitchell interview on October 3, 2013. Washington State Historical Society, 18-Oct-13. https://wshs-collections.s3.us-west-2.amazonaws.com/2013.5.22.2.pdf.

Ramirez, Alfred. B727 Pressurization: General Description. Alfred Ramirez, 03-Aug-2016. https://www.youtube.com/watch?v=J3qDknQaQp4.

Rinella, Joseph F. *Lakes of Oregon*. Vol. 5, *Marion County*. US Geological Survey, 1977. https://pubs.er.usgs.gov/publication/70199343.

Rose, Brian. Interview with FBI agent Roy Rose. Brian Rose, 24-Mar-2012. https://vimeo.com/39145668.

Seattle Approach Control. Document 2013.5.15.5: "Digital document, transcript of radio communication between Northwest Orient Airlines flight 305 and Seattle-Tacoma International Airport, Reno International Airport." Washington State Historical Society, 2012. https://wshs-collections.s3.us-west-2.amazonaws.com/2013.5.15.5.pdf.

Shulters, M. V. *Lakes of Oregon*. Vol. 2, *Benton, Lincoln, and Polk Counties*. US Geological Survey, 1974. https://pubs.usgs.gov/unnumbered/70199339/report.pdf.

Shulters, M. V. *Lakes of Oregon*. Vol. 3, *Hood River, Multnomah, Washington, and Yamhill Counties*. US Geological Survey, 1975. https://pubs.usgs.gov/unnumbered/70199341/report.pdf.

Shulters, M. V. *Lakes of Oregon*. Vol. 4, *Clackamas County*. US Geological Survey, 1976. https://pubs.usgs.gov/unnumbered/70199342/report.pdf.

Sytsma, Mark. *Atlas of Oregon Lakes*. Portland State University, 1985–2020. https://oregonlakesatlas.org/map.

Turi, Robert, Charles M. Friel, Robert B. Sheldon, and John P. Matthews. *Descriptive Study of Aircraft Hijacking*, Criminal Justice Monograph III.5. Sam Houston State University, 1972. https://files.eric.ed.gov/fulltext/ED073315.pdf.

US Air Force. *United States Air Force Statistical Digest, Fiscal Year 1953*. Dept of the Air Force, 1953. https://media.defense.gov/2011/Apr/05/2001329931/-1/-1/0/AFD-110405-030.pdf.

US Army Corps of Engineers. *Report of the Chief of Engineers*. US Army, 1974, North Pacific Division. US Government Printing Office, 1975. https://usace.contentdm.oclc.org/digital/collection/p16021coll6/id/525.

US Department of Health and Human Services, Public Health Service, National Center for Health Statistics. Anthropometric Reference Data and Prevalence of Overweight, United States, 1976–80. DHHS, 1987. https://www.cdc.gov/nchs/data/series/sr_11/sr11_238.pdf.

US Environmental Protection Agency. *National Lakes Assessment*. National Aquatic Resource Surveys. US Environmental Protection Agency, 2020. www.epa.gov/national-aquatic-resource-surveys/nla.

US Geological Survey. National Water-Quality Assessment (NAWQA): 1991–2012. US Geological Survey, 2020. www.usgs.gov/mission-areas/water-resources/science/national-water-quality-assessment-nawqa-1991-2012.

US Government. Federal Register: 29 Fed. Reg. 8453 (July 7, 1964). US Government Printing Office, 07-Jul-64. www.loc.gov/item/fr029131/.

Willamette Aviation. Seattle / Salt Lake ARTCC Low Altitude. Willamette Aviation, 2020. www.willametteair.com/images/seattleartcc_sectors.gif.

**Journal articles**

Boeing Commercial Airplane Company. "Pressure Bumps." *Boeing Airliner*, Mar/Apr 1967.

Kaye, Thomas G., and Mark Meltzer. "Diatoms Constrain Forensic Burial Timelines: Case Study with DB Cooper Money." *Scientific Reports*, 3-Aug-20. https://doi.org/10.1038/s41598-020-70015-z.

McGowan, Sam. "Loadmaster Evolution." *Air Force Magazine*, 01-Dec-2011.

Murray-Leslie, C. F., D. J. Lintott, and V. Wright. "The Spine in Sport and Veteran Military Parachutists." *Annals of the Rheumatic Diseases* 36, no. 4 (1977): 332–342. https://ard.bmj.com/content/annrheumdis/36/4/332.full.pdf.

**Monographs**

Bustamante, A. C., 9513, and Aerospace Nuclear Safety Department 9510, Sandia Laboratories. *Free-Fall Rotation and Aerodynamic Motion of Rectangular Plates*. Document reference SC-RR-68-132. Springfield, VA: US Department of Commerce, Aug-68. https://apps.dtic.mil/dtic/tr/fulltext/u2/a395124.pdf.

Cowpey, R. W. *Radioactive Plankton from the Columbia River*. Richland, WA: General Electric, 29-Mar-51.

Frey, Bruce E., Ruben Lara-Lara, and Lawrence F. Small. *Final Report on the Water Column Primary Production Work Unit of the Columbia River Estuary Data Development Program.* Corvallis, OR: Columbia River Estuary Data Development Program (CREDDP), Feb-84.

Wallick, Lorna, Ronald Campbell, Vicki Morris, and Richard S. LeGore. *Interim Report: Study Area Vi–C, Columbia River.* Seattle, WA: Parametrix, 31-Jan-75.

**News articles**

AP. "Decal's Link to Hijacker Discounted." *Register Guard,* 19-Jan-79. https://vault.fbi.gov/D-B-Cooper /d.b.-cooper-part-42-of-48/view.

AP. "Treasure Hunters Fail to Find More Cooper Loot." *Daily News,* 22-Feb-80. https://vault.fbi.gov/D-B-Cooper /d.b.-cooper-part-43-of-48/view.

Cloherty, Jack. "D. B. Cooper DNA Results: 'Not A Match,' Another Inconclusive Lead in Decades-Long Investigation." ABC News, 08-Aug-11. https://abcnews.go.com/US/db-cooper-dna-results-match/story?id=14258726.

*The Columbian* Staff and AP. "No Hunt Set for Skyiacker." *The Columbian,* 19-Jan-79. https://vault.fbi.gov/D-B-Cooper /d.b.-cooper-part-42-of-48/view.

DuBeth, Donna. "Beach Residents Groan." *Daily News,* 13-Feb-80. https://vault.fbi.gov/D-B-Cooper /d.b.-cooper-part-43-of-48/view.

Gantenbein, Douglas. "Find Spurs D. B. Cooper." *The Columbian,* 18-Jan-79. https://vault.fbi.gov/D-B-Cooper /d.b.-cooper-part-42-of-48/view.

Struck, Myron. "FBI Geologist Favors Washougal Landing for D. B." *The Columbian,* 16-Mar-80. https://vault.fbi.gov/D-B-Cooper /d.b.-cooper-part-43-of-48/view.

Noceda, Kristofer." Livermore Man Recaps Encounter with D. B. Cooper." *Patch*, 5-Aug-2011. https://patch.com/california/livermore/livermore-man-recaps-encounter-with-db-cooper.

Zheng, Yuxing. "Oswego Lake Set to Begin Slowly Draining on Sept. 5 for Sewer Project Work." *The Oregonian,* 27-Aug-10. www.oregonlive.com/lake-oswego/2010/08/oswego_lake_set_to_begin_slowly_draining_on_sept_5.html.

# ACKNOWLEDGMENTS

The author extends warmest thanks to the following individuals who generously helped with facts, images, comments, and corrections: Bob Bogash, Bruce Kitt, Claudia Tausz, Cliff Ammerman, Gwen Whiting, Joe Leeker, Johnny Kirkley, Mark Logan, Martha Einan, Peter Schilling, and Robert Nicholson.

A big thank-you to Michael Grigsby for driving up to Battle Ground and taking photographs of the VORTAC.

Many thanks to Flight 305 passenger Daniel Rice for permission to use three verses from his poem "D. B. Cooper."

To the members of the web groups Aviastar, Aviation Stack Exchange, Boeing 727 Group | Facebook, Dropzone, F-106 Delta Dart Forum, Oldschool Skydiving Group | Facebook, Pilots of America, Southern Air Transport Group | Facebook, and the DB Cooper Forum, who replied to my posts or whose posts inspired my ideas, many thanks.

I acknowledge the efforts of the CIA, FAA, FBI, National Archives and Records Administration, US Air Force, US Army Corps of Engineers, and US Geological Survey to respond to my FOIA requests. Thanks in particular to Alan Billings of the FAA for establishing that in 1971, the Victor 23 airway was 8 nautical miles wide, and to Heather A. Hall of the Corps of Engineers for retrieving their aerial photographs of the dredging at Tena Bar.

To the surviving passengers and crew of Flight 305: your statements to the FBI and to private researchers were critical to my understanding of the events of November 24, 1971, and I apologize for any misinterpretations.

Finally, my thanks to you the reader, for accompanying me on this journey. You are the other half of the "we" that has appeared throughout this story.

All errors and omissions are my own. As Harry Truman used to say: *The buck stops here*.

# INDEX

*a: denotes reference in an appendix table*
*e: denotes reference in an endnote*
*i: denotes reference in the caption of an image*
*t: denotes reference in a table*

**Concepts**



**Events**



**Objects and materials**

**Organizations**

**Persons**

**Places**

**Publications**